CONTENTS

INDEX TO THE FIGURES

A description of the Figures — maps — which accompany the
text, is as follows:

INTRODUCTION

The Niagara, St. Catharines & Toronto Railway is one of the foremost examples in Canada of an intensively developed and closely integrated transportation system. It operated local street railways, interurban lines, carload and LCL freight, lake steamers, a large motor coach system and even an amusement park. The NS&T and predecessors include almost the first electric railway in Canada (the first to have operated uninterruptedly), and certainly the last interurban passenger service. Each aspect of the company's operations was co-ordinated with others to form a transportation system which, while comparatively small in area, was very active in operation, and several distinct types of passenger business (local, commuter, inter-city and excursion) were developed. The methods by which these different types of business were catered to, and by which the several aspects were made to supplement and complement each other, as well as the historical background and development of the system, make up the substance of this book.

The study has been divided into a small number of fairly broad headings, based on the function of the various components in the overall picture, and the manner in which they were thought of by the management. In so complex an organization, of course, watertight divisions are impossible, and a certain amount of overlapping is inevitable. In most cases, a chronological narrative style has been adopted, the better to view the subject as a living and developing entity.

The basic research for this book was performed in the University of Toronto Library, particularly in its collections of early railway and electrical industry periodicals and of bygone newspapers on microfilm. Additional work was done in the St. Catharines Public Library. Much documentary material not usually available to studies of this kind was rescued from a basement storeroom behind the furnace when the St. Catharines carhouse building was vacated in 1964. This material was invaluable in giving, in many instances, a "view from within", and in fact "kick-started" preparations for this book. This material is now in the Ontario Electric Railway Historical Association archives.

Thanks are due for photographs to many sources, as individually noted both in photo captions and below. Useful information was obtained in 1965 conversations with Mr. J.D. Knowles and Mr. P. Leger of Toronto, and Mrs. H.E. Battel, Mrs. W.M. Willis and Mr. E.V. Snell of St. Catharines. Photo selection for this edition was made by Mr. E.A. Wickson of Toronto, whose ability to choose appropriate illustrations knows no bounds. Many of the new images and updated information made available forty years later were not available when the original book was published in 1967. By appointing Ted Wickson as photo editor, Railfare*DC Books demonstrated their deep commitment, by engaging knowledgeable individuals in the task of bringing back to life interesting railway and transit subjects, and with a high quality result.

This book is dedicated to all employees of the Niagara St. Catharines & Toronto Railway over the years, and particularly to the late Mr. J.R. Empringham, Superintendent of the line, who courteously took time to read the manuscript, to make many useful suggestions and set numerous errors straight. Unfortunately, he passed away before being able to write the introduction he hoped to contribute.

John M. Mills, Toronto
November 2007

Photographs and Illustrations

In addition to the individuals named by the author in the above introduction, editor Ted Wickson gained the assistance of many people who provided visual and informational support in this revised and expanded edition of John Mills' original book. His thanks, and those of the publisher and author are extended to the following.

There were many institutions who helped, including: Archives of Ontario; Upper Canada Railway Society; Ontario Electric Railway Historical Association; Niagara Falls Public Library; Fort Erie Public Library, C. Robert Craig Memorial Library, and St. Catharines Museum, with special thanks to curator Arden Phair; CRHA Archives, with special thanks to Peter Murphy; Library and Archives Canada, with special thanks to Nathalie Rahal; and Canadian Urban Transit Association.

Thanks are extended to these individuals, who provided access to their own photos or their collections: Bill Hood; Jack Knowles; John Bromley, especially for his digital optimizing of early colour slides by J.W. Hood; Andy Douglas; Adam Zhelka; Dick Vincent; Johan Wigt; Al Paterson; Bob Chambers; Don McCartney; John Burtniak, who provided exceptional visual support in offering unique material soon to be accessioned by St. Catharines Museum; Fred Angus, who also made the Addison Lake collection available prior to its accessioning by CRHA Archives; John Humiston; Bill Volkmer; Ron Ritchie; Bill Pharoah; Bob Sandusky, who was most helpful in the sheer volume of images and equipment drawings he provided as well as his efforts in optimizing his digital images and chasing down missing information; Rich Krisak; Colin Hatcher helped with car roster information; also images were received from photo editor Ted Wickson, as well as from author John Mills.

Other helpful individuals were Colin Churcher, Tom Grumley and Bruce Curry, with much-appreciated advice which enabled Ted Wickson to streamline his research in Ottawa at LAC and Robert Craig Library; John Thompson, for sharing his knowledge of many potential contributors; Andy Panko, for his extensive knowledge of railways in the Niagara Peninsula and the day spent with Ted exploring and explaining evidence of NS&T infrastructure present and lost; book designer Ian Cranstone, who performed miracles with enhancement of photos and various artifacts.

John M. Mills

NIAGARA, ST. CATHARINES & TORONTO RAILWAY

A Canadian National Electric Railways Subsidiary

Railfare ✴ DC Books

ABOUT THE AUTHOR

John Mills was born in Toronto in 1931, and has lived there all his life. He graduated from the University of Toronto in 1952. Shortly thereafter, John entered the business world, but found that a commercial career was not for him, and soon returned to the University of Toronto as an administrative staff member. Being a compulsive researcher, he found this to be an ideal workplace environment, as it provided him with unrestricted access to the university's enormous collection of information, books and artifacts.

The author is a founding member of the Ontario Electric Railway Historical Association, and is an honourary life member. The OERHA operates the *Halton County Radial Railway*, featuring historic electric transit vehicles in action at their museum near Milton, Ontario.

John has written several books on electric railway subjects, including *Traction on The Grand* and *Cataract Traction*. Several others are in preparation. Besides being interested in railways, John is equally fascinated by steamboats, and is the author of *The New Mills List*. This is a listing, with statistics and other details, of over 6000 Canadian coastal and inland steamers from the beginning, covering the period from 1809 up to 1930. The definitive edition was published, to John's great satisfaction, by The Marine Museum of the Great Lakes at Kingston in 1999.

In addition to his transportation hobby, John's great joy in life is travelling the world. He hopes you will enjoy your own travels back to a bygone era, through the fascinating transportation system that was the *Niagara, St. Catharines & Toronto Railway*.

As one of the founding members of the Ontario Electric Railway Historical Association, author John Mills frequently dons his motorman's uniform, and helps to operate one of the many electric cars at the Halton County Radial Railway streetcar museum near Milton, Ontario. Photo taken June 2004 at the OERHA's fiftieth anniversary celebration.
(J.M. MILLS COLLECTION)

Book designed and typeset in Adobe Garamond Pro, ITC Garamond, and Myriad MM.
Overall book design by Ian Cranstone, Osgoode, Ontario.
Graphic grid and outside covers designed by Primeau & Barey, Montreal, Quebec.
Printed and bound in Canada by AGMV Marquis.
Distributed by LitDistCo.

Legal Deposit, *Bibliothèque et Archives nationales du Québec* and the National Library of Canada, 1st trimester, 2008.

Library and Archives Canada Cataloguing in Publication
Mills, John M.
Niagara, St. Catharines & Toronto Railway : a Canadian National Electric Railways subsidiary : an illustrated history of electric transit in Canada's Niagara peninsula / John M. Mills.

Includes bibliographical references and index.
ISBN 978-1-897190-27-2 (pbk.).—ISBN 978-1-897190-28-9 (bound)

1. Niagara, St. Catharines & Toronto Railway—History.
2. Railroads—Ontario—History. I. Title. II. Title: Niagara, St. Catharines and Toronto Railway.

HE2810.N5M54 2007   385'..0971338   C2007-906195-8

We acknowledge the financial support of the Government of Canada through the Book Publishing Industry Development Program (BPIDP) for our publishing activities.

For our publishing activities, **Railfare ❄ DC Books** gratefully acknowledges the financial support of The Canada Council for the Arts, and of SODEC.

Canada Council   Conseil des Arts
for the Arts   du Canada

Société de développement des entreprises culturelles
Québec ✛✛

The involvement of, and assistance from, the CN Lines Special Interest Group in the preparation of this book is acknowledged.

Railfare ❄ DC Books

Ontario office:
1880 Valley Farm Road, Unit #TP-27, Pickering, ON L1V 6B3

Business office and mailing address:
Box 666, St. Laurent Station, Montreal, QC H4L 4V9
email: railfare@videotron.ca   web: www.railfare.net

Opposite (inset): J.R. Empringham, Superintendent, NS&T.
(CANADIAN URBAN TRANSIT ASSOCIATION)

Top: Car 134 poses with crew on the Grantham Division, May 1928.

Bottom: New car 305 and crew on Bridge Street 1926.
(BOTH PHOTOS THIS PAGE W.S. FLATT COLLECTION)

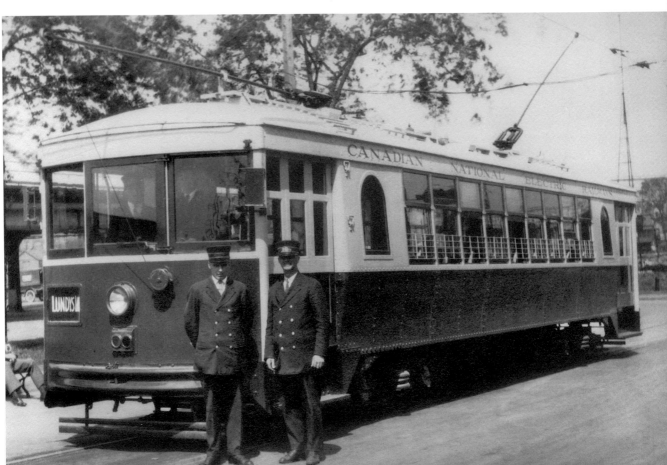

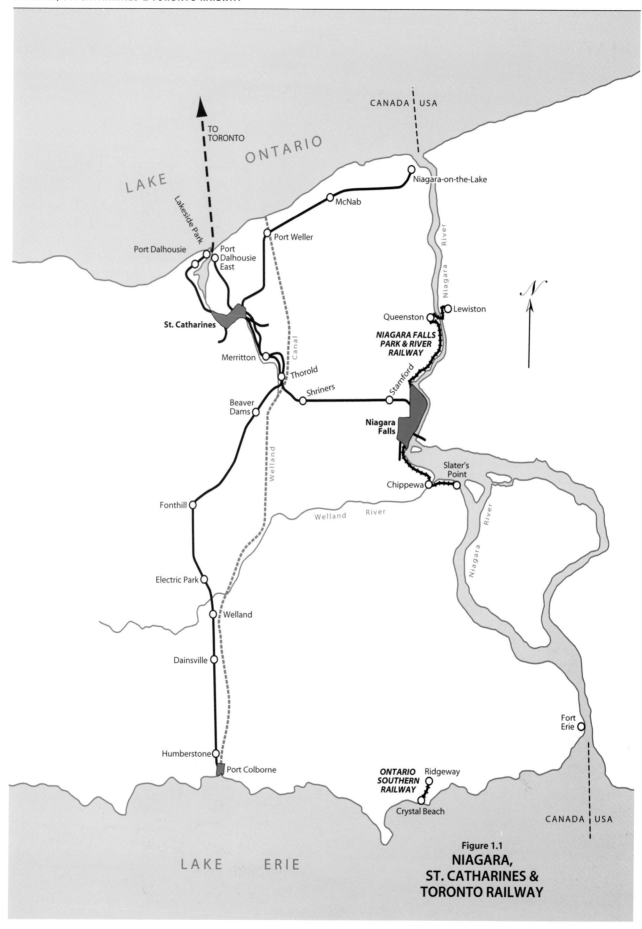

Figure 1.1
**NIAGARA,
ST. CATHARINES &
TORONTO RAILWAY**

CHAPTER 1

St. Catharines Street Railway (1879)
St. Catharines, Merritton & Thorold St. Ry. (1882)
Port Dalhousie, St. Catharines & Thorold St. Ry. (1893)

CHRONOLOGICALLY, the first section of the NS&T system was the St. Catharines local line, originating in December 1874 when the St. Catharines Street Railway Co. was chartered to build a horsecar line in the towns and villages of Port Dalhousie, St. Catharines, Merritton and Thorold, and Grantham Township. The Company was promoted by Dr. L. S. Oille, a local entrepreneur whom we shall meet again later.

On November 1st 1879, a short line was opened from Welland House at Ontario Street along St. Paul and Queenston streets to Hennessey's Corner at Thorold Road. Among the provisions of the twenty-year franchise was that a maximum speed of six MPH and a minimum of four MPH was required, and that sleighs could be used in the winter if necessary. The town council could specify service frequency but "not oftener than once in 40 minutes." The original 30-lb. rails were shaped like the letter "L" and the car wheels had no flanges. Cars were turned bodily at each end of the run by small turntables in the roadway. The carhouse was on the south side of St. Paul Street near Bond Street.

In 1880, extensions were built via Geneva Street to the Welland Railway station at Welland Avenue, and via Thorold Road to Merritton. In the following year, tracks were built up Ontario Street and the turntable relocated to the corner of King Street; the Merritton line was further extended to Front Street in Thorold. The latter extension, opened officially on April 18th 1882, later became the "Low Line" of the NS&T. The minimum curve radius was 35 feet and, including several minor "dips," the total elevation to be climbed by cars bound for Thorold was about 370 feet. The short cars (ten-foot body) in most cities would have been hauled by a single horse but two were used here, and on busy days it was company policy to allow the teams to rest on alternate trips.

In June 1881, the company was reorganized and sold to Edward A. Smyth. A year later its name was changed to describe more accurately the area served by the extended line. It was exempted from municipal taxes, originally for an eight-year period but later extended several times.

In the local directory dated June 1887 appears the little road's final timetable as a horse railway:

"Cars leave Welland House every 40 minutes from 5:50 a.m. till 10 p.m.; leave Thorold from 6:45 a.m. till 11 p.m. City service and Geneva Street branch leave Welland House every 30 minutes connecting with trains on the Welland branch."

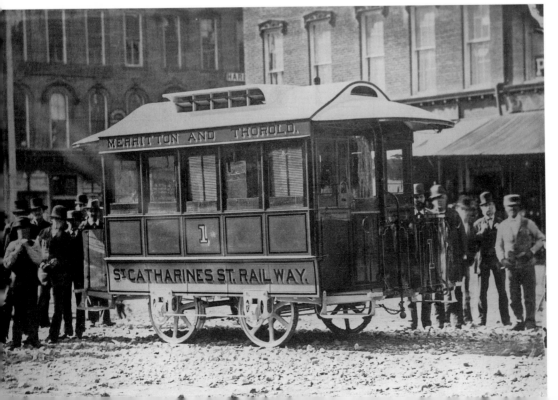

Number 1 of the St. Catharines Street Railway: the first horse-drawn streetcar in the city of St. Catharines, the service starting November 1st 1879. (B. WEST COLLECTION)

Electrification

It was always recognized that animal haulage was inefficient in the conditions prevailing, but no really successful electric line had yet been commercially operated for more than a very short time anywhere in the world. In fact, the first experimental electric railway using even remotely modern technology had been set up at an exhibition in Germany in 1879. The problems, therefore, were many and formidable. No previous electrification had been attempted on a line whose operating characteristics were so severe, and the St. Catharines project attracted attention both on this continent and abroad. Formal permission for the momentous change to electrification was given by the Town in June 1887.

The Van Depoele system was used, involving double overhead wires carrying a heavy four-wheeled "traveller" connected to the car by a flexible cable. When the traveller dewired (not an infrequent occurrence) the conductor restored it with an implement described as "a refined hay fork." Span wires were used where the line was laid in the centre of the road, with bracket arms on roadside sections in Merritton and Thorold. Standard wire height was nineteen feet and all insulators were of wood.

The horsecars had been built by the local firm of Patterson & Corbin whose plant was on the south side of Queenston Street just east of Geneva. The company was established as a carriage builder in 1874; large-scale streetcar construction was added in 1891 and expanded in 1895. Seventy men were employed at the peak. Cars built by Patterson & Corbin were used literally from coast to coast in Canada but the company had over-reached itself; it went bankrupt and closed down in 1897.

The horsecars were modified for electric operation with equipment furnished by Canadian General Electric Co. A 500-volt fifteen-HP motor was mounted on the front platform beside the driver (who, therefore, came to be called "motorman") on the closed cars. An early article in the trade press reported, "The brushes used are peculiar, consisting of two pieces of brass riveted together, with a space left between the ends which are turned up to receive a piece of electric light carbon. As the copper was never scraped off the carbon, the noise made by the grinding on the commutator was anything but a song of the sirens." When an electrical fault occurred in the motor, says the same article, "the section in trouble was nonchalantly cut out and the commutator bars were connected across with fine wire. Some of these cripples would run thus and stand up to their work for months with 6 or 7 sections cut out."

Opposite Top: St. Catharines Street Railway No. 4. Its motor, situated on the front platform, drove the front wheels through a chain drive. The car also featured two retractable brooms which could be lowered to sweep the track clear ahead of the wheels. (FROM *TROLLEY CAR TREASURY*)

Opposite Bottom: StCM&T open car 10, posed in front of the Patterson & Corbin plant, Queenston Street near Geneva, in Van Depoele days. Note motorman, situated in centre of car: it appears that he could not operate the hand brake. (H.E. BATTEL COLLECTION)

The motor drove a countershaft on which were mounted two sprocket wheels ten inches in diameter, driving corresponding twenty-inch sprocket wheels on the axles by means of an endless chain. Speed was governed by a box rheostat. In order to prevent the magnetism of the motor from stopping passengers' watches, the front platform was sheeted throughout with zinc. The cars had longitudinal seating for twelve or fourteen. On the open cars the control position was in the centre of the body directly over the axles, the same control being used in both directions. This curious arrangement meant that the motorman could not apply the brakes whose handles were located in the normal position on the platforms. The carhouse was on St. Paul Street opposite Mary Street.

A generating plant was built at Lock 12 of the old Welland Canal in Merritton, close to the centre point of the line. For two weeks each spring, the water was let out of the canal for cleaning, and the horses had to return to work. Alternative arrangements were made about 1900 for power supply during the cleaning period. The original Van Depoele generator was soon replaced by a Canadian General Electric machine.

The turntables continued in use but were removed about 1896. Even in electric days, a spare team was kept at the bottom of the hill on Thorold Road at Eastchester as the Van Depoele cars could not be relied upon to get up to Queenston Street on their own. It is understood that the equine "helpers" were rather often required.

Electric service was started in St. Catharines in September 1887, and through to Thorold on October 5th. Four ten-foot closed cars and three open cars were the original equipment, in addition to two trailers, which were probably former horsecars. Car service started at 6:45 AM, ran every 40 minutes, and ended at 11:00 PM.

Successful Operation

After the line had been running for a short time, the prominent US trade magazine *Electrical World*, reported on....

"....the electric railway system at St. Catharines, Ontario now working so successfully on the Van Depoele system. The line is 116 yards short of six miles in length. It is one succession of grades and curves, and one of the heaviest grades is on a curve. There are a number of grades of 6 feet in the hundred, and one of 400 feet in length 7 feet in the hundred. In fact, in the whole six miles, there is one straight run of 1500 feet on the level. The company has at present, five motor cars, 15 h.p. each.

"It is equipping a car every two weeks and intends by the first of May to have 12 motor cars running. The road was very hard on horses on account of the grades, and as the company gets its water-power from the Welland Canal at a nominal figure — 90 cents per h.p. per annum for 400 h.p. — the saving by the change to electric motors is greater than it would be to use steam

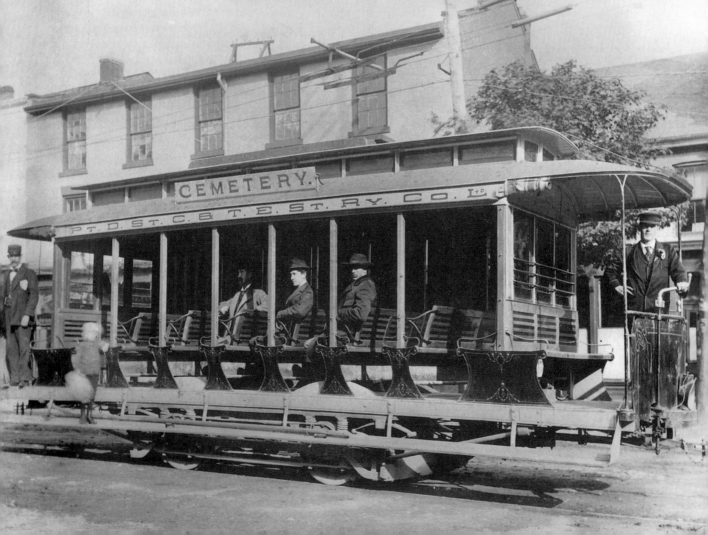

to generate the current. The secretary of the road has calculated that the company saves by the change, after deducting the interest on the electric plant, about $18 a day.

"But this is not all. As the company is able to give the public cleaner cars and more rapid transit, the passenger business has increased by about 35 percent. The motors are placed on the front platform of the horsecars and the drivers had no difficulty in learning how to handle the machines. The company has not had a single mishap of any consequence to its electrical machinery, and though the municipal authorities were very slow to give it permission to adopt electricity, they approve of the change. The drivers and conductors seem to have more respect for themselves than they did in the horsecars — more polite to passengers. In fact, aside from the business and saving to the company in operating expenses, Mr. E.A. Smyth, of the company, says he would not have the care and trouble of a stable full of horses on any account......It is found that five electric cars do as much work as eight horse-cars." (January 7th 1888)

In September 1888, the company calculated its daily expenses, exclusive of wages, as follows:

Power Station		Road	
Power	$ .83	Oil and waste	$1.00
Oil and waste	.20	Brushes	.30
Labour	3.00	Travellers	.30
Depreciation	3.70	Labour	2.00
		Repair Materials	1.70
		Deprec. on cars	6.30
		Deprec. on line	2.00

The separate item of expense for brushes might be noted. This resulted from the fact that carbon brushes had not yet been developed. Copper or bronze was used, the brushes bearing on imperfectly-shaped commutators which acted as a grinder, quickly wearing the brushes away so that it was sometimes necessary to replace them after every trip.

Development And Reorganization

The new line was immediately very popular and shortly after it opened, the company ordered three larger open cars from Patterson & Corbin. This brought the total rolling stock to twelve cars (four closed, six open, two trailers), a roster exceeded, at that time, only by the eighteen cars of the Seashore Electric Railway, a Daft-equipped line at As-

Opposite Top: Crew posing with open-side car Number 15 at carhouse 1907. (PUBLISHER'S COLLECTION)

Opposite Bottom: Port Dalhousie St. Catharines & Thorold Electric Street Railway open car c1895 (note double overhead of original Van Depoele installation). (LIBRARY AND ARCHIVES CANADA E004665772)

bury Park, New Jersey. The new cars repeated the unusual motorman's position at the centre of the car.

The Victoria Lawn line was opened late in 1888. This was located on the south side of the street, and used light T-rail instead of the older flat rail; this was the first T-rail on the system. It was promoted by the Niagara & St. Catharines Street Railway Company but was taken over by the StCM&T. before completion. The Geneva Street trackage built in 1880 was included in the electrification, but was removed or allowed to disintegrate before 1890. The Welland Railway had been taken over by the Grand Trunk in 1882, and it is probable that this led to a decline in the importance of its station as a terminal point. (The Geneva Street branch had no other purpose at this time). In 1892-94, T-rail replaced flat rail on most of the company's tracks.

A new three-track wooden carhouse was opened at this time incorporating offices, crew rooms, machine shop and two pits under one of the tracks. Battery-operated electric light was installed.

In October 1892, the company was sold to George Dawson and Henry C. Symmes, who had previously been involved in an abortive project to build a huge marine railway to transport ships across the Chignecto Isthmus in Eastern Canada. Considerable confusion has been caused between H. C. Symmes, the partner (who later sold his interest to Dawson), and H. D. Symmes who was Secretary-Manager of the company throughout its life. The new management again changed the company's name.

Early in 1893 permission was obtained to make an extension along Ontario Street to the north limits of the town but the exact date of construction is uncertain; it is thought to have been 1896.

Modernization

The Van Depoele system was not entirely satisfactory. The weight of the motor (about 1500 lbs.) caused the lightly-built platforms to sag badly so that chains and sprockets would not mesh correctly; also the motorman on open cars had no control over the brakes. The traveller was also troublesome, as it tended to dewire frequently, hitting the roof of the car with a loud crash and giving Van Depoele cars a reputation for leaky roofs. Overhead frogs at switches were impracticable, and cars meeting at sidings would stop and exchange travellers. Therefore, in the spring of 1896 the Van Depoele system was scrapped and conventional (Sprague) technology — a spring-loaded pole with its trolley wheel riding under the wire — substituted. The redundant negative wire was at first used as a feeder but was soon removed.

The entirely different appearance and larger size of the new cars suggests that they were newly built, though parts of the old cars may have been incorporated. It is known that General Electric type 1200 motors, the most powerful then available, were purchased. (Some of the new cars were used very briefly on the Van Depoele overhead.)

By the end of 1896, therefore, the pioneer system had been brought into line with what had become standard practice, except that the town of Thorold refused permission to lay T-rail on Front Street. The condition of the old flat-rail track became so bad that in April 1899 service had to be temporarily cut back to Regent Street while emergency repairs were made. New rail was not laid here until about 1900.

Life-saving fenders replaced the primitive "cow-catchers" in 1896 and during the next two years rudimentary block signals and a company-owned telephone despatching system were installed.

A reduced fare of five cents was in effect on summer evenings between St. Catharines and Thorold (normally ten cents), and "trolley parties" using chartered cars grew to three or four a week by 1895. Small parks were operated in Merritton and near the end of the Victoria Lawn line. The area was still so rural in many places that the company was having trouble with claims for cattle killed by the cars on Queenston Street. A package freight service was provided to premises along the tracks. Bulky articles were handled on flat trailers in a sort of street-railway mixed train. The first Sunday service was operated on May 23rd 1897; however, a few cars had run on Sunday mornings previously to take worshippers to church.

After trying unsuccessfully to prevent the new NS&T company from building its Port Dalhousie line, Dawson sold out to the larger company in May 1901 and, after certain legal technicalities were overcome, the two companies were formally amalgamated on July 8th 1902.

CHAPTER 2

St. Catharines & Niagara Central Railway

A COMPANY bearing this name was originally incorporated in Ontario in 1881 to build a steam railway from the Niagara River through St. Catharines and Hamilton to Toronto. Early records are quite indefinite, but it seems that part of the line may have been in use as early as 1884 on a makeshift basis, hauling materials for the construction of the new (third) Welland Canal. In 1887 the project was taken over by Dr. Lucius S. Oille, late of the St. Catharines Street Railway. The first train from Niagara Falls to Thorold ran on October 12th 1887; this section of the line was completed first in order to qualify for a $20,000 subsidy from Thorold. The rest of the line was formally opened into St. Catharines on July 11th 1888. Trains wyed outside St. Catharines and backed up Raymond Street to James; in Niagara Falls they similarly wyed and backed to the Michigan Central station.

At first, St. Catharines was an enthusiastic supporter of the NCR, as it was commonly known, since its competition had forced a reduction in Grand Trunk freight rates. A Canadian Pacific Railway connection was always hoped for.

The new management applied for a Dominion charter (with its attendant possibility of a subsidy), which was granted with all provisions retroactive to 1881. A subsidy of $3,200 per mile for twelve miles was duly received and the town of St. Catharines agreed to guarantee the interest on $96,000 in railway bonds, receiving in return enough stock to make it one of the major shareholders. As the line was now under Dominion jurisdiction, it was inspected by a representative of the Railway Committee of the Privy

Council (the Board of Railway Commissioners had not yet been formed) and declared "officially open for traffic" on December 20th 1888. This date is often incorrectly given as the actual opening date.

Abortive Extension Plans

An arrangement was made in 1890 with the city of Hamilton for financial assistance in the amount of $275,000 if the line were completed to Toronto by July 1st 1892. In September of that year another attempt was made to finance an extension through the guarantee by Hamilton of the interest on $125,000 in company bonds, or alternatively through an outright grant. This was rejected by the voters in April 1893. In November 1894 it was arranged that control of the company would be purchased by a group headed by W. F. Forsyth of Boston, President of the Hamilton Radial Electric Railway. The HRER was an ambitious project that seems to have been a gamble by a group of investors to build a railway line and sell it to the Canadian Pacific, which was anxious to make a connection with US railroads at the Niagara River. Accordingly, the HRER would have involved a steam-operated main line from Niagara Falls to Toronto, with a branch to Brantford and Woodstock, or farther, and a number of electric branches to such places as Galt and Guelph.

These ambitious plans were thwarted when the CPR participated in construction of the Toronto, Hamilton & Buffalo line. The Forsyth interests therefore defaulted on payment and the deal was not finalized on the intended date (January 27th 1895). The railway then (in public at least) changed its goal to a TH&B connection at Smithville or Fenwick, and hoped to lease itself to the latter company. Nothing came of this either. The company's corporate name was changed at this time to "Niagara, Hamilton & Pacific" but this seems never to have been generally used, and the company continued to refer to itself as the "Niagara Central Railway" or the "Niagara Central Route" even into NS&T days.

Opposite Top: Front Street, Thorold c1910.
(JOHN BURTNIAK COLLECTION, ST. CATHARINES MUSEUM)

Opposite Bottom: Car 54 at Merritton station (first) c1905.
(JOHN BURTNIAK COLLECTION, ST. CATHARINES MUSEUM)

Bottom: Niagara Central train on Raymond Street, near James — the St. Catharines terminal.
(B. WEST COLLECTION)

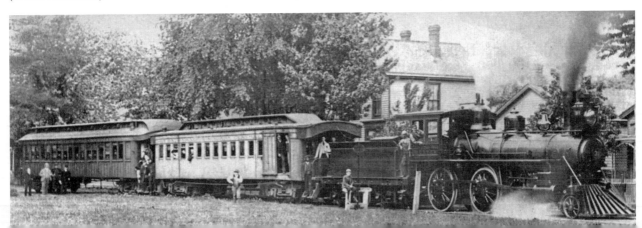

N.S. &T. Station, Thorold, Ont.

Troubled Waters

These disappointments caused the directors to split into two factions, one led by Dr. Oille and the other by the vice-president, Captain Neelon. One magazine commented in February 1896, with fine Victorian understatement, that the directors were "not in the most perfect harmony" and indeed they were not, for the dispute culminated in the Neelon faction walking out of the 1896 annual general meeting in a body, followed by a public assault on Oille by Neelon in St. Catharines streets. The president wished to weather the storm, electrify, and proceed with extension plans, while Neelon wanted to salvage at least part of the investment by selling out, even to the Grand Trunk, which alarmed the city of St. Catharines.

The company reported that it handled 65,916 tons of freight in the year ending June 30th 1896, and 20,817 passengers (down from 26,605 in two years). The two daily passenger trains left James Street and 8:40 AM and 3:44 PM, returning from the MCRR station in Niagara Falls at 10:15 AM and 5:41 PM.

Early in 1897, after a conference showed that the Hamilton Grimsby & Beamsville Electric Railway was not interested in closing the Beamsville–St. Catharines gap on the Niagara Central's terms, Dr. Oille and four other directors resigned and Captain Neelon became president; however he died only a year later.

While all this was going on, the property was falling into a condition of extreme decrepitude, and it became an object of amusement. A local paper in 1896 reported that "Recently, the only engine in commission on the Niagara

Central Railway burst some flues, and consequently the rolling stock of the company was forced to take a short holiday." Finally, the virtually ownerless line was thrown into receivership on June 9th 1897 with the manager, Richard Wood, as receiver. At this time there were 12.35 miles of track and the company was in debt to the extent of $243,330, exclusive of accrued interest.

A further blow was sustained in the same month of June when the Grand Trunk, after a long period of determined opposition from the Niagara Central, was granted permission to build a siding into the Riordan Paper Mills in Thorold; this crossed the NCR track and deprived the latter of most of the revenue from what was its largest single shipper.

Company Sold

The railway was offered for sale in June 1898. Some confusion arose while two intending purchasers vied with each other, auction-style, after the supposed closing date. The property was finally sold on July 11th to another Neelon, George M. of St. Catharines for just $35,000 plus assumption of outstanding debt. Neelon paid ten

WE HANDLE THE AMERICAN EXPRESS.

St. Catharines and Niagara Central R'y.

TRAINS EAST.

STATIONS.	Miles from St. Catharines	57 Buffalo Express.	59 Mixed.
		A. M.	P. M.
St. Catharines............... Dep	0	8.40	3.15
Merritton	3	8.53	3.26
Thorold	5	9.05	3.37
Stamford	10	9.13	3 55
Niagara Central Junction	11	9.22	4 00
Clifton ....Arrive	12	9.25	4 03
Niagara-on-the-Lake...... .Arrive			6.05
Clifton, M. C. R............Dep.	12	9.30	5.12
Niagara Falls...................	13	9.36	
Chippawa	16	9.46	
Black Creek....................	22	9 56	
Fort Erie......................	29	10.00	
Black Rock....................	30	10.15	
Buffalo, Exchange st .....Arrive	34	10.30	6.20

☞When you are ordering Goods from Toronto or Montreal be sure that your orders are marked "Ship via C. P. R., M. C. R. and St. C. & N. C. R'y."

TRAINS WEST.

STATIONS.	Miles from Buffalo.	56 Mixed.	58 Buffalo Express.
		A. M.	P. M.
Buffalo....................Dep.	0	7.07	4.35
Black Rock....................	4	7.20	4.50
Fort Erie......................	5	7.25	4.55
Black Creek....................	12	7.39	5.10
Chippawa......................	13	7.49	5.21
Niagara Falls..................	21	7.59	5.30
Clifton...................... ...Arrive	22	8.05	5.36
Niagara-on-the-Lake...... .....Dep.		9.00	
Clifton, M. C. R .... Dep.	22	10.15	5.41
Niagara Central Junction....... ...	23	10.18	5.44
Stamford	24	10.23	5.49
Thorold......................	29	10.38	6.00
Merritton......................	31	10.48	6.10
St. Catharines..............Arrive	34	11.00	6.20

Take the St. C. & N. C. R'y for Niagara Falls and Buffalo Good Coaches. No Change. Quick Time. Patronize your own Railway

When ordering Goods from New York or Great Britain, mark your order

Care of Merchants Dispatch Company at New York,
and Michigan Central Railway and St. Catharines & Niagara Central Railway.

Top: NS&T 82 at Shriner's. Travelling in car No. 130, the photographer snapped this shot just before its trolley-pole rope obscured the view of No. 82.
(H.E. BATTEL COLLECTION)

Opposite: StC&NC 1894 timetable.
(JOHN BURTNIAK COLLECTION, ST. CATHARINES MUSEUM)

percent down and quickly resold the company to Haines Brothers of New York, for a commission of $1,000 and a job with the company (he became General Passenger Agent of the NCR).

Hardly had the new owners come into effective possession when passenger service was closed down in August 1898 by order of Dominion authorities, owing to the poor condition of much of the trestlework. Freight service was also discontinued about the same time. The company took immediate steps to patch things up so that a partial freight service could be resumed on November 16th of the same year, and passenger service was restored on February 1st 1899, apparently using borrowed equipment. Three daily trips were shown on the first timetable, leaving James Street at 9:10 AM, 1:00 and 4:30 PM, returning from Niagara Falls at 10:00 AM, 1:40 and 6:00 PM. The mid-day trip was later dropped to simplify the task of overhead construction.

On April 15th 1899 the company was once again sold, this time to Messrs. Colvin, Powers and Herbert, and transferred by them on October 1st to a new corporation, the Niagara, St. Catharines & Toronto Railway Company. This last step was purely a legal technicality as the owners were the same, and it merely marked the final termination of the Niagara Central's receivership. Thus was laid the foundation on which the NS&T transportation system was to be built.

CHAPTER 3

Niagara Falls, Wesley Park & Clifton Tramway Company

THE City of Niagara Falls is an amalgamation of two formerly independent villages. The town of Clifton (close to the Falls) had been renamed "Niagara Falls" in 1881; the village of Drummondville was confusingly renamed "Niagara Falls Village" in 1882. The two were finally amalgamated in 1904. The city at first retained within its boundaries the original separate business districts, and to a certain extent this is still the case. This reduced the demand for transportation in the unified town, and before being taken over by the NS&T, the local line was of comparatively minor importance.

The Niagara Falls, Wesley Park & Clifton Tramway Company was incorporated in August 1886 to operate a street railway in Niagara Falls and Stamford Township. On December 6th of the same year 3¾ miles of line was opened, starting at Culp Avenue and running via Main Street, Ferry Street, Victoria Avenue, Simcoe, St. Lawrence, Morrison, Welland, Queen, Erie and Bridge streets to River Road. 30- and 45-lb. rail was used, and the company eventually owned ten cars and forty horses, which were housed in barns on Simcoe Street at Buckley Avenue. Turntables were used at route termini but were removed quite early.

The company was never very prosperous; in later years it suffered from being an anachronistic horsecar line in a very electricity-conscious city, particularly after 1892 when the Niagara Falls Park & River Railway was opened as an electric line. According to its public statements, after 1890 the tramway company was always just on the verge of electrification.

In 1895, the railway was purchased by another company with the same name, promoted by W. Kyle of Toronto, J. M. Brinker of Niagara Falls, New York (promoter of the Gorge Line) and A. E. Schoelkoff, then active in power developments on the American side. Their plans for electrification were not carried out.

In 1897, possible competition appeared when the town, dissatisfied with the Tramway Company's plodding ways, tacitly encouraged the efforts of a Toronto group planning to build an electric line using the franchise of the Niagara Falls & Drummond Turnpike Road Company, which included street railway powers.

Canadian Control

The owners of the company at this time became embroiled in certain financial problems with the Niagara Gorge line. Unwilling to invest the capital for electrification, they sold out in January 1897 to A. G. Hanan and E. Davis of Niagara Falls, Ontario. Announcements indicated that

electrification was, as usual, "imminent", but nothing was immediately done.

Early in 1899 the NS&T system was taking shape, and an informal understanding seems to have been reached between the two companies. The Tramway Company requested permission to electrify and extend a belt line running on Bender Street, Falls Street and Clifton Hill, which would have brought the rails to almost exactly the site of the future Tower Inn Terminal. While this extension was not built, there is little doubt that it was inspired by the NS&T, and around the end of 1899 the Tramway Company was purchased by the NS&T. In April 1900, a contract was awarded by the new management to a New York firm to electrify the line. It was then almost the last

horsecar operation in Canada; only the Sarnia line lasted longer. Four new cars were ordered from the Ottawa Car Company and it is possible that additional cars were received second-hand from USA but they do not appear on any available equipment records. Electric operations began at last on August 15th 1900. It is probable that the circuitous routing of the tracks was changed in 1900 when the interurban entrance via Victoria, Queen, Erie and Bridge streets was built, though whether or not the earlier route was electrified is uncertain.

In 1901 the company, which then had 4.3 miles of track, was formally absorbed by the NS&T. The Niagara Falls local line was known as the "Wesley Park Division" as late as 1940.

Top: Car 111 on Queen Street, Niagara Falls c1910. From a postcard mailed in 1916.
(PUBLISHER'S COLLECTION)

Opposite: NS&T car 306 rounding corner of Bridge and Erie streets, 1938.
(AL PATERSON COLLECTION)

Right: NS&T car 5 (Ottawa Car 1900), built for Niagara Falls local lines, at Welland Street Yard, St. Catharines c1915.
(LIBRARY AND ARCHIVES CANADA E004666262)

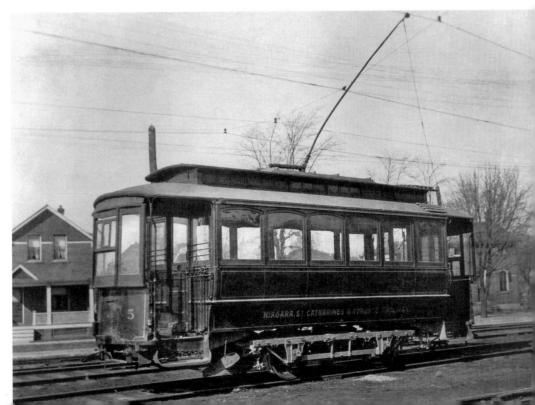

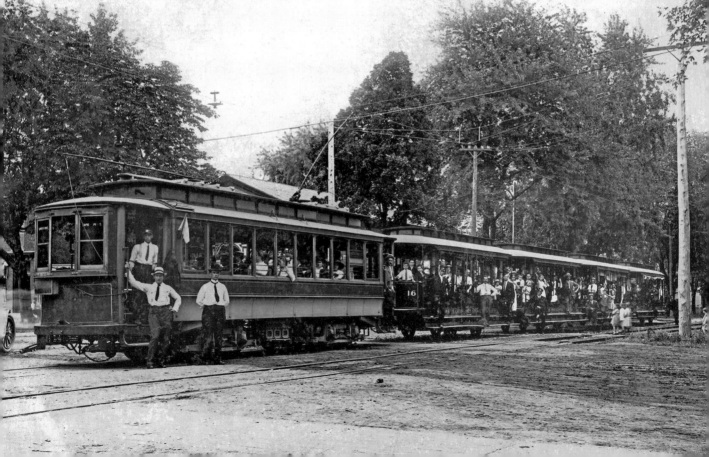

CHAPTER 4

NS&T — General Information

THE Niagara, St. Catharines & Toronto Railway Company was incorporated in 1899 to take over the property of the St. Catharines & Niagara Central Railway. The owning interests were those in control of the Hudson Valley Railway, an interurban network in upstate New York north of Albany. Despite the American ownership, Chairman of the Board was Z. A. Lash of Toronto, a close associate of Mackenzie and Mann (who built the Canadian Northern Railway), evidence of the early interest of these enterprising partners in the Niagara Peninsula.

Between 1899 and 1902 the company completed the framework on which its subsequent development was based, as detailed in later chapters. The present chapter deals with events affecting the company as a whole in its more than six decades of existence.

Extensions Proposed

The first act of the new company, undertaken in April 1900, was to start construction of the Port Dalhousie line, over the strong objections of the local street railway company, which had not yet been taken over. Port Dalhousie, at the foot of the Welland Canal, was the departure point for the Toronto lake boats, with adjacent small picnic grounds and amusement area known as Lakeside Park. By 1902 the railway completed its acquisition of these marine and park interests, to be operated under the name Niagara, St. Catharines & Toronto Navigation Company (described further in later chapters).

Plans were announced in 1902 for the Hamilton extension. This was to branch from the Port Dalhousie line at Barnesdale, run parallel to the lakeshore to Twenty-Mile Creek, then along the Queenston & Grimsby Stone Road to a crossing over the Grand Trunk Railway near Beamsville and a junction with the Hamilton Grimsby & Beamsville Electric Railway. A branch from Beamsville to St. Anns and Smithville was provided for; this was an interesting reversion to the abortive Niagara Central proposal, and reflects the continuing wish of residents of the Niagara Peninsula for an alternative to the Grand Trunk monopoly. Haines Brothers were also promoting an interurban between Hamilton and Brantford, and a major interurban system would have been produced if their plans had come to pass.

Opposite Top: NS&T open car 51 c1905.
(LIBRARY AND ARCHIVES CANADA E004665776)

Opposite Bottom: Train consisting of motor car and trailers 14-17, with large charter group, is westbound on King Street at Queen Street, Niagara-on-the-Lake c1913. Michigan Central Railroad is adjacent track. See other views, same location, pages 80 and 81.
(LIBRARY AND ARCHIVES CANADA E004666261)

A draft agreement, never executed, reveals the NS&T proposal that cars of both companies would run through from Hamilton to Niagara Falls, at a mileage payment of 1.75 cents when running over the other company's line. The NS&T, unlike the HG&B, would have used the Hamilton Radial's terminal at James and Gore streets, and preliminary plans were made for a wye and for expansion of the small station. A separate freight station was planned on TH&B property near Trolley Street (now Gage Avenue). A long bridge would have been required over Sixteen-Mile Creek, and arrangements were made to purchase a five-span bridge from the New York Central, which had just removed it from its main line at Herkimer, New York.

Control Returns To Canada

A minor depression in 1903-04 was probably responsible for failure of these plans, because the New York owners encountered financial difficulties and sold out to a Toronto group. Two Canadian Northern men joined the Board; other directors were associated with Sir William Mackenzie in Toronto electric utility promotion. This led to the incorporation of the Toronto, Niagara & Western Railway, which would have built a St. Catharines–Toronto interurban along the right-of-way of the Toronto Power Company's new transmission line. This project was kept alive for some years, with the later addition of a union interurban terminal at Yonge Street (close to CPR's North Toronto Station) for use by the Toronto, Niagara & Western, the Toronto & York Radial, the Toronto Suburban Railway and the Toronto Eastern Railway — all Mackenzie properties.

In 1908, control of the NS&T passed to the Canadian Northern Railway (CNoR), which had previously a forty percent interest, and all directors were CNoR men. It was thenceforward operated as a semi-autonomous unit of the Canadian Northern system, and its financing was handled, in the peculiar style of the CNoR, by Mackenzie, Mann & Company. It was not until 1915 that the NS&T was shown as a constituent company of the Canadian Northern system in the yearly financial statements.

More Extension Plans

Still another proposal in 1913 was for an even more ambitious line running around Hamilton Bay instead of across the Beach in order to provide better station and yard locations. Three tremendous bridges, each over 110 feet high, would have been required over valleys east of Vineland. This line would have joined the NS&T near Thorold. A second line would have run from Fonthill through Caledonia to Brantford, and the NS&T was assessed part of

Top: *S.S. Dalhousie City* alongside NS&T freight shed and passenger station at Port Dalhousie dock c1920.
(NIAGARA FALLS (ONTARIO) PUBLIC LIBRARY)

Opposite Top: Port Dalhousie dock, electric cars and steamer *Garden City* c1910.
(LIBRARY AND ARCHIVES CANADA E004666260)

Opposite Bottom: Freight motor 14 c1920.
(LIBRARY AND ARCHIVES CANADA E004665774)

Bottom: Line car 30, just outshopped c1921.
(JOHN BURTNIAK COLLECTION, ST. CATHARINES MUSEUM)

the cost of a new bridge in Brantford which the new line would use. These extensions would undoubtedly have been steam-operated, only the NS&T charter rights being used.

After World War I, the Province of Ontario's Hydro-radial scheme (of which more later) included a Toronto–St. Catharines line, and thus it was not until 1923 that the project for a Toronto extension was finally dropped.

As can perhaps be sensed, the motives for Canadian Northern interest in the NS&T changed as the goals of Mackenzie and Mann expanded. At first a regional Prairie carrier, the Canadian Northern soon resolved to become a transcontinental system in order not to remain dependent on its competitors who also provided its connections both east and west. The CNoR development took place at the same time as the expansion and consolidation of public utilities in Ontario. Some of the same men were closely involved in both schemes, among them Mackenzie and others inside the Canadian Northern's inner circle. In carrying out these enormous plans, they made use of the means at hand, e.g. something would be done by a utility corporation that was to be shared at a later date, perhaps, by a railway corporation under arrangements to be made later. These long-range plans were sometimes carried out, sometimes abandoned and sometimes replaced by others, so that there were always corporate bits and pieces lying around waiting for their time to come, or ignored as being part of a purpose that had not come to pass.

These characteristics were all present with respect to the NS&T. Partly by accident and partly by design, the system was vital to its owners from two points of view, neither of which had very much to do with providing electric railway service to the eastern Niagara Peninsula. First, it would help to bring electric power from Niagara to Toronto, the cornerstone of Mackenzie's utilities empire, and second, it would help to bring Canadian Northern trains from Toronto to Niagara, considered essential for the long-term prosperity of the railroad.

Meanwhile the CNoR undertook an expansion program for the NS&T. Within five years, it had built the two longest interurban lines and completed unification of the various components of the system. In 1905 an office building and waiting room, a rather ugly corrugated-

N. St. C. & T. RY. No. 14.

iron structure, was built on St. Paul Street; car storage and repair facilities were centralized on the former Niagara Central freight yard property on Welland Avenue. The system was quite profitable, with operating ratios hovering around fifty per cent. Track mileage was increasing rapidly: 47.7 miles (1913); 60.9 miles (1914); 75.2 miles (1922). In 1915 the company attempted to buy the little-used Michigan Central line from Fort Erie to Niagara-on-the-Lake but was unsuccessful.

Hydro-radials

Under the energetic urging of Sir Adam Beck, the Hydro-Electric Power Commission of Ontario, about the time of World War I, promoted a number of Hydro-operated radial railways in southern Ontario. These were to be high-class electric lines built and managed by the Hydro Commission but paid for by the municipalities through which they would run. The financing was to be done by a special bond issue in each municipality, which would have to be approved by the voters. These proposals always became the centre of intense political fighting, made worse by Beck's habit of entering the fray with enormous absence of tact. Favourable votes had to be recorded in municipalities representing 85 percent of the financing before any particular line could be built.

The Toronto–Hamilton–St. Catharines line was in an advanced state of planning by 1921, and the HEPC was

Top: Military parade and car 105, St. Paul Street, St. Catharines 1915.
(PUBLISHER'S COLLECTION)

Opposite: Car 100 and steamer *Lakeside* were featured in this 1901 NS&T brochure.
(R.J. SANDUSKY COLLECTION)

Bottom: Car 105, crew and passengers at St. Catharines c1918.
(H.E. BATTEL)

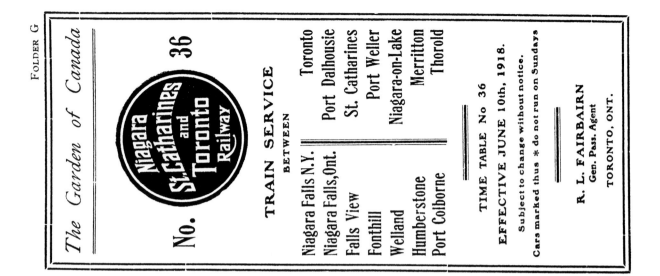

The Garden of Canada — Folder G

No. 36 — Niagara St. Catharines and Toronto Railway

TRAIN SERVICE BETWEEN

Niagara Falls N.Y. — Toronto
Niagara Falls, Ont. — Port Dalhousie
Falls View — St. Catharines
Fonthill — Port Weller
Welland — Niagara-on-Lake
Humberstone — Merritton
Port Colborne — Thorold

TIME TABLE No 36 — EFFECTIVE JUNE 10th, 1918.
Subject to change without notice. Cars marked thus * do not run on Sundays

R. L. FAIRBAIRN, Gen. Pass. Agent, TORONTO, ONT.

MERRITTON AND THOROLD DIVISION

GOING EAST—UP

LEAVE	*am	*	*	*	*	*	*	*	*	*	*	*			pm												
McKinnon's			6 10	6 30	6 50	7 10	7 30	7 50	8 10	8 30	8 50	9 10	AND EVERY 20 MINUTES UNTIL		12 10	12 30	12 50	1 10	1 30	1 50	2 10	2 30	2 50	3 10	AND EVERY 20 MINUTES UNTIL	10 50
General Office	5 40	6 00	6 20	6 40	7 00	7 20	7 40	8 00	8 20	8 40	9 00	9 20			12 20	12 40	1 00	1 20	1 40	2 00	2 20	2 40	3 00	3 20		11 00
Calvin Street	5 45	6 05	6 25	6 45	7 05	7 25	7 45	8 05	8 25	8 45	9 05	9 25			12 25	12 45	1 05	1 25	1 45	2 05	2 25	2 45	3 05	3 25		11 05
Lincoln Avenue	5 50	6 10	6 30	6 50	7 10	7 30	7 50	8 10	8 30	8 50	9 10	9 30			12 30	12 50	1 10	1 30	1 50	2 10	2 30	2 50	3 10	3 30		11 10
Centre Switch	5 55	6 15	6 35	6 55	7 15	7 35	7 55	8 15	8 35	8 55	9 15	9 35			12 35	12 55	1 15	1 35	1 55	2 15	2 35	2 55	3 15	3 35		11 15
G. T. R. Bridge	5 58	6 18	6 38	6 58	7 18	7 38	7 58	8 18	8 38	8 58	9 18	9 38			12 38	12 58	1 18	1 38	1 58	2 18	2 38	2 58	3 18	3 38		11 18
Cotton Mill	6 00	6 20	6 40	7 00	7 20	7 40	8 00	8 20	8 40	9 00	9 20	9 40			12 40	1 00	1 20	1 40	2 00	2 20	2 40	3 00	3 20	3 40		11 20
Town Line	6 05	6 25	6 45	7 05	7 25	7 45	8 05	8 25	8 45	9 05	9 25	9 45			12 45	1 05	1 25	1 45	2 05	2 25	2 45	3 05	3 25	3 45		11 25
Thorold	6 10	6 30	6 50	7 10	7 30	7 50	8 10	8 30	8 50	9 10	9 30	9 50			12 50	1 10	1 30	1 50	2 10	2 30	2 50	3 10	3 30	3 50		11 30

GOING WEST—DOWN

LEAVE	*am	*	*	*	*	*	*	*	*	*	*	*			pm												
Thorold	6 10	6 30	6 50	7 10	7 30	7 50	8 10	8 30	8 50	9 10	9 30	9 50	AND EVERY 20 MINUTES UNTIL		12 10	12 30	12 50	1 10	1 30	1 50	2 10	2 30	2 50	3 10	AND EVERY 20 MINUTES UNTIL	11 30
Town Line	6 15	6 35	6 55	7 15	7 35	7 55	8 15	8 35	8 55	9 15	9 35	9 55			12 15	12 35	12 55	1 15	1 35	1 55	2 15	2 35	2 55	3 15		11 35
Cotton Mill	6 20	6 40	7 00	7 20	7 40	8 00	8 20	8 40	9 00	9 20	9 40	10 00			12 20	12 40	1 00	1 20	1 40	2 00	2 20	2 40	3 00	3 20		11 40
G. T. R. Bridge	6 22	6 42	7 02	7 22	7 42	8 02	8 22	8 42	9 02	9 22	9 42	10 02			12 22	12 42	1 02	1 22	1 42	2 02	2 22	2 42	3 02	3 22		11 42
Centre Switch	6 25	6 45	7 05	7 25	7 45	8 05	8 25	8 45	9 05	9 25	9 45	10 05			12 25	12 45	1 05	1 25	1 45	2 05	2 25	2 45	3 05	3 25		11 45
Lincoln Avenue	6 30	6 50	7 10	7 30	7 50	8 10	8 30	8 50	9 10	9 30	9 50	10 10			12 30	12 50	1 10	1 30	1 50	2 10	2 30	2 50	3 10	3 30		11 50
Calvin Street	6 35	6 55	7 15	7 35	7 55	8 15	8 35	8 55	9 15	9 35	9 55	10 15			12 35	12 55	1 15	1 35	1 55	2 15	2 35	2 55	3 15	3 35		11 55
General Office	6 40	7 00	7 20	7 40	8 00	8 20	8 40	9 00	9 20	9 40	10 00	10 20			12 40	1 00	1 20	1 40	2 00	2 20	2 40	3 00	3 20	3 40		12 00
McKinnon's	6 50	7 10	7 30	7 50	8 10	8 30	8 50	9 10	9 30	9 50	10 10	10 30			12 50	1 10	1 30	1 50	2 10	2 30	2 50	3 10	3 30	3 50		12 00 Barn

* Cars marked thus do not run on Sundays

PORT DALHOUSIE DIVISION

NORTH BOUND

LEAVE	*am	*	*	*	*	*	*						pm														AND EVERY 30 MINUTES UNTIL			
St. Catharines	6 00	6 30	7 00	7 30	8 00	8 30	9 00	9 30	10 00	10 30	11 00	11 30	12 00	12 30	1 00	1 30	2 00	2 30	3 00	3 30	4 00	4 30	5 00	5 30	6 00	6 30		10 30	11 00	12 00
Barnesdale	6 10	6 42	7 12	7 42	8 12	8 42	9 12	9 42	10 12	10 42	11 12	11 42	12 12	12 42	1 12	1 42	2 12	2 42	3 12	3 42	4 12	4 42	5 12	5 42	6 12	6 42		10 42	11 12	12 12
Port Dalhousie Arrive	6 20	7 00	7 30	8 00	8 30	9 00	9 30	10 00	10 30	11 00	11 30	12 00	12 30	1 00	1 30	2 00	2 30	3 00	3 30	4 00	4 30	5 00	5 30	6 00	6 30	7 00		11 00	11 30	12 30

SOUTH BOUND

LEAVE	*am	*	*	*	*	*	*					pm															AND EVERY 30 MINUTES UNTIL			
Port Dalhousie	6 20	7 00	7 30	8 00	8 30	9 00	9 30	10 00	10 30	11 00	11 30	12 00	12 30	1 00	1 30	2 00	2 30	3 00	3 30	4 00	4 30	5 00	5 30	6 00	6 30	7 00		11 00	11 30	12 30
Barnesdale	6 30	7 12	7 42	8 12	8 42	9 12	9 42	10 12	10 42	11 12	11 42	12 12	12 42	1 12	1 42	2 12	2 42	3 12	3 42	4 12	4 42	5 12	5 42	6 12	6 42	7 12		11 12	11 42	12 42
St. Catharines		7 30	8 00	8 30	9 00	9 30	10 00	10 30	11 00	11 30	12 00	12 30	1 00	1 30	2 00	2 30	3 00	3 30	4 00	4 30	5 00	5 30	6 00	6 30	7 00	7 30		11 30	12 00	1 00
Merritton	6 54																													
Thorold	7 00																													

* Cars marked thus do not run on Sundays.

CEMETERY DIVISION

EAST BOUND

LEAVE	*am	*	*	*	*	*	*	*	*	pm																
General Office	6 20	7 00	7 40	8 20	9 00	9 40	10 20	11 00	11 40	12 20	1 00	1 40	2 20	3 00	3 40	4 20	5 00	5 40	6 20	7 00	7 40	8 20	9 00	9 40	10 20	11 00
Hennessey's Corner	6 26	7 06	7 46	8 26	9 06	9 46	10 26	11 06	11 46	12 26	1 06	1 46	2 26	3 06	3 46	4 26	5 06	5 46	6 26	7 06	7 46	8 26	9 06	9 46	10 26	11 06
Arrive Victoria Lawn	6 33	7 13	7 53	8 33	9 13	9 53	10 33	11 13	11 53	12 33	1 13	1 53	2 33	3 13	3 53	4 33	5 13	5 53	6 33	7 13	7 53	8 33	9 13	9 53	10 33	11 13

WEST BOUND

LEAVE	*am	*	*	*	*	*	*	*	pm																	
Victoria Lawn	6 40	7 20	8 00	8 40	9 20	10 00	10 40	11 20	12 00	12 40	1 20	2 00	2 40	3 20	4 00	4 40	5 20	6 00	6 40	7 20	8 00	8 40	9 20	10 00	10 40	11 20
Hennessey's Corner	6 47	7 27	8 07	8 47	9 27	10 07	10 47	11 27	12 07	12 47	1 27	2 07	2 47	3 27	4 07	4 47	5 27	6 07	6 47	7 27	8 07	8 47	9 27	10 07	10 47	11 27
Arrive General Office	6 53	7 33	8 13	8 53	9 33	10 13	10 53	11 33	12 13	12 53	1 33	2 13	2 53	3 33	4 13	4 53	5 33	6 13	6 53	7 33	8 13	8 53	9 33	10 13	10 53	11 33

Cemetery Cars do not run past General Office.

MAIN LINE
EAST BOUND

MILES	LEAVE	*am	*	*							pm						*									
0.0	St. Catharines	5 35	6 00	6 41	7 00	8 00	9 00	10 00	11 00	12 00	1 00	2 00	3 00	4 00	4 30	5 00	6 00	7 00	8 00	9 00	10 00	11 00	12 00
2.9	Lincoln Ave.	5 46	6 12	6 46	7 12	8 12	9 12	10 12	11 12	12 12	1 12	2 12	3 12	4 12	4 38	5 12	6 12	7 12	8 12	9 12	10 12	11 12	12 12
4.0	Merritton	5 52	6 18	6 52	7 18	8 18	9 18	10 18	11 18	12 18	1 18	2 18	3 18	4 18	4 46	5 18	6 18	7 18	8 18	9 18	10 18	11 18	12 18
6.0	Thorold	6 00	6 24	7 00	7 24	8 24	9 24	10 24	11 24	12 24	1 24	2 24	3 24	4 24	4 52	5 24	6 24	7 24	8 24	9 24	10 24	11 24	12 24
12.7	Stamford		6 37		7 37	8 37	9 37	10 37	11 37	12 37	1 37	2 37	3 37	4 37	5 07	5 37	6 37	7 37	8 37	9 37	10 37	11 37	12 37
13.8	N., St. C. & T. Junc.		6 41		7 41	8 41	9 41	10 41	11 41	12 41	1 41	2 41	3 41	4 41	5 09	5 41	6 41	7 41	8 41	9 41	10 41	11 41	12 41
	Niagara Falls Ont.		6 50		7 50	8 50	9 50	10 50	11 50	12 50	1 50	2 50	3 50	4 50	5 20	5 50	6 50	7 50	8 50	9 50	10 50	11 50	12 50
	Niagara Falls, N.Y. (Int. Ry.)		7 10		8 10	9 10	10 10	11 10	12 10	1 10	2 10	3 10	4 10	5 10	....	6 10	7 10	8 10	9 10	10 10	11 10	12 10	

WEST BOUND

MILES	LEAVE	*am	*						pm					*									
0.0	Niagara Falls, N.Y. (Int. Ry.)	....	6 40	7 40	8 40	9 40	10 40	11 40	12 40	1 40	2 40	3 40	4 40	....	5 40	6 40	7 40	8 40	9 40	10 40	....	11 40	....
0.0	Niagara Falls, Ont.	....	7 00	8 00	9 00	10 00	11 00	12 00	1 00	2 00	3 00	4 00	5 00	5 30	6 00	7 00	8 00	9 00	10 00	11 00		12 00	1 00
1.1	N., St. C. & T. Junc.	....	7 09	8 09	9 09	10 09	11 09	12 09	1 09	2 09	3 09	4 09	5 09	5 41	6 09	7 09	8 09	9 09	10 09	11 09		12 09	1 09
7.8	Stamford	....	7 13	8 13	9 13	10 13	11 13	12 13	1 13	2 13	3 13	4 13	5 13	5 43	6 13	7 13	8 13	9 13	10 13	11 13		12 13	1 13
9.8	Thorold	6 00	7 26	8 26	9 26	10 26	11 26	12 26	1 26	2 26	3 26	4 26	5 26	5 57	6 26	7 26	8 26	9 26	10 26	11 26		12 24	1 26
10.9	Merritton	6 06	7 32	8 32	9 32	10 32	11 32	12 32	1 32	2 32	3 32	4 32	5 32	6 03	6 32	7 32	8 32	9 32	10 32	11 32		12 30	1 32
13.8	Lincoln Ave.	6 10	7 38	8 38	9 38	10 38	11 38	12 38	1 38	2 38	3 38	4 38	5 38	6 12	6 38	7 38	8 38	9 38	10 38	11 38		12 37	1 38
	St. Catharines	6 30	7 50	8 50	9 50	10 50	11 50	12 50	1 50	2 50	3 50	4 50	5 50	6 20	6 50	7 50	8 50	9 50	10 50	11 50		12 47	1 50

* Cars marked thus do not run Sundays.

DRUMMONDVILLE AND FALLS VIEW DIVISION

Leave CATHOLIC CHURCH—*5.23, *5.38 and *5.53 a.m.
Leave BRIDGE STREET—*6.00, *6.15, *6.30, *6.45 a.m, then every 15 minutes until 11.45 last car 12.30 a.m.
Leave MONTROSE—*5.45, *6.00, *6.15, *6.30, *6.45, *7.00, *7.15, then every 15 minutes until 12.15; last car 1.00 a.m.

    * Cars marked thus do not run on Sundays.   All time tables subject to change without notice.

Steamer "DALHOUSIE CITY"
SUNDAY BOAT SERVICE
Effective JUNE 30th

Leave Port Dalhousie 9.30 a.m.   **Leave Toronto 7 p.m.**

Time Table Between Niagara Falls, N.Y., and Toronto
SEASON 1918
Daily Except Sunday (Weather Permitting)

NIAGARA FALLS TO TORONTO			TORONTO TO NIAGARA FALLS	
LEAVE	a m		LEAVE	p m
Niagara Falls, N.Y. (Int. R.)	6 40		Toronto	5 00
Niagara Falls, Ont.	7 00		Port Dalhousie	7 30
Port Colborne	6 08		St. Catharines	8 00
Welland	6 33		Welland .... Arr.	9 00
St. Catharines	8 00		Port Colborne ...... Arr.	9 24
Port Dalhousie	8 30		Niagara Falls, Ont. .. Arr.	8 50
Toronto .... Arr.	10 30		Niagara Falls, N.Y ... Arr.	9 10
			(Int. Ry)	

Navigation will close on or about December 1st

PORT COLBORNE DIVISION

MILES	SOUTH BOUND	*am					pm								
0.0	Thorold	6 00	7 30	8 30	9 30	10 30	12 00	1 30	3 00	4 30	6 00	7 00	8 30	10 00	11 30
6.8	Fonthill	6 18	7 48	8 48	9 48	10 48	12 18	1 48	3 18	4 48	6 18	7 18	8 48	10 18	11 48
11.0	Welland	6 30	8 00	9 00	10 00	11 00	12 30	2 00	3 30	5 00	6 30	7 30	9 00	10 30	12 00
17.3	Humberstone	6 47	8 16	9 16	10 16	11 16	12 46	2 16	3 46	5 16	6 46	7 46	9 16	10 46	12 16
18.8	Port Colborne ...... Arr.	6 57	8 24	9 24	10 24	11 24	12 54	2 24	3 54	5 24	6 54	7 54	9 24	10 54	12 24

MILES	NORTH BOUND	*am					pm								
0.0	Port Colborne	6 08	7 30	8 30	9 30	10 30	12 00	1 30	3 00	4 30	6 00	7 00	8 30	10 00	11 30
1.5	Humberstone	6 16	7 38	8 38	9 38	10 38	12 08	1 38	3 08	4 38	6 08	7 08	8 38	10 08	11 38
7.8	Welland	6 33	7 54	8 54	9 54	10 54	12 24	1 54	3 24	4 54	6 24	7 24	8 54	10 24	11 54
12.0	Fonthill	6 41	8 08	9 08	10 08	11 08	12 38	2 08	3 38	5 08	6 38	7 38	9 08	10 38	12 08
18.8	Thorold ...... Arr.	7 08	8 24	9 24	10 24	11 24	12 54	2 24	3 54	5 24	6 54	7 54	9 24	10 54	12 24

* Cars marked thus do not run on Sundays.

LAKE SHORE DIVISION

Stop No.	NORTH BOUND	*AM	*					PM												
43	General Office	6 00	7 00	8 00	9 00	10 00	11 00	12 00	1 00	2 00	3 00	4 00	5 00	6 00	7 00	8 00	9 00	10 00	11 00
48	Carleton Street	6 15	7 15	8 15	9 15	10 15	11 15	12 15	1 15	2 15	3 15	4 15	5 15	6 15	7 15	8 15	9 15	10 15	11 15
54	Port Weller	6 23	7 23	8 23	9 23	10 23	11 23	12 23	1 23	2 23	3 23	4 23	5 23	6 23	7 23	8 23	9 23	10 23	11 23
58	McNab	6 28	7 28	8 28	9 28	10 28	11 28	12 28	1 28	2 28	3 28	4 28	5 28	6 28	7 28	8 28	9 28	10 28	11 28
60	Colemans	6 31	7 31	8 31	9 31	10 31	11 30	12 31	1 31	2 31	3 31	4 31	5 31	6 31	7 31	8 31	9 31	10 31	11 31
74	Creek Road	6 34	7 34	8 34	9 34	10 34	11 34	12 34	1 34	2 34	3 34	4 34	5 34	6 34	7 34	8 34	9 34	10 34	11 34
	Niagara	6 44	7	8 44	9 44	10 44	11 44	12 44	1 44	2 44	3 44	4 44	5 44	6 44	7 44	8 44	9 44	10 44	11 44

Stop No.	SOUTH BOUND	AM	*					PM												
74	Niagara	7 00	8 00	9 00	10 00	11 00	12 00	1 00	2 00	3 00	4 00	5 00	6 00	7 00	8 00	9 00	10 00	11 00	12 00
60	Creek Road	7 10	8 10	9 10	10 10	11 10	12 10	1 10	2 10	3 10	4 10	5 10	6 10	7 10	8 10	9 10	10 10	11 10	12 10
58	Colemans	7 13	8 13	9 13	10 13	11 13	12 13	1 13	2 13	3 13	4 13	5 13	6 13	7 13	8 13	9 13	10 13	11 13	12 13
54	McNab	7 16	8 16	9 16	10 16	11 16	12 16	1 16	2 16	3 16	4 16	5 16	6 16	7 16	8 16	9 16	10 16	11 16	12 16
48	Port Weller	7 21	8 21	9 21	10 21	11 21	12 21	1 21	2 21	3 21	4 21	5 21	6 21	7 21	8 21	9 21	10 21	11 21	12 21
43	Carleton Street	7 29	8 29	9 29	10 29	11 29	12 29	1 29	2 29	3 29	4 29	5 29	6 29	7 29	8 29	9 29	10 29	11 29	12 29
	General Office	7 44	8 44	9 44	10 44	11 44	12 44	1 44	2 44	3 44	4 44	5 44	6 44	7 44	8 44	9 44	10 44	11 44	12 44

Opposite and Top: NS&T public timetable No. 36. (TED WICKSON COLLECTION)

purchasing rights-of-way and making other preliminary expenditures to the eventual amount of almost one million dollars. In November of that year the Canadian National Railway Company gave the Commission an option on the entire NS&T system, the purchase price to be $3,544,374. A meeting of seventeen area municipalities held on December 1st endorsed the Hydro scheme with enthusiasm. However, the provincial government, in the grip of a post-war economy drive, was much less enthusiastic than was Sir Adam and refused its approval of the financing arrangements for the radial scheme. Another municipal meeting on December 22nd unanimously expressed its "extreme indignation and regret" and strongly urged that the project "be gone ahead with" immediately. What proved to be the final blow occurred at the 1922 municipal elections when favourable votes were recorded in places that would assume less than fifty percent of the radial's cost.

Nationalization

By 1917, wartime conditions and tight money policies spelt doom for the incomplete Canadian Northern empire. The NS&T, as a constituent company, was included in the assets that the Dominion Government took over as

Opposite Top: Panorama of St. Catharines yard.
(J.D. KNOWLES)

Opposite: St. Catharines Terminal platforms c1946.
(J.J. WIGT COLLECTION)

Opposite Bottom: Interior of St. Catharines shops with cars 61 and 83, June 1947.
(J.D. KNOWLES)

Bottom: Toronto Suburban Railway car 107, built by NS&T in 1925, on a test run on Welland Avenue at Geneva Street in St. Catharines. This car later became NS&T car 83.
(R.J. SANDUSKY COLLECTION)

its price for extricating the parent system from its hopeless financial position. In July 1917, the government, already holding forty percent of CNoR stock, decided that further aid could only be granted on condition that it be given the remainder of the stock or, in other words, that the government, rather than Mackenzie and Mann, should own the Canadian Northern system. After prolonged negotiations, on September 6th 1918 Sir William Mackenzie and Sir Donald Mann resigned from the system that they had, in a little over twenty years, built up from literally nothing. On December 20th, the name was changed to the Canadian National Railway Company. Thus the Dominion Government found itself in the somewhat incongruous position of operating local street railway services and an amusement park.

Plans for the Future

In November 1922, E.W. Oliver, General Superintendent of the line, presented an exhaustive report on the company's operations and prospects for the guidance of the highest officials of the Canadian National. Much of the preliminary work had been done by H.R. Vercoe. Based on twelve years' results and a forecast of future conditions, it made far-reaching recommendations intended to guide company policy in the 1924-27-improvement period. The very optimistic tone with which the report was written was the result of the fact that the year 1921 — the last previous year for which operating statistics were available — appeared to mark yet another in an ever-increasing annual sequence of traffic gains. Unfortunately, 1921 proved to be the company's peak year. Thereafter, even as improvements were being made based on the assumption that conditions would continue to advance, the passenger load began a twenty-year decline that was to reduce it by more than half. The basic cause, of course, was the rapid spread of

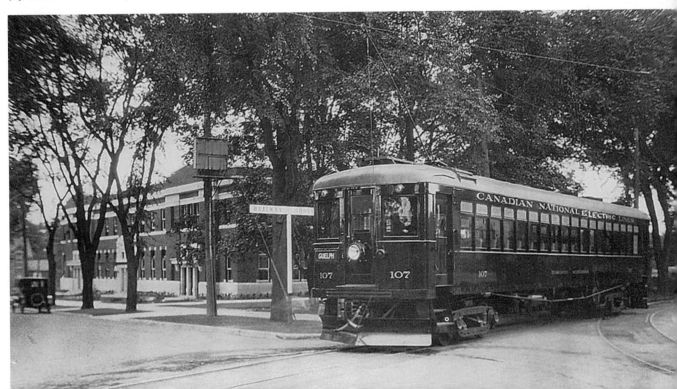

paved highways and motor vehicles, something not envis-
aged in the report. Another omission, possibly caused by
the fact that its authors were railway people rather than
transportation people, is that nowhere was there a single
mention of the motorbus.

One of the company's continuing problems was the fact
that it operated in many different municipalities, each with
a separate franchise and a council ever vigilant for trans-
gressions, real or imagined. While the Hydro-Radial proposals were pending, most of these franchises had expired,
but operations were continued on an ad-hoc basis. The
new franchises, when negotiated, usually required much
new capital investment. The company's physical condition was deteriorating and a rolling stock shortage developed, largely owing to a great increase in passenger volume
(*1903*: 1,204,000; *1913*: 3,887,000; *1923*: 7,553,000) that
was particularly noticeable on the local lines.

Canadian National Electric Railways

After the collapse of the Hydro-Radial plans, the CNR
took steps to unify the NS&T, the Toronto Suburban
Railway and the incomplete Toronto Eastern under one
management. The result was the formation in November
1923 of the Canadian National Electric Railways, with
headquarters in Toronto. The NS&T did not become fully
integrated with the others until 1925, since there were still
a few shares outside CNR control. The Oshawa Railway,
the Thousand Islands Railway (steam) and the Montreal &
Southern Counties Railway were closely associated, though
never a corporate part of the CNER. Use of the CNER
name was short-lived and was replaced by that of the parent Canadian National Railways about the end of 1928.

Expansion and Modernization

Under CNER management, a four-year $2½-million
modernization program was undertaken for the NS&T
District. Notable capital items included new interurban
terminals, route extensions, new cars and virtually complete track rehabilitation of local lines. Track mileage increased from 85.77 (*1922*) to 104.29 (*1928*). The wisdom
of investing so much money in such an enterprise at that
time is open to question. As Mr. J. R. Empringham, for
many years Superintendent of the line, was to remark 25
years later, "If this work of rehabilitation had been left for
another two or three years, it is possible that it never would
have been done at all, and a bus service would have been
established at that time for a much smaller expenditure
than was made on cars and tracks." It is fair to point out,
however, that the failure to anticipate the rapid spread of
automotive transport was not at all unique to the NS&T.

Details of the new facilities will be found in subsequent
chapters, and it is only necessary to indicate here that the
railway reached its peak in this period, as far as geographical
extent and physical condition are concerned. With so much
capital tied up in the system, which it soon appeared could

Opposite Top: Track construction at St. Paul and Geneva streets,
September 1925.
(H.E. BATTEL COLLECTION)

Opposite Bottom: Old track at St. Paul Street station before
rehabilitation 1925.
(H.E. BATTEL, J.J. WIGT COLLECTION)

Bottom: 300s (eight cars), led by car 305, newly outshopped at
St. Catharines shops, 1926.
(H.E. BATTEL)

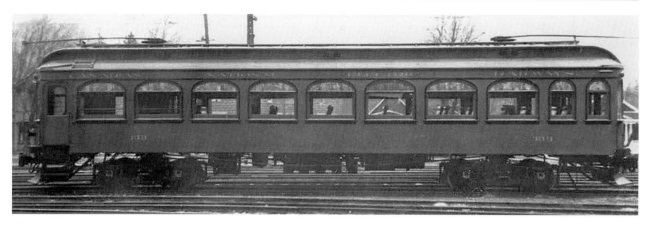

never be entirely recovered, it was found necessary to maintain a policy of strict economy in all aspects of NS&T financing. Thereafter, the task of management was essentially to do what needed to be done while employing the absolute minimum of new capital. As an example of this policy in practice, the local lines remained a rail operation long after the time when other similar railways had been converted, purely from a desire to avoid investment in buses.

The car shops on Welland Avenue were expanded as a car-building centre for all CNR electric lines, and, in addition to its own cars, the shop built equipment for Toronto Suburban, Oshawa Railway, Montreal & Southern Counties and for parent CNR (battery and self-propelled cars). It also assembled twelve new cars shipped in pieces from Cincinnati. The amount of such work done probably did not justify the investment involved in setting up the shop. The carhouse and yard property was expanded over the years to occupy an area of approximately 3½ acres. (Oshawa line car 45 at the Halton County Radial Railway Museum at Milton, Ontario is now the only car in existence that was built at St. Catharines shops.)

A characteristic of the 1920s was the great development of tourist travel. The NS&T was in a good position to exploit this because it served Niagara Falls and operated lake steamers; indeed it was forced to emphasize this because of its small resident population. Many of the 1924-27 changes, therefore, were aimed at improving the NS&T's competitive position in this regard. Agreements were made with bus lines in Ontario and New York, and with steamer lines on Lake Erie. One tour offered a great novelty: an airplane ride. By such means the company was quite successful in attracting excursion business. For large special parties originating on the American side, USA-based International Railway Company interurbans sometimes ran through to Port Dalhousie, in Canada.

The lucrative through-passenger traffic from Toronto to the Falls area had always been a very competitive market. The Grand Trunk (CNR) served the inconvenient uptown Bridge Street station, while Canada Steamship Lines (formerly Niagara Navigation Company) used dock facilities at Queenston where connections were made with cars of the Niagara Falls Park & River Railway for direct service to the major Falls attractions.

Top: Car 133 at St. Catharines prior to its retirement in 1935. (B. SCHUFF COLLECTION)

Opposite Top: Train of cars 131 & 134 on the Falls Subdivision, passing Niagara Tower as they arrive at St. Catharines, July 20th 1947. (JOHN HUMISTON, S7235)

Opposite Bottom: Car 120 loading on St. Paul Street c1927. (CRHA, FONDS R.F. CORLEY)

Direct interurban bus service from Toronto to Niagara Falls (and Buffalo) was inaugurated by the Toronto Transportation Commission in 1926; however travel times were not competitive with the cross-lake marine service and electric railway connections. The TTC saw great potential in traffic to the Niagara region and, in 1927, established Gray Coach Lines (GCL) as a wholly-owned subsidiary to exploit this and other tourist markets in Ontario. When the new divided highway "Queen Elizabeth Way" was completed in 1940, GCL offered more frequent scheduled express trips and very competitive travel times when compared with NS&T's co-ordinated marine and railway service.

The NS&T's first bus was operated on February 1st 1929 in St. Catharines in lieu of proposed rail extensions. The first such operation outside the city started on January 15th 1931 replacing Lake Shore Division interurban service. Buses were lettered "Canadian National Transportation Ltd." but operated by the NS&T as an integral part of its system. They were always "coaches" in company parlance and, in number of vehicles operated, eventually overshadowed the rail operation.

In addition to acting as freight feeder for the CNR, the NS&T participated in its passenger ticketing arrangements. Many passengers used punch-out multiple-ride commutation tickets. Those for use on the Welland Division had an unusual double-punching arrangement for through rides to Main Line points: one punch was made on each line, or both punches on the Welland Division if the ride were confined to that line.

An unusual feature was the practice of showing the name of the Division rather than the destination on the cars. Thus, until 1955, they were signed "Welland Div." (later simply "Welland") or "Lake Shore Div." Port Dalhousie cars carried "Port Dalhousie" in both directions.

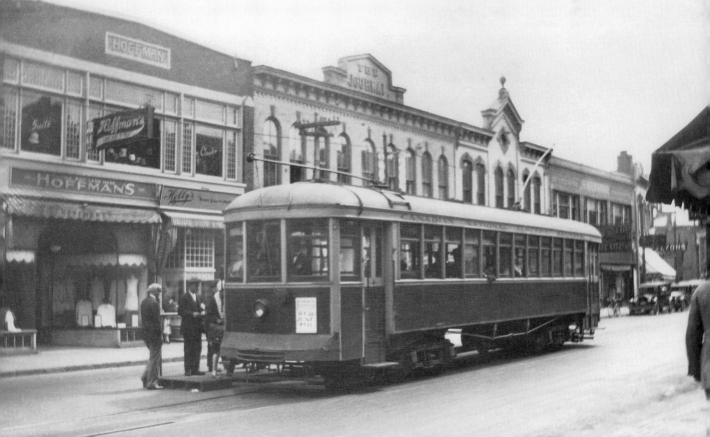

Depression

As an economy measure, wages were reduced 10 per cent in 1932 and a further 5 per cent early in 1934. As conditions began to improve, the 1934 reductions were wiped out in the following year and increases were subsequently made in steady progression. In 1935 the company had 310 employees, though this number was increased for the summer season. The peak number of passengers was almost 8 million in 1921; this dropped slowly to 6 million in 1929 and then plummeted to a low of about 2½ million in 1933. It inched up to 4½ million in 1940. Then war conditions made themselves felt: 6½ million (1941); 9½ million (1942); 12½ million (1943); 13 million (1944); 14 million (1945-46). The post-war peak was reached in 1948 (14,670,000) after which a definite decline began.

The worst snow conditions in the history of the railway occurred in 1936. By mid-March all snow-fighting equipment of both the railway and the city of St. Catharines had been put away for the summer. However, about 9:00 AM on Tuesday, March 17th, heavy snow began to fall. Many cars had become snowbound by noon. The snow continued to fall until about twenty inches had accumulated. Not a wheel turned in St. Catharines. By Saturday, a start had barely been made on digging out, when a further sixteen inches fell.

After a week, an attempt was made to plow Niagara Street using a borrowed railway wedge plow propelled by two electric locomotives. Half a day was needed to plow one-third of a mile; the weather conditions and depth of snow were such that the bottom layer had turned to ice so tough that it often derailed the plow; the vehicle could usually be re-railed, however, by backing it along the grooves it had made in the ice. New flangeways had to be cut by pick and shovel after the overlaying snow and ice had been removed. When salt was finally used (over city objections) on St. Paul Street, the resultant slush was so deep that it spread into stores fronting on the street. Nearly two weeks passed before normal service was resumed.

New Rule Book

Between 1936 and 1939, several unfortunate collisions occurred. The rule book then in effect had been introduced in 1918 and not revised since; it was obsolete and had generally not been issued to employees. Operations were conducted by verbal instructions and frequent "Bulletins" having the force of rules. The many extra sections and the close headways in effect on single-track lines greatly

Opposite Top: Collision between cars 66 and 41 at Thorold on October 11th 1939.
(H.E. BATTEL COLLECTION)

Opposite Bottom: Car 325 and two other 320s behind loading at Port Dalhousie dock 1941.
(AL PATERSON COLLECTION)

increased the chance of accident and required constant vigilance. It is perhaps remarkable that so few serious accidents did occur. The most serious of the collisions referred to are as follows:

Aug. 30th 1936: Head-on collision at Shriner's, Main Line; 9 injured. Eastbound car over-ran meet.

Sept. 1st 1937: Rear-end collision at Ormond Street bridge, High Line. Third section ran into second section stopped by fire on trestle.

June 29th 1939: Head-on collision between cars 320 and 322 near Corbetts, Port Dalhousie line; 26 injured. Northbound car over-ran meet.

Oct. 11th 1939: Head-on collision between car 66 and express motor 41 running extra, High Line, Thorold. 1 killed, 9 injured.

After the 1939 accidents, the permissible distance between sections of a train was increased from 1200 feet to 2000 feet, and an intensive study of the situation was undertaken. The rules had to provide for concentrated movements of fifteen or even twenty cars, for restrictions imposed by terminal trackage layouts, and for frequent stops at crossroads. The imposition of the standard CNR rule book was ordered by the Board of Transport Commissioners, but was never put into effect because it was completely unsuited to an operation of this type.

A revised code of rules was therefore made effective in April 1940, following CNR practice wherever possible. The most fundamental differences, perhaps, were provisions for running extra trains in sections (an unknown concept on steam railways), elimination of the "five-minute rule" (which required a minimum five-minute interval between trains — obviously inappropriate on an interurban line), and the establishment of fixed meeting points. The distinctions between superior and inferior directions were largely eliminated, as were references to operation in reverse, all cars being double-ended. At meeting points, trains carrying signals for a following section had to stop on the switch until the following section had arrived, thus preventing an opposing train from proceeding. (The interpretation of this rule in the particular circumstances prevailing at Lake and Louisa streets on the Port Dalhousie line was always a problem: because the St. Catharines end of the line was a large loop through city streets, the motorman of the first car of an outbound multi-car move had no way of knowing whether the last car of that move had passed inbound. Hence the requirement to call the dispatcher.) The "Divisions" became "Subdivisions" and the Main Line was rechristened "Falls Subdivision". To assist in avoiding confusion, the older designations are used throughout this review.

Top: Car 301 in "sunburst" livery on Bridge Street, Niagara Falls, June 1939. A rare view of one of these Cincinnati lightweights in this 1930s paint scheme.
(R.T. VINCENT)

Opposite Top: Car 304 southbound on Victoria Avenue at Stamford Street, Niagara Falls, July 20th 1946.
(JOHN F. HUMISTON S7218)

Opposite Bottom: Car 80 laying over at Thorold station, September 17th 1951.
(W.S. FLATT, ANDY DOUGLAS COLLECTION)

Temporary Bus Replacements, then Wartime

During the late 1930s, a trend to reduce or eliminate the company's rail passenger operations became evident. Ways and means, along with economic aspects, were under consideration as early as 1933. The St. Catharines local lines (except for Port Dalhousie) were discontinued in 1939, followed in 1940 by the Main Line. In 1941 the steamer subsidiary and Lakeside Park were offered for sale (but not sold). Other abandonments would have occurred but for World War II which forced resumption of the discontinued services in 1942.

By 1940 the system was fully extended. A few examples will indicate this. On Civic Holiday (August 1940), one afternoon Port Dalhousie trip ran in five sections; in the evening, because one of the steamers arrived on a "moonlight cruise" just as the Lakeside Park dance hall was preparing to close, an eight-car trip was necessary. It is recorded that 22 cars were prepared for service on the Victoria Day weekend of 1941, "just in case." On May 24th, the 10:25 PM trip ex-Port Dalhousie was run in five sections while on Dominion Day all Port Dalhousie trips were doubled and some in the afternoon were tripled. Two lightweight city cars had to be pressed into service on boat-connection runs.

The railway was sometimes called upon to handle extremely large concentrated loads. One of the largest occurred on July 27th 1942 when an estimated 5,000 employees of Atlas Steel Company of Welland held their annual picnic at Lakeside Park. On this occasion, bus service replaced Port Dalhousie cars from 6:30 AM to 1:00 PM during the northward picnic movement, and again from 6:30 PM during the return movement; as well, the local lines had buses for a few trips so that their cars could be used for the picnic. Twenty-four cars were involved, making two trips in concentrated groups at 8:30 and 11:20 AM to simplify the despatching. These were the seven 320s, four 130s in two trains, four 60s in two trains, 82, and a mixture of 100s and 300s. Welland Division cars operated south of Welland only, while this cavalcade, loaded on the TH&B interchange siding, was setting out. One car shuttled back and forth between Thorold and Welland as best it could, meeting excursion trains at all sidings. Line cars were stationed at Thorold and Fonthill in case of emergency; maintenance men stood by at Thorold and flagmen protected busy highway crossings. Fortunately, no problems occurred.

Similar movements took place at other times, including one as late as August 1949 when about 1,600 people were moved from Port Colborne and Welland to Lakeside Park in ten cars and twenty buses. This occasion is interesting in that NS&T honoured employee tickets issued by Atlas Steel on its regular services between Welland and Port Dalhousie throughout the day.

The "Big Snow" of December 12th to 14th 1944 greatly increased the problems of an already fully-extended system. The difficulties were particularly severe on the interurban lines, where windblown drifts up to nine feet in depth were formed. On three occasions the lines were blocked several hours. Since the Main Line ran east and west, while the Welland line ran north and south, drifting occurred

somewhere on the system no matter what the wind direction. With the holiday period following closely upon the problem snows, it was difficult to keep enough cars on the road to fulfill the schedules. Particular trouble arose when motormen tried to stop on slippery, snowy rail by reversing the electric motors, with resultant motor failures for which there were no replacements, thus causing the cars to be kept out of service until the motors could be rewound.

Contractions Begin

During and after the war, alterations to the St. Catharines carhouse, particularly to the former car-building shop, provided more space for bus storage and maintenance. Eventually, only two tracks remained for rail vehicles.

In 1947-48 an extensive survey explored the immediate dieselization of freight and abandonment of passenger services. Of the 93.3 miles of track then operated, a long-range plan suggested elimination of 37.2 miles. This included all trackage subsequently abandoned between 1948 and 1961, plus a section of the High Line. For various reasons the plans were not carried out in full, or yet as quickly as had been expected, but by 1950 most of the system had become freight-only or was abandoned altogether. At the end of World War II car miles and bus miles had been approximately equal (1¼ million each), but by 1950 car miles were down to 250,000 and bus miles up to 2¾ million. Practically speaking, the rail operations were now a rather extended

Opposite Top: Car 623 southbound on Welland Division at Beaver Dams shelter, March 14th 1959.
(R.J. SANDUSKY)

Opposite Bottom: Sweeper No. 22 (built by NS&T 1920) at St. Catharines yards, March 28th 1959.
(J.D. KNOWLES)

Bottom: Line car 30 with snowplows (front and rear) attached, on line car siding, Welland Avenue, St. Catharines. March 28th 1959.
(J.D. KNOWLES)

freight switching service, though the remainder of the trackage was intact and in operation, and was available for railway enthusiast excursions which became frequent in later years. The management was very co-operative with enthusiast groups, and passenger cars appeared at one time or another on every track and spur on the line.

As the bus system expanded, passenger operators could be called on to run either buses or electric cars, sometimes both in the same day. By 1948, most employees thought of themselves primarily as bus drivers (except, of course, for the freight crews) and indeed the standard cap badge read "Canadian National Transportation Ltd." It is interesting to note that passenger operators and freight men belonged to different unions, the former to the transit union and the latter to the railway brotherhoods. Non-operating employees were organized in four other unions.

The Latter Days

Track 1 of the St. Catharines Terminal was removed shortly after World War II to provide room for buses, and Track 2 was removed in 1951. The remaining tracks were, in effect, storage tracks. Part of the large waiting room was altered in 1954 for use as a bank branch. In 1955, the building, long a "white elephant" from the railway standpoint, was sold and the offices moved to the carhouse.

Following the abandonment of the Welland Division passenger service in March 1959, little time was lost in converting the rest of the system to diesel operation. The last six passenger and express cars left for the London reclamation yard on August 13th of that year. Three freight motors were sent to Oshawa for a few years more of service and, by early 1960, all regular freight operation was handled by CNR diesels. Two freight motors remained in serviceable condition and were used in the St. Catharines area whenever one of the assigned diesels was not available. Electric operation dwindled as the weeks went by, and finally simply expired in July 1960 on a date that has not been recorded.

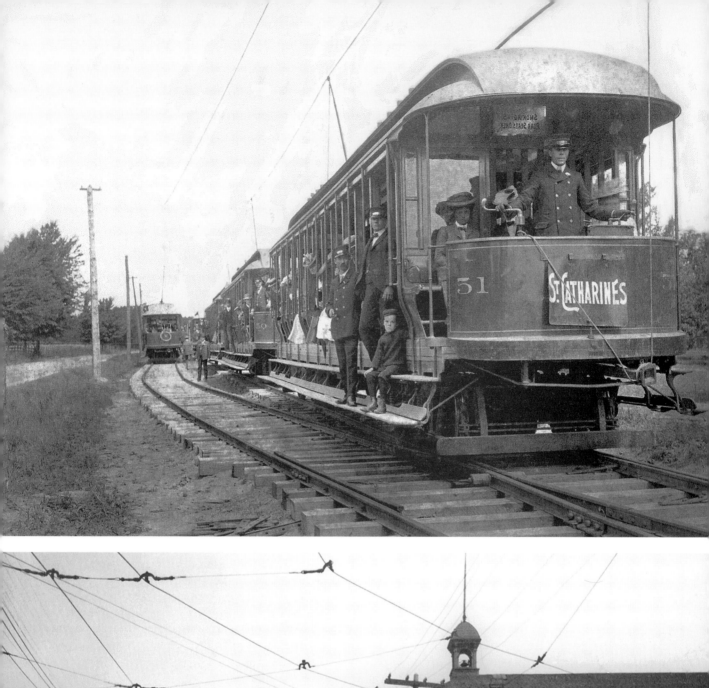

CHAPTER 5

NS&T — The Main Line

WHEN the St. Catharines & Niagara Central passed to NS&T ownership on October 1st 1899, it was with the intention of electrification and extension to Port Dalhousie and Beamsville. Originally the Port Dalhousie line was to leave St. Catharines via Lake Street and run direct to the port, but this was soon changed to the Louisa Street routing so that the same entrance could serve both the Port Dalhousie and Beamsville lines.

Electrification work began in the same month of October. On June 18th 1900, with the work almost completed, construction started on an extension on James Street from Raymond to St. Paul. This was held up by an injunction (soon dissolved) when the local street railway challenged the right of the NS&T to use this street, on which the street railway claimed to have franchise rights through a dormant subsidiary. On July 14th of the same year, work started on what was known as the "Louisa Street cutoff."

Service Begins

Power was first activated on July 9th 1900, but all was not well and modifications were necessary. A trial electric trip between St. Catharines and Thorold on July 17th was followed by a formal inspection trip over the whole line the following day. Public service began with little fanfare on July 19 between James and Raymond and Michigan Central Railroad Junction, Niagara Falls. Through cars operated every two hours, and local service amounting to 26 cars a day was run as far as Thorold.

The electric cars quickly gained in popularity and on July 22nd, the first Sunday, many trips had to be doubled. This was also the first day on which cars ran over the new extension to St. Paul Street where a small station was located on the northwest corner. The tracks veered to the west side of the street at this point for loading purposes.

New tracks on Queen, Erie and Bridge streets in Niagara Falls were opened on July 31st 1900 and this date is sometimes given as the date of completion of the Main Line.

Main Line electrification used two 2/0 wires of figure-8 section suspended about a foot apart over the centre of the track, and either wire could be used in either direction. It is not known when this unusual arrangement was re-

placed by conventional single overhead with feeder cable. Power was supplied at a pressure variously described as 11,000 and 12,000 volts by a high-tension line along the right-of-way and reduced to trolley voltage by substations in St. Catharines and Stamford. (A third substation was later built at Thorold.) The first interurban cars were given the Nightingale storage-air brake system and the cars did not have compressors. A large air reservoir on each car was charged at St. Catharines before every departure, and the motorman had to make his air last for the round trip.

Steam power was continued for freight service until about 1912, though switching was performed by electricity almost from the beginning.

The Service Develops

The Port Dalhousie line was ready for operation on February 26th 1901, completing the first stage of the new management's plans. New trackage on Louisa, Lake and James streets allowed Main Line and Port Dalhousie cars to run either to the St. Paul and James terminal or through the edge of town via the Louisa Street cutoff. Cars may have run through between Niagara Falls and Port Dalhousie for a short time but the two lines were soon separated and the subsequent history of the latter line appears in the St. Catharines local lines chapter.

Before the Main Line opened, arrangements had been made with the Niagara Falls Park & River Railway for operation of special NS&T trains from Bridge Street across to Niagara Falls, New York. Regular NS&T schedules terminated at Bridge Street but after 1906 the NFP&R provided a regular shuttle service to the American side.

In St. Catharines an interurban waiting station was built about 1906 on the former St. Paul Street carhouse property and was used until 1924. Main Line cars reached this station via Geneva Street while Port Dalhousie cars used James Street. The original Niagara Central station at Raymond Street had been sold and a large residence built on the site.

The High Line

The territory between Thorold and St. Catharines is very uneven, and it is necessary to climb the Niagara Escarpment. The Niagara Central had a large amount of timber trestlework in this area, and it had deteriorated badly despite recent repairs. Therefore some of the structure at the top of the grade in Thorold was removed and the tracks laid on the ground in a straighter alignment where the trestles had swung considerably to the east. Much of the remaining timberwork was rebuilt in steel and con-

Opposite Top: Car 51 and second sections, possibly at Port Dalhousie West, July 1900.
(JOHN BROMLEY COLLECTION)

Opposite Bottom: St. Catharines terminal and St. Paul Street looking east c1920.
(AL PATERSON COLLECTION)

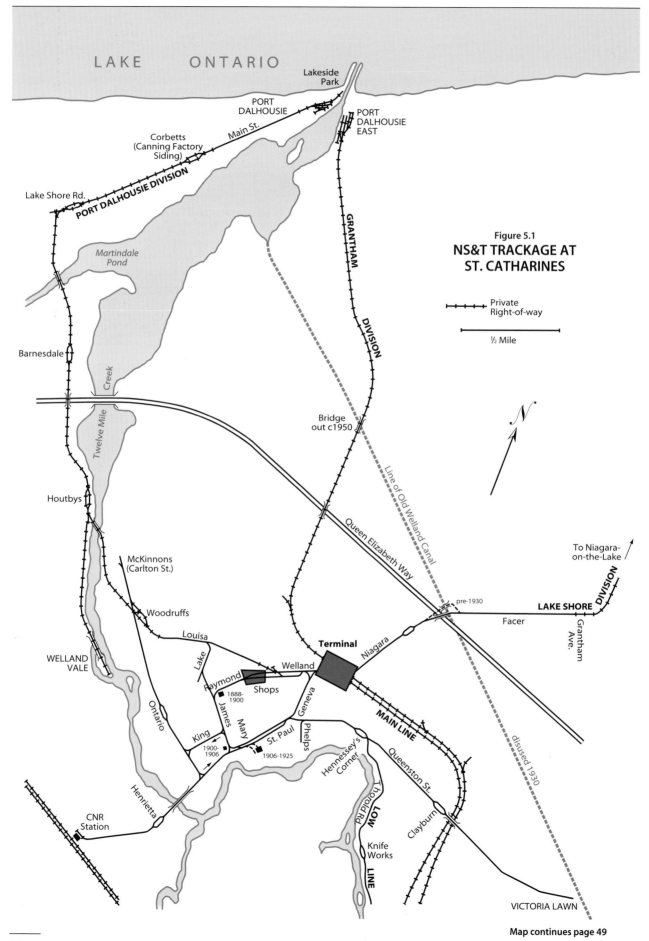

LAKE ONTARIO

Lakeside Park

PORT DALHOUSIE

PORT DALHOUSIE EAST

Corbetts (Canning Factory Siding)

Main St.

GRANTHAM DIVISION

PORT DALHOUSIE DIVISION

Lake Shore Rd.

Figure 5.1
NS&T TRACKAGE AT ST. CATHARINES

Private Right-of-way

½ Mile

Martindale Pond

Barnesdale

Creek

Twelve Mile

Bridge out c1950

Line of Old Welland Canal

N

Houtbys

McKinnons (Carlton St.)

Queen Elizabeth Way

To Niagara-on-the-Lake

Woodruffs

pre-1930

LAKE SHORE DIVISION

Louisa

Lake

Facer

Grantham Ave.

WELLAND VALE

Ontario

Raymond

Shops

Terminal

Welland

Niagara

1888-1900

James

Geneva

King

Mary

1900-1906

St. Paul

1906-1925

Phelps

MAIN LINE

disused 1930

Henrietta

Hennessey's Corner

Queenston St.

Thorold Rd.

LOW LINE

CNR Station

Knife Works

Clayburn

VICTORIA LAWN

Map continues page 49

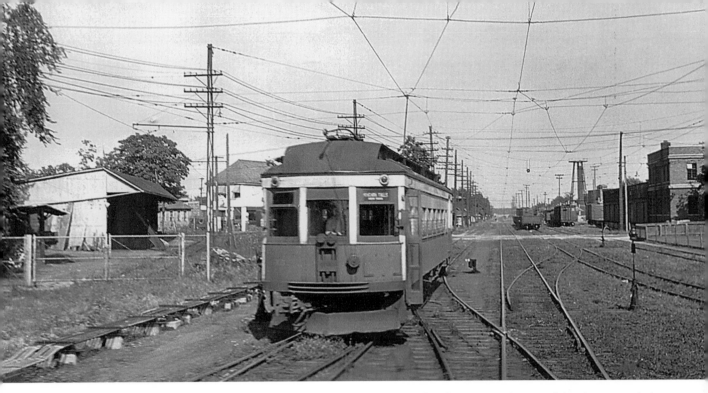

Top: Car 132 seen head on from approaching train,
near Niagara Street Tower, July 1940.
(ADDISON LAKE COLLECTION, COURTESY FRED ANGUS)

crete or became filled in over the years. However, the elevation remained. It is that phenomenon that led to the Main Line being known as the "High Line", to distinguish it from the Thorold local line on city streets, which was the "Low Line." New bridges were obtained second-hand from American railroads and were installed over Front and Ormond streets The last lengthy trestle section, extending a half-mile north of the CNR overpass in Merritton, was filled in about 1925; as late as 1947, a further 265-foot trestle was filled in. Eventually, of the 5.11 miles between St. Catharines and Thorold, more than half (2.7 miles) was on high fill or bridges, which were almost continuous between mile 2.7 and mile 4.5.

Considerable difficulty had been experienced in the winter of 1906-07 with settlement of the fills that had replaced trestles during 1905. Several times, freight service had to be suspended for two or three days as all freight cars were in use strengthening and restoring the fills to grade.

Improvements

An interchange with the Grand Trunk Railway (over which the Wabash Railroad had trackage rights) was installed at Stamford in 1905, and a station was built at this point. This structure burnt down on April 2nd 1916 and was replaced by a larger one. Another large station was opened in Thorold in March 1913. In 1906 the Main Line received 80-lb. rail replacing the old 56-lb. material, which was not standing up well under heavy traffic. A new bridge was installed over the GTR at Merritton and a few minor line relocations were made in Merritton and Thorold.

Serious delays were being encountered about 1912 in

Niagara Falls where interurbans and local cars used the same single line. The company therefore proposed to build a separate interurban track from MCRR Junction to River Road directly, but the outbreak of World War I caused abandonment of the idea.

Six new interurban cars, at first numbered 129-134, were built in 1914 by Preston Car & Coach Company, and were ever afterwards known as the "Main Line cars" by employees. They were designed for luxury service and had oak interiors inlaid with white holly. Additional features included electric heat (a rarity in 1914), "deadman" control and what would now be called "picture windows." They were intended for use in two-car trains with a combine and a passenger car in each train, and were the only multiple-unit cars on the property until 1927. The smoking compartment in the passenger cars (129-131) had a narrow passage to one side so that one did not have to walk through the smoking section; the baggage section in the combines (132-134) occupied a similar position so that there was a baggage door on one side only. Car 129 was renumbered 135 in 1920.

A swing bridge was built in 1915 at the site of the future Welland Ship Canal just west of Shriner's. However, such were the delays in completion of the canal that it was not until 1930 that the bridge was called upon to pass its first commercial vessel. 1921 was the top year for Main Line passenger business, with almost exactly three million being carried. At the time of the 1922 report previously mentioned, great optimism was shown for the future of interurban business, since Main Line loads had almost tripled in three years. After 1921, the trend was definitely downwards, reaching about 1½ million in 1928 and only 250,000 in 1939. On the Main Line, as on other lines, the hopes on which the report's recommendations were based proved almost entirely false.

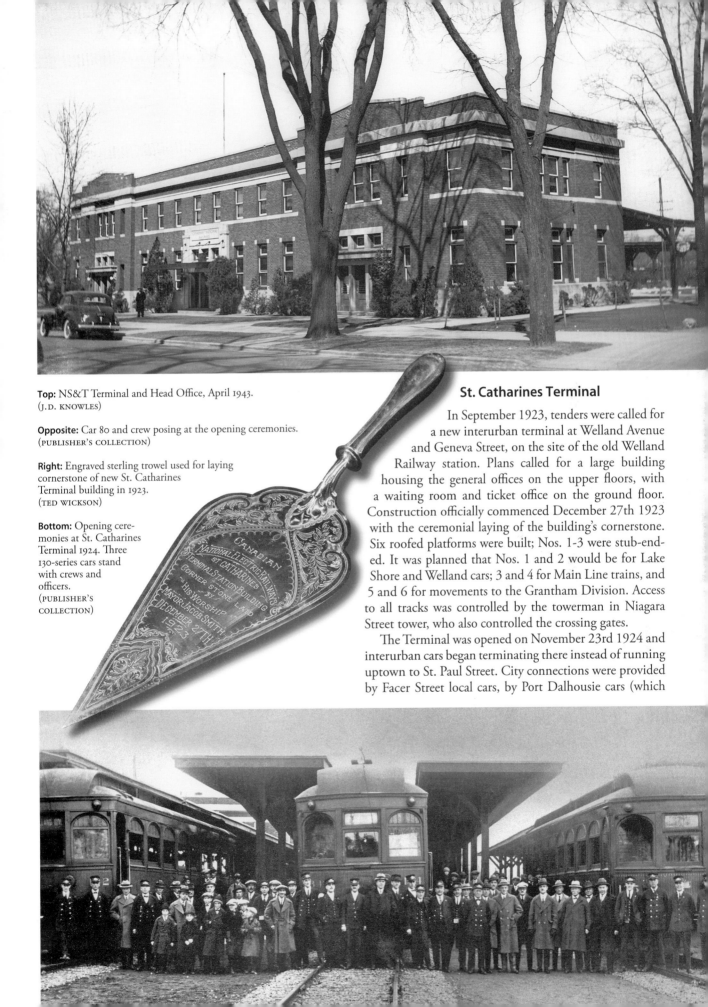

Top: NS&T Terminal and Head Office, April 1943. (J.D. KNOWLES)

Opposite: Car 80 and crew posing at the opening ceremonies. (PUBLISHER'S COLLECTION)

Right: Engraved sterling trowel used for laying cornerstone of new St. Catharines Terminal building in 1923. (TED WICKSON)

Bottom: Opening ceremonies at St. Catharines Terminal 1924. Three 130-series cars stand with crews and officers. (PUBLISHER'S COLLECTION)

St. Catharines Terminal

In September 1923, tenders were called for a new interurban terminal at Welland Avenue and Geneva Street, on the site of the old Welland Railway station. Plans called for a large building housing the general offices on the upper floors, with a waiting room and ticket office on the ground floor. Construction officially commenced December 27th 1923 with the ceremonial laying of the building's cornerstone. Six roofed platforms were built; Nos. 1-3 were stub-ended. It was planned that Nos. 1 and 2 would be for Lake Shore and Welland cars; 3 and 4 for Main Line trains, and 5 and 6 for movements to the Grantham Division. Access to all tracks was controlled by the towerman in Niagara Street tower, who also controlled the crossing gates.

The Terminal was opened on November 23rd 1924 and interurban cars began terminating there instead of running uptown to St. Paul Street. City connections were provided by Facer Street local cars, by Port Dalhousie cars (which

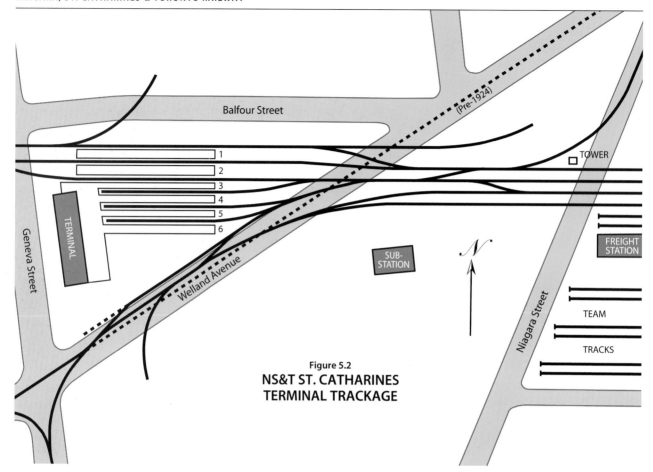

**Figure 5.2
NS&T ST. CATHARINES
TERMINAL TRACKAGE**

never used the terminal) and by a new local line running between the terminal and the Canadian National Railways station. The old station, occupying valuable business-district land with a 129-foot frontage on St. Paul Street was closed and sold.

The new building was never used as intended. The disadvantage of losing a prominent uptown location far outweighed any advantage of having a terminal on the Grantham Division. Also, an extra fare now had to be paid to reach city points, as required by the "service-at-cost" franchise. So little traffic originated at the Terminal, in fact, that at certain hours tickets were sold in the despatcher's office. The original proposal to run Welland Division cars through to St. Catharines was not carried out, since a third car would have had to be added to the run.

Bus Competition

The first bus competition was felt on the Main Line in 1925, when a highway service started between Niagara Falls and Stamford, and was very soon extended to St. Catharines. This ultimately became part of Canada Coach Lines and was one of the reasons for retention of Main Line service until 1940, since the NS&T did not have operating rights on the main highways. The buses ran to uptown St. Catharines, and in an effort to compete on better terms, Main Line cars resumed uptown operation on December 8th 1927, looping via Geneva, St. Paul, James and Raymond

streets. The city agreed to forego the local fare technically due, provided that city passengers were not carried on the interurbans. (The city's interest stemmed from the fact that the rate of fare on the local lines was governed, in theory at least, by their financial results). Transfers were issued to local lines at each end of the line, and persons boarding interurban cars with transfers had an equivalent amount deducted from their interurban fare.

If for any reason the Main Line train was late, it would be terminated and sent back from the Terminal. A separate car then carried passengers over the uptown loop. This procedure was known as "stubbing around town" and, at times of heavy traffic, especially during World War II, a stub car would meet all trains at the Terminal. Lake Shore Division cars continued to use the Terminal until they were discontinued.

Grantham Division Electrification

During 1924-25, the Merritton–Port Dalhousie (East) branch of the CNR was electrified at a cost of $135,000. This was the oldest part of the NS&T system since it had originated in 1859 as the Welland Railway, built because the shallow draft of the Welland Canal at the time required that part of a ship's cargo be removed and forwarded by rail while the ship transited the canal. It was formally leased to the NS&T on January 1st 1926 though the electrification had been completed the previous summer. The installation used a new overhead construction intended to be

Map continues page 44

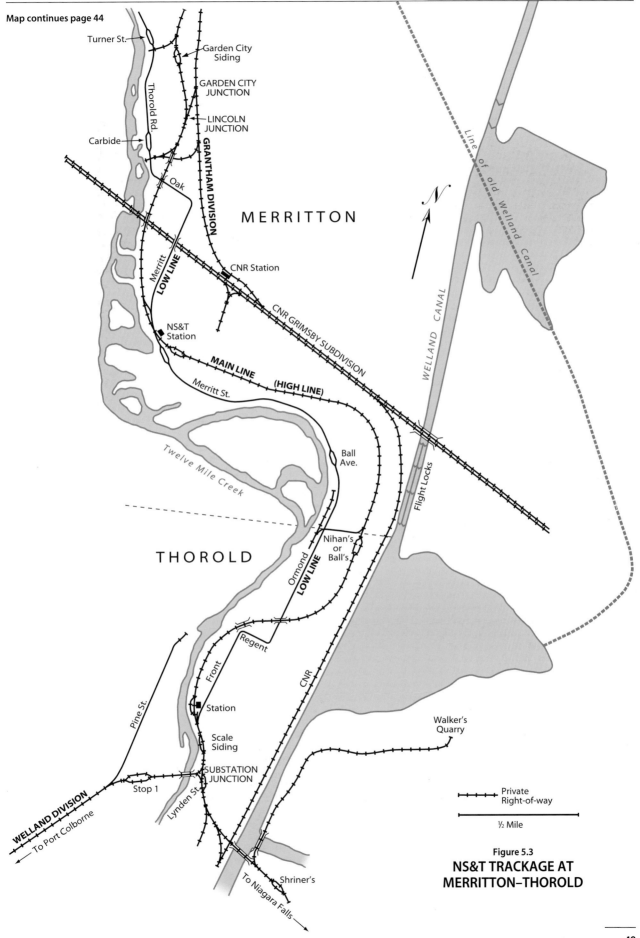

Figure 5.3
**NS&T TRACKAGE AT
MERRITTON–THOROLD**

standard for the Canadian National Electric lines, involving inclined catenary suspended from steel towers 330 feet apart. A specially-made messenger cable consisted largely of aluminum but contained a seven-strand steel core for strength. The same overhead style was used on part of the Montreal Terminals electrification. The electrification was mainly intended for improvements in freight service but it also provided a new high-speed line to dockside at Port Dalhousie East, thus saving considerable time over the former route through city streets to Lakeside Park. Grantham Division track could be used as double track with the Main Line between St. Catharines and Lincoln Junction, but the volume of freight traffic usually prevented such operation.

The CNR facilities at Port Dalhousie East were expanded into a four-track yard with some freight sidings (bulk coal was handled at this point, among other things), and a large passenger shelter was built. Until the boat connection was given over to buses in 1945, steamers docked first at Port Dalhousie East for Niagara Falls passengers, then turned around and docked again at Lakeside Park for local

Top: Two 130-series cars looking northeast at the Tower Inn Terminal c1939.
(JOHN BURTNIAK COLLECTION, ST. CATHARINES MUSEUM)

Opposite Top: Cars 132 and 135 on the main line crossing Welland Avenue, approaching Niagara Street Tower July 20th 1946.
(JOHN F. HUMISTON S7238)

Opposite: Locomotive 19 on the main line at Niagara Street tower looking east, July 20th 1946.
(JOHN F. HUMISTON S7233)

Opposite Bottom: Cars 132 and 135 run as Train 208 on Welland Avenue in front of St. Catharines Terminal, July 20th 1946.
(JOHN F. HUMISTON S7248)

Bottom: Billboard at Niagara Falls Lower Arch Bridge, March 31st 1946.
(J.D. KNOWLES 20276)

passengers. Completion of this project permitted about 25 minutes to be cut from Niagara–Toronto times, resulting in a schedule of about 3¼ hours for the lake crossing and the rail journey to the Falls. No local passenger service was ever provided on the Grantham Division.

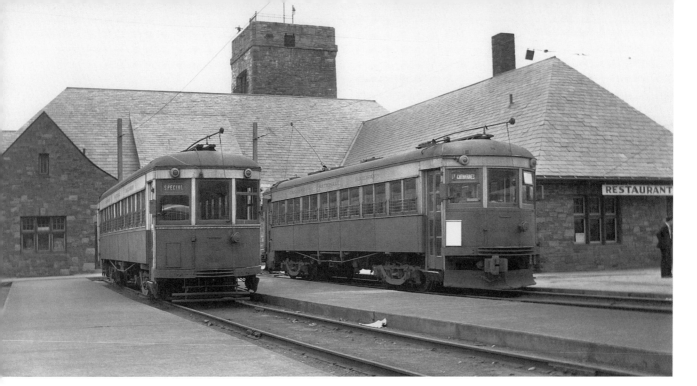

Tower Inn Terminal

The Terminal situation in Niagara Falls was still unsatisfactory, with interurban and local cars competing for track space on the single line to Bridge Street; furthermore, the station was poorly located for tourist traffic. Consequently, one of the provisions of the new franchise was the construction of an interurban terminal. At first a small one-storey building was considered, but revised plans were prepared for a stone building (ingeniously designed to make the most of a rather small site) whose architecture was said to be derived from an English country inn. The feature of the building was a tall observation tower overlooking the Falls. It was without doubt the most outstanding terminal in Canada, and one of the finest electric line stations anywhere. The best description comes from the magazine *Electric Transportation* at the time of its opening in July 1928:

"Rough-faced multi-colored stones of random sizes and shapes used for the exterior were obtained from various quarries and from the site itself, preference being given to stones which have mineral stains on the faces. The roof has been covered with a mixture of slates which, when weathered, will have a much similar effect to the stone walls . . . . . . The woodwork and plaster of the three grouped gables at the corner (facing the Falls) is treated in the traditional black and white manner.

"Set at a slight elevation from the street, the building is on a broad flagged terrace, the slope of the terracing and the space between that and the sidewalk being grassed. The tower is the dominant feature from whatever point the building is viewed, and in this has been placed the broad splayed main entrance.

"To reach the tower lookout the entrance has been arranged from an angle of the waiting room, and a

Top: Two 60-series cars on adjacent tracks at Tower Inn Terminal c1939.
(J.W. HOOD COLLECTION)

Opposite Top: Tower Inn Terminal, looking northwest from River Road, 1928.
(J.J. WIGT COLLECTION)

Opposite Bottom: Car 123 and GCL bus wait at Tower Inn Terminal in 1940.
(AL PATERSON COLLECTION)

stairway leads to a balcony over the entrance to the cafeteria and thence through the wall of the tower to a concrete stair leading to the lookouts, where one of the best views of the Falls may be obtained.

"Plans for the Terminal were prepared by J. Schofield, Architect, C.N. Railways, and the construction was under the direction of E.W. Oliver, Manager."

The Terminal had three stub tracks plus one passing to the north of the building to connect with NFP&R trackage on River Road. At the same time interurban cars began running on a private right-of-way line beside a new street, called Newman Hill, from Victoria Avenue descending through a rock cut to the edge of the gorge where the Terminal was located. The construction of this new line was very costly, involving over half a million dollars for less than half a mile of line.

The provision of two such ambitious terminals for an interurban route just thirteen miles long can only be explained in terms of anticipated traffic increases that never materialized. These various changes greatly reduced street running and speeded schedules, and in order to take full advantage of them, multiple-unit control was installed on most interurban cars in 1927-28. Only the six 130s had previously been so equipped.

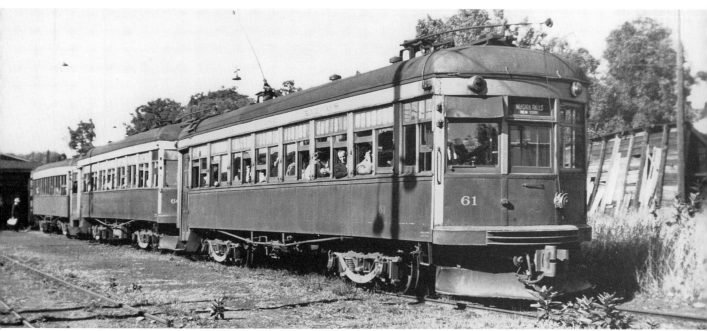

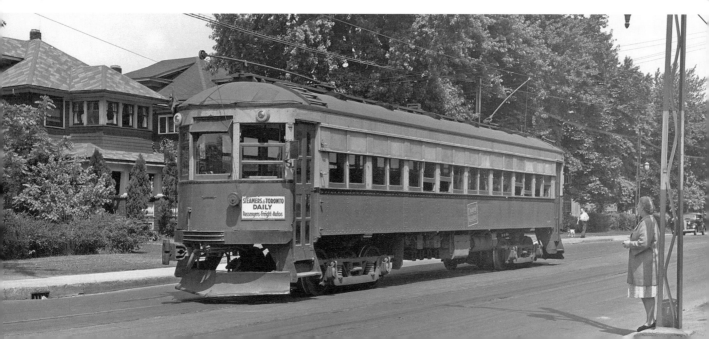

Top: Cars 135, 134 and 130 at Tower Inn Terminal. Photograph taken from the observation tower of the station, July 1940, two months before terminal's forced closure. Note stockpile of highway construction materials stored on the former through track on north side.
(LLOYD G. BAXTER)

Opposite Top: Car 83 on main line passes Niagara Falls carhouse on July 14th 1946. North American Cyanamid plant is in the background.
(J.D. KNOWLES 20284)

Opposite: Cars 61, 60 and 62 work the boat train at Port Dalhousie East, August 1944.
(J.W. HOOD)

Opposite Bottom: Car 80 on Victoria Avenue at Stamford Street, Niagara Falls, July 20th 1946.
(JOHN F. HUMISTON S7208)

Falls View Bridge

In the summer of 1929, a special day excursion fare of fifty cents was introduced between St. Catharines and Niagara Falls, and arrangements were made with the International Railway Company for all Main Line trains to operate through to the IRC terminal in Niagara Falls, New York with direct connection to High Speed Line interurbans for Buffalo. This potentially valuable arrangement did not last long, however, as the Falls View (Honeymoon) Bridge was beginning to show its age, and at almost the same time a newly-imposed weight restriction would keep all interurban equipment except the 60s off the bridge. Even this limited operation ceased suddenly in July 6th 1932 owing to the approaching abandonment of the NFP&R and to further bridge deterioration. A bus shuttle was substituted since forty percent of Main Line passengers were bound on international journeys. In 1934 a bridge speed limit of ten MPH and a gross weight limit of twelve tons were imposed, even on bus crossings. When boarding eastbound vehicles, NS&T passengers, in buying tickets,

commonly said only "Ontario" or "New York," the words "Niagara Falls" being thought unnecessary under the circumstances.

Reduced depression-era loads meant that normal Main Line service was being provided by the higher-numbered 60s (60-63 were on the Welland Division), assisted by 82 and 130, which had been converted for one-man operation. One-man crews took over Main Line runs on August 16th 1931, although two men continued to be used on the first and last cars of multi-car moves. Cars nos. 65 and 67 were specially modernized for shuttle service across the Falls View Bridge.

On January 27th 1938 the bridge was swept away by a huge ice jam, and thereafter the Lower Arch Bridge (Whirlpool Rapids Bridge) became the only route, other than purely railway bridges, across the river. Tower Inn Terminal, while still well located for tourist traffic, was now most inconvenient for international business. Main Line cars therefore sometimes ran over the old route to Bridge Street, and at such times connecting service from the Terminal would be provided by a spare city car.

In an astonishing display of legalized vandalism, on September 27th 1940 Tower Inn Terminal, less than fourteen years old, was closed and torn down, and the double track leading to it was abandoned. Both these changes were at the instigation of the Ontario highways authorities who were then engaged in building the Queen Elizabeth Way, the province's first modern divided highway. The railway right-of-way was paved over the following January, and became the eastbound lane of the QEW down the hill. A bus station was built on the site of the terminal. Gray Coach Lines, which had served the old Tower Inn Terminal, became a major tenant at the new bus terminal, along with Canada Coach Lines. Interurban cars then resumed full-time operation to the foot of Bridge Street and block signals were installed on the single-track approaches.

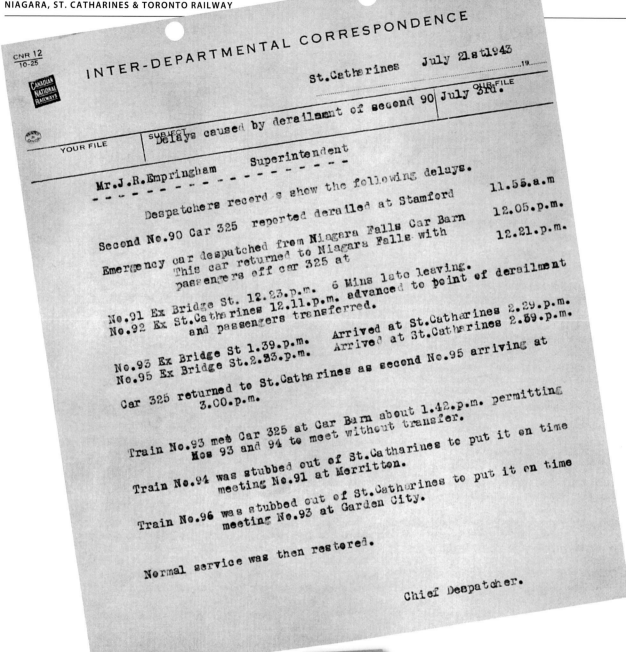

INTER-DEPARTMENTAL CORRESPONDENCE

CNR 12
10-25

St.Catharines   July 21st1943

OUR FILE
second 90 July 3rd.

YOUR FILE   SUBJECT Delays caused by derailment of second 90

Mr.J.R.Empringham   Superintendent

Despatchers records show the following delays.

Second No.90 Car 325 reported derailed at Stamford   11.55.a.m

Emergency car despatched from Niagara Falls Car Barn   12.05.p.m.
This car returned to Niagara Falls with   12.21.p.m.
passengers off car 325 at

No.91 Ex Bridge St. 12.23.p.m. 6 Mins late leaving.
No.92 Ex St.Catharines 12.11.p.m. advanced to point of derailment
          and passengers transferred.

No.93 Ex Bridge St 1.39.p.m.   Arrived at St.Catharines 2.29.p.m.
No.95 Ex Bridge St.2.23.p.m.   Arrived at St.Catharines 2.59.p.m.

Car 325 returned to St.Catharines as second No.95 arriving at
          3.00.p.m.

Train No.93 met Car 325 at Car Barn about 1.42.p.m. permitting
          Nos 93 and 94 to meet without transfer.

Train No.94 was stubbed out of St.Catharines to put it on time
          meeting No.91 at Merritton.

Train No.96 was stubbed out of St.Catharines to put it on time
          meeting No.93 at Garden City.

Normal service was then restored.

                                                Chief Despatcher.

Service Suspended

Main Line passenger service was discontinued on November 27th 1940 except for one round trip for commuters; this was abolished on June 10th 1941 with Board of Transport Commissioners approval of the abandonment and delivery of new buses, but the track was left intact. Carload freight continued, as did rush hour passenger service over the High Line from St. Catharines to Thorold, and occasional special interurban movements to Niagara Falls were made. Through business to the American side was greatly reduced by wartime border crossing restrictions imposed on July 1st 1940. As well, in late 1942 the Dominion Transit Controller ordered interurban bus carriers to discontinue all routes exceeding 50 miles. Gray Coach through service to the Falls was then suspended,

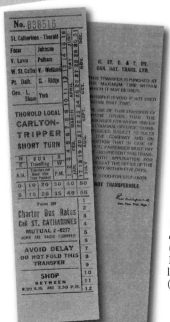

Top: The intricacies of a delay on the NS&T.
(ONTARIO ELECTRIC RAILWAY HISTORICAL ASSOCIATION ARCHIVES)

Opposite Top: Cars 132 and 131 make a photo stop crossing Ormond Street Bridge on the high line, September 1947.
(J. M. MILLS)

Opposite: Eastbound car 623 crosses fourth Welland Canal bridge on a fan trip in July 1956.
(R. J. SANDUSKY)

Opposite Bottom: A 120-series car, inbound on the low line (Front Street), is about to turn onto Regent Street adjacent to the high line bridge over Front Street c1918.
(H. E. BATTEL)

leaving passengers originating in Toronto the option of using the steam railways or NS&T's lake boats and local streetcar and bus connections to the Falls.

Service Resumed

As the war situation worsened, the Transit Controller requested resumption of NS&T rail services as a conservation measure, and the Main Line cars went back to work on November 15th 1942. However, daily rush-hour service between Niagara Falls and McKinnon's, St. Catharines, recommended previously, had begun on April 27th 1942, so that the actual period of total suspension was less than a year. Lacking their proper terminal, interurban cars merely ran to the end of the Victoria Avenue double track at Newman Hill, returning to the carhouse for layover if necessary. Connections were made at Bridge and Victoria with buses for Niagara Falls, New York. Interurban cars would sometimes run beyond Newman Hill to Clifton Hill, the nearest point to the Falls tourist area, but this was not encouraged as it often delayed local cars on the single

Top: Flagging a Main Line movement of eastbound cars 134 and 135 across the Queen Elizabeth Way, 1946.
(J.D. KNOWLES 20277)

Opposite: Notice of scheduled extra cars on Main Line before official resumption of full passenger service. "Scheduled extras" were an unusual feature. Note complicated footnotes required to operate street car services under interurban rules.
(ONTARIO ELECTRIC RAILWAY HISTORICAL ASSOCIATION ARCHIVES)

Bottom: Car 130 on a charter at Merritton station, looking northwest, July 4th 1953.
(JOHN F. HUMISTON T2678)

track. The company attempted to rent some land on Ferry Street, south of Clifton Hill, for a small station and interurban layover point, but terms could not be arranged.

In view of the coming abandonment, no grade separation or even crossing protection was provided at the Queen Elizabeth Way near Niagara Falls. A flagman was carried on one-man cars, and he assisted in changing ends at Niagara Falls in order not to delay local cars. At other

MERRITTON

NIAGARA, ST. CATHARINES AND TORONTO RAILWAY

BULLETIN NO. 9.

St. Catharines, Ont.,
September 11th, 1942.

To Passenger Car and Coach Operators,
Freight Trainmen and All Others Concerned.
- -

The undermentioned extra cars will operate in conjunction with schedule in Time Table No. 57:-

Dai. Ex. Sat. Sun. "D" P.M.	Dai. Ex. Sat. Sun. "D" P.M.	Dai. Ex. Sat. Sun. "F" P.M.	Dai. Ex. Sat. Sun. "E" P.M.	Dai. Ex. Sat. Sun. "D" P.M.	Dai. Ex. Sun. "A" A.M.	Dai. Ex. Sun. "C" A.M.	Dai. Ex. Sun. "B" A.M.	Dai. Ex. Sun. "A" A.M.			Dai. Ex. Sun. "A" A.M.	Dai. Ex. Sun. "B" A.M.	Dai. Ex. Sun. "C" A.M	Dai. Ex. Sat. Sun. "D" P.M.	Dai. Ex. Sat. Sun. "E" P.M.	Dai. Ex. Sat. Sun. F P.M.	Dai. Ex. Sat. Sun. "D" P.M.	Dai. Ex. Sat. Sun. "D" P.M.
-	5.07	5.06	5.06	-	7.07	7.07	7.07	-	L. McKinnons	A.	6.47	6.48	6.48	4.56	4.58	4.58	-	-
-	-	5.08	5.08	-	-	-	7.09	-	Ontario st. Diamond		-	6.46	6.46	4.54	4.56	4.56	-	-
-	-	5.13	5.13	-	-	-	7.13	-	A. King and Ontario	L.	-	6.42	6.42	4.50	4.52	4.52	-	-
-	5.11	-	-	-	7.11	7.11	-	-	L. Woodruffs	A.	6.45	-	-	-	-	-	-	-
-	5.13	-	-	-	7.13	Note	-	-	Lake and Louisa		6.42	-	-	-	-	-	-	-
-	5.15	-	-	-	7.15	"C"	-	-	A. Welland Ave. (D. Trk.)	L.	6.39	-	-	-	-	-	-	-
6.05	5.20	Note	Note	4.15	-	-	Note	5.15	L. St. Catharines (Ter.)	A.	6.35	Note	Note	4.42	Note	Note	5.53	7.55
-	"F"	"E"	-	-	-	"B"	-		Hayes Steel		6.27	"L"	"M"	4.35	"X"	"X"	5.44	-
6.15	5.30	-	-	4.25	-	-	-	5.24	Merritton		6.25	-	-	4.30	-	-	5.42	7.45
6.23	5.35	-	-	-	-	-	-	5.28	Thorold		6.21	-	-	-	-	-	5.38	7.40
6.41	-	-	-	-	-	-	-	5.50	A. Bridge Street	L.	6.00	-	-	-	-	-	-	7.20
P.M.	P.M.	P.M.	P.M.	P.M.	A.M.	A.M.	A.M.	A.M.	THIS IS NOT A WORKING TIMETABLE		A.M.	A.M.	A.M	P.M.	P.M.	P.M.	P.M.	P.M.

Note "C" – This car will operate as a section of Port Dalhousie trains Nos. 7 and 12 on School Days only. Operator will see proper classification signals are displayed before proceeding.

Note "E" – This car will operate as a section of 5.14 P.M. Victoria Lawn Car - St. Paul and William to Victoria Lawn and return. Returning to Barn via James and Raymond Streets.

Note "F" – This car will operate as a section of 5.15 P.M. Facer St. Car - St. Paul and William to Facer St. and return to Terminal Station and Car Barn via Welland Avenue.

Note "L" – This car from Victoria Lawn to McKinnons.   Note "M" – This car from Facer St. to McKinnons.

Note "X" – These cars from Car Barn via Welland Ave.-Geneva-St.Paul-James-King-Ontario.

Note "B" – This car to Car Barn via Ontario-St.Paul-James and Raymond.

Trains operating on Welland and Falls Subdivisions will operate as Extra trains according to Rule.

Port Dalhousie Subdivision train No. 5 must stop at Lake and Louisa, wait for car from Niagara Falls and display classification signals - Lake and Louisa to Woodruffs.

Extra train leaving Bridge St. at 6.00 A.M. for McKinnons will, on arrival at St. Catharines, meet Port Dalhousie Subdivision train No. 2 at Terminal Station or on Welland Ave. Double Track, and operate as a section of Port Dalhousie train No. 5 - Lake and Louisa to Woodruffs.

(OVER)

Bulletin No. 9, cont'd.   Page No. 2.

Extra train leaving Merritton at 4.30 P.M. will, on arrival at St. Catharines, proceed to McKinnons via Geneva St.-St. Paul St.- James St.- King St. and Ontario St.

Cars operating from McKinnons at 7.07 A.M. and 5.07 P.M. via Port Dalhousie Subdivision to Welland Ave. must meet Northward trains Nos. 7 and 47 at Woodruffs and then proceed via Louisa St. and Welland Ave.

Cars operating eastward on Ontario St. must make sure all scheduled cars have arrived before leaving McKinnons.

PORT DALHOUSIE SUBDIVISION

Motorman of Train No. 5 must protect following sections as provided in Rule 96, and all sections must register at Lake and Louisa.

Motorman of Train No. 7 must ascertain from Operators at Woodruffs if they are required to carry classification signals for car mentioned in Note "C".

Cars not operating as a section of a regular train, or having train order meet, M U S T clear the time of regular trains in both directions as required by Rule.

Motormen of cars operating to or from McKinnons via Port Dalhousie Subdivision M U S T report to Despatcher at Woodruffs and if they fail to run as scheduled, will operate under Despatchers instructions.

By Order,

J. R. EMPRINGHAM,

Superintendent.

Top: Eastbound car 80 on Falls Subdivision arriving at
Thorold, July 20th 1946.
(JOHN F. HUMISTON S7206)

Opposite Top: Car 130 on a charter on Grantham Subdivision,
at Lakeshore Bridge, Port Dalhousie East, July 4th 1953.
(JOHN F. HUMISTON T2687)

Opposite Bottom: NS&T main line meet at Shriners Siding
east of Welland Canal, October 1st 1946. Car 135, heading
three-car NRHS charter, stands at booth for telephone to
dispatcher; regular car 82 behind. Car 83 is bound for
St. Catharines, with usual end-of-train red flag.
(J.D. KNOWLES 20279)

times, the flagman was stationed in a shanty at the crossing. Work had actually started on an overpass in 1940, but
was stopped and the fill material carted away when final
abandonment was decided on.

Wartime Traffic

Substantial traffic increases were recorded and, late in 1943,
operation of the 130s in two-car trains became standard
procedure; this remained so, on weekends at least, until
the end. Most of these fine cars had been all but retired for
several years before the war, but were reconditioned and
returned to service.

Most of the area traversed by the NS&T was highly in-
dustrialized or urban in character, and apart from the Falls
itself, almost entirely without scenic attraction. A sample of
typical lineside scenery is contained in this description of a
trip over the High Line written during the latter days:

> "The cars set out for a run over the remarkable line to
> Thorold, past the mountains of pulp logs at the Merrit-
> ton paper mills, past Hayes Steel, over the bridges and
> the high embankment and the CNR overpass, past the
> stagnant muddy ponds of various improbable colours,
> up the long climb overlooking the Merritton wartime
> housing and within sight of the twin flight locks of
> the Welland Canal, over the twisting fill with its vari-
> ous bridges above a residential section of Thorold and
> across the through truss bridge which spans the main

street of Thorold at a very acute angle, finally to rumble
along the trestle at second-story level a few feet away
from the rear of buildings along the west side of Front
St., and emerge at Thorold station, opposite an old
stone mill building built in 1827 and located on the
west side of the old Welland Canal." (J.D. Knowles)

In the 1946 season, and in some cases in 1945 also, Niagara Falls boat connections were provided by bus, and
the steamers did not dock at Port Dalhousie East at such
times. However, electric cars were sometimes pressed into
service to handle large-scale movements. The "Port East"
passenger shelter was torn down in 1951. St. Catharines
connections from Lakeside Park were always by streetcar.

Final Abandonment

Inevitably, the Main Line passenger service was again abandoned, this time permanently, on September 13th 1947,
the last trip being made by cars 132 and 135 in train. The
track continued in use for deadhead movements of local
cars, and for carload freight to the area near Bridge Street.
This was given over to the CNR in December 1947 and,
after the Niagara Falls local lines overhead had been dismantled, the diamond at the Stamford crossing was removed, breaking the rail connection. Rail east of Shriner's
was lifted during April 1948 and rush-hour trips as far as
Thorold were continued for a short time.

Canada Coach Lines offered to buy out the Niagara
Falls–St. Catharines coach route at this time, but the offer
was refused and Canadian National Transportation Ltd.
buses took over from the electric cars. This ceased after
December 3rd 1955 when CNT and Canada Coach Lines
agreed that CCL would provide all highway service, while
CNT would take over international bridge crossings.
Freight service was retained as far as Walker's Quarry, just
west of Shriner's, but was terminated and the swing bridge
over the Welland Canal removed in 1964. The Thorold
NS&T station has been demolished and the old Welland
Canal filled in, so that very little trace of this once-busy
location remains.

CHAPTER 6

NS&T — Welland Division

THE Welland Division, destined to be the last segment of the system to have passenger service, was projected primarily for its freight potential. The line was opened in stages: from a junction with the Main Line, a short distance from Thorold, to Fonthill on June 1st 1907; to the Welland River on May 4th 1908; across the river on a timber trestle to the new station in October 1908; and to its terminal in rented quarters at Elm and Kent Streets, Port Colborne, on August 2nd 1911. Tracks were laid on the road (Elm Street) south of Borden Street through Humberstone and Port Colborne. Apart from the Welland River trestle, there were no major engineering works on the line. Tracks were laid with 60-lb. rail, but the northerly five miles received 80-lb. relay rail in 1919. Plans were prepared for an extension to Crystal Beach and Fort Erie, but nothing came of them.

Very fruitful arrangements were made in 1909 with the Toronto Hamilton & Buffalo, and in 1914 with the Michigan Central (NYC) for freight interchange at Welland. Particularly before the creation of the unified Canadian National system, these connections formed the mainstay of NS&T freight revenue.

Normal passenger service was hourly with two cars, scheduled to meet at Electric Park, a short distance north of Welland.

Opposite: Lady alighting from car 622, 1958-59.
(BOB CHAMBERS)

Bottom: Car 105 or 106 on Welland line in Thorold, c1910.
(PUBLISHER'S COLLECTION)

(There never was a park at Electric Park, and indeed the name was not used until 1940 when all meeting points had to be named in accordance with the new rule book adopted at that time.) At Thorold, where connections were made with the Main Line, Welland cars terminated on a special siding which dead-ended at the south wall of the station. The heaviest passenger load was experienced in 1920 when just over 1.3 million fares were paid.

Port Colborne Station

The Canadian National station at Port Colborne was originally located east of the canal, a logical point for operating purposes but very inconvenient for passengers. In 1925, therefore, a new station was built in the centre of town at King Street. Two blocks of new trackage allowed NS&T cars to terminate at the new station; operation to this point began on March 1st 1926. The cars ran only to the street line of King Street at first, pending changes to CNR trackage caused by construction of the new Ship Canal. They were extended to a point opposite the station in 1929 at which time the old station at Elm and Kent streets was closed and the agent moved to Humberstone; this station in turn was closed in 1932 and torn down. One source of delay in completing the move to the new station was the necessity of serving several freight customers south of the CNR. Eventually this service was taken over along with about 4000 feet of track by the CNR in December 1929, and the NS&T crossing removed.

The *Red Onion*

On May 1st 1927, the CNR ended passenger and express service on its parallel line to the east of the canal. As a substitute, a new service was inaugurated on the NS&T connecting with CNR trains at Merritton. Equipment was obtained second-hand from abandoned interurbans in Ohio and comprised express cars 40 or 41 hauling No. 90, the only trailer on the system. No. 90 had motorman's controls and could be run as the first car in a train. Initially, this train was run twice daily, leaving Merritton at 7:00 AM and 4:20 PM, returning from Port Colborne at 8:25 AM and 6:45 PM. In 1929 a third service using regular interurban cars was tried for a short time but was soon dropped. It left Merritton at 10:10 AM and returned from Port Colborne at 2:45 PM. The express-car-cum-trailer was popularly known as the "Red Onion" by Port Colborne residents, suggesting that it was not held in high regard. A rough ride was often given, since the trailer was much lighter than the motor, resulting in all coupler slack action being felt by the passenger as a virtually continuous buffeting and jolting.

The passenger trailer was discontinued on April 25th 1937 and replaced by bus service. This was operated by the NS&T with revenue guaranteed by the CNR as had been the case with the rail service. The CNR guarantee on the bus was withdrawn in April 1955 and the bus itself discontinued in July, but the rail express service continued until 1958.

Considerable delay was encountered in obtaining new orders at Thorold, changing ends, and switching from High Line to Grantham Division at Lincoln Junction. Therefore, in 1929, some thought was given to electrifying an almost-disused CNR spur terminating close to the NS&T Merritton station. This would have allowed regular Welland Division cars to make the connection, eliminating the special operation. No action was taken owing to the cost of trackage rearrangements.

Top: Locomotive 10 and flatcar 207 during construction of the Welland Division at Fonthill, 1908. (H.E. BATTEL COLLECTION)

Opposite Top: Express car 40 and trailer 90 (*Red Onion*) c1929. (W.S. FLATT COLLECTION)

Opposite: Former trailer 90 as residence at Grimsby, Ontario c1938. (J.W. HOOD)

Opposite Bottom: Car 90 at St. Catharines in 1935, its retirement year. (B. SCHUFF COLLECTION)

The Thirties

One-man crews took over Welland Division cars on July 5th 1931. Cars 60-63 were used, assisted by No. 132 and, later, by No. 80. These cars had all been built with one door in each vestibule, in the right rear corner according to the direction of operation. When they were modified for one-man, no second door was provided and passengers boarded through the left front door. Since there was little street operation, no danger arose from this rather unusual situation. Main Line cars loaded through the right front door, so that equipment assignments tended to be rather inflexible at this time.

A careful survey was made in the summer of 1935 with a view to total abandonment of the line, but the conclusion was that money would be lost rather than gained by this step. Reducing or eliminating passenger service was also ruled out.

In 1937, street trackage in Humberstone was relaid with welded 85-lb. relay rail, but too little ballast was applied, allowing the rail to get out of alignment and breaking some of the welded joints. This resulted in serious electrolysis problems; therefore, in 1951-52 the whole installation was again rebuilt with new ties and ballast. Bad power conditions owing to increased freight business

caused a new substation to be built at Humberstone in 1936. Another low power spot was a half-mile of 1.2 per-cent grade against southbound trains, starting at Fonthill station. A new substation was therefore built here in 1938 to eliminate "doubling the hill." This situation had been anticipated as far back as 1922 when it had been proposed to erect catenary overhead as far as Fonthill to improve the feed from Thorold substation.

In later years, a signal installation designed to protect switching movements was added in Humberstone and Port Colborne. A short-lived earlier installation between Scanlan's and Electric Park was removed about 1940.

Top: Southbound NS&T car 67 passes Thorold substation as it starts the 18.6 mile run to Fonthill, Welland and Port Colborne, March 31st 1946.
(J.D. KNOWLES 20597)

Opposite Top: Car 63 southbound at Dainsville near CNR crossing, July 20th 1946.
(JOHN F. HUMISTON S7204)

Opposite Bottom: Cars 132 and 135 (main line) and car 61 (Welland Division) at Substation Junction, June 15th 1946.
(J.W. HOOD)

Bottom: Car 63 at CNR Port Colborne station, looking east towards canal lift bridges, July 20th 1946.
(JOHN F. HUMISTON S7203)

In 1938, some trackage was rearranged at Port Colborne and more facilities were added for electric cars, which previously had often been held up by CNR switching moves using the same track.

While one-man operation was the rule after 1931, it was necessary to flag across the private crossing of an industrial railway north of Port Colborne as the NS&T was the junior railroad at the crossing. A flagman rode back and forth between Welland and Port Colborne, flagging over this crossing and working the manual interlocking at the CNR crossing south of Welland. A frequent source of delay was the heavy-traffic New York Central crossing at Welland, since the NYC operated many particularly long freight trains which had to run slowly here because of a speed restriction over the canal drawbridge.

Main Line traffic experienced a great boom during World War II but the Welland line never needed more than hourly single cars. Starting on December 12th 1943, a morning commuter run was scheduled from Stop 4 on the Welland Division to McKinnon's. It is not known how long this car continued to operate but it was, so far as is known, the only regularly scheduled car ever to run through from Welland Division points to St. Catharines without change of cars at Thorold.

Following the Main Line abandonment in 1947, the old 60s were displaced by larger steel cars. These cars had doors on both sides at each end, but Welland passengers were by now so accustomed to boarding from the left that it was not until June 1953 that this practice was officially terminated.

Early Post-War Years

Track was relocated and the level raised in 1947 between mile 1.4 and mile 2.1 in connection with a Hydro project to increase the generating capacity of the DeCew Falls station. About this time, several miles of the original 60-lb. rail were replaced by 85-lb. steel salvaged from the Main Line; the CNR interchange track at Port Colborne was relocated to clear Canal lands. (Much CNR freight originating at Port Colborne was turned over to the NS&T for delivery at Merritton Transfer to reduce the demand for CNR switching at Port Colborne.)

Top: NS&T Welland depot with southbound car 82 on Thorold–Port Colborne run. September 7th 1950.
(J.D. KNOWLES)

Opposite Top: Car 82 is northbound approaching Substation Junction, Thorold, on September 7th 1950, crossing old swing bridge over Welland Canal feeder, having almost completed the 18.6 mile run from Port Colborne on Lake Erie.
(J.D. KNOWLES)

Opposite Bottom: Line car 31 on Elm Street, Humberstone, c1955.
(JOHN F. BROMLEY)

Right: Express car 41 in siding photographed from passing car. 1950s.
(ROGER JENKINS, J.J. WIGT COLLECTION)

Top: Power-off situation at Stop 15, Welland Division, January 1958. Borrowed CNR plow 55307, pushed by motor 21, has just clipped a span pole with its wing. It will take three days to restore traction power. (BOB CHAMBERS)

Bottom: Car 83 at Humberstone, c1958-59. (BOB CHAMBERS)

Opposite Top: Car 83 southbound for Port Colborne, crossing the New York Central tracks at Welland, March 14th 1959. (J.D. KNOWLES 20967)

Opposite Bottom: The operator of car 83 on a fantrip phones the dispatcher before venturing down the Pine Street spur, May 9th, 1955. (J.M. MILLS)

The management wished to drop passenger service as early as 1948; one suggestion was to abandon the line between Welland and Humberstone, and station a freight motor at Port Colborne to switch the "orphaned" section. It was thought that a disused CNR engine shed might serve as a makeshift shelter for the electric engine. However, the question of providing adequate highway replacement for the passenger service was to prove an obstacle for some years to come, since there was no paralleling highway north of Welland. In the event, service was in fact continued until reduction in passenger loads had made the question irrelevant.

Evening service was reduced in December 1954 and notice was given of an eighty percent service cut to be effective on March 25th 1955, but this was cancelled by the Board of Transport Commissioners which required consultation with the municipalities concerned. The traditional hourly service therefore continued. Passenger loads had dropped to an average of about 625 a day, however, and on July 2nd 1956 service was cut, though less drastically than had been proposed. Cars now ran hourly only between 2:00 and 6:00 PM with service every two hours in the morning; there was no evening or Sunday service.

New Cars

It seems strange to record that, while service was being slashed, new cars were obtained, but such is indeed the case. The condition of the 80s, which had been pounding back and forth on the NS&T's less than perfect trackwork for upwards of thirty years, had reached the point where action was required. Forced to continue rail service, in August 1955 three of the four 620-series cars (Nos. 620, 622, 623) were transferred from the Montreal & Southern Counties Railway (along with matching trailer 220, obtained for parts only). These cars had been built in 1930 by the Ottawa Car Company for a short-lived modernization of the Windsor, Essex & Lake Shore Rapid Railway.

Top: CNR mixed passenger train 219 (Fort Erie–Stratford) with Mikado 3422 and NS&T car 620 at Port Colborne, 1958. (BOB CHAMBERS)

Opposite Top: M&SC 623 and 621 at St. Lambert, June 11th 1955. (AL PATERSON COLLECTION)

Opposite Bottom: Car 623 lays over at Thorold, March 3rd 1956. (AL PATERSON COLLECTION)

Bottom: NS&T schedule board, Port Colborne station, 1958. (BOB CHAMBERS)

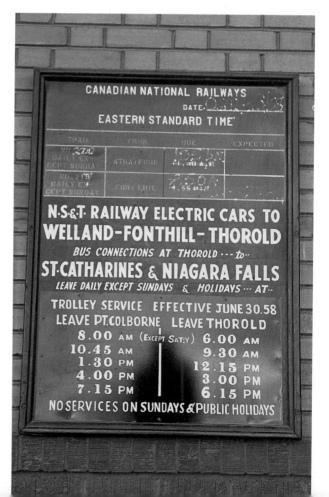

This line closed down after only two years and the cars were stored in Windsor until they went to Montreal in December 1939 for use on the M&SC's interurban line to Granby, Quebec. Except for one car built in 1947 for the Grand River Railway, they were the most modern interurban cars in Canada.

A slightly incongruous feature of the Welland Division was a lift bridge at Welland South that apparently spanned nothing at all. When built it had crossed a navigable feeder to the old canal; however when the new Ship Canal was opened in 1930, the feeder became redundant and was filled in, so that all traces of it had disappeared except the "bridge over nothing", which remained in place until 1957.

Opposite Top: Car 82 crosses the "bridge over nothing" (see text above), May 9th 1955.
(R.J. SANDUSKY)

Opposite Bottom: Motorman seated at the controls of car 82, November 21st 1954.
(R.J. SANDUSKY)

Bottom: Car 83 at Welland, 1958-59.
(BOB CHAMBERS)

The Last Interurban

Traffic continued to dwindle; passenger loads dropped from 350,000 (1953) to 95,000 (1957). In the summer of 1958, the schedule was cut to only five trips a day. Finally, with losses approaching $3,500 a month, all passenger service was terminated on March 28th 1959. This was the last interurban passenger service in Canada, and the last on this continent that did not depend on commuter business into a large city. To this extent at least, it was the last "true interurban".

The official last run left Thorold at 6:15 PM on March 28th in three sections. In the lead was NS&T-built 83 with the official party. This car was deliberately chosen because, on August 15th 1931 as car 107, it had made the last run on the Toronto Suburban Railway's Toronto–Guelph line. The second section was 620, pressed into service for one trip because of the number of last-ride passengers; one of these was a lady who had ridden the first car 52 years before. The final car was 623, the regular car for the afternoon. Car 83 remained in Port Colborne while the official party indulged themselves in a banquet. The other two cars operated the final northbound revenue trip.

THE NIAGARA, ST. CATHARINES AND TORONTO RAILWAY COMPANY

CANADIAN NATIONAL TRANSPORTATION LIMITED

R. B. Smith
Superintendent, Bus Services

St. Catharines, Ont.
January 23, 1959.
File No. 3205-2.

Dear Sir:

Please be advised that, in accordance with Board of Transport Commissioners for Canada, Order No. 96824, dated at Ottawa,
Friday, the 9th day of January, A. D. 1959, all passenger train
service at present provided by the Niagara, St. Catharines and
Toronto Railway Company (Canadian National Railways) between Port
Colborne and Thorold, in the Province of Ontario, and all inter-
mediate points on the said line will be discontinued effective
upon completion of service on Saturday, March 28, 1959.

Copy of bus schedule to supplement rail service, effective
Monday, March 30th, 1959, will be forwarded as soon as available.

Superintendent, Bus Services.

City Clerk, St. Catharines
City Clerk, Niag.Falls
City Clerk, Welland
Town Clerk, Port Dalhousie
Town Clerk, Merritton
Town Clerk, Thorold
Town Clerk, Pt.Colborne
Twp.Clerk, Grantham
Twp.Clerk, Thorold
Twp.Clerk, Stamford
Twp.Clerk, Crowland
Twp.Clerk, Humberstone
Twp.Clerk, Pelham
Vill.Clerk-Fonthill
Ticket Agt.NS&T, St.Cath.
Ticket Agt.NS&T Niag.Falls
Agent, NS&T Fonthill
Agent, NS&T Welland
Agent, CNR, Thorold
Agent, CNR Pt.Colborne
Agent, CNR St.Catharines
CTA CNR St.Catharines
Agent CNR, Welland
Agent, CNR, Merritton
Agent, CNR, Niag.Falls
Dist. Engr. Toronto
Can. Transit, Toronto

Agent, C.N.Exp.St.Catharines
Agent, C.N.Exp. Welland
Agent, C.N.Exp.Port Colborne
Trainmaster, St.Catharines
Supt. Road Transport, Toronto
Gen.Pass.Agt. Toronto
Elec. Supvr. St.Cath.
Supt. Motive Power-Toronto
Auditor, Pass. Accts. - Montreal
Ticket Bureau, Montreal
Asst. Engr. St. Catharines
Asst. Rdm. St. Catharines
Storekeeper, St. Catharines
Supvr. Frt.Trn.St.Cath.
Revenue Clerk, St. Catharines
Supvr. Buses - Niag.Falls
Supt. C.N.Exp. Toronto
Gen.Supt.C.N.Exp. Toronto
Genl.Supt. Toronto
Baggage Agt. Toronto
Supt. London
Asst. Supt. Hamilton
Gen. Supt. Trans., Toronto
Supt. Invest. Toronto
Public Relations - Toronto
Chamber of Commerce, St.Cath
C.P.R.St.Cath.

Toronto Star, St.Cath.
St.Catharines Standard
Toronto Rail Fans

Top: Car 623 southbound on the Welland River trestle, 1958.
(BOB CHAMBERS)

Opposite: Notice of discontinuance of service.
(R.J. SANDUSKY COLLECTION)

The following day, an excursion was sponsored by the Upper Canada Railway Society of Toronto, the last of many extending over a period of more than 25 years (see Chapter 19 for additional photos and reminiscences of the first UCRS excursion over the NS&T in 1943). One of the co-ordinators of the final fantrip was the author. Its itinerary is worth noting in detail as it is typical of the diverse routings possible on the NS&T's track system. Leaving the St. Catharines carhouse, the two cars (83 and 623) proceeded to Merritton to meet the CNR train from

Toronto, then ran through to Port Colborne via Lincoln Junction with a side trip over the short Commonwealth Electric Company spur at Welland. Returning to St. Catharines, the cars made their way to St. Paul and Geneva streets for lunch; this was always a tricky move because the Geneva Street track was laid on the "southbound" side of the street instead of being centred.

In the afternoon the trip proceeded to the end of track on the former Port Dalhousie line, with the inevitable "photo run" at Martindale Pond trestle. The cars separated on return to St. Catharines; No. 623 ran to Merritton with train-connection passengers while No. 83 traversed the Grantham Division as far as the tracks had been cleared of snow, which was about half-way to Port Dalhousie East. Car 83 returned to St. Catharines at 5:50 PM and No. 623 about ten minutes later, just as the sun was setting, end-

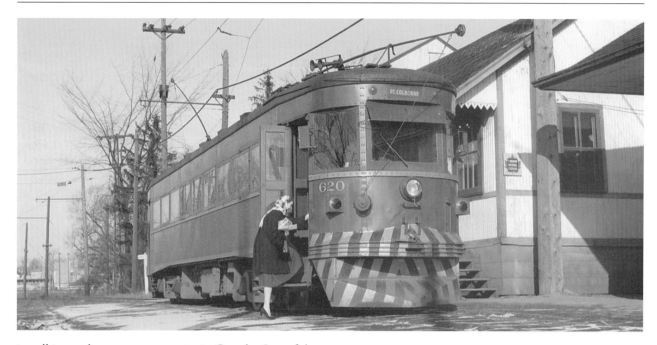

ing all interurban passenger service in Canada. One of the participating motormen, a veteran of many such excursions, was observed to stand silently for a few minutes, staring at the closed doors through which No. 623 had just disappeared; then he shrugged his shoulders slightly, remarked "Well, that's that" to no one in particular, and silently trudged away.

Top: Lady boarding southbound car 620 at Welland, 1958-59. (BOB CHAMBERS)

Opposite: Motor 20 and "funeral procession" at Port Dalhousie East, 1959. (*ST. CATHARINES STANDARD*, J.J. WIGT COLLECTION)

Bottom: NS&T motorman Russ Cudney and last day rider 1959. (BOB CHAMBERS)

CHAPTER 7

NS&T — Lake Shore Division

ONE of the more frequently projected of the many proposed lines in the Niagara Peninsula was one from St. Catharines to Niagara-on-the-Lake (known commonly as "Niagara"). This was vigorously pushed by residents of the area to the extent that in 1903, a bonus of $15,000 and exemption from taxes for twenty years was offered as an inducement by the tiny village. Nothing happened until 1911, however. In that year a gigantic plan was announced for the improvement of the Welland Canal, then hopelessly outdated and unable to pass ships more than 250 feet in length. The new canal would have a relocated outlet to Lake Ontario, following the course of Ten-Mile Creek to Port Weller, instead of striking across country to Port Dalhousie. New freight traffic would be generated by the building of harbour facilities and locks.

Opposite Top: Postcard view of Michigan Central Railroad Niagara-on-the-Lake station and dock, c1915. MCRR never exploited the Toronto–Niagara Falls business, as most passengers crossing on vessels of Canada Steamship Lines (*Chippewa, Cayuga,* etc.) preferred to disembark upriver at Queenston where good connections were made with the Niagara Falls Park & River Railway (IRC). (JOHN BURTNIAK COLLECTION, ST. CATHARINES MUSEUM)

Opposite Bottom: The first car to Niagara-on-the-Lake, November 1913. View looking east on King Street at Queen Street at 'end of steel'. Michigan Central branch is in foreground. (H.E. BATTEL COLLECTION)

Bottom: Postcard view of Michigan Central Railroad steam-hauled passenger train, looking east on King Street towards the river, at Niagara-on-the-Lake c1920. MCRR train has just left the station and is crossing Queen Street headed for Niagara Falls. Track on left is the NS&T (see also photo on opposite page at same location). (NIAGARA FALLS (ONTARIO) PUBLIC LIBRARY)

Therefore, on December 2nd 1912, the first sod was turned in the construction of a line leaving St. Catharines via Welland Avenue, Niagara and Facer streets and in a direct line to Port Weller, then following the Lake Shore Road to Niagara. The original intention was to enter the town along Mississauga and Queen streets, but this proved impracticable and the line was built on King Street, where a Michigan Central branch was already laid. There were therefore two parallel single tracks on this unpaved street. The station, on leased land at Market Street, was similar in appearance to those at Thorold and Welland and is still to be seen, in use as a residence but unmistakable in outline.

Service Starts

The line was built by railway forces. It was not until December 1st 1913 that it was officially open for traffic. Even then, ballasting was not complete; it had been open on an informal basis as far as McNab during September to handle the fall fruit harvest. 80-lb. rail was used as far as Port Weller and 65-lb. beyond, where much of the line was built on or adjacent to the highway. There were several timber trestles up to 420 feet in length. Hourly service was usually provided, though this interval was widened to ninety minutes towards the end.

A large volume of traffic was handled, particularly during World War I, to Niagara Military Camp. Much of this wartime traffic was carried in railway troop trains handled to Niagara-on-the-Lake by electric motors (one on each end of the train), passing through the streets of St. Catharines en route.

As originally built, the line crossed five GTR tracks on Welland Avenue on the extremely acute angle of 32

Top: Car 130 near lock No. 1 c1914-1920.
(J.J. WIGT COLLECTION)

Opposite: Lakeshore Division car 80 (rebuilt from car 100) poses on the new bridge over the fourth canal, c1925.
(LIBRARY AND ARCHIVES CANADA E004666254)

Bottom: Locomotive No. 1 or No. 7 and steam railway coaches (troop train from Niagara-on-the-Lake) on Welland Avenue, c1916.
(LIBRARY AND ARCHIVES CANADA E004665759)

degrees. An elaborate interlocking plant was required and specially designed catenary overhead was installed because of the wide span on which no support could be provided. Upon electrification of the former GTR line (old Welland Railway) as the Grantham Division, this crossing was removed and the electric line diverted along Niagara Street to its junction with the Grantham Division, which it crossed on a series of crossovers under control of the Niagara Street tower.

Until 1930, the line crossed the old Welland Canal near the intersection of Facer and Niagara streets on a wood-floored swing bridge so narrow that electric cars could use it only if there was no automobile traffic on the bridge. This was almost exactly on the spot where the Queen Elizabeth Way overpass was later built.

Service Ends

Only five trips a day were being run at the end, with the cars terminating at the Terminal and not running uptown. Local service was provided as far as Carlton Street by the Facer Street local line. With the end of canal construction and the onset of the depression, passenger service was dis-

Top: Car 68, lettered "Canadian National Electric Railways" at St. Catharines Terminal c1929.
(CRHA, FONDS R.F. CORLEY)

Opposite Top: Cars 135 and 134 on fantrip at disused swing bridge over former third Welland Canal, southbound on the Grantham Division, July 1940. By now it was completely filled in and virtually invisible. The third canal had opened in 1881. Its replacement's construction commenced in 1913, and the last section opened in 1932.
(S. MCGUIRE, FRED ANGUS COLLECTION)

Opposite Bottom: Chartered car 83 at Port Weller (end of track after 1931), in July 1956. Welland Canal drawbridge is in the background.
(R.F. GLAZE)

Bottom: Car 68 at St. Catharines shops, August 7th 1940. Cars 68 and 69 had been used on the Lake Shore Division to Niagara-on-the-Lake.
(J.D. KNOWLES)

continued on January 15th 1931 and the tracks beyond Port Weller abandoned. The Facer Street line continued as a rail operation as far as Grantham Avenue with hourly cars to Carlton Street for a few years. The replacement bus operation was subsequently turned over to a private operator, in April 1932.

For a time in 1942, passenger service was restored on an experimental basis, five trips daily being run to Port Weller. Car 60 was used with a one-man crew, and the resultant left-side loading on Niagara and Facer streets caused some confusion. In 1962, freight operation through the streets ended when a non-electrified line was built passing under the new Garden City Skyway, which carries the Queen Elizabeth Way over the Canal.

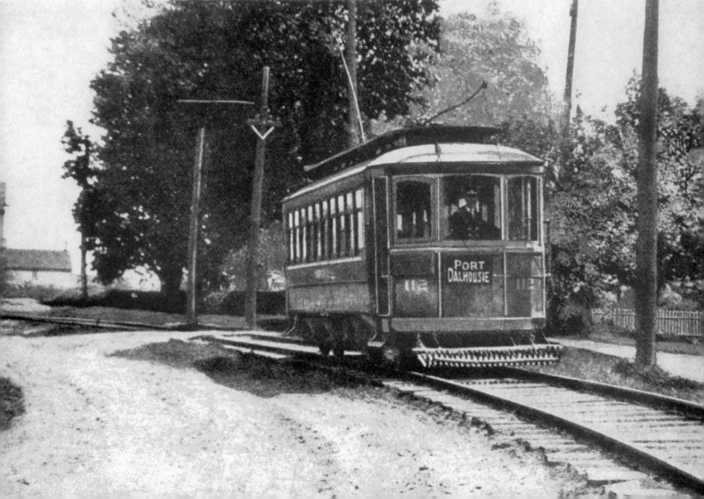

CHAPTER 8

NS&T — St. Catharines Local Lines

AT the time the local line was taken over, it consisted of the original and most important line, the Thorold "Low Line" from Woodruff's on Ontario Street to Thorold station. A second line ran to the Victoria Lawn Cemetery on Queenston Street. The Port Dalhousie line, built by the NS&T before the amalgamation, was operated as part of the local lines. It was almost interurban in character (the territory west of the old canal was never built-up) but was included in the St. Catharines fare area, which the Low Line was not. There was a half-mile of street running in Port Dalhousie; most of the remainder was roadside trackage, except for the canal crossing and its approaches. The canal itself was disused for navigation purposes, but occasionally the NS&T bridge had to be swung to pass dredges, as the waterway was a tailrace for the DeCew Falls generating station. A picturesque wooden trestle spanned Martindale Pond.

Statistics for the year ending June 30th 1903 were still being reported in the name of the Port Dalhousie, St. Catharines & Thorold and showed 6.82 miles of track operated by eight cars. 252,079 passengers were carried and the operating ratio was 58.3 percent.

In 1903, a spur was built up Lake Street to Wellington to serve a canning factory, and the curve radius at Lake and Louisa was widened by passing over a vacant corner lot in order to accommodate standard railway freight cars. In the previous year the tracks on James Street had been connected to those on St. Paul Street (a separate franchise was required for this single curve) which retained their roadside location at this point. Track was laid in 1907, apparently for the second time, on Geneva Street. Tracks had been built here in 1880 and later electrified, but seem to have passed out of use; the rebuilding was prompted largely by a desire to give freight service in the area. In 1911, the Ontario Street line was extended from Woodruff's to Carlton Street to improve service to the McKinnon Industries manufacturing facilities.

New Franchise

A new franchise was negotiated with the town of Thorold effective December 18th 1911, providing for an annual payment to the town of $1,000, and requiring a five cent fare within its limits. As the old franchise had expired on

November 28th, service on the Low Line in Thorold was suspended pending the new agreement. High Line service was not affected as it had its own right-of-way and required no franchise.

Much of the Port Dalhousie line was relaid in 1907 with 80-lb. rail, although the on-street section retained its 56-lb. steel. This was a very busy line, carrying up to 75 or even more cars a day over the single track. A new station and freight shed were opened at Lakeside Park in 1912 as the two lake steamers, including the new (1911) *Dalhousie City*, had developed a substantial freight and express traffic.

In 1913 the frequency of service on the Low Line was increased, and four cars (which eventually became 101-104) were purchased second-hand. These were "Philadelphia Standards" built in 1903, part of a fleet of hundreds of almost identical cars. At the same time it was proposed to extend the Low Line by double-tracking to Substation Junction and building a new line south along the canal towards, but this idea was given up during World War I even though a franchise had been granted in 1914.

The last extension in St. Catharines was opened on November 26th 1917 as far as the Grand Trunk "Western Hill" station, over a new high-level viaduct known as Burgoyne Bridge. Volunteer lady conductors were used on the first day, and the total receipts for the day ($79.79) were turned over to an organization planning the "Great War Veterans' Club House." The special fare for the day was "ten cents and upwards" and no transfers were accepted.

The Early Twenties

The Merritton franchise provided for relocation of Low Line tracks from the centre to the side of the road from Thorold Road through the centre of town. A section of track was relocated in 1922 on the hilly stretch between the Thorold boundary and Ball Avenue, but owing to the war and subsequent uncertainties, the rest of the agreement was not carried out. In 1922, the Board of Railway Commissioners ordered the rest of the work to be done; however, there remained one other section of street trackage between Walnut Street and the Main Line crossing, and this was never relocated.

In common with many of the municipalities through which the railway ran, the St. Catharines franchise expired shortly after WWI. There ensued a period of uncertainty as to the future ownership of the system, as mentioned elsewhere, and during this period the company was unwilling to invest any capital. By 1922, therefore, the local lines were badly run down, particularly the trackage.

Opposite Top: Car 112 in the east end, c1905.
(J.W. HOOD COLLECTION)

Opposite Bottom: Car 112 outbound to Port Dalhousie, c1915.
(J.M. MILLS COLLECTION)

Top: St. Paul Street 1919.
(NIAGARA FALLS (ONTARIO) PUBLIC LIBRARY D418171)

Opposite Top: Postcard view of car 53 turning off St. Paul onto James c1910.
(PUBLISHER'S COLLECTION)

Opposite Bottom: Car 102 on St. Paul Street, St. Catharines 1927.
(T. WALLING, R.T. VINCENT COLLECTION)

Bottom: Open car 51 and closed car 109 at Port Dalhousie dock c1910.
(LIBRARY AND ARCHIVES CANADA E004665775)

Much of the city track had been built with a foundation consisting essentially of two parallel concrete beams, rather than a single slab. Heavy traffic had pounded this track out of alignment, producing a condition that no amount of maintenance work could correct. Paving was crumbling, and as the entire railway was single-track, it suffered badly from congestion, particularly on the approaches to the St. Paul Street interurban station. This situation was wors-

ened with the opening of the Burgoyne Bridge; the general improvement of highways in the area threw more vehicular traffic onto narrow St. Paul Street which was part of Ontario provincial highway No. 8. It was recognized that the situation was unsatisfactory, but several years were to pass before it was improved.

Routes in 1922 were:

"Low Line": via Queenston, St. Paul and Ontario to Carlton Street (twenty minute headway),

Grand Trunk: west of interurban station only (twenty minutes),

Victoria Lawn: east of interurban station only (thirty minutes),

Port Dalhousie: via Louisa, Lake and James to station (thirty minutes)

Service on the future Facer Street route was provided by hourly Lake Shore Division cars operating via Niagara, Welland, Geneva and St. Paul to the station.

Rehabilitation

Agreement was finally reached in 1925 for a new St. Catharines franchise, to be perpetual except that the city could buy the company out at the end of any five-year period. It was based largely on a franchise adopted two years earlier in Ottawa, and provided for a thorough rebuilding of the local lines and for a fare increase. The Merritton and Thorold franchises had not expired, however, and these towns refused to accept the revised fares. The company was unwilling to proceed with many of the improvements until it was assured of adequate revenue, and a joint application was made by the railway and the city of St. Catharines for a Board of Transport Commissioners order imposing the higher fare on the entire area. The order was duly issued, the fare raised on March 8th 1926, and the company proceeded to rebuild the system along its original lines.

Even before the increase went into effect, during 1925 a single track was built on King Street between James and Ontario, and St. Paul was double-tracked between James and Geneva. West of James, the street was considered too narrow for double track, so the existing single track was used for eastbound movements while westbound cars were diverted to parallel King Street. An additional benefit was the formation of a loop around the James–King–Ontario–St. Paul block where cars could be turned to avoid changing ends in the congested uptown area. Port Dalhousie cars now looped via Welland Avenue, Geneva, St. Paul, James and Lake Streets

At the same time, the old interurban station was abandoned; re-rerouting of the local lines eliminated almost all two-way running on single track in the uptown area. Track extensions were proposed on Geneva and Lake Streets as far as Carlton Street, with a line on Carlton from Geneva to Ontario. This loop line was never built, since by the time the bulk of the rehabilitation was completed, the motorbus had come into its own, and the company's first bus service was eventually established in this area by buying out a private operator.

In 1926, a complete rebuilding of existing trackage was carried out, with much new rail laid on St. Paul Street West, Queenston, Geneva, Louisa, Niagara and Ontario streets and Welland Avenue, the latter being double-tracked west of Geneva Street and through the carhouse yard.

Opposite: Highway 8 (St. Paul Street), St. Catharines, looking west from the Lincoln Hotel entrance canopy (similar to that of Hotel Leonard across the street) on April 24th 1937 (ARCHIVES OF ONTARIO RG 14-162-3, 723S, A07605)

One-Man Operation

One-man operation of the local lines began on June 7th 1926 and all local cars were modified during 1926-27. Four of the twelve new Cincinnati curve-side cars were assigned to St. Catharines, but the higher riding habit in Niagara Falls led to the assignment of most of the new equipment there. Two-man operation continued on the Low Line for some time owing to zone-fare collection problems.

1925 was the peak pre-World War II year for the St. Catharines local lines, with about 2,700,000 passengers. This was an increase from 1,300,000 ten years earlier and at the time seemed to justify the investment in rehabilitation.

In 1927, the Low Line was re-routed to the CNR station and Victoria Lawn cars were changed to run on Ontario Street. The former separate line between the CNR and the Terminal was eliminated. In the same year Mr. G. E. Patterson, partner in the early car-building firm of Patterson & Corbin, died; his funeral entourage was conveyed to Victoria Lawn Cemetery, appropriately, by chartered streetcar. Streetcars were often chartered for funeral parties in the early days, and the practice continued in a small way almost to the end of rail service, latterly mostly for a group of Armenians living near one of the local lines.

Low Line Abandoned

The town of Merritton had never been favourably disposed towards the railway, and in 1929 there occurred a remarkable example of railway-municipal disagreement. The expiry date of the franchise, which affected only the Low Line, was July 28th 1929. An argument developed over whether or not it was renewable, and if so, on what terms. The railway took the position that in the absence of any new agreement, the terms of the old one automatically continued in force. This was based on a section of the Ontario Railway Act providing that when a franchise expired, the municipality must either grant a new one or buy out the operation. The town maintained that the railway had no rights on its streets after July 28th, and started negotiations for a private bus service. Unfortunately for the town, this plan received a temporary setback when the bus operator sold out to a larger concern.

In December 1929, the town secured an injunction forcing the railway off the streets on January 1st 1931; the judge asserted that the Ontario act did not apply as the NS&T was a Dominion corporation. The railway appealed and the line kept running, but the appeal was dismissed and the end of service was set for May 31st 1931.

The day before rail service was to end, the NS&T discovered that the substitute bus line had no operating permit for the route in question. By direct appeal to the Premier of Ontario, the railway arranged for temporary operating authority and hastily borrowed four buses from Toronto. On May 31st, normal Low Line service ended as scheduled and the following day, the four borrowed buses

Top: Car 327 on Geneva Street, summer 1949.
(R.T. VINCENT)

Opposite Top: Car 130 at CNR station on NRHS Buffalo Chapter fantrip on September 14th 1947.
(J.D. KNOWLES)

Opposite Bottom: Car 323 with portable city headlight at the outer end of Facer Street on June 19th 1943. This car was destroyed by fire at Houtby's Siding in 1945 due to a lightning strike.
(J.D. KNOWLES)

Bottom: Four 320-series "Washington" cars and car 61 on Port Dalhousie line at Holtby's Siding on the Civic Holiday (August 2nd) 1941.
(J.D. KNOWLES 20600)

began running between Merritton and Thorold, while rail service continued over the Low Line to the crossing in Merritton, thence over the High Line to Thorold. This makeshift arrangement lasted only until the delivery of seven buses on order, at which time all Low Line service then terminated, ending the oldest continuously-operated electric line in Canada. Facer Street cars replaced the Low Line to the CNR station.

Upon abandonment of the Lake Shore Division in 1931, Facer Street cars were extended to Carlton Street for a short time. By 1935, base service had become twenty minutes to Grantham Avenue with an hourly extension to Carlton Street. All trips beyond Grantham Avenue had been dropped by 1938.

On July 1st 1932 cash fares were raised to ten cents, the ticket rate remaining at four for 25 cents. A survey had shown that expenses averaged 22 cents per car-mile while revenues were 15 cents. A supplementary agreement to the franchise legalized this change. At this time the local lines were served by a great variety of old cars, most of which had been somewhat modernized in 1920 (in appearance at least). The Port Dalhousie line was in the capable hands of the 320-series "Washington" cars, the most versatile cars the company ever had; they were equally at home in local or suburban service and were often used as Main Line extras.

In 1936, Victoria Lawn–Ontario Street cars carried about 1,000 passengers daily; Facer Street–CNR about 800; Port Dalhousie about 1,250 (many more in summer) and buses replacing the Low Line about 2,000.

Port Dalhousie Line

After 1940, the Port Dalhousie line operated under the standard rulebook in many respects, so that the cars could be seen with green or white flags when required. All cars were given marker lights and flag brackets in 1940. A "Bulletin" (reproduced on page 59) shows the complicated rules necessary to operate rush hour extras under this system, and also shows the way in which one car was made to fill what amounted to two or three separate schedules.

This line was always difficult to operate, being subject to heavy seasonal loads to Lakeside Park both day and night, as there was a popular dance hall there. Base service was usually twenty minutes in summer, half-hourly in winter, although during the depression a 45-minute headway was in effect for a time. "Doubles" (i.e. two cars closely following on the same schedule) were a routine matter, and extras often resulted in operation of scheduled trips with up to six sections. Before the 1940 rules revision, at such times a man would be stationed at each passing track to be sure that all sections of each movement had arrived before movement in the other direction began. A further complication was the fact that the lead car of such a movement arriving at Lake and Louisa outbound, could not tell whether all sections of his movement had passed inbound. It was therefore always compulsory to call the despatcher on arrival at this point.

Another problem was narrow Main Street, Port Dalhousie, where parked cars often caused traffic jams that further hindered operations. The dance hall was well-patronized by St. Catharines people; at about 12:30 AM, extras would load at Lakeside Park running through to Victoria Lawn and Facer Street, avoiding late-night transfers uptown. When freight motors, as often happened, were operating as the second section on a passenger schedule,

Opposite Top: Cars 325, 321 and 320 inbound at Canning Factory Siding for meet with train 79, July 20th 1946. (JOHN F. HUMISTON S7242)

Opposite Bottom: Cars 327 and 328 on adjacent tracks at Port Dalhousie dock, looking east, July 20th 1946. (JOHN F. HUMISTON S7246)

one of the freight crew would ride the passenger car to ensure that the "section following" flags were observed. Under the circumstances, it is indeed surprising that block signals were never installed.

McKinnon's Extras

A very heavy rush-hour movement occurred during shift-change times at McKinnon Industries Limited, a General Motors subsidiary at the outer end of Ontario Street. In addition to the regular Ontario Street cars and Thorold South buses that terminated there, extras would load for operation through to Facer Street, and to Thorold via the High Line. These would avoid uptown traffic by using the Louisa Street cut-off. Because local line cars had improper flange characteristics for open-track service, 320s or interurban cars were therefore used, which is why 130s or even the 61-foot 80s could be seen in this local line operation (and as Lakeside Park extras). Car assignments on the NS&T were often determined on the basis of expediency. After 1945, only extras bound for the High Line used the cut-off.

In January 1941, the diamond at the Ontario Street crossing was removed, thus requiring any access to McKinnon's to be only from the Port Dalhousie line. It was restored in September 1942 when local line service was resumed, and removed finally in April 1948.

Service Suspended

Uptown congestion continued to increase, especially on St. Paul Street which was only 33 feet wide in places. Pressure for removal of the rails began in 1936 and steadily increased, until finally on February 26th 1939 the Facer Street–CNR and Victoria Lawn–Ontario Street lines were replaced by bus service, leaving only Port Dalhousie cars to traverse uptown streets, along with Main Line movements for a few months more. All tracks were left in place and the agreement with the city covering the substitution allowed the company to use street cars in rush hours and in winter snow. The cars were placed in storage or sent to Niagara Falls, where local line service continued. This change had been delayed as long as possible in an attempt to make maximum use of the new trackage on which so much money had been spent scarcely ten years before.

SC 560
3-36

NIAGARA ST. CATHARINES TORONTO RAILWAY

LOCAL LINE REPORT

DATE _____ 19____

FARE BOX NUMBER	CAR OR COACH NUMBER	TIME LEAVING	TERMINAL OR CHANGE OFF POINT	TIME ARRIVING	AUDIT OFFICE
		M	CAR BARNS	M	
		M		M	
		M		M	
		M		M	
		M		M	
		M		M	
		M		M	
		M		M	
		M		M	
		M		M	
		M		M	
		M		M	
		M		M	
		M		M	
		M		M	
		M		M	
		M		M	

COLLECTIONS

TRANSFERS	PASSES	OTHER LINES TICKETS

SPEEDOMETER READING
TRANSFERS AND PASSOUT CHECKS ISSUED

FORM	COMMENCING	CLOSING	FORM	COMMENCING	CLOSING
290			296		
291			297		

SPEED O METER

OPERATOR _____ NO. _____

FROM _____ TO _____

LUNCH RELIEF OPERATOR _____ M _____ M _____

Service Resumed

As World War II conditions worsened, the Dominion Transit Controller requested resumption of some local service in St. Catharines as well as on the Main Line, as a conservation measure. This was not in the form of an order, but was complied with; an additional reason probably was the small size of Depression-era buses. At any rate, the faithful streetcars went back to work on April 1st 1942 on Facer Street and Victoria

Lawn, daily except Sunday, looping uptown around the James–King–Ontario block. Reading the correspondence files, one might almost think the management was happy to see some real transportation again, instead of all those buses! Sunday service was resumed on September 13th. Rush hour service was provided on Ontario Street by Victoria Lawn cars; some rush-hour cars operated to the CNR Station, but not as a normal rule since the bus route had been extended well beyond the end of track. From April to June 1943, an experimental service was instituted between Port Weller and McKinnon's via the Louisa Street cut-off at a separate ten-cent fare, but did not prosper.

As with most transit systems, women were hired to keep the service running when male employees went to war. The first female bus driver started work on September 3rd 1943 and the first female motorman on April 6th 1944. The use of women on streetcars was not at first undertaken because of doubts that they would be strong enough to handle the trolley retrievers in the event of dewirements, but this fear proved groundless when one determined lady successfully persuaded the management to let her try.

Local Line Abandonment

With the end of the war, Victoria Lawn and Facer Street lines resumed normal bus operation on March 30th 1946. Most of the old cars were scrapped and the curve-side cars sent to Niagara Falls to ease maintenance problems there. However, cars 106 and 124 remained in serviceable condition in St. Catharines and continued on extra runs (as did the 320s) for two years more. The last dates of passenger service were as follows:

Victoria Lawn — September 9th 1947
Ontario Street — September 9th 1947
Facer Street — May 7th 1948
CNR Station — March 30th 1946

Opposite Top: Operator of car 312 northbound at Canning Factory Siding on Port Dalhousie line replaces dewired trolley pole as southbound car 303 speeds past, c1948.
(J.D. KNOWLES 20621)

Opposite Bottom: Crowded car 312 returning from Port Dalhousie at Canning Factory Siding, October 5th 1948.
(BILL BAILEY, A. DOUGLAS COLLECTION)

The end of Victoria Lawn–Ontario Street service was unplanned, and resulted from the rails on Queenston Street being covered with a layer of "Colas" road-surfacing material. The last car to operate became stranded when it "lost its ground" on this material. The last actual trips over the CNR and Ontario Street lines were railway enthusiasts' excursions on September 14th and November 30th 1947 respectively. Overhead was dismantled in 1949 and the redundant tracks paved over. The Port Dalhousie line continued to run on Geneva, St. Paul and James Streets, and Facer Street trackage was continued in freight service, often being traversed by excursions as long as these trips were possible.

By 1948, the accumulated deficit on local line operations under a supposedly "service-at-cost" franchise since 1925 had reached almost $1,500,000. Fares were raised to three for 25 cents on February 10th 1949.

Port Dalhousie Line Ends

Conversion of the Port Dalhousie line was delayed for two years pending agreement about track removal and repaving, and the company's rights and responsibilities after the tracks were abandoned. After the 320s were sent to Montreal in 1947 there was really no suitable equipment for this line. The curve-side lightweights were most often used, but were prone to derailment on open track, and lacked proper ground clearance for operation in snow. Therefore, nos. 67 and 68 were sometimes used, as were cars 327 and 328, the two derelict bodies that had been reconditioned for wartime use. Finally, on March 1st 1950, buses took over as required by a 1949 franchise renewal. The last car was No. 302 which reached the carhouse at 2:00 PM on that day. Pending Board of Transport Commissioners approval, a daily trip had to be operated; this left St. Catharines at 5:35 AM and was run using one of the Welland interurban cars before it began its day's work. This franchise run was terminated on August 6th of the same year, and the final

Top: NS&T car 80 at Port Colborne, July 1955.
(KENNETH F. CHIVERS, C. ROBERT CRAIG MEMORIAL LIBRARY,
CI-BWI399)

trip over the line was an employees' picnic to Lakeside Park on August 16th. The street trackage in Port Dalhousie and the terminal tracks at Lakeside Park were removed in October. The remainder was retained to serve on-line freight shippers and was destined to form part of the itinerary of the railway's last passenger operation on March 29th 1959. Tracks were abandoned beyond McKinnon's in 1965-66.

Canadian National Transportation Ltd. turned over the charter coach business to Canada Coach Lines in 1959, but continued to provide local bus service until September 1st 1961 when all routes in the area were taken over, along with 35 buses, by the St. Catharines Public Utilities Commission following annexation of Port Dalhousie, Merritton and part of Grantham Township by the city of St. Catharines. The PUC leased the carhouse and was its last occupant, moving out in April 1964, long after the last of the track had been removed. The building was demolished in April 1965 to make way for a shopping centre.

Niagara, St. Catharines & Toronto Railway
Canadian National Transportation Ltd.
12-Ride Commutation Ticket

36555

TO	Stop No.	From	Expiry Date	
Pt. Dalhousie	40	★	Feb.	Jan
St. Cath'rines	50	★	Apr	Mar
Merritton	51	★	Jun	May
Thorold	60	★	Aug	July
Stop	61	★	Oct	Sept
Stop	62	★		Nov
Stop	63	★		
Stop	64	★	2	1
Stop	65	★	4	3
Stop	66	★	6	5
Stop		★	8	7
N'g.Falls,Ont.			10	9
Canal Bridge	53	★	12	11
Stone Road	54	★	14	13
Ont. Paper Co	80A	★	16	15
Windle Vill.	68	★	18	17
Bl.H'se Corn.	69	★	20	19
Jct. 26 and Garner Rd.	71	★	22	21
Well. Chem. Works	72	★	24	23
			26	25
			28	27
			30	29
				31

Ticket is good only when presented by the purchaser for 12 continuous rides between stations punched, with transfer to or from Local Lines in the City of St. Catharines or Niagara Falls, Ont., when commencing or completing journey in these cities.

Ticket must be presented to operator on Interurban or Local Division where trip is started who will punch out one number and issue transfer check. Fare 30¢, if destination is on another Division.

Ticket is not good after date of expiry punched in margin and will be taken up for the cash ride.

Form 153 ML

5	10	15	20	25	30
35	40	45	50	55	60
65	70	75	80	85	90
95	$1	$2	$3	$4	

Year
1944—19
1946—1945

ORDER NO. 74951

THE BOARD OF TRANSPORT COMMISSIONERS FOR CANADA

...NDAY, THE 31ST DAY OF
JULY, A. D. 1950.

...GH WARDROPE,
...sst. Chief Commissioner.
. SYLVESTRE, K.C.,
Deputy Chief Commissioner.
. M. MACPHERSON,
Commissioner.

IN THE MATTER OF the
application of The Niagara,
St. Catharines and Toronto
Railway Company, hereinafter
called the "Applicant Company,"
under Sections 33, 34, 165A,
312 and all other relevant
sections of the Railway Act,
and under Sub-section 3 of
Section 2 of the Canadian
National-Canadian Pacific Act,
1933, for an Order:
(1) authorizing the Applicant
Company to discontinue the
operation of its electric
passenger trains in and between
the City of St. Catharines, the
Township of Grantham, the Township of Louth and the Town of
Port Dalhousie, in the Province
of Ontario; and
(2) approving the abandonment
by the Applicant Company of 6.72
miles of its lines of railway in
the City of St. Catharines, in
the Township of Grantham and the
Town of Port Dalhousie, as shown
in red and yellow on plan
No. 8.1.L-3, dated September 20,
1946, revised to July 19, 1950,
and as shown in black on plan
No. 13.80A-A8, dated October 31st,
1949, on file with the Board
under file No. 27528.4:

UPON reading the submissions filed--

IT IS ORDERED

1. That the Applicant Company be, and it is hereby,
authorized to discontinue the operation of its electric passenger
trains in and between the City of St. Catharines, the Township
of Grantham, the Township of Louth and the Town of Port Dalhousie,
in the Province of Ontario,

2. That the abandonment of operation of 6.72 miles of
the Applicant Company's lines of railway in the City of
St. Catharines, in the Township of Grantham and the Town of Port

74951

-2-

74951

Dalhousie, as shown in red and yellow on plan No. 8.1.L-3, dated
September 20, 1946, revised to July 19, 1950, and as shown in
black on plan No. 13.80A-A8, dated October 31st, 1949, on file
with the Board under file No. 27528.4, be, and it is hereby,
approved.

(SGD.) A. SYLVESTRE,
Deputy Chief Commissioner,
The Board of Transport Commissioners for Canada.

BOARD OF TRANSPORT COMMISSIONERS FOR
CANADA
Examined and certified as a true copy
under Section 23 of "The Railway Act."

P. F. Baillargeon

Secretary, Board of Transport
Commissioners for Canada,
OTTAWA, August 1st, 1950.

74951

800

BOARD OF TRANSPORT COMMISSIONERS FOR CANADA

OFFICE OF THE SECRETARY

OTTAWA, August 2, 1950.

JPS.   File 27528.4

Dear Sir,

I enclose herewith certified copy of Order of the
Board No 74951 dated July 31, 1950.
Please acknowledge receipt.

Yours truly,

P. F. Baillargeon
SECRETARY

N.L. Graham, Esq.,
Clerk & Treasurer,
Corp of the town of
Port Dalhousie, Ont.

Top: Authorization for abandonment of lines in St. Catharines,
Grantham Township, Louth Township and Port Dalhousie.
(CREDIT)

320S TO MONTREAL

Top: 320, 325 and 326 at Port Dalhousie dock, July 1941.
(AL PATERSON COLLECTION)

Bottom: Car 325 on Geneva Street, St. Catharines, February 21st 1943.
(R.T. VINCENT)

Opposite Top: Montreal & Southern Counties No. 321 southbound on McGill Street passing a Montreal Tramways Company Presidents' Conference Committee (PCC) Car No. 3542 c1950.
(AL PATERSON COLLECTION)

Opposite Bottom: M&SC No. 321, a local car from Montreal South, on Common Street turning into Des Soeurs Grises (McGill Street Terminal), Montreal, Quebec, June 1947. Note that the car still wears the NS&T red and grey uniform instead of M&SC dark green.
(WILLIAM C. JANSSEN, A. DOUGLAS COLLECTION)

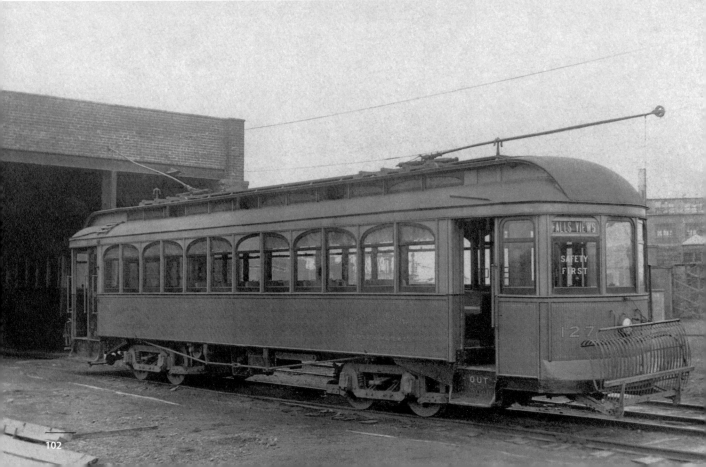

CHAPTER 9

NS&T — Niagara Falls Local Lines

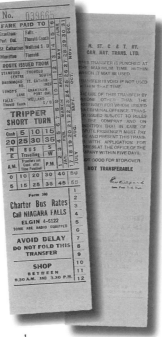

At about the time that the NS&T assumed control, the Niagara Falls local line was extended to the foot of Bridge Street over tracks built as an entrance for Main Line interurbans, passing the Grand Trunk station and terminating at the Lower Arch Bridge. This remained the terminal for local cars until abandonment.

Statistics for the year ending June 30th 1903 were still being reported in the name of the Niagara Falls Wesley Park & Clifton Tramway; they listed 4½ miles of track served by six cars. 349,672 passengers were carried and the operating ratio was 53.8 percent. Early in 1906, the line was extended southerly from Falls View to the Michigan Central yard at Montrose, about ⅔ mile.

In 1918 the city, with no previous warning to the company, announced that at the annual municipal elections on New Year's Day, 1919, the voters would be asked to approve of the city taking over the line at the end of the franchise in March 1920. The vote was in favour, but the city took no further action and it seems likely that this was only a move intended to strengthen its hand in the coming franchise negotiations. A new agreement was eventually ratified by the voters in March 1924. This provided for an increase in fares from five cents to seven cents (four tickets for 25 cents) on July 1st. An interesting feature was the inclusion of four different schedules of fares, each one higher than the last, to take effect automatically according to the financial position of the operation. This clause was invoked once, when on August 8th 1929 fares were increased to eight cents (seven tickets for fifty cents) but it fell into disuse under the combined effects of depression and war.

On December 10th 1919 the car barn was badly damaged by fire, destroying two new cars (124 and 125) and a plow. The replacement structure was a very small one with a capacity of only two cars, without servicing facilities.

Cars were therefore always deadheaded to St. Catharines when any work needed to be done.

Rehabilitation

The new franchise called for new cars, reconstruction of trackage, an extension on Lundy's Lane and construction of a new terminal to get interurban trains off Bridge Street. In 1926 eight of the twelve new curve-side lightweight cars, the last new cars purchased, were assigned to Niagara Falls where they performed all normal service. One-man operation was introduced with these cars on June 7th 1926. Tower Inn Terminal has been mentioned previously, and for two or three years, a local service originated here, running up Newman Hill and to a popular observation tower at Falls View. Unfortunately it did not attract tourist traffic as had been hoped, and later became simply a shuttle between the Terminal and Victoria Avenue. It was cancelled altogether during the depression.

All trackage on the former horsecar line was reconstructed. New girder rail was installed on paved sections. All was single track except for Victoria Avenue, which was doubled as far as Newman Hill. A wye was installed at Ferry and Stanley streets as the branchoff point for a new line to extend north to connect with the Main Line. The exten-

Opposite Top: Postcard view of car 110 on Main Street c1910. (PUBLISHER'S COLLECTION)

Opposite Bottom and Right: Preston-built "Prairie" type car 127 in rare grey livery from late World War I era, shown in Niagara Falls at carhouse and on street with crew.
(OPPOSITE BOTTOM: LIBRARY AND ARCHIVES CANADA E004668766; RIGHT: ADAM ZHELKA COLLECTION)

sion was never built and the wye was disconnected about 1936. Beyond Murray Street the rails were laid at the side of the road, but the passing siding on Livingstone Street went out onto the roadway. During the reconstruction, part of the service was provided by old buses borrowed from Toronto, which were not popular with the patrons.

The Lundy's Lane extension, projected at various times since 1895, was mostly outside the city in Stamford Township. Construction of this line was started before any of the other new work, and the line was opened as far as Winery Road (now Mouland Street) on February 15th 1925. Stub service was provided while work was proceeding elsewhere, following which half-service was operated on each branch, giving 7½ minute headways downtown. Later, base service intervals on each branch were widened to twenty minutes.

In 1929-30 the company suffered from the city's failure to regulate competing bus services as required by the franchise; further difficulty was experienced with a taxi company which ran more or less established routes on carline streets at a flat 25 cent fare, in defiance of franchise and city by-law alike. Cab drivers actively solicited passengers on NS&T property in front of, and even inside, Tower Inn Terminal. This was finally eliminated by city police, but not until several years had passed. Ticket rates were changed on June 10th 1934 from seven for fifty cents to four for 25 cents, partly to combat the competition referred to above, but partly also because of public resistance, under depression conditions, to paying out more than 25 cents at a time for tickets.

On several occasions during the depression, merchants of the city combined to hold a city-wide "shopping day," when the fare would be cut to five cents for the day. The increased business generated by the sales meant that there was little reduction in revenue, and, in addition, information was gained that proved useful in fending off politically-inspired demands for a permanent nickel fare. Interestingly, these one-day concessions constituted a change in an approved fare, and had to be the subject of an amendment to an established tariff, complete with the full panoply of Transport Board approval and published bulletins.

Wartime

Unlike other parts of the system, the Niagara Falls local lines were not changed to bus operation, but unquestionably would have been if the war had not intervened. The lightweight cars were offered to the Toronto Transportation Commission in 1939-40. The TTC seriously considered them as a replacement for the old wooden cars on

Top: Postcard view of car 124 at Michigan Central Victoria Park station, Niagara Falls c1919.
(NIAGARA FALLS (ONTARIO) PUBLIC LIBRARY, DI2793)

Opposite Top: Car 123 after rebuilding at Niagara Falls Terminal July 20th 1940.
(AL PATERSON COLLECTION)

Opposite Bottom: Car 107 on Victoria Avenue, outbound to Montrose, April 1943.
(J.W. HOOD)

Left: One of the lightweight cars outbound at Main and Ferry Streets, Niagara Falls, June 23rd 1947.
(J.D. KNOWLES)

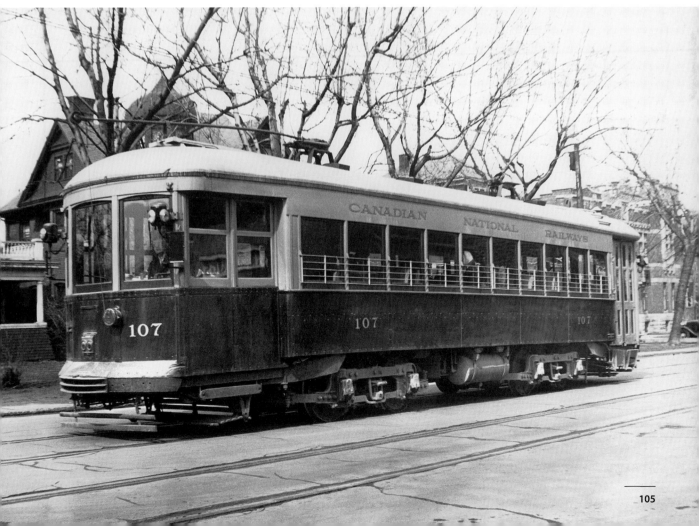

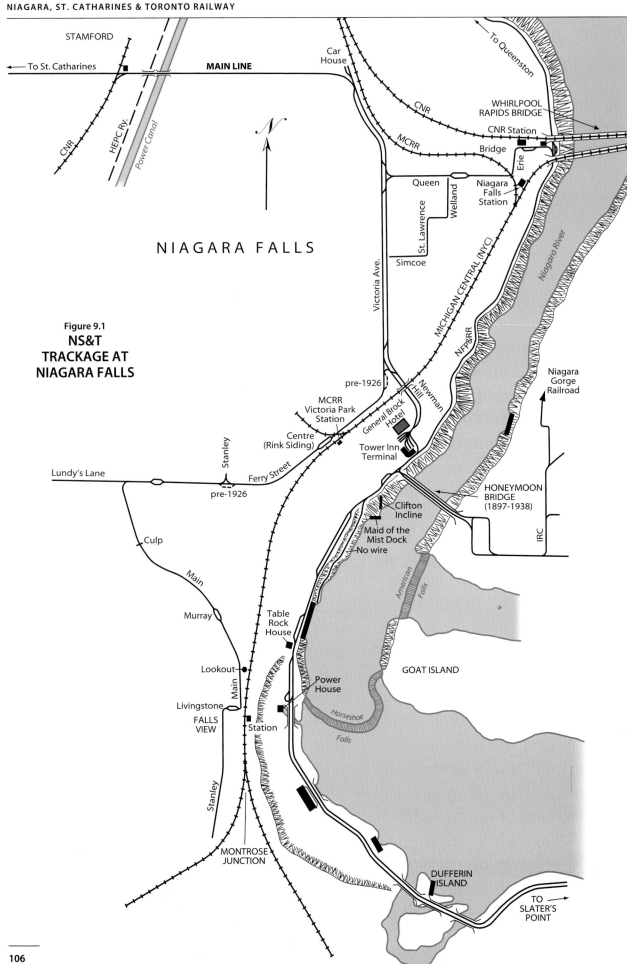

Figure 9.1
**NS&T
TRACKAGE AT
NIAGARA FALLS**

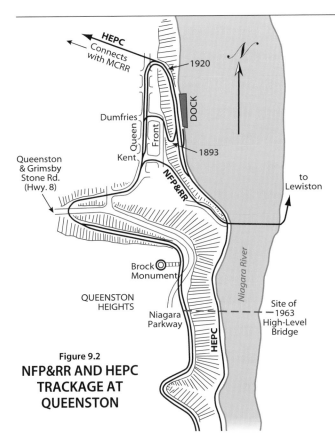

Figure 9.2

NFP&RR AND HEPC TRACKAGE AT QUEENSTON

the Weston Road line, but finally rejected them because of clearance problems — they did not have the tapered vestibules required by Toronto's double-track curves. Had this offer been accepted, the Falls local lines would have been abandoned and the Main Line probably torn up.

In June 1942, the Victoria Avenue double track was extended from Queen Street north along the interurban line to eliminate operating problems as far as the carhouse. This extension incorporated a former passing track.

By the end of 1942, the accumulated deficit under the franchise, supposedly giving service-at-cost with a guaranteed (but modest) profit, amounted to almost exactly a million dollars. Even in 1932 — the best year in the history of the local lines — the surplus was only $900. These results were in spite of an increase in passengers from 960,000 (*1939*) to 3,050,000 (*1946*).

Abandonment

It was intended to replace the streetcars in May 1946, but postwar shortages delayed the change until the following year. On May 12th 1947 the Lundy's Lane line was abandoned beyond the Main and Ferry junction, since the built-up area had grown beyond the end of track and local residents were clamouring for service. Stamford Township

(text continues on page 112)

Left: 300-series car inbound on Montrose line, Niagara Falls c1944. (BRO. BERNARD POLINAK, S.J., COLLECTION OF RICHARD A. KRISAK)

Bottom: Freshly-outshopped express car 40, resplendent in CNR red, undergoes testing in St. Catharines yard c1944. (ANTHONY J. KRISAK, COLLECTION OF RICHARD A. KRISAK)

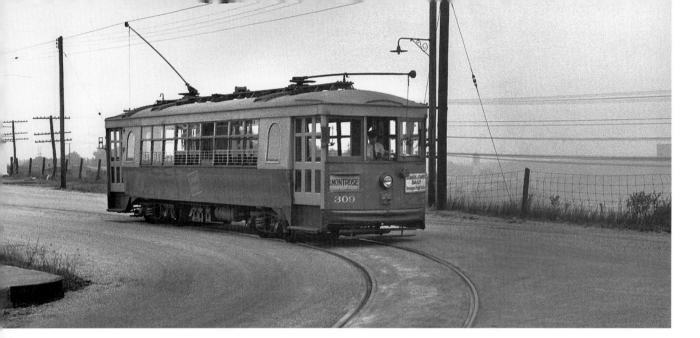

Opposite Top: Car 309 outbound at Portage and Livingstone (beside New York Central tracks, — see middle photo, same page) July 20th 1946. (JOHN F. HUMISTON S7214)

Opposite: NYC Mohawk — "extra south" at Falls View, July 20th 1946. (JOHN F. HUMISTON S7215)

Opposite Bottom: 300-series car has just turned from Livingston Street to Portage Road, looking east c1946. Note disused Falls View siding in foreground. (J.D. KNOWLES)

Top: Car 309 lays over on Bridge Street at River Road, July 20th 1946. (JOHN F. HUMISTON S7216)

Bottom: Car 302 at Montrose Terminal, July 20th 1946. (JOHN F. HUMISTON S7213)

NIAGARA-ST. CATHARINES & TORONTO RAILWAY COMPANY

TIME TABLE

Effective October 1st 1938

MAIN LINE DIVISION
St. Catharines-Niagara Falls

WELLAND DIVISION
Thorold-Port Colborne.

NIAGARA FALLS LOCAL DIVISION
Niagara Falls, Ontario

VICTORIA LAWN DIVISION
Queenston Street to McKinnons.

FACER STREET DIVISION
Facer Street to C.N.R. Depot.

PORT DALHOUSIE DIVISION
St. Catharines to Port Dalhousie

THOROLD COACH ROUTE
St. Catharines-Merritton-Thorold

GENEVA-YORK COACH ROUTE

NIAGARA-YORK COACH ROUTE
St. Catharines Belt Lines

All time Eastern Standard Time except during period of Daylight Saving in St. Catharines, when all routes will operate on Daylight Saving Time.

Subject to change without notice.

NIAGARA, ST. CATHARINES AND TORONTO RAILWAY CO.
ST. CATHARINES, ONTARIO
3000—Nights, Sundays, Holidays, 3010

St. Catharines-Thorold Coach Route
St. Catharines—Merritton—Thorold

EASTBOUND

Glen Ridge & William	St. Paul & Geneva	Thorold Road	Town Line	Thorold
a.m.	a.m.	a.m.	a.m.	a.m.
......	5.54	6.01	6.13	6.16
......	6.14	6.21	6.33	6.36
6.34	6.39	6.41	6.53	6.56

First trip from Glen Ridge 8.10 a.m.
On Sundays, 9.50 a.m.

AND EVERY 20 MINUTES TO

Glen Ridge & William	St. Paul & Geneva	Thorold Road	Town Line	Thorold
p.m.	p.m.	p.m.	p.m.	p.m.
10.50	10.54	11.01	11.13	11.16
11.10	11.14	11.21	11.33	11.36
11.30	11.34	11.41	11.53	11.56

WESTBOUND

Thorold	Town Line	Queenston	St. Paul & Geneva	Ontario	Glen Ridge
a.m.	a.m.	a.m.	a.m.	a.m.	
6.20	6.23	6.35	6.37	6.43	......
6.40	6.43	6.55	6.57	7.03	......
7.00	7.03	7.15	7.17	7.23	......

First trip to Glen Ridge 8.03 a.m.
On Sundays 10.43 a.m.

AND EVERY 20 MINUTES TO

Thorold	Town Line	Queenston	St. Paul & Geneva	Ontario	Glen Ridge
p.m.	p.m.	p.m.	p.m.	p.m.	p.m.
11.20	11.23	11.35	11.37	11.43	......
11.40	11.43	11.55	11.57	12.03	......
12.00	12.03	12.15	12.17	12.23	......

Geneva-York Coach
St. Paul St., Geneva Street, St. Patrick Street, McGhie Street, Russell Ave., York Street, Welland Ave., Ontario Street.

St. Paul & William	Term'l Station	St. Paul & Geneva	Russell & York	St. Paul & William
a.m.	a.m.	a.m.	a.m.	a.m.
	6.22	6.28	6.34	
6.34	6.40	6.42	6.48	6.54
6.54	7.00	7.02	7.08	7.14
7.14	7.20	7.22	7.28	7.34

AND EVERY 20 MINUTES TO

St. Paul & William	Term'l Station	St. Paul & Geneva	Russell & York	St. Paul & William
p.m.	p.m.	p.m.	p.m.	p.m.
11.20	11.34	11.40	11.42	11.48

On Sundays, first trip at 10.22 a.m. from Terminal Station.

Niagara-York Coach
St. Paul Street, Niagara Street, Maple Street, Wiley Street, Russell Ave., York Street, Welland Ave., Ontario Street.

St. Paul & William	Term'l Station	St. Paul & Geneva	Welland & Niagara	Russell & York	St. Paul & William
a.m.	a.m.	a.m.	a.m.	a.m.	a.m.
7.04	7.10	7.12	7.18	7.24	
7.24	7.30	7.32	7.38	7.44	

AND EVERY 20 MINUTES TO

St. Paul & William	Term'l Station	St. Paul & Geneva	Welland & Niagara	Russell & York	St. Paul & William
p.m.	p.m.	p.m.	p.m.		
10.24	10.30	10.32	10.38		
10.44	10.50	10.52	10.58		

NO SUNDAY SERVICE

Victoria Lawn Cemetery Division
Queenston Street, St. Paul Street, James Street, King Street, Ontario Street to McKinnons.

EASTBOUND

McKinnons	William & St. Paul	St. Paul & James	St. Paul & Geneva	Victoria Lawn
a.m.	a.m.	a.m.	a.m.	a.m.
		5.56	5.59	6.08
6.08	6.14	6.16	6.19	6.28
6.28	6.34	6.36	6.39	6.48
6.48	6.54	6.56	6.59	7.08

AND EVERY 20 MINUTES TO

McKinnons	William & St. Paul	St. Paul & James	St. Paul & Geneva	Victoria Lawn
p.m.	p.m.	p.m.	p.m.	p.m.
11.28	11.34	11.36	11.39	11.48
11.48	11.54	11.56		

On Sundays, first car at 9.56 a.m. from St. Paul and James Street

WESTBOUND

Victoria Lawn	St. Paul & Geneva	St. Paul & James	Ontario & King	McKinnons
a.m.	a.m.	a.m.	a.m.	a.m.
			6.03	6.08
6.08	6.17	6.20	6.23	6.28
6.28	6.37	6.40	6.43	6.48
6.48	6.57	7.00	7.03	7.08

AND EVERY 20 MINUTES TO

Victoria Lawn	St. Paul & Geneva	St. Paul & James	Ontario & King	McKinnons
p.m.	p.m.	p.m.		p.m.
11.28	11.37	11.40		11.43
11.48	11.57	12.00		

On Sundays, first car at 10.03 a.m. from Ontario and King Street

Facer St. Division
Facer Street, Niagara Street, Welland Ave., Geneva Street, St. Paul Street, James Street, Ontario Street, St. Paul Street West to C.N.R. Depot.

WESTBOUND

Grantham Ave.	Term'l Station	St. Paul & James	Ontario & St. Paul	C.N.R. Depot
a.m.	a.m.	a.m.	a.m.	a.m.
	5.55	6.00	6.04	6.08
6.09	6.15	6.20	6.24	6.28
6.29	6.35	6.40	6.44	6.48
6.49	6.55	7.00	7.04	7.08

AND EVERY 20 MINUTES TO

Grantham Ave.	Term'l Station	St. Paul & James	Ontario & St. Paul	C.N.R. Depot
p.m.	p.m.	p.m.	p.m.	p.m.
11.09	11.15	11.20	11.24	11.28
11.29	11.35	11.40		
11.49	11.55	12.00		

On Sundays, first car at 9.55 a.m., from Terminal Station

EASTBOUND

C.N.R. Depot	William & St. Paul	St. Paul & James	Term'l Station	Grantham Ave.
a.m.	a.m.	a.m.	a.m.	a.m.
		6.01	6.07	
6.09	6.14	6.21	6.27	
6.29	6.34	6.41	6.47	
6.49	6.54	7.01	7.07	

AND EVERY 20 MINUTES TO

C.N.R. Depot	William & St. Paul	St. Paul & James	Term'l Station	Grantham Ave.
p.m.	p.m.	p.m.	p.m.	p.m.
11.09	11.14	11.21	11.27	
11.29	11.34	11.41	11.47	

On Sundays, first car at 10.01 a.m. from Terminal Station

PORT DALHOUSIE DIVISION
St. Catharines to Port Dalhousie
FALL, WINTER and SPRING

NORTHBOUND

St. Caths. Terml..	St. Paul & James	Lake & Louisa	Barnes-dale	Port Dalhousie
a.m.	a.m.	a.m.	a.m.	a.m.
†5.45	5.55		6.04	6.14
†6.35	6.40	6.44	6.49	6.56
†6.56	7.01	7.06	7.15	7.27
†7.26	7.31	7.36	7.45	7.57
*†7.56	8.01	8.06	8.15	8.27
8.51	8.56	9.01	9.10	9.22
9.56	10.01	10.06	10.15	10.27
AND EVERY HOUR TO				
p.m.	p.m.	p.m.	p.m.	p.m.
12.26	12.31	12.36	12.45	12.57
12.56	1.01	1.06	1.15	1.27
AND EVERY HALF-HOUR TO				
8.26	8.31	8.36	8.45	8.57
8.56	9.01	9.06	9.15	9.27

Saturday only, half-hour service to 10.56 p.m.
AND EVERY HOUR TO

11.56	12.01	12.06	12.15	12.27

†Daily except Sunday. *Daily.

SOUTHBOUND

Port Dalhousie	Barnes-dale	Lake & Louisa	St. Caths. Terml.	James & St. Paul
a.m.	a.m.	a.m.	a.m.	a.m.
†6.15	6.25		6.36	6.40
†7.05	7.15	7.22	7.26	7.31
†7.35	7.45	7.52	7.56	8.01
†8.05	8.15	8.22	8.26	8.31
*8.30	8.40	8.47	8.51	8.56
*9.35	9.45	9.52	9.56	10.01
AND EVERY HOUR TO				
p.m.	p.m.	p.m.	p.m.	p.m.
12.35	12.45	12.52	12.56	1.01
1.05	1.15	1.22	1.26	1.31
AND EVERY HALF-HOUR TO				
9.05	9.15	9.22	9.26	9.31
9.35	9.45	9.52	9.56	10.01
AND EVERY HOUR TO				
a.m.	a.m.	a.m.	a.m.	a.m.
12.35	12.45	12.52	12.56	1.01

Saturdays only, half-hour service to 11.35 p.m.
†Daily except Sunday. *Daily.

SUMMER ONLY
First Wed. in June to Labor Day inclusive, first two trip same as above—then every half hour 6.56 a.m. to 12.56 p.m.; then every 20 minutes leaving Terminal Station at 16, 36 and 56 minutes after each hour until 10.56 p.m.; then every half-hour until 11.56 p.m. Saturdays only 12.28 a.m.

Port Dalhousie to St. Catharines 6.15 a.m., then every half-hour, 7.05 a.m. to 12.35 p.m.; then every 20 minutes at 15, 35 and 55 minutes after each hour until 10.55; then 11.05 and every half-hour until 12.35 a.m. Saturdays only, 1.05 a.m.

On Sundays, first car from St. Catharines 7.56 a.m. and from Port Dalhousie 8.35 a.m.

STEAMERS
"Dalhousie City" and "Northumberland"
Daily Service to Toronto
May 20th to Sept. 17th (1939)
Enquire for schedule.—Any Local Agent or Phone 3000, St. Catharines
Phone 3010—Nights, Sundays, Holidays

MAIN LINE DIVISION
St. Catharines, Merritton, Thorold, Niagara Falls

EASTBOUND

James & Geneva St.Paul Sts.	St. Cath. Terminal	Merritton	Thorold	Niagara Falls Ont.	Niagara Falls N.Y.
a.m.	a.m.	a.m.	a.m.	a.m.	a.m.
5.55	5.45	5.54	5.58		
	6.05	6.13	6.18	6.43	6.57
	6.37	6.46	6.50		
6.55	7.05	7.13	7.18	7.43	7.57
AND EVERY HOUR TO					
p.m.					
11.55	12.05	12.13	12.18	12.43	12.57

Late evening trips:

p.m.	p.m.	p.m.	p.m.	p.m.	p.m.
11.36	11.48	11.44	11.50	11.53	11.59
12.00	12.12	11.56	12.02	12.05	12.11
12.24	12.36	12.08	12.14	12.17	
		12.20	12.26	12.29	
		12.32	12.38	12.41	
		12.44	12.50	12.53	

On Sundays, first car at 6.55 a.m.

Transfers given to Niagara Falls Local Cars without extra charge.

Passengers paying 10 cents cash fare on St. Catharines Local Cars and Buses will be issued transfer to Main Line and amount deducted from Main Line Fare.

WESTBOUND

Niagara Falls N.Y.	Niagara Falls Ont.	Thorold	Merritton	St. Caths. Terml.	James & St. Paul
a.m.	a.m.	a.m.	a.m.	a.m.	a.m.
6.58	7.11	7.36	7.40	7.48	7.55
7.58	8.11	8.36	8.40	8.48	8.55
AND EVERY HOUR TO					
a.m.					
12.58	1.11	1.36	1.40	1.48	1.55

On Sundays, first car at 7.58 a.m.

Transfers given to St. Catharines Local Cars and Buses without extra charge.

Passengers paying fare on Niagara Falls Local Cars will be issued transfer to Main Line and amount deducted from Main Line Fare.

NIAGARA FALLS LOCAL CARS

SOUTHBOUND

Bridge St.	Queen & Victoria	Newman Hill	Main & Ferry	Winery Road	Montrose Road
a.m.	a.m.	a.m.	a.m.	a.m.	a.m.
5.32	5.35	5.41	5.44	5.50	6.00
5.41	5.44	5.50	5.56	6.02	6.12
5.47	5.50	5.56	6.02	6.14	6.24
5.53	5.56	6.02	6.08	6.26	6.36
6.05	6.08	6.14	6.20	6.26	6.38
6.17	6.20	6.26	6.32	6.38	
6.12					
AND EVERY 12 MINUTES TO					
p.m.	p.m.	p.m.	p.m.	p.m.	p.m.
11.00	11.05	11.08	11.14	11.20	11.24
11.12	11.17	11.20	11.26	11.32	11.36
11.24	11.29	11.32	11.38	11.44	12.00
11.36	11.41	11.44	11.50	11.56	12.10
11.48	11.53	11.56	12.02	12.08	12.24
12.00	12.05	12.08	12.14	12.20	
12.12	12.17	12.20	12.26		
6.12					

NORTHBOUND

Montrose Road	Winery Road	Main & Ferry	Newman Hill	Queen & Victoria	Bridge St.
a.m.	a.m.	a.m.	a.m.	a.m.	a.m.
5.50	5.56	6.02	6.05		6.11
6.00	6.14	6.20	6.26	6.29	6.35
6.12	6.26	6.32	6.38	6.41	6.47
6.24					
AND EVERY 12 MINUTES TO					
p.m.	p.m.	p.m.	p.m.	p.m.	p.m.
11.24	11.20	11.32	11.38	11.41	11.47
	11.32	11.38	11.44		

(continued)

SUNDAYS ONLY
SOUTHBOUND — First trip leaves Bridge St. 6.12 a.m., Main and Ferry 6.32 a.m., Montrose 6.41 a.m. Second Trip 6.42 a.m., Main and Ferry 7.02 a.m., Winery Road 7.09 a.m. Service every half-hour from Bridge St. .12 car going to Montrose and 42 car going to Winery Road until 10.12 a.m. then every 15 minutes to both Montrose and Winery Road to 11.12 p.m. then 11.27 to Winery Road; 11.42 to Montrose and 12.12 a.m. to Winery Road.

NORTHBOUND—First trip from Montrose 6.41 a.m.; Main and Ferry 6.52; Bridge St. 7.11; First trip from Winery Road 7.15 a.m.; Main and Ferry 7.22; Bridge St. 7.41 and every half-hour to 10.34 a.m. from both Montrose and Winery Road and every 15 minutes at 49, .04 and .19 until 11.34 p.m. from Montrose; 11.49 from Winery Road; 12.04 a.m. Montrose and 12.34 Winery Road. Last two trips to Queen and Victoria only, arriving 12.21 a.m. and 12.51 a.m.

NIAGARA FALLS MOTOR COACH— Lower Arch Bridge
Route—Tower Inn Terminal, Newman Hill, Victoria Ave., Centre St., McDonald St., Fourth Ave., Bridge St., Queen St., Lower Arch Bridge and International Rly. Terminal, Niagara Falls, N.Y.

Operates one complete trip each hour, leaving Tower Inn 6.28 a.m. (Sundays 7.28 a.m.) to 12.28 a.m. and leaving I. R. C. Terminal 6.58 a.m. (Sundays 7.58 a.m.) until 12.58 a.m. Connection is made with Main Line Division Cars in both directions at Victoria Ave., and Queen St. (Catholic Church).

Note:—On Sundays October to April inclusive, first trip to cross Lower Arch Bridge leaves Tower Inn at 12.28 p.m. and I. R. C. 12.58 p.m. Trips prior to that on Sundays terminate at foot of Bridge St.

WELLAND DIVISION
Thorold, Fonthill, Welland, Port Colborne. Take Main Line Niagara Falls to Thorold and transfer; also either Main Line or Buses, St. Catharines to Thorold and transfer.

SOUTHBOUND

Thorold	Fonthill	Welland	Pt. Colborne
a.m.	a.m.	a.m.	a.m.
6.00	6.18	6.30	6.51
7.36	7.51	8.02	8.24
8.36	8.51	9.02	9.24
AND EVERY HOUR TO			
p.m.			
11.36	11.51	12.02	12.24

On Sundays, first car at 8.36 a.m.

NORTHBOUND

Pt. Colborne	Welland	Fonthill	Thorold
a.m.	a.m.	a.m.	a.m.
6.12	6.35	6.45	7.02
7.31	7.54	8.05	8.23
8.31	8.54	9.05	9.23
AND EVERY HOUR TO			
p.m.			
11.31	11.54	12.05	12.23

On Sundays, first car at 8.31 a.m.

Opposite and Top: 1938 public timetable. (J. W. HOOD COLLECTION)

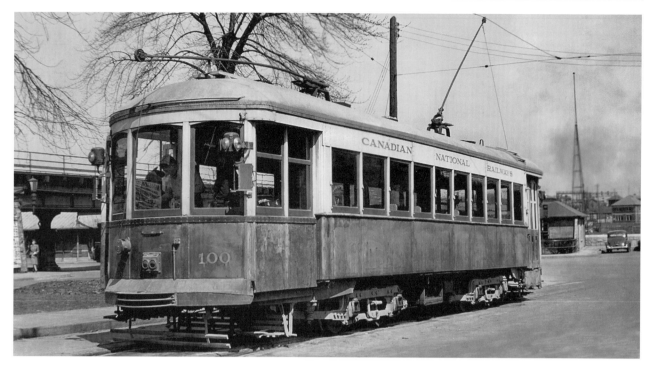

Top: Car 100 lays over on Bridge Street c1944.
(CRHA, FONDS R.F. CORLEY)

Bottom: Car 306 on Victoria Avenue, August 13th 1947.
(AL PATERSON COLLECTION)

was now as anxious to get rid of the car line as it had been to obtain it, 25 years before. Rail removal began after an enthusiasts' excursion the following day, and Lundy's Lane cars turned back near Main and Ferry, with a shuttle bus providing service beyond.

Finally on the afternoon of November 26th 1947, amid much ceremony, car 312 terminated the history of the Niagara Falls local lines. The cars were deadheaded back to St. Catharines over the moribund but intact Main Line, and trackage was removed or paved over by the city.

Canadian National Transportation Ltd. provided local bus service in the Niagara Falls–Stamford area until 1960, when the newly-formed Greater Niagara Transit Commission took over the service with a fleet of twelve new buses.

Top: Colour postcard view of St. Paul Street station, St. Catharines c1907.
(ST. CATHARINES MUSEUM N1087)

Bottom: Car 623 street running in Humberstone, July 26th 1958.
(J.W. HOOD)

Top: Car 83 at Scanlans shelter, March 14th 1959.
(R.J. SANDUSKY)

Bottom: Car 80 southbound passing Electric Park on a regular run, November 1st 1953.
(R.J. SANDUSKY)

Top: Car 83 at semaphore signal near Michigan Central crossing, March 14th 1959.
(R.J. SANDUSKY)

Bottom: Interior of car 83, March 14th 1959.
(R.J. SANDUSKY)

Top: Car 83 at Beaver Dams, July 1958.
(RON RITCHIE)

Bottom: NS&T car 83, Fonthill, Ontario, April 8th 1955.
(RON RITCHIE 1874)

Top: NS&T car 620 near Welland, Ontario, June 24th 1956. (BILL VOLKMER)

Bottom: Cars 83 and 623, on railfan charter, pause for photo stop at Fonthill, July 4th 1958. (BILL VOLKMER)

Top: Car 620 on the Grantham Division crosses the Queen Elizabeth Way on an October 9th 1955 fantrip.
(R.J. SANDUSKY)

Bottom: Cars 83 and 623 on the last day, at Thorold, March 29th 1959.
(J.W. HOOD)

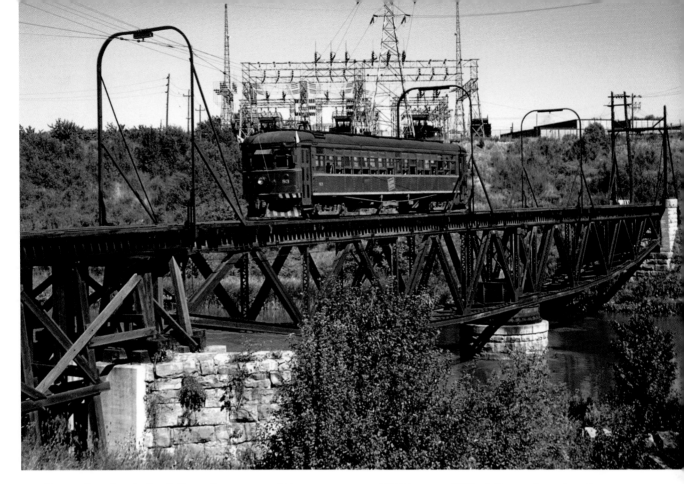

Top: Car 83 outbound on the Port Dalhousie line crossing 12 Mile Creek (old Welland Canal), September 8th 1957.
(R.J. SANDUSKY)

Bottom: NS&T car 130 at Welland, Ontario, September 9th 1953.
(BILL VOLKMER)

Top: Freight motor 19 running light at Packard Electric Company siding, June 1956.
(RON RITCHIE)

Bottom: Freight motor 14 at St. Catharines yard, April 8th 1955.
(RON RITCHIE)

Top: NS&T sweeper 23 is seen at Port Colborne on September 25th 1955, where it cleared the lengthy paved track on Elm Street. (J.D. KNOWLES)

Bottom: Former NS&T (CNT) Fitzjohn bus outshopped for CNR maintenance of way service April 1955. (RON RITCHIE)

Top: Freight motor 16 on the Pine Street spur, Thorold, August 1956. (J.D. KNOWLES)

Bottom: Freight motor 17 at St. Catharines yard in the 1950s. (J.D. KNOWLES)

Top: Express car 41 at St. Catharines shops, August 24th 1952.
(J.W. HOOD)

Bottom: By July 26th 1958 photo, car 41 had been repainted in green.
(J.W. HOOD)

Top: Car 130 at St. Catharines shops, August 24th 1952. (J.W. HOOD)

Bottom: Less than a decade later, car 130 languishes at Rail City, an ill-fated privately-run tourist attraction in Sandy Pond, New York, 1960. (C. ROBERT CRAIG, C. ROBERT CRAIG MEMORIAL LIBRARY, C2-CS212)

Top: Car 620 "as delivered" from M&SC, near Welland, January 1957. Note spoked pilot, soon plated over. (J.D. KNOWLES)

Bottom: Car 80 at Port Colborne, August 24th 1952. (J.W. HOOD)

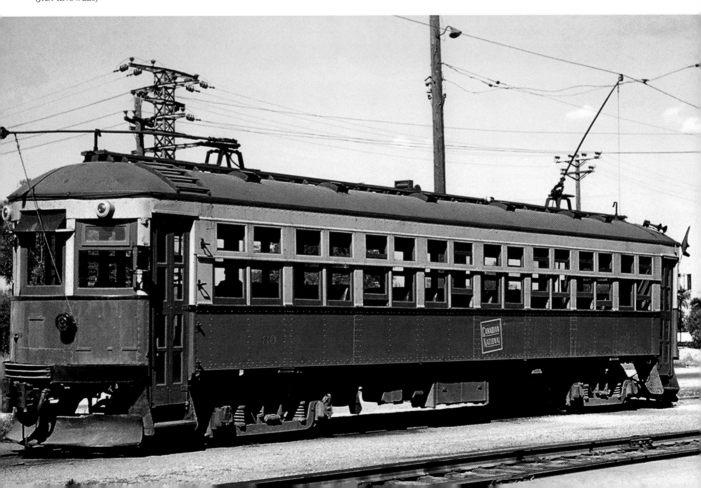

Top: Car 134 on the Port Weller line July 24th 1948.
(J.W. HOOD)

Bottom: Line car 30 at St. Catharines shops July 24th 1948.
(J.W. HOOD)

Top: Car 623 at Martindale Pond trestle inbound, August 31st 1958.
(BILL VOLKMER)

Bottom: Postcard view of Niagara Gorge Railroad car
at Queen Victoria Park, Niagara Falls, c1915.
(JOHN BURTNIAK COLLECTION, ST. CATHARINES MUSEUM)

CHAPTER 10

NS&T Navigation Company

ONE of the first organized passenger services between Toronto and Port Dalhousie was begun about 1884 by the St. Catharines, Grimsby & Toronto Navigation Company, one of the many shipping enterprises of A.W. Hepburn of Picton, Ontario. Two steamers were used, *Empress of India* (built 1876) and, later, *Garden City* (built 1892). Connections were made at Port Dalhousie East with the Grand Trunk branch that later became the Grantham Division, but some steamers locked up the old (second) Welland Canal and docked at the foot of Welland Avenue in St. Catharines.

In 1892 a competitor appeared on the scene when the new steamer *Lakeside*, formerly running in a ferry service to Pelee Island on Lake Erie, was transferred to Lake Ontario. At first, a rate agreement was made between the operators, but a rate war soon broke out, eventually forcing the earlier line out of business and the Lakeside Navigation Company was alone in the field by the end of 1898. Since 1896, *Garden City* had been running between Buffalo, New York and Crystal Beach, Ontario.

Meanwhile, *Lakeside* had been unable to handle all the business offering. Thus, in 1899 and 1900, the owners chartered the steamer *Lincoln* to run in conjunction with her. At this time the Lakeside Navigation Company was bought out by a group headed by Z.A. Lash of Toronto; Mr. Lash was a close associate of Mackenzie and Mann and soon became Chairman of the Board of the NS&T Railway. The Lakeside Navigation Company name was duly changed to NS&T Navigation Company, and in 1902 it became a wholly-owned subsidiary of the NS&T Railway. (The service was later operated under the name "Canadian National Steamers" but there was no corporate change.) The *Lincoln* changed places with *Garden City* on the Buffalo–Crystal Beach run for 1901, and the Port Dalhousie service settled down with *Garden City* and *Lakeside*.

Dalhousie City Built

Traffic was steadily increasing, especially with the introduction of electric service to Niagara Falls in 1901. The Canadian Northern Railway, as ultimate owner, found it necessary to replace *Lakeside* by a larger steamer. The result was *Dalhousie City*, built at Collingwood in 1911 and one

Opposite Top: Postcard view of *Lakeside* at Port Dalhousie dock, c1902. (DON McCARTNEY COLLECTION)

Opposite Bottom: Postcard view of *Garden City* at Toronto harbour, c1912. (DON McCARTNEY COLLECTION)

of the last of the "day boats" to be built for the Great Lakes. She was originally to have been named simply *Dalhousie*, but the name was altered to resemble *Garden City*. She was 193 feet long, while *Lakeside* was only 121 feet, but a more significant indication of size is the register tonnage (which represents not weight but carrying capacity); here the respective figures were 752 and 220. The new ship's boiler capacity was rather limited and speed somewhat low; a moderate increase was achieved by the installation of a redesigned propeller around 1921. An upper shade deck was also installed at the same time.

During World War I, the lake passenger trade generally did not experience any sudden upsurge of business (as later occurred in World War II), and there was, in addition, a very severe coal shortage towards the end of the war. The result was that *Garden City* was laid up in 1917 and later sold.

Northumberland

Dalhousie City carried on alone until 1920, when there appeared on Lake Ontario one of the most interesting vessels ever to operate on the Lower Lakes. The steamer *Northumberland* had been built in Newcastle-on-Tyne, England, in 1891 for the Charlottetown Steam Navigation Company service across Northumberland Strait between Prince Edward Island and the Nova Scotia mainland. The Navigation Company sold out to the federal Government in 1916, and in 1920 *Northumberland* moved to Lake Ontario. Her port of registry, emblazoned with her name in a burst of gold scrollwork on her stern, remained Charlottetown throughout her life.

She was put in service opposite *Dalhousie City* with little alteration, but that winter she was rebuilt by the Toronto Drydock Company. Most cabins were removed, upper deck made suitable for lake excursion service, and much of her lower deck was converted from freight space to crew facilities. A shade deck was built in 1927 abaft her funnel, completely ruining her former racy yacht-like appearance. In the late 1930s a large amount of fundamental reconstruction work was undertaken, because of her age, but she retained her original engines and boilers throughout her life.

The Boats Compared

Northumberland was a faster and more manoeuvrable vessel than her running mate, being a twin-screw steamer. In addition she was more comfortable, since *Dalhousie City* had a reputation as a "roller" in rough weather; in fact bilge keels were fitted soon after entering service in an attempt to counteract this tendency. On the other hand, *Northumberland* had been designed for a different type of service, so

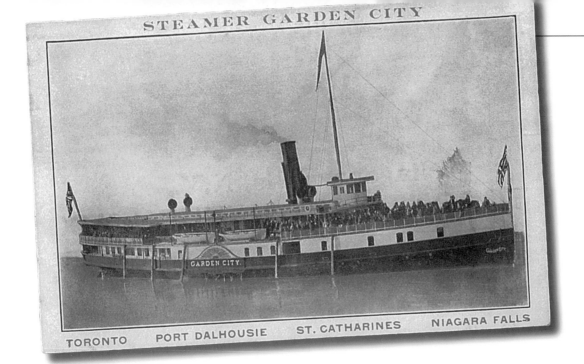

STEAMER GARDEN CITY

TORONTO   PORT DALHOUSIE   ST. CATHARINES   NIAGARA FALLS

GARDEN CITY.

it suffered somewhat from inconvenient interior arrangements and very restricted open deck space; the upper works were not built out beyond the steel hull as was the practice with Lower Lakes excursion steamers. She was also more expensive to run, burning an average of about 4.4 tons of coal per crossing, contrasted with *Dalhousie City's* 3.5 tons. *Northumberland* had two triple-expansion engines with cylinders 17½", 27½" and 46" with 33" stroke; total indicated horsepower 2,500 on 160 lb. of steam pressure. Nominal speed was 14 MPH.

Dalhousie City had one triple-expansion engine with cylinders 18", 28½" and 38" with 30" stroke; total indicated horsepower 1,520 on 186 lb. of steam pressure. Nominal speed was 12 MPH (speeds on the Lakes were not expressed in knots). Crossing times were 2 hours 10 minutes and 2½ hours respectively.

The Toronto dock after 1927 was at the foot of York Street (York Street Slip), waiting room and office space being rented from adjacent Terminal Warehouses Limited. The vessels had previously docked at the foot of Yonge Street on the old waterfront, at a wharf obliterated by landfill operations; its actual position was northeast of the Harbour Commission building.

Top: Postcard view of *Garden City* showing her original appearance c1900.
(ADAM ZHELKA COLLECTION)

Opposite Top: Stern view of *Garden City* leaving Port Dalhousie c1910.
(LIBRARY AND ARCHIVES CANADA C11740)

Opposite Bottom: Toronto Transportation Commission picnic. *Dalhousie City* docking at Port Dalhousie, July 29th 1926. By 1927, TTC was operating Toronto Island ferries and future picnics were held at Hanlan's Point, closer to home.
(TTC COLLECTION, CITY OF TORONTO ARCHIVES, 4454)

Bottom: Fuzzy but unique postcard view of *Garden City*, dock and town panorama looking southwest from Port Dalhousie East c1910.
(JOHN BURTNIAK COLLECTION, ST. CATHARINES MUSEUM)

THE NIAGARA ST. CATHARINES & TORONTO
RAILWAY COMPANY
1931-1932   N 846
PASS — Mr. A. J. Grant —
Engineer, Welland Canal —
GOOD ON BOAT ONLY
UNTIL DECEMBER 31ST, 1932   UNLESS OTHERWISE ORDERED AND SUBJECT TO CONDITIONS ON BACK
VALID ONLY WHEN COUNTERSIGNED BY
F. A. JOHNSON, E. W. OLIVER OR
H. H. ROLLO
                            H. W. Thornton
                            PRESIDENT

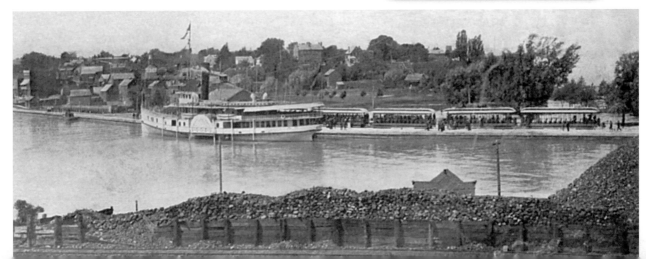

Top: Postcard view of *Dalhousie City*, NS&T freight sheds, town, looking north up third canal c1920.
(JOHN BURTNIAK COLLECTION, ST. CATHARINES MUSEUM)

Opposite Top: *Northumberland*, as delivered, at Yonge Street dock, 1920.
(H.E. BATTEL COLLECTION)

Opposite Bottom: Port side of *Northumberland* at Toronto harbour in 1940.
(AL PATERSON COLLECTION)

Bottom: Postcard view of beachfront scene looking west.
(JOHN BURTNIAK COLLECTION, ST. CATHARINES MUSEUM)

The Canadian Northern Railway faced insurmountable financial difficulties after WWI and saw control of its vast transportation empire gradually assumed by the federal government. As part of this collapse, CNoR's cross-lake service and Lakeside Park came under government control in 1918 and were soon absorbed into the Canadian National Railways family. NS&T lake boats then began to carry the "Canadian National Steamers" banner. The Navigation Company was the only division of the NS&T whose business continued to grow during the 1920s. In 1921 about 185,000 passengers were carried, and about 270,000 in 1929.

On the Promenade Deck

The Dalhousie City

The Ladies' Room

Top and Left: Cover and excerpts from 1913 brochure showcasing the scenic attractions to be found on the NS&T, showing the interior features of the *Dalhousie City*. (ONTARIO ELECTRIC RAILWAY HISTORICAL ASSOCIATION ARCHIVES)

Opposite Top: Port side of *Dalhousie City* at Toronto harbour c1940. (CNR PHOTO 32675)

Opposite Bottom: Car 57 and sisters (screens, end loading) at Lakeside Park c1916. (JOHN BURTNIAK COLLECTION, ST. CATHARINES MUSEUM)

Lakeside Park

Lakeside Park, Port Dalhousie, was developed by the company about 1902 and became an important source of traffic for both steamers and electric cars, particularly for organized groups. In 1903 there were about 200,000 visitors, ninety percent of whom had been carried by NS&T services. When *Northumberland* was put on the route, a substantial traffic increase was noted, and in 1922 the area of the park was doubled to over twelve acres. For a year or two, park operation was undertaken by the Canadian Railway News Company, which added many new rides and other attractions. The NS&T resumed operation of the expanded park on its own account in 1923.

A further increase in steamer revenues occurred in 1925-26 with the Grantham Division electrification. The planned effect was to reduce the Toronto–Niagara time to about 3¼ hours, compared with 3¾ hours via Queenston (Canada Steamship Lines). With these various stimulants, business remained fairly good on the NS&T route during the depression. The company's steamers were smaller and less expensive to operate than those of the competing CSL; this was a decided advantage when traffic fell during the depression; NS&T was able to continue a two-ship service with four or five trips daily long after CSL reduced sailing to one lake boat, *Cayuga*, when *Chippewa* was laid up after the 1936 season.

Toronto–St. Catharines Steamers

Official Number	Name	Builder	Date	Dimensions	Tonnage Gross	Reg.	In Service Toronto–St. Catharines	Ultimate Fate
72998	*Empress of India*	Mill Point, Ontario	1876	180x36x11	579	336	1884-1898	Broken up about 1918
100055	*Garden City*	Toronto	1892	178x26x11	637	401	1892-1896 & 1901-1917	Broken up 1936?
90778	*Lakeside*	Windsor	1888	121x26x9	348	220	1892-1911	Sank 1929
92735	*Lincoln*	Hamilton	1888	130x26x9	337	219	1899-1900	Burnt 1920
130312	*Dalhousie City*	Collingwood	1911	193x37x21	1256	752	1911-1949	Burnt 1960
96937	*Northumberland*	Newcastle, England	1891	220x33x20	1255	542	1920-1948	Burnt 1949

Note: Data given is at time of Toronto–St. Catharines service

Special Arrangements

On weekends, the last trip of the day was scheduled to arrive in Toronto in the small hours of the morning and was met by a lineup of TTC streetcars destined for several different routes covering much of the city. The ship's passenger load figure was radioed ahead to enable the appropriate number of cars to be on hand.

Special party business was actively solicited. 150 such groups, totalling 41,000 passengers, were handled in 1947 alone. A complex schedule of reduced mid-week and excursion fares was in effect. As late as the end of World War II, a children's day-return ticket from Toronto to Niagara Falls could be bought for less than $1.00. Despite the competitive position, relations between the CSL and the NS&T were quite friendly, and when the occasion required it, one company's tickets would be honoured on the other service and accounted for later. Sometimes, for large groups, one of the NS&T steamers would make special trips from Hamilton to Port Dalhousie. Such trips were made eleven times in 1947, and over 8,000 passengers were carried. One of the Cobourg–Rochester train ferries, operated by a company partly owned by the CNR, would sometimes be borrowed to replace the absent steamer on the Toronto run.

In line with the reduction of passenger service planned for 1940-41, and in view of operating deficits in 1939 and 1940, the entire Navigation Company, along with Lakeside Park, was offered for sale as a going concern in October 1941. A concrete offer was received but the prospective purchaser was unable to raise the money. In August 1943, the sale was again advertised, but this time no offers were received. The ships and the park were considered to be a single entity; thus the disposal of only one ship would be a

Opposite: Stern view of *Northumberland* docked at Port Dalhousie July 20th 1946.
(JOHN F. HUMISTON S7245)

severe blow to the undertaking as a whole. The Navigation Company in itself was not particularly profitable; it did return a modest profit during the war, but increased labour costs brought about a deficit after 1946.

Northumberland Burnt

The two-ship operation was continued until 1949, since passenger loads were holding relatively steady, and would have been continued longer except for a major disaster. On June 2nd of that year, *Northumberland* was destroyed by fire at Port Dalhousie, the day before she was scheduled to start her summer's work. The fire began about 6:00 AM in the aft section of the boat. Fresh paint helped the fire to spread rapidly despite strenuous efforts of the crew, most of whom were newly signed-on. Some trouble had been experienced with electrical circuits a short time previously, but investigation failed to trace the cause to an electrical failure. In fact, the cause was never officially established, but there is reason to believe that it was a cigarette carelessly discarded in a storage room.

The sudden end of this popular vessel left the company with only the slower of its two steamers, which could readily make only two round-trip sailings a day. Emergency arrangements were made with Canada Steamship Lines and the CNR to look after special-party commitments that could not be handled by one steamer. *Dalhousie City* carried on as best she could for the 1949 season, making two trips weekdays and three on weekends.

At the end of the season, the decision was taken to abandon the service. It is interesting to note that the 1949 loss was slightly less than 1948, but the reduced service had an adverse effect on revenues of Lakeside Park and connecting land transport. *Dalhousie City* was sold to Inland Lines Limited of Montreal, leaving Port Dalhousie for the last time on April 21st 1950. Renamed *Island King II*, she was used in excursion service out of Montreal until, on November 24th 1960, she too was destroyed by fire while laid up for the winter at Lachine, Quebec. Lakeside Park was sold to its former manager for operation in his own interest, and declined in importance thereafter; it is now a municipal park.

Top: *Dalhousie City* entering Port Dalhousie harbour at lighthouse c1940.
(MARINE HISTORICAL SOCIETY OF DETROIT, PUBLISHER'S COLLECTION)

Opposite Top: A Toronto newspaper columnist commemorates the end of Toronto–Port Dalhousie steamer service, and Mr. J.R. Empringham, Superintendent of the line, replies. Further comment would be superfluous.
(ONTARIO ELECTRIC RAILWAY HISTORICAL ASSOCIATION ARCHIVES)

Opposite Bottom: Car 82 meets *Dalhousie City* at Port Dalhousie East, July 1939.
(ADDISON LAKE COLLECTION, COURTESY FRED ANGUS)

Bottom: Busy days at Port Dalhousie East: Car 82 and one of the Evans "Road Railers" meet *Northumberland* c1937.
(H.E. BATTEL COLLECTION)

Bon Voyage
By Frank Tumpane

The era of the passenger steamship on Lake Ontario is almost ended and with it will go one more pleasant facet of Toronto life.

News that the Dalhousie City has been sold leaves but one ship, the Cayuga, on cross-lake runs out of Toronto.

The Dalhousie City ran between Toronto and Port Dalhousie and there must be tens of thousands of Torontonians who went aboard her for the first boat trip of their lives. She sailed out of Toronto from 1911 to 1949, loaded with children on church and school picnics each with a supervisory detachment of harassed adults.

The automobile gradually pushed the lake steamer into the background. Now the triumph is nearly complete. It's easier to hop into the family car and drive to a picnic place than to travel across the lake.

Only it isn't as much fun.

Some of us have vivid memories of the Dalhousie City which we considered an enormous ship. We thought the Mauretania and the Dalhousie City must be very much alike.

On a fine summer day, she left the dock on her first trip at 8:15 in the morning and that was the trip to catch. It was exciting to arrive on the street car and watch her sitting there, white and magnificent, with the thin stream of smoke emerging from her funnel.

The adults were encumbered with the picnic boxes which contained sandwiches, cake, cookies, olives and pickles, all of this covered with white napkins. But you could run on ahead and up the gangplank. The grown-ups liked to sit still on deck, but for you the thrill was that you never had to sit still.

There were a graet many things to see on the Dalhousie City and on the Northumberland, her sister ship, destroyed last year by fire. The engines were splendid and they were oiled by an engineer with a long-spouted can who poked ceaselessly among the gauges, valves and pistons.

There was a lunch counter where you paid double the city price for everything. You were warned not to eat the food, for parents considered it was stale and most likely contaminated.

There was a small forward cabin with a card table at which it was rumored some of the sports played for money. This cabin was walled with mirrors, one of which bore the name of the ship in gold letters.

You could race from one end o those lake ships to the other, peering for the first glimpse of the far

shore and sort of hating it when you saw it. Down on the lower deck you could lean over and watch the green water scudding past.

As you grew older and more sophisticated you spent a lot of time on the dance floor near the stern, watching the dancers and envying them. The years were counted off in hit tunes: Yes, We Have No Bananas; Barney Google, Tea for Two, Girl of My Dreams, and Let a Smile Be Your Umbrella on a Rainy, Rainy Day.

In early June, your high school sponsored a picnic to Port Dalhousie, the first one of the season. Everybody looked forward to it for a couple of months. Nobody carried lunches on the high school picnic. Nearly everybody smoked cigarets for the first time openly and brazenly. The minority of smooth, glib-talking fellows made tremendous conquests with the girls which they discussed for weeks afterward. Boys and girls would start going steady after a meeting on the Dalhousie City and often the great love would last the entire summer.

Then the day would arrive (often sometime in your 20th or 21st year) when you would look at the Dalhousie City or the Northumberland or the Cayuga and be shocked at how it had shrunk in size.

Sometimes you would long to shed your new-found world-weariness and return to the illusions of only a few years before. But once you lose something like that it is gone forever.

And now the Dalhousie City herself has gone.

THE NIAGARA, ST. CATHARINES AND TORONTO RAILWAY CO.
CANADIAN NATIONAL STEAMERS

J. R. EMPRINGHAM
SUPERINTENDENT

ST. CATHARINES, ONT.

February 15th, 1950
3900-1

Mr. Frank Tumpane,
The Globe and Mail,
Toronto, Ontario.

Dear Mr. Tumpane:

Your recent article in the Globe and Mail entitled "Bon Voyage", which has reference to the passing of the Dalhousie City has been read with much interest. Your story gives an excellent cross-section of the many thousands of people who, in the past 30 years, have travelled on the Dalhousie City, and the Northumberland, on their annual picnics to Lakeside Park, Port Dalhousie.

The loss of the Northumberland by fire, and subsequently it being scrapped, and the sale of the Dalhousie City, are to me like losing old friends. I have had the responsibility for the operation of the two ships for over 25 years, and have travelled back and forward hundreds of times with special parties such as those referred to in your article. Until 1932 I was located in Toronto and when a summer holiday or week-end came around, our children, when they were growing up, always wanted to spend the day on the lake.

I wanted you to know that the article has been read and is appreciated.

Yours very truly,

J. R. Empringham

Superintendent.

JRE:VW

CHAPTER 11

NS&T — Freight and Express

From the beginning, the NS&T eagerly sought to expand its freight and express business, since it was a Canadian Northern Railway outpost in Grand Trunk Railway territory. It achieved considerable success, as indicated by these figures of tonnage handled: *1897 (steam)*: 74,000; *1903*: 92,248; *1908*: 112,597; *1913*: 344,660; *1929*: 666,179. Traffic remained remarkably steady despite the growth of road transport. In 1905, freight revenue was half the amount of passenger revenue, but by 1918, it grew to 450 percent.

After the Niagara Central was electrified, most freight work continued to be handled by steam engines until about 1910. Freight cars could be accommodated on all parts of the system except the Niagara Falls local lines, and the part of the St. Catharines lines that had originated with the PDSC&T. Freight was often moved at night on the main lines; such night service was compulsory on many spurs in St. Catharines. The first available equipment list (April 1901) shows one electric locomotive for switching, one steam locomotive for road freight work, and fifteen flat cars.

The first freight yard was the former Niagara Central facility at Welland Avenue and Clark Street, St. Catharines; a moderate-sized wooden freight shed was built on the north-west corner of the property. However, business soon outgrew this yard and, being in a residential area, certain classes of freight, by city regulation, could not be handled.

In 1913, there were some sixty industrial sidings on the line. Some of the more important trackage built for freight service was as follows: Walker's Quarry, Thorold (1901); Welland Vale spur, Port Dalhousie line (1909); Pine Street spur, Thorold (1910); Interlake Tissue Mills spur, Merritton (1913); Phelps Street spur, St. Catharines (1916).

In 1913, the line owned thirty box cars, thirty gondolas, sixteen flat cars and two cabooses. The latter were No. 36 (a converted box car) and No. 40, both of which were replaced in 1918 by former Canadian Northern cabooses nos. 2516 and 3605 renumbered 33 and 34 (not to be confused with cabooses 33 and 34 of 1948). In later years, CNR cabooses that were often borrowed tended to stay for some time because the stoves had to be grounded before they could be safely used on electrified tracks. Up to 1922, while the NS&T was a Canadian Northern enclave with no connection to the rest of the system, it had quite a number of CNoR freight cars for on-line use, but later, when the Canadian National system was consolidated, there was no longer any need for this, and separate assignments largely ceased. Because of the frequent borrowings, freight equipment is not shown in the equipment roster, but the following are known to have been assigned to the NS&T in earlier years:

Box cars 225-234.

Coal cars 300-308, purchased 1910.

Coal cars 30561-30579 and 30781-30799 (odd numbers), ex-Canadian Northern.

(Most of the above were scrapped in 1919-22)

Cinder cars 1000-1003, disposed of in 1930

Flat cars 1004, 1005, ex-CN 11145 and 614810 in 1927. Disposed of in 1939 after long retirement. 1004 had "tool-house" body.

One of the first actions of the Canadian Northern management was to start work on the Welland Division to provide freight connections with the Toronto, Hamilton & Buffalo Railway (Canadian Pacific Railway) and Michigan Central

Opposite Top: Freight motor 18 works at St. Catharines freight yard, believed to in 1940s.
(H.E. BATTEL COLLECTION)

Opposite Bottom: Freight motor 12 and employees in St. Catharines yard c1920.
(JOHN BURTNIAK COLLECTION, ST. CATHARINES MUSEUM)

Right: 1935 NS&T freight ad.
(JOHN BURTNIAK COLLECTION, ST. CATHARINES MUSEUM)

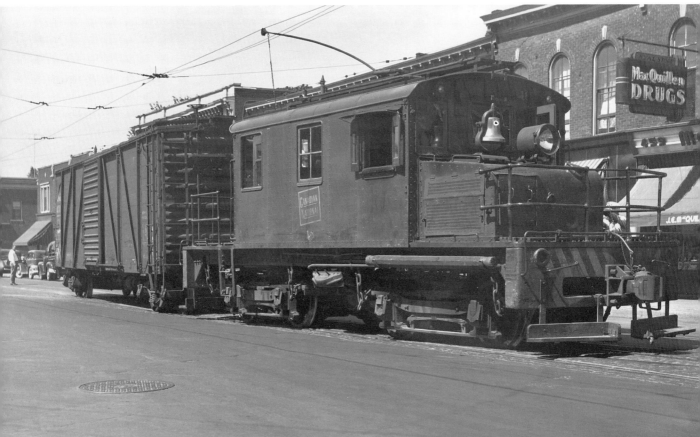

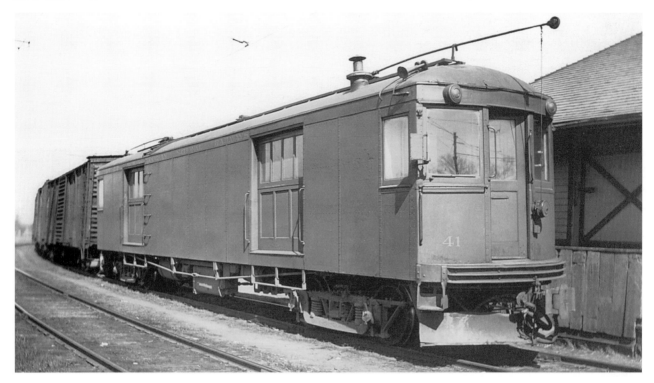

Top: Express car 41 at Fonthill station, boxcars in tow, September 1938. (ADDISON LAKE COLLECTION, COURTESY FRED ANGUS)

Opposite Top: Freight motor 14 entering Welland Avenue while coming from McKinnon's, 1950. (R.T. VINCENT)

Opposite Bottom: Freight motor 18 on St. Paul Street, west of Geneva, July 13th 1949. (R.T. VINCENT)

(New York Central) at Welland. These interchanges were established in 1909 and 1913. Much revenue came from the Welland–St. Catharines haul, but this was lost in 1922 when NS&T, now integrated into the Canadian National system, began large-scale interchange with its former competitor in St. Catharines.

Consolidation

The principal aim of the 1924-27 rehabilitation was to eliminate the now-needless duplication of freight facilities, and to make the NS&T the only CNR freight distributor in the area. A larger freight yard was opened beside the Main Line in September 1924 with a freight shed at Niagara Street. The CNR Merritton–St. Catharines–Port Dalhousie branch was electrified for the NS&T as were four tracks of the CNR's Merritton yard. The old freight shed on Welland Avenue was demolished and the site used for expansion of car-storage tracks.

In addition to carload freight, the NS&T looked after express and less-than-carload freight, and carried mail in sacks on Welland Division express cars and on regular Port Dalhousie passenger cars.

A considerable volume of package freight was handled on the Toronto steamers, though this greatly diminished when the Grand Trunk ceased to be a competitor. Much of this traffic was fruit in season, which was soon largely lost to motor trucks except during World War II. As a depression traffic incentive, in 1932 a bargain rate of 25 cents per 100 lb. was introduced between St. Catharines/Merritton/Thorold and Toronto, via steamer, guaranteeing next-morning delivery. The building of the new Welland Canal brought much new business to the line, about 10,000 carloads of cement alone being handled in the 1920s. Carload freight made up the bulk of the regular business included auto parts, iron, pulpwood, paper products, coal, stone and coke.

The following were the normal freight runs about 1941:

1. Switch Merritton Transfer to St. Catharines several times daily.
2. AM: cars from #1 to McKinnon's; PM: Port Dalhousie East line.
3. Thorold wayfreight and switch at Thorold.
4. McKinnon's switcher.
5. St. Catharines switcher, assist Merritton transfer.
6. PM and evening, direct to Port Colborne as switcher.
7. PM and evening, Port Dalhousie (west) line, assist Merritton transfer.
8. Overnight, wayfreight Thorold–Welland, then to Niagara Falls if traffic offering.

Wartime Business

Beginning in 1941, express and LCL business greatly increased with introduction of restrictions on motor transport. In 1942 the morning Merritton–Port Colborne express-

car trip had to be doubled using both nos. 40 and 41, one hauling a box car which was usually dropped at Welland. This wasteful system was altered in 1943 when the morning CNR train from Toronto began hauling two CNR express cars, which were dropped at Merritton. One of these contained packages and mail for Thorold, Fonthill and Port Colborne and this was trans-shipped to the NS&T car. The other CNR car contained only Welland items; it was hauled there as a trailer and left for the day.

In 1946 two additional tracks of the Merritton yard were electrified, making six in all. At this time, over 400 freight cars were handled each weekday.

The Main Line was abandoned in November 1947. In order to permit removal of the track, in the following month the CNR took over switching for a small area near Bridge Street, the only part of the Main Line east of Shriner's that had any appreciable freight business. In 1954, Port Colborne was established as an "outpost", with a freight motor stationed there, returning to St. Catharines weekly for servicing. For many years, much CNR business originating at Port Colborne was turned over to the NS&T for delivery at Merritton Transfer.

Express Problems

Car 40 suffered severe body deterioration and was withdrawn from service in December 1954. Both nos. 40 and 41 were actually old wooden cars, though steel sheathing gave them a relatively up-to-date appearance. After No. 40 was withdrawn, if car 41 was not available, express traffic would be accommodated in a CNR express car handled to the CNR Welland station in a steam-powered freight train. Meanwhile, the NS&T stores truck would cater to local business. The afternoon express run was handled by truck

Top: Car 82 was converted to an express motor in 1956 to replace car 40. At St. Catherines shops, September 8th 1957. (J.D. KNOWLES)

Opposite Top: Freight motor 21 and consist on Elm Street, Humberstone, May 9th 1955. (R.J. SANDUSKY)

Opposite Bottom: Freight motor 20 and consist, c1950. (J.M. MILLS COLLECTION)

for a few months to save mileage on No. 41, but later in 1955 the rail service was restored and serious consideration given to obtaining express car 504 from Montreal along with the passenger cars. This was ruled out because the cost of shipment and double-ending was not considered justified. Therefore passenger car 82 was modified, its seats removed, windows blocked and a wide door cut in each side, taking its place in the express service when No. 41 was laid up.

The Merritton–Port Colborne mail contract was cancelled on October 1st 1956, and the railway gave consideration to transferring the express business to trucks. No. 82 was somewhat poorly adapted for this service, being centre-drive. As it was often necessary to push CNR express cars (sometimes all the way to Thorold), extra men were required as "lookouts" on each side since the motorman could not see past the corners of the car being pushed. No action was immediately taken, but in March 1958 car 41 was also withdrawn owing to body deterioration. No. 82 was used for three weeks, during which the visibility problem caused an extra wage bill of $138; these costs resulted in the service finally being given over to trucks. In this, as in other instances, the impression is one of sheer reluctance to part with the good old rail service.

CHAPTER 12

NS&T — Power Supply

THE original power house was a hydraulic station in Merritton built by the St. Catharines Street Railway. A potential of 300 HP was available on a 12'-6" head of water, only 125 HP of which was originally exploited. A rental of $300 annually was paid to the Dominion Government for the privilege of using Welland Canal water. This station was enlarged in 1902 when the NS&T took over but was soon outgrown and was sold to a local industry in 1906.

At first the consolidated NS&T obtained its power from the Niagara Falls hydraulic plant of the Electrical Development Company, an affiliate of the Toronto Railway Company. This was taken over in 1921 by the Hydro-Electric Power Commission of Ontario which continued to supply energy until the end of 1925. On the first day of 1926 the feed was switched to the Canadian Niagara Power Company upon the offer of an exceptionally low rate. By the terms of its agreement for use of Niagara water, this US-owned firm had to sell in Ontario a certain percentage of the power that was generated in Ontario, and having just lost a major customer (Canadian Carborundum Company at Niagara Falls), it had to find another major replacement user.

The original two substations, each of 300 kW capacity, were at Stamford and at Welland Avenue and Court Street, St. Catharines. As previously mentioned, double overhead was installed without feeders, but even after conventional single overhead was substituted, feeders were rarely installed until much later. In 1906, Thorold Substation was built (at "Substation Jct.") to replace the hydraulic plant, and, in 1910, Welland Substation was opened.

With the building of the Lake Shore Division, a small substation was built at Niagara-on-the-Lake. At St. Catharines, an additional rotary converter was set up in temporary quarters until a larger building was erected in 1914. Two 500 kW rotaries had been acquired in 1913, one for Niagara-on-the-Lake and one for St. Catharines. Upon installation of the latter machine, one of the 300 kW units was moved to Niagara Falls.

In 1914, the substation situation was as follows:

    Niagara Falls, 2 converters, 600 kW
    Thorold, 2 converters, 1,000 kW
    St. Catharines, 2 converters, 1,000 kW
    Welland, 1 converter, 500 kW
    Niagara-on-the-Lake, 1 converter, 500 kW

By 1925, this had become:

    Niagara Falls, 3 converters, 1,100 kW
    Thorold, 2 converters, 1,000 kW

    St. Catharines, 3 converters, 1,750 kW
    Welland, 2 converters, 1,000 kW
    Niagara-on-the-Lake, 1 converter, 500 kW
    (automatic)

Another 1000 kW was added at St. Catharines in 1926 by transfer of equipment from the abandoned city lines of the Toronto Suburban Railway, and around this time another 500 kW was added at Niagara Falls. No action was taken on the Welland Division since freight business there had been reduced. However, the power situation was never satisfactory; in 1936 a substation was opened at Humberstone using a 1000 kW rotary from St. Catharines, which in turn was replaced by the 500 kW unit from Niagara-on-the-Lake (now closed). The Humberstone building was without utility connections and water had to be delivered in pails by passenger cars. This station was usually "on line" for only one shift a day, when freight switching was going on at this end of the line.

Automatic substation control equipment was installed as opportunity allowed, in order to reduce wage costs; usually only one of several converters in a station would be modified, and staffing reduced to a single shift a day. This equipment was installed on one machine at Welland in 1936, and, in 1944, on one machine at each of Thorold and St. Catharines.

For many years, electrolysis damage was being encountered by the Bell Telephone Company south of Welland. After prolonged investigation, it was eventually traced to minute ground currents from the deteriorating street trackage in Humberstone and Port Colborne. These stray currents were being conveyed north by canal waters, which they reached via the Port Colborne interchange and the CNR canal drawbridge.

Welland Division power supply was further improved in 1938 by the construction of a small substation at Fonthill. Consideration had been given to erecting, as feeder, some aluminum messenger cable salvaged from the Toronto Suburban's Guelph interurban line. However, it was considered preferable to purchase the automatic equipment from Maidstone Substation of the abandoned Windsor, Essex & Lake Shore, part of which had been obtained second-hand in 1930. It is interesting to note that the new cars built for the same WE&LS modernization turned up 25 years later on the Welland Division, taking power from the same substation.

During the war, the power situation became critical, but fortunately in 1943 two converters with associated equipment were purchased from the London Street Rail-

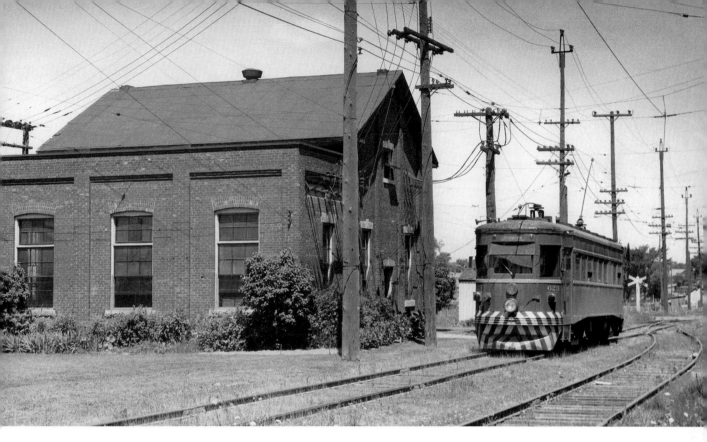

way; this had become an all bus operation in late 1940. One of these was installed at St. Catharines after the 750 kW unit there was badly damaged by lightning, and the other replaced a similar machine at Niagara Falls, damaged beyond repair by a massive insulation failure.

On November 30th 1945 the Canadian Niagara Power Company contract expired, but was extended on a year-to-year basis because of the contemplated dieselization. A new contract was arranged in 1954 on terms that took account of the greatly reduced peak load requirements.

Niagara Falls substation closed in November 1947, and the remaining stations were closed down on conversion to diesel power in 1959-60.

Top: Car 623 on excursion, passing Thorold substation on the former Main Line, July 29th 1956. (R.J. SANDUSKY)

Bottom: Car 328 northbound just after crossing the former swing bridge at the Welland Vale spur, June 27th 1947. (J.D. KNOWLES)

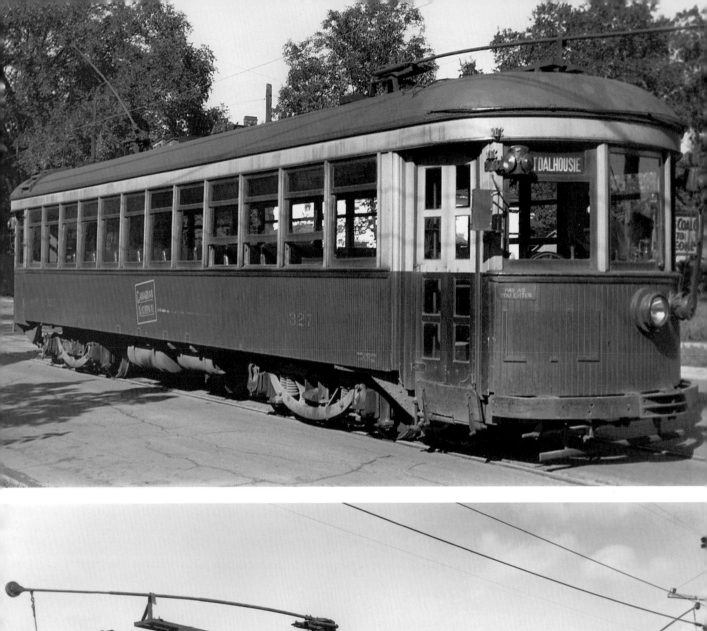

CHAPTER 13

NS&T — Car Equipment

THE four double-truck cars built for the NS&T in 1899 were among the earliest heavy interurban cars in Canada. The bodies were built by the Ottawa Car Company but, as was the practice at the time, trucks, brakes and control equipment were installed by the purchaser. One reference states that the original equipment comprised one-year-old steam coaches electrified; this idea is not correct but no doubt arose from the practice just referred to.

It has not been possible to compile an accurate roster of local lines equipment before 1900. Later records tend to lump all single-truck cars together as if they were all identical, which is certainly not the case. The following is an approximation:

St. Catharines, Merritton & Thorold Street Ry.:

1-4   Closed cars. Built as horse cars by Patterson & Corbin 1879. Electrified 1887. 10-foot body. Weight as electric cars 6 tons. Probably scrapped 1896.

5-7   Open cars. History as 1-4. 16-foot body, weight 7 tons.

8-10   Open cars. Built as Van Depoele electric cars by Patterson & Corbin 1888. Some sources say rebuilt as conventional electric cars but photos show later cars quite different. Probably scrapped 1896.

Port Dalhousie, St. Catharines & Thorold Street Ry. and Niagara, St. Catharines & Toronto:

1-4   Closed cars. Built as conventional electric cars by Patterson & Corbin 1896. See NS&T list.

5-6   Closed cars. Built by Ottawa 1900 for Niagara Falls.

11,12   Open cars. Built as conventional electric cars
14,15   by Patterson & Corbin 1896. See NS&T list.

16,17   Open cars. Built by Ottawa 1900 for Niagara Falls.

Opposite Top: Car 327 eastbound on Welland Avenue, St. Catharines on September 14th 1947. NS&T 327 and 328 were made from the stripped bodies of Oshawa Railway 81 and 80. (J.D. KNOWLES)

Opposite Bottom: Car 622 (ex M&SC and WE&LS) on Upper Canada Railway Society charter, posed south of Beaver Dams on the Welland line, September 28th 1958. White flags denoted an unscheduled extra. The usual red tail flag was also displayed. (J.D. KNOWLES)

Other closed cars were obtained second-hand for Niagara Falls but no record of them has been found. Even the number of cars is doubtful (probably between four and six); if there were four, they could have been Nos. 7-10.

In 1911, the roster consisted of 39 passenger cars, sixteen freight cars and four locomotives. Two years later this had increased to 42 passenger cars, 36 freight cars and six locomotives. The first piece of gasoline-powered equipment was a 2-ton Reo truck purchased in 1917, permitting retirement of: "one horse, two lorries, manure box, three sleighs, one lumber wagon, harness, rain covers, two pair blankets, two wagons, one team and one mare."

In the last years of Canadian Northern ownership, cars 1, 18, 19 and 38 (old series, see equipment list) were assigned CNoR numbers 61003, 61005, 61007 and 61009 but these seem to have been for inventory purposes only.

Swain Valuation

In 1917, an extremely detailed inventory was made of all Canadian Northern Railway properties, in preparation for transfer to the Dominion Government, by Professor G. C. Swain of Harvard University. This was to plague the management in later years since all equipment changes had to be expressed in terms of this valuation, and new cars were not accounted for as such, but rather as increases in the value of a given car number. So the Washington cars acquired in 1927 appear on some records under the number of the older NS&T cars whose electrical equipment they inherited. This also accounts for the first steel interurban being given the number 82, while two later acquisitions were given lower numbers, 80 and 81. This practice has rendered the compilation of an all-time roster very difficult, and further complication is caused by the fact that many early records had disappeared as early as 1913, so that any record of the origin of second-hand cars purchased before that time comes from sources outside the NS&T. The 1920 renumbering, following so closely after the Swain valuation, sometimes causes uncertainty as to just which car is referred to in such records that do survive. As a final source of uncertainty, there is the extensive rebuilding of many cars during the 1920s. For all these reasons, the information provided may appear to conflict with that shown in other sources, but is believed to be substantially correct as of December 1924 for cars on the roster at that time (except for some of the 60s rebuilt later in the decade).

Colours

Equipment colours varied considerably over the years. Originally dark Pullman green, by the time of World War I and for some time after, cars were painted a sober grey with black trim. (The latter scheme frustrated Valentine & Sons postcard publishers and others who frequently hand tinted early black and white cards — they sometimes applied a more colourful but arbitrary livery to brighten up this rolling stock cloaked in grey.) In 1921 Pullman green was again adopted by the Canadian National; by 1926 this had become olive green and cream. About 1933, a dark red colour was adopted (quite similar to the famous Canadian Pacific maroon) for some interurbans, but city cars and the 60s were light red and yellow-cream. After 1939, bright vermilion and a pale tawny colour called "desert sand" became standard; some city cars were still green at this time. With the advent of the 620s in 1955, standard CNR coach green was used. With so many changes, two or more colour schemes would be in effect at the same time; thus only nos. 130 and 132 of the "Main Line cars" ever appeared in red and grey, and car 132 was repainted dark red afterwards; express car 41 went directly from dark red to CNR green while No. 40 remained red to the end. Locomotives were black, but received green cabs in the 1950s. Service equipment was black or box-car red, and in later years the sweepers and line cars were bright orange for better visibility.

Rebuilding and Renumbering

To make them suitable eventually for one-man operation, in 1920 most of the local lines equipment was rebuilt — one car (old No. 114) by Preston Car & Coach and the rest by Ottawa Car. Platforms were lengthened about 18", manually-operated folding doors installed, omnibus sides made straight, steel sheathing added, roof rebuilt to arch style and windows rebuilt to more modern appearance. (No. 114 was less radically altered.) Cars had to be borrowed on occasion from the International Railway Company to maintain service during this process. In order to standardize, in 1924 the old trucks and motors were discarded and almost all cars given Taylor trucks and either GE 214 or GE 216 motors. Safety-car equipment and air-operated doors were added for one-man operation between 1927 and 1929.

There was a general renumbering of equipment in December 1920. A key to the old and new numbers appears in the roster beginning on page 154. Under the revised scheme, St. Catharines cars were numbered 100-119 with Niagara Falls cars 120 and above. Most local line cars were second-hand from various sources except for two pairs, 100+112 and 105+106; also 120+122 were not built to NS&T order but were unused when acquired.

A new rule book took effect in 1940, and most cars were given extinguishing headlights, flag brackets and marker lights. Interurban cars had received pneuphonic horns in place of air whistles in 1929. These were more easily heard at a distance and required less compressed air for operation.

New Cars

The 1922 report (described in Chapter 4) recommended the purchase of ten second-hand city cars and ten new interurbans. What appeared were twelve new city cars and one interurban, while four interurbans, seven suburban cars and two express cars came second-hand in 1925-27.

With the arrival of the 300s and 320s, a reassignment of cars was made. Nos. 104, 112 and 301-308 went to Niagara Falls; Nos. 100-102, 105-107, 113, 114, 120-124, 309-312 and 320-326 to St. Catharines. Nos. 103 and 108-111, not modernized, were held "in reserve". Nos. 120-124, the largest city cars, were used on the Low Line, 320-326 on Port Dalhousie, and 113 and 114 (temporarily renumbered from 68 and 69) on the Lake Shore Division.

In 1935, Toronto Suburban Railway cars 107 and 108, which had been built at St. Catharines ten years before, came back for conversion to 600-volt and rebuilding as NS&T one-man cars 83 and 84. Nothing was immediately done to 107, but 108, a combine, went to Montreal and was violently mutilated by being cut off at the baggage door. A perfectly flat wooden end was installed and the car used by the Montreal & Southern Counties as a snow plow, with the passenger interior intact but for the removal of the seats. No. 107 was stored for some years but was shopped when World War II traffic increases began. Early in 1943, it went into service as No. 83 using the trucks from car 80 and 600-volt electrical equipment from car 133. No. 80 then acquired the trucks of retired car 81.

Road-Railers

In 1937 the NS&T acquired one of the CNR "Autorailers" built by Evans Products Company of Detroit, Michigan. This was an attempt to produce a bus-type vehicle that would run equally well on roads and rails. Two other such vehicles were obtained in 1938. They were actually the property of the CNR and never officially formed part of the NS&T roster. They were largely used for special parties originating on the American side and bound for boat connections, to avoid having to change from bus to car after crossing the bridge. However, they were too light to operate spring switches and it proved difficult to keep the rail guide mechanism in repair. Therefore they came to be used exclusively as buses with the rail equipment removed, but they were really unsatisfactory in this service as well, owing to restricted driver visibility.

Flexibility

Through an extremely flexible system of car assignments, a typical NS&T interurban car might begin its day's work running an extra trip or two in rush hour service on the Main Line, then go to Port Dalhousie East and make a trip to the Falls with boat passengers, returning with passengers destined to a mid-afternoon sailing. It might then

Top: Line truck c1940 (former bus).
(J.W. HOOD)

make a rush-hour trip to Thorold as a McKinnon's extra, then deadhead to Niagara Falls and bring back the excursion passengers it had taken there earlier. It might then make an extra trip or two on the Port Dalhousie line with passengers from Lakeside Park, by which time our hypothetical car would have been in more or less continuous operation for about eighteen hours.

Passenger service on the Oshawa (Ontario) Railway was abandoned in 1940. Cars 82 and 83, wooden cars built by Ottawa Car in 1923, were transferred to St. Catharines for rehabilitation. This was not done, and the bodies were discarded in November 1941. (The body of car 83 survived and is awaiting restoration at the Halton County Radial Railway Museum at Milton, Ontario.) Less than two years later the increased wartime traffic had created a such a critical rolling stock situation that two bodies then in use as storehouses in Oshawa (formerly OR 80 and 81, both originally from Edmonton) were taken to St. Catharines, eventually reappearing as nos. 327 and 328. The explanation for not shopping nos. 82 and 83 may be that they were not really suitable for use on the NS&T, having wooden seats and non-standard trucks and motors; at the time they could be used only on the Port Dalhousie line where they were not specifically required. As the war progressed, it become impossible to obtain new buses, so greater expense in reconditioning used or retired equipment became justified.

The entire 320-series was sent to the Montreal & Southern Counties in 1947, becoming base-service equipment on the St. Lambert–Montreal South line.

Scrapping

When the Port Dalhousie line was abandoned, the M&SC considered acquiring some NS&T cars to replace its aging 100-series suburban cars, but the 300-series lightweights were held to be too slow and light, and the others were rather wide for operation over the Victoria Bridge; in any case they were little improvement over the 100s. Trucks and electrical equipment from some of the older cars were, however, taken for spares.

The only NS&T passenger car to escape scrapping was No. 130, which was transferred to Rail City, an ill-fated privately-run tourist operation on New York Route 3 at Sandy Pond, where it sat, unattended and exposed for many years. Eventually the tourist operation there folded, and the car, which had acquired a decidedly decrepit appearance due to neglect, was eventually scrapped. The body of car 135 had earlier been purchased by a railway enthusiast and moved to Lambeth, Ontario, but unfortunately was allowed to deteriorate and was eventually scrapped. The remaining cars were sent to the CNR reclamation yard at London for scrapping, except for freight motors 16, 17, 18 and sweeper 22, which went to Oshawa for another few years of service.

Freight Locomotives

Number	Pre-1920 Number	Builder	Year	Weight Tons	Disposition	Notes
	1	NS&T	1901		Scr. 1916	Flat, small cab, switcher only. Scr. 1916, body parts to #11.
7	600	Montreal Street Ry.	1901		Sold	Flat, small cab. ex Shawinigan Fallls Terminal Ry. 1912, Written off 1928, sold to used equipment dealer. Resold Cornwall #7 1931.
I-8		Baldwin/Westinghouse	1912?	32	Scr. 1924	Acquired used, wrecked and scrapped 1924.
II-8	605	NS&T		44	Scr. 1960	Built by NS&T from unknown source, probably used some equipment from I-8.
9	602	NS&T	1912		Scr. 1933	Built by NS&T from flat car. Switcher only.
10	603	NS&T	1918			Built by NS&T from flat car, again rebuilt 1924. Steeple-cab in final configuration. To Cornwall #8 1935, rebuilt as plow there 1946.
11	604	NS&T	1916	28	Scr. 1928	Built by NS&T 1916 with many parts from #1.
12	601	Baldwin/Westinghouse	1914?		Sold 1930	To WE&LS #9 1930, to Cornwall #9 1942.
14	606	General Electric	1914	40	Scr. 1960	Rebuilt by NS&T 1943.
15		NS&T	1925	50	Scr. 1960	
I-16		NS&T	1925	50	Scr. 1960	To M&SC 325 1925, returned as NS&T 19 1936.
II-16		National Steel Car	1918	50	Sold	ex HEPC Queenston Construction Ry. (# uncertain) 1926, rebuilt with new cab 1930. To Oshawa 1960. To Noranda Mines Ltd. 1965.
17		National Steel Car	1918	50	Scr. 1964	ex HEPC Queenston Construction Ry. #E-9 1926. To Oshawa 1960.
18		Baldwin/Westinghouse	1918	55		ex HEPC Queenston Construction Ry. #E-21. To T&YRR (Hydro) #2 1924. To NS&T 1927. To Oshawa #18 1960. To Connecticut Electric museum (Warehouse Point) 1965
19	see I-16					
20		General Electric	1914	55	Scr. 1960	ex South Brooklyn Ry. #6 1938 in trade with used equipment dealer for Toronto Suburban #300, unusable as 1200 volt
21		Canadian Locomotive Co.	1927	60	Scr. 1960	ex M&SC #327 1941.

Note: 600-series numbers probably for inventory purposes only.

Opposite: Locomotive No. 17, former Hydro Electric Power Commission No. E-9 used for digging the Queenston-Chippewa Power Canal, at St. Catharines shops, August 25th 1956. (J.D. KNOWLES)

Top: Locomotive No. 1, c1902. (J.M. MILLS COLLECTION)

Bottom: Freight motor No. ii-8 at St. Catharines shops, September 8th 1957. A spare, it was also loaned to Oshawa Railway. (J.D. KNOWLES)

Roster of Equipment

Top: Side running boards went out of fashion around the time of World War I. The open interurbans were converted to end-loading cars with wire mesh sides by Preston in 1916, including this 50-series car.
(J. FREYSENG COLLECTION)

Opposite: Car 58 as originally built with crew, c1901.
(J.W HOOD COLLECTION)

Number	Pre-1920 Number	Builder	Year	Seats	Length	Body Length	Width	Height	Weight	Motors	
	1	Patterson & Corbin	1896?	22	27'0"				17,840	GE1200	
	2	Patterson & Corbin	1896?	22	27'0"				17,840	GE1200	
	3	Patterson & Corbin	1896?	22	28'0"				17,840	GE1200	
	4	Patterson & Corbin	1896?	22	28'0"				17,840	GE1200	
	5	Ottawa	1900	22	28'0"				17,840		
	6	Ottawa	1900	22	28'0"				17,840		
	11	Patterson & Corbin	1896?	45	27'0"				16,700	GE1200	
	12	Patterson & Corbin	1896?	45	27'0"				16,700	GE1200	
	14	Patterson & Corbin	1896?	45	27'0"				16,700	GE1200	
	15	Patterson & Corbin	1896?	45	27'0"				16,700	GE1200	
	16	Ottawa	1900	45	27'0"				16,700		
	17	Ottawa	1900	45	27'0"				16,700		
1 to 17: Information (except for building data) given as it appears in official records). 11 to 15 perhaps trailers later.											
	50	Crossen	1900	52	43'0"	33'0½"	10'0"		34,000	GE57	
51	51	Crossen	1900	52	43'0"	33'0½"	10'0"		34,000	GE57	
	I-52	Crossen	1900	52	43'0"	33'0½"	10'0"		34,000	GE57	
53	53	Crossen	1900	52	43'0"	33'0½"	10'0"		34,000	GE57	
54	54	Crossen	1900	52	43'0"	33'0½"	10'0"		34,000	GE57	
55	55	Crossen	1900	52	43'0"	33'0½"	10'0"		34,000	GE57	
56	56	Crossen	1900	52	43'0"	33'0½"	10'0"		34,000	GE57	
57	57	Crossen	1900	52	43'0"	33'0½"	10'0"		34,000	GE57	
58	58	Crossen	1900	52	43'0"	33'0½"	10'0"		34,000	GE57	
59	59	Crossen	1900	52	43'0"	33'0½"	10'0"		34,000	GE57	
50 to 59: 1916 rebuilding by Preston changed them to centre-aisle, end-loading cars with wire mesh on sides. 50 and 52 burnt at Preston 1917; 51 and 57 scrapped 1928, rest 1931-32. Existence of a No. 59 questionable.											
II-52			1903?							GE45	
II-52: Originally single-end, open on right side only, known officially as "semi-open car." Open side later partly enclosed. Of the several sources suggested for this car, the most likely (to the author at least) is that it was supplied by Preston in replacement for cars 50 and 52 (burnt at the factory before delivery)											

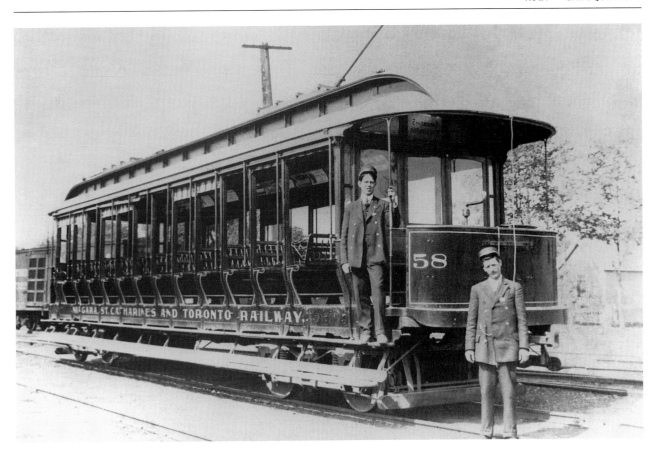

Control	Truck	Truck Wheelbase	Truck Centres	Type	Disposition	Notes
				Closed City	Scr. 1918	
				Closed City	Scr. 1918	
				Closed City	Scr. 1919	
				Closed City	Scr. 1919	
	Jones			Closed City	Scr. 1918	This information is known to be incomplete. Six cars were used in Niagara Falls and eight in St. Catharines.
	Jones			Closed City	Scr. 1918	
				Open City	Scr. 1918	
				Open City	Scr. 1918	
				Open City	Scr. 1919	
				Open City	Scr. 1919	
	Jones			Open City	Scr. 1919	
	Jones			Open City	Scr. 1919	

Control	Truck	Truck Wheelbase	Truck Centres	Type	Disposition	Notes
K-10	Taylor	6'0"	26'6"	Open Interurban	—	Burnt 1916 at Preston plant.
K-10	Taylor	6'0"	26'6"	Open Interurban	Scr. 1928	
K-10	Taylor	6'0"	26'6"	Open Interurban	—	Burnt 1916 at Preston plant.
K-10	Taylor	6'0"	26'6"	Open Interurban	Scr. 1933	
K-10	Taylor	6'0"	26'6"	Open Interurban	Scr. 1933	
K-10	Taylor	6'0"	26'6"	Open Interurban	Scr. 1933	
K-10	Taylor	6'0"	26'6"	Open Interurban	Scr. 1933	
K-10	Taylor	6'0"	26'6"	Open Interurban	Scr. 1928	
K-10	Taylor	6'0"	26'6"	Open Interurban	Scr. 1933	
K-10	Taylor	6'0"	26'6"	Open Interurban	Scr. 1928	

Control	Truck	Truck Wheelbase	Truck Centres	Type	Disposition	Notes
				Semi-Open Int.	Scr. 1933	ex London & Lake Erie 1923.

and was probably rebuilt from an open car of the Preston & Berlin Railway.

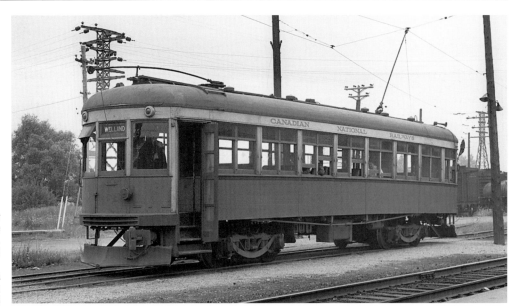

Right: Car 63 laying over at Port Colborne on the morning of July 20th 1946. (JOHN F. HUMISTON S7202)

Bottom: Car 67 in a post-war view. (CRHA, FONDS R.F. CORLEY)

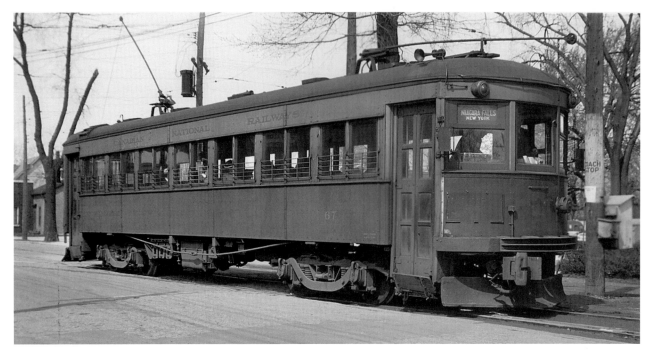

Number	Pre-1920 Number	Builder	Year	Seats	Length	Body Length	Width	Height	Weight	Motors	
60	60	Niles	1912	54	50'7"	38'1½"	9'6½"	12'10"	58,960	GE216	
61	61	Niles	1912	54	50'7"	38'1½"	9'6½"	12'10"	58,960	GE216	
62	62	Niles	1912	54	50'7"	38'1½"	9'6½"	12'10"	58,960	GE216	
63	63	Niles	1912	54	50'7"	38'1½"	9'6"	12'10"	58,960	GE216	
60-63: Two-car motor-trailer sets built for London & Lake Erie, among the first arch-roof cars in Canada. Formerly 93-95 (trailers), 97-99 (motors), not necessarily renumbered in order. All used as motors by NS&T.											
64		Preston	1908	56	50'2"	38'0"	8'10"	12'4½"	55,520	GE57	
65		Preston	1908	44	50'2"	38'0"	8'10"	12'4½"	48,000	WH93?	
66		Ottawa	1906	56	50'2"	38'0"	8'10"	12'4½"	48,000	WH93?	
67		Ottawa	1906	48	50'2"	38'0"	8'10"	12'4½"	48,000	WH93?	
68		Preston	1908	54	51'0"	38'0"	8'10"	12'7½"	54,380	GE80	
69		Preston	1908	54	51'0"	38'0"	8'10"	12'7½"	54,380	GE80	
64-69: Formerly railroad-roof. 66 and 69 trucks to line cars 31 and 30 1939. Other identical cars went from London to Oshawa.											

Top: Seldom-photographed car 66 after modifications at St. Catharines 1925. (W.C. BAILEY COLLECTION)

Left: Car 66 outshopped in NS&T livery c1919 or 1920. (LIBRARY AND ARCHIVES CANADA E004665763)

Control	Truck	Truck Wheelbase	Truck Centres	Type	Disposition	Notes
K-35	Baldwin	6'6"	25'9½"	Interurban	Scr. 8/1947	ex London & Lake Erie 1915.
K-35	Baldwin	6'6"	25'9½"	Interurban	Scr. 11/1947	ex London & Lake Erie 1915
K-35	Baldwin	6'6"	25'9½"	Interurban	Scr. 1942	ex London & Lake Erie 1915, retired 1936.
K-35	Baldwin	6'6"	25'9½"	Interurban	Scr. 11/1947	ex London & Lake Erie 1915.
K-6	Brill 27E	6'0"	26'0"	Interurban	Scr. 1941	ex London & Lake Erie #80 1920. Rebuilt 1925.
WH D202	Brill 27E	6'0"	26'0"	Interurban	Scr. 7/1946	ex London & Lake Erie #82 1920. Rebuilt 1925.
WH D202	Brill 27E	6'0"	26'0"	Interurban	Scr. 1940	ex London & Lake Erie #54 1920. Rebuilt 1925.
WH D202	Brill 27E	6'0"	26'0"	Interurban	Scr. 6/1951	ex London & Lake Erie #56 1920. Rebuilt 1925.
K-6	Brill 27E	6'0"	26'0"	Interurban	Scr. 9/1950	ex London & Lake Erie comb. #84 1920, re#113.
K-6	Brill 27E	6'0"	26'0"	Interurban	Scr. 1942	ex London & Lake Erie #88 1920, re#114.

60-series: Much rebuilt in the 1920s and internal company records are inconsistent. 69 "reconstructed" 1920; all re-motored 1924; 64-67 extensively remodelled 1925; 64, 65 and 67 MU control 1927; 64 and 67 remodelled and platforms raised 1928; 65 and 67 modernized (new seats etc.) 1929; all eventually one-man.

Top: Car 81 (II-81) at St. Catharines yard c1930. (W.S. FLATT COLLECTION)

Right: Car 108 or 109 outshopped at St. Catharines, c1909. (AL PATERSON COLLECTION)

Number	Pre-1920 Number	Builder	Year	Seats	Length	Body Length	Width	Height	Weight	Motors	
70	108	Brill	1906?	52	46'0"	34'0"	9'0"		61,000	GE90	
71	109	Brill	1906?	52	46'0"	34'0"	9'0"		61,000	GE90	
70-71: "Temporarily renumbered until reconstructed into local cars". Note: cars 108 and 109 were never rebuilt.											
I-80	100	Ottawa	1899	50	48'0"	37'0"	9'0"		57,000	GE57	
II-80		Kuhlman	1915	64	57'6"	41'6"	8'7½"	13'0½"	69,740	GE214	
II-80: Rebuilt 1939 to eliminate baggage section, truck bolster being moved to suit. Train doors removed and two side doors changed to folding air-operated, then left-side loading as one-man car for Welland Division. Following collision with 82 in May 1941, rebuilt from 2-door right-hand drive to 4-door centre drive, then also available for Main Line.											
I-81	102	Ottawa	1899	50	48'6"	37'0"	9'0"		57,000	GE57	
II-81		Niles	1915	64	57'6"	41'6"	8'7½"	13'0"	68,740	GE214	
II-81: Retired 1936, trucks to II-80 1942, body sold 1945.											

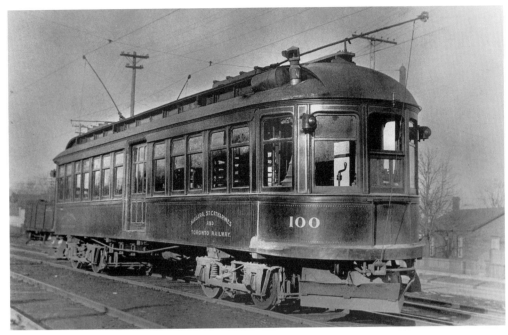

Left: Car 100 at
St. Catharines c1918.
Built by Ottawa in
1899, this car would be
renumbered 1-80 in 1920,
and was scrapped in 1927.
(AL PATERSON COLLECTION)

Bottom: Car 82 at
Port Dalhousie East in
1930s livery, c1940.
(CRHA, FONDS
CHARLES BRIDGES)

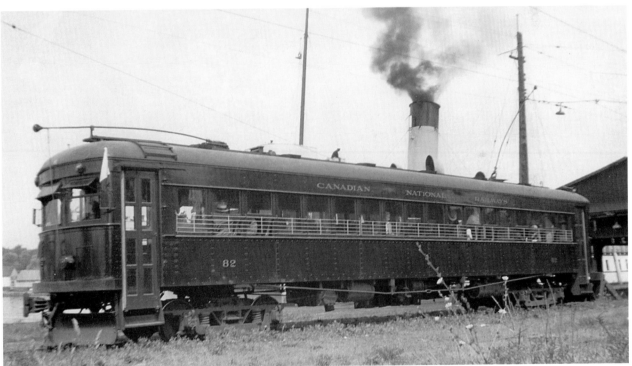

Control	Truck	Truck Wheelbase	Truck Centres	Type	Disposition	Notes
K-35	Brill 27E	6'6"	22'3"	Semi-Conv.	Scr. 1929	ex Boston & Northern Street Ry. 1909.
K-35	Brill 27E	6'6"	22'3"	Semi-Conv.	Scr. 1933	ex Boston & Northern Street Ry. 1909.
K-35	Taylor	6'0"	27'7"	Combine	Scr. 1927	
GE M	Baldwin	6'10"	31'9"	Steel Interurban	Scr. 1956	ex Cleveland & Eastern #56 1926.
II-80, 81: Official records give same data for both cars (very unlikely). Both originally combines. Trucks of 80 to 83 1942; 80 received trucks from derelict 81.						
K-35	Taylor	6'0"	27'7"	Combine	Scr. 1927	
GE M	Baldwin	6'10"	31'9"	Steel Interurban	Scr. 1945	ex Cleveland & Eastern #57 1926.

Top: Car 83 on enthusiasts' charter at Michigan Beach, Port Dalhousie East, normally a freight line only. September 8th 1957. (J.D. KNOWLES)

Left: Interior of car 83, November 30th 1947. (J.D. KNOWLES)

Number	Pre-1920 Number	Builder	Year	Seats	Length	Body Length	Width	Height	Weight	Motors	
I-82	103	Ottawa	1899	50	48'6"	37'0"	9'0"		57,000	GE57	
II-82		NS&T	1925	72	61'9"	43'10"	9'0"	12'1½"	80,000	GE214	
83		NS&T	1925	72	62'3"	43'0"	9'2"	12'11"	80,000	GE214	

82: Intended as first of ten cars. No others built. Rebuilt as express car 1956.
82-83: built on standard CNR underframe designed for gas-electric cars etc., hence flat end contour (similar to Toronto Suburban #108).

90		Niles	1910?	48	48'0"						
91		Niles	1907	48	49'0"						
100	118	Brill	1912	40	40'9"	28'0"	8'6"	11'4½"	43,500	GE216	
101	119	Brill	1903	40	40'9"	28'0"	8'6"	11'4½"	43,500	GE216	
102	120	Brill	1903	40	40'9"	28'0"	8'6"	11'4½"	43,500	GE216	
103	121	Brill	1903	40	40'9"	28'0"	8'6"	11'4½"	43,500	GE216	
II-104	122	Brill	1903	40	40'9"	28'0"	8'6"	11'4½"	43,500	GE80	

101-104: ex Philadelphia Rapid Transit Co. #2055, #2060, #2062, #2092 1913 (not necessarily renumbered in order).

	I-104										
105	105	Kuhlman	1905	40	39'0"	28'0"	8'3"	11'11"	38,000	GE57	
106	106	Kuhlman	1905	40	39'0"	28'0"	8'3"	11'11"	38,000	GE57	

Left: Car 104 c1910.
This car was constructed
from two single-truck cars
spliced together in 1904.
(H.E. BATTEL COLLECTION)

Bottom: Car 120 c1915.
This car was renumbered
102 in 1920.
(AL PATERSON COLLECTION)

Control	Truck	Truck Wheelbase	Truck Centres	Type	Disposition	Notes
K-35	Taylor	6'0"	27'7"	Combine	Scr. 1927	
GE M	Baldwin	6'6"	37'0"	Steel Interurban	Scr. 1959	Rebuilt express 1956.
GE M	Baldwin	6'6"	37'0"	Steel Interurban	Scr. 1959	ex TSR #107 1935.
HL	Taylor			Int. Trailer	Scr. 1935	ex Cleveland, Painesville & Eastern 1927.
HL				Interurban	Scr. 1935	ex Cleveland & Eastern #21 1926.
K-28	Taylor	4'8"	16'0"	City	Scr. 11/1946	Rebuilt 1920; 1-man 1928.
K-28	Taylor	4'8"	16'0"	City	Scr. 11/1946	2nd hand 1913; 1-man 1928.
K-28	Taylor	4'8"	16'0"	City	Scr. 11/1946	2nd hand 1913; 1-man 1928.
K-28	Taylor	4'8"	16'0"	City	Scr. 1933	2nd hand 1913; sand car later.
K-28	Taylor	4'8"	16'0"	City	Scr. 1935	2nd hand 1913; 1-man 1926.
					Scr. 1918	Built from two single-truck cars spliced 1904.
K-10	Taylor	6'0"	15'11"	City	Scr. 12/1940	2nd hand 1919; 1-man 1928. Ret. 1934.
K-10	Taylor	6'0"	15'11"	City	Scr. 11/1946	2nd hand 1919; 1-man 1928. Sand car 1945.

Top: Car 114 after rebuilding at Preston Works 1914. (R. NEUBURGER COLLECTION)

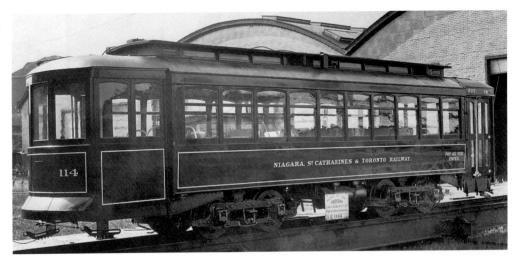

Bottom: Car 124 at the outer end of Facer Street city line on May 20th 1947. (J.D. KNOWLES)

Number	Pre-1920 Number	Builder	Year	Seats	Length	Body Length	Width	Height	Weight	Motors	
	107										
107	110	Brill		40	39'0"	28'0"	8'3"		44,000	GE216	
108	111	Brill		40	39'0"	28'0"	8'3"		44,000	GE216	
	112										
	113										
109	114	Brill		40	39'0"	28'0"	8'3"		44,000	GE216	
110	115	Brill		40	39'0"	28'0"	8'3"		44,000	GE216	
111	116	Brill		40	39'0"	28'0"	8'3"		44,000	GE216	
II-112	117	Brill	1912	40	40'9"	28'0"	8'6"	11'4½"	43,500	GE216	
100-series: Particulars varied greatly over the years because of rebuildings, which usually changed their appearance completely.											
113		Preston									
114		Preston									
120	123	Preston	1914	40	46'9"	33'2"	9'0"		49,500	GE216	
	124	Preston	1914	40	46'9"	33'2"	9'0"		49,500	GE216	
	125	Preston	1914	40	46'9"	33'2"	9'0"		49,500	GE216	
121	126	Preston	1914	40	46'9"	33'2"	9'0"		49,500	GE216	
	127	Preston	1914	40	46'9"	33'2"	9'0"		49,500	GE216	
122	128	Preston	1914	40	46'9"	33'2"	9'0"		49,500	GE216	
120 to 122: Originally Preston "Prairie-type" cars built for Saskatoon but not used there as too heavy for bridges. Virtually unrecognizable in their final form.											

Top: Rarely photographed car 112 at St. Catharines, May 20th 1932. (O.P. MAUS)

Bottom: Car 120 c1920 after rebuilding. (W.S. FLATT COLLECTION)

Control	Truck	Truck Wheelbase	Truck Centres	Type	Disposition	Notes
						Burnt 1916. Rebuilt baggage car 1918. Re#40 1920 but unused.
K-28	Taylor	4'8"	15'11"	City	Scr. 11/1947	2nd hand 1910. 1-man 1928.
K-28	Taylor	4'8"	15'11"	City	Scr. 1928	2nd hand 1910.
					Sold 1921	Sold to Chatham, Wallaceburg & Lake Erie 1921.
						Not accounted for.
K-28	Taylor	4'8"	15'11"	City	Scr. 1933	2nd hand 1910. Rebuilt Preston 1920.
K-28	Brill	4'0"	15'11"	City	Scr. 1928	2nd hand 1912.
K-28	Taylor	4'8"	15'11"	City	Scr. 1928	2nd hand 1912.
K-28	Taylor	4'8"	16'0"	City	Scr. 1935	1-man 1927.
						ex 68.
						ex 69.
K-28	Taylor	4'8"	22'2"	City	Scr. 1941	Steel sheathed 1920-21.
K-28	Taylor	4'8"	22'2"	City		Burnt Niagara Falls December 10th 1919.
K-28	Taylor	4'8"	22'2"	City		Burnt Niagara Falls December 10th 1919.
K-28	Taylor	4'8"	22'2"	City	Scr. 1941	
K-28	Taylor	4'8"	22'2"	City		Burnt December 1918.
K-28	Taylor	4'8"	22'2"	City	Scr. 1941	Steel sheathed 1920-21.

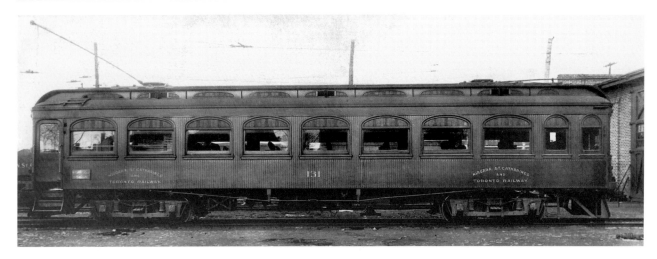

Top: Car 131, September 1920.
(AL PATERSON COLLECTION)

Bottom: Car 134 in St. Catharines yard, 1939.
(ADDISON LAKE COLLECTION, COURTESY FRED ANGUS)

Opposite Top: Car 132 at Port Colborne, December 1939.
(ADDISON LAKE COLLECTION, COURTESY FRED ANGUS)

Opposite Bottom: Car 132 at Substation Junction, Thorold on May 3rd 1941, starting the 18.6 mile run to Port Colborne. It was a straight passenger car, as the express compartment was used as a smoker. A walled-off side passage bypassed the smoker, so there was not an express door on the opposite side.
(J.D. KNOWLES)

Number	Pre-1920 Number	Builder	Year	Seats	Length	Body Length	Width	Height	Weight	Motors	
123	141	Southern	1918	44	44'0"	30'6"	8'4"	12'8½"	48,300	GE216	
124	142	Southern	1918	44	44'0"	30'6"	8'4"	12'8½"	48,300	GE216	
130	130	Preston	1914	64	58'0"	45'3"	9'6"	13'7"	75,400	GE214	
131	131	Preston	1914	64	58'0"	45'3"	9'6"	13'7"	75,400	GE214	
135	129	Preston	1914	64	58'0"	45'3"	9'6"	13'7"	75,400	GE214	

130, 131, 135: Passenger cars. Had Pullman-style smoker in separate compartment with side corridor, copied from I-80 to 82. 130 rebuilt 4-doors for one-man operation. Upper sash blocked off 1947 and "picture windows" became half-size smaller sash. 130 retired 1954; 131 and 135 scrapped 1949.

Number	Pre-1920 Number	Builder	Year	Seats	Length	Body Length	Width	Height	Weight	Motors	
132	132	Preston	1914	64	58'0"	45'3"	9'6"	13'7"	75,400	GE214	
133	133	Preston	1914	64	58'0"	45'3"	9'6"	13'7"	75,400	GE214	
134	134	Preston	1914	64	58'0"	45'3"	9'6"	13'7"	75,400	GE214	

132 to 134: Combines. Unusual baggage section occupying position of smoker above, door on one side only. 132 rebuilt one-man, steel sheathed and upper sash plated over, left-side loading as one-man car, also used as two-man car on Main Line, scrapped 1949. 133 scrapped 1942 after long retirement,

Control	Truck	Truck Wheelbase	Truck Centres	Type	Disposition	Notes
K-28	Taylor	4'8"	19'4"	City	Scr. 10/1946	ex Columbia (SC) Gas & Elec. Co. #111 1919.
K-28	Taylor	4'8"	19'4"	City	Scr. 10/1947	ex Columbia (SC) Gas & Elec. Co. #112 1919.
GE MK	Taylor	6'6"	34'8"	Interurban		Rebuilt to 1-man 4-door. Ret. 1954. Preserved Sandy Pond NY but allowed to decay.
GE MK	Taylor	6'6"	34'8"	Interurban	Scr. 1949	
GE MK	Taylor	6'6"	34'8"	Interurban	Scr. 5/1949	
GE MK	Taylor	6'6"	34'8"	Int. Combine	Scr. 4/1949	Rebuilt to 1-man steel sheathed.
GE MK	Taylor	6'6"	34'8"	Int. Combine	Scr. 1942	Ret. 1935
GE MK	Taylor	6'6"	34'8"	Int. Combine	Scr. 1950	

134 scrapped 1950.

Top: Car 303 at
St. Catharines yard,
August 1947.
(R.T. VINCENT)

Right: Interior of
car 303 c1946.
(CRHA, FONDS R.F. CORLEY)

Number	Pre-1920 Number	Builder	Year	Seats	Length	Body Length	Width	Height	Weight	Motors	
301		NS&T/Cincinnati	1926	44	42'6"	31'6"	8'6½"	10'5½"	32,700	WH508A	
302		NS&T/Cincinnati	1926	44	42'6"	31'6"	8'6½"	10'5½"	32,700	WH508A	
303		NS&T/Cincinnati	1926	44	42'6"	31'6"	8'6½"	10'5½"	32,700	WH508A	
304		NS&T/Cincinnati	1926	44	42'6"	31'6"	8'6½"	10'5½"	32,700	WH508A	
305		NS&T/Cincinnati	1926	44	42'6"	31'6"	8'6½"	10'5½"	32,700	WH508A	
306		NS&T/Cincinnati	1926	44	42'6"	31'6"	8'6½"	10'5½"	32,700	WH508A	
307		NS&T/Cincinnati	1926	44	42'6"	31'6"	8'6½"	10'5½"	32,700	WH508A	
308		NS&T/Cincinnati	1926	44	42'6"	31'6"	8'6½"	10'5½"	32,700	WH508A	
309		NS&T/Cincinnati	1926	44	42'6"	31'6"	8'6½"	10'5½"	32,700	WH508A	
310		NS&T/Cincinnati	1926	44	42'6"	31'6"	8'6½"	10'5½"	32,700	WH508A	
311		NS&T/Cincinnati	1926	44	42'6"	31'6"	8'6½"	10'5½"	32,700	WH508A	
312		NS&T/Cincinnati	1926	44	42'6"	31'6"	8'6½"	10'5½"	32,700	WH508A	

301 to 312: Shipped in pieces from Cincinnati and assembled by NS&T. Steel parts not treated against corrosion and body deterioration serious in later years. In 1948 four cars were scrapped and the rest renumbered: 304, 306 and 308 became 301, 310 and 311. This placed remaining cars in groups

320		Brill	1917	52	48'4"	36'0"	8'5"	12'6½"	56,200	GE216	
321		Brill	1917	52	48'4"	36'0"	8'5"	12'6½"	56,200	GE216	
322		Brill	1917	52	48'4"	36'0"	8'5"	12'6½"	56,200	GE216	
323		Brill	1917	52	48'4"	36'0"	8'5"	12'6½"	56,200	GE216	
324		Brill	1917	52	48'4"	36'0"	8'5"	12'6½"	56,200	GE216	
325		Brill	1917	52	48'4"	36'0"	8'5"	12'6½"	56,200	GE216	
326		Brill	1917	52	48'4"	36'0"	8'5"	12'6½"	56,200	GE216	
327		Preston	1914								
328		Preston	1914								

327 to 328: Built for Edmonton Radial Railway. Sold to Oshawa Railway as 80, 81, eventually tool sheds. To St. Catharines 1943, motorized with parts from 62 and 64. Originally single-end but double-ended in Oshawa. Doors not cut in "closed" side until NS&T rebuilding when original long rear (double-door)

620		Ottawa	1930	50	31'2"	37'8"	8'5½"	12'10"	68,000	WH548	
622		Ottawa	1930	50	31'2"	37'8"	8'5½"	12'10"	68,000	WH548	
623		Ottawa	1930	50	31'2"	37'8"	8'5½"	12'10"	68,000	WH548	

Top: Oshawa Railway car 80 in 1939, just before abandonment of streetcar service. This and sister car 81 would, in 1944, become NS&T nos. 328 and 327 respectively. Modifications by NS&T included shortening vestibules by the width of one door.
(AL PATERSON COLLECTION)

Control	Truck	Truck Wheelbase	Truck Centres	Type	Disposition	Notes
K-35	Cinti.	5'0"	21'6"	Lightweight City	Scr.	
K-35	Cinti.	5'0"	21'6"	Lightweight City	Scr. 1950	
K-35	Cinti.	5'0"	21'6"	Lightweight City	Scr. 1950	
K-35	Cinti.	5'0"	21'6"	Lightweight City	Scr. 1950	Re#301 1948.
K-35	Cinti.	5'0"	21'6"	Lightweight City	Scr.	
K-35	Cinti.	5'0"	21'6"	Lightweight City	Scr. 1950	Re#310 1948.
K-35	Cinti.	5'0"	21'6"	Lightweight City	Scr. 1950	Re#311 1948.
K-35	Cinti.	5'0"	21'6"	Lightweight City	Scr.	
K-35	Cinti.	5'0"	21'6"	Lightweight City	Scr. 1950	
K-35	Cinti.	5'0"	21'6"	Lightweight City	Scr.	
K-35	Cinti.	5'0"	21'6"	Lightweight City	Scr.	
K-35	Cinti.	5'0"	21'6"	Lightweight City	Scr. 1950	
301 to 303 and 309 to 312, possibly for franchise purposes as 309 to 312 were numbers originally assigned to St. Catharines in 1926. Remaining cars given trolley bridges, 14-foot poles and, where not already installed, marker lights for use on Port Dalhousie line, scrapped May-September 1950.						
K-35	Brill	6'0"	21'10"	Suburban	Scr. 1956	ex Washington, VA. To M&SC 1947.
K-35	Brill	6'0"	21'10"	Suburban	Scr. 1956	ex Washington, VA. To M&SC 1947.
K-35	Brill	6'0"	21'10"	Suburban	Scr. 1956	ex Washington, VA. To M&SC 1947.
K-35	Brill	6'0"	21'10"	Suburban	Scr. 1945	ex Washington, VA.
K-35	Brill	6'0"	21'10"	Suburban	Scr. 1956	ex Washington, VA. To M&SC 1947.
K-35	Brill	6'0"	21'10"	Suburban	Scr. 1956	ex Washington, VA. To M&SC 1947.
K-35	Brill	6'0"	21'10"	Suburban	Scr. 1956	ex Washington, VA. To M&SC 1947.
				City	Scr. 9/1950	ex Oshawa No. 81, 1944.
				City	Scr. 9/1950	ex Oshawa No. 80, 1944.
platform shortened to match original front platform. Scrapped 1950, trucks and motors to M&SC along with those from 68. Similar cars from Edmonton to Toronto & York Radial Railway, Scarborough Division.						
HL	Natl. Steel Car	6'6"	26'6"	Interurban	Scr. 1959	ex M&SC 1956.
HL	Natl. Steel Car	6'6"	26'6"	Interurban	Scr. 1959	ex M&SC 1956.
HL	Natl. Steel Car	6'6"	26'6"	Interurban	Scr. 1959	ex M&SC 1956.

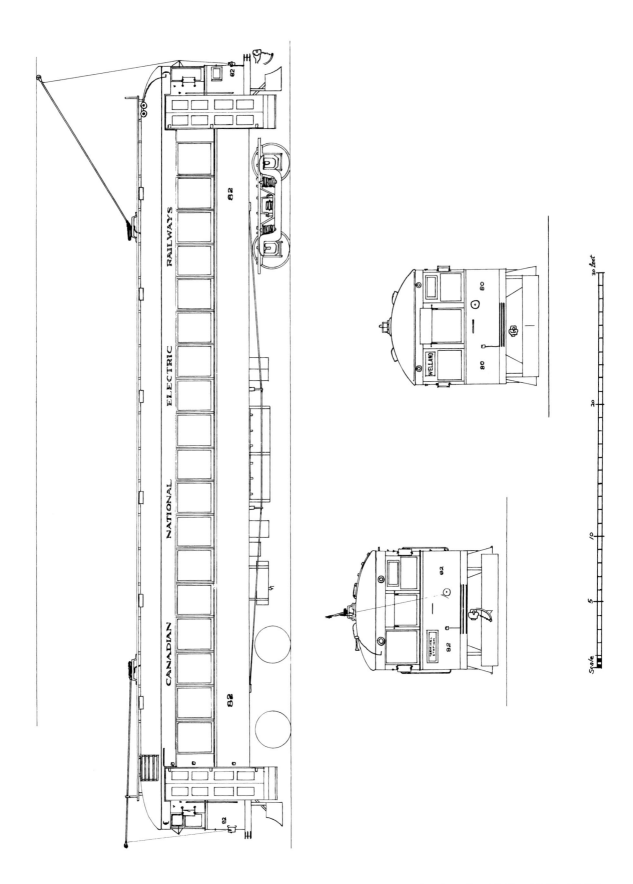

Drawings of cars 80, 82 and 320 by J. M. Mills

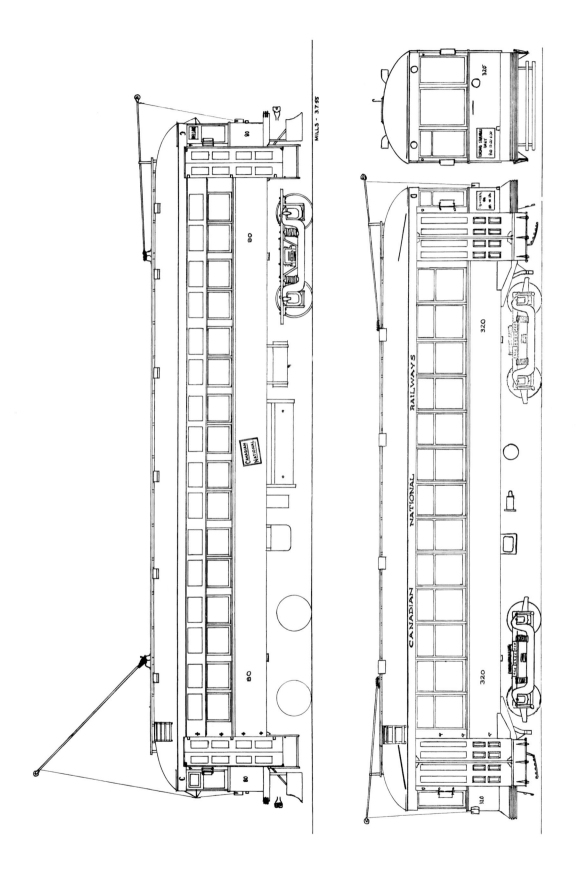

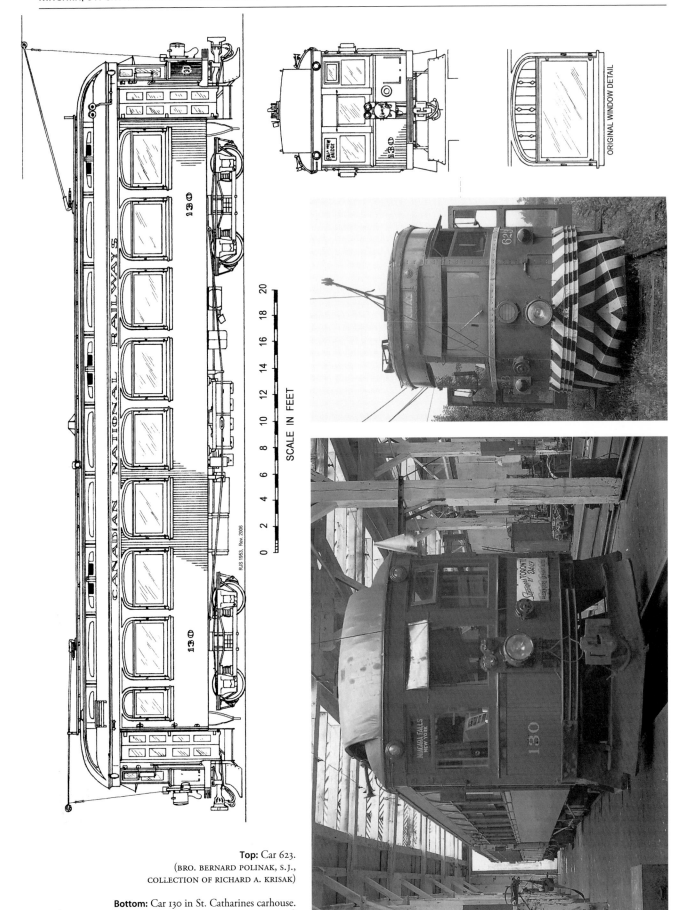

ORIGINAL WINDOW DETAIL

CANADIAN NATIONAL RAILWAYS

RJS 1953. Rev. 2006

SCALE IN FEET

0 2 4 6 8 10 12 14 16 18 20

Top: Car 623.
(BRO. BERNARD POLINAK, S.J.,
COLLECTION OF RICHARD A. KRISAK)

Bottom: Car 130 in St. Catharines carhouse.
(ANTHONY J. KRISAK, COLLECTION OF RICHARD A. KRISAK)

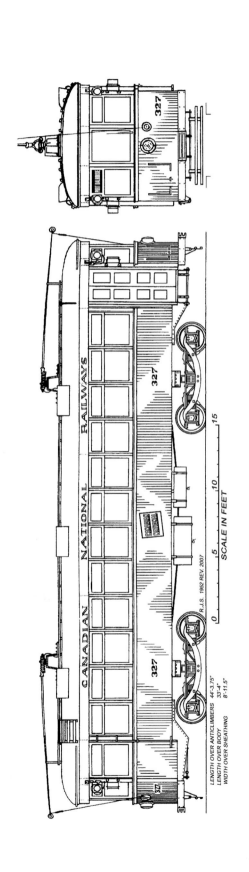

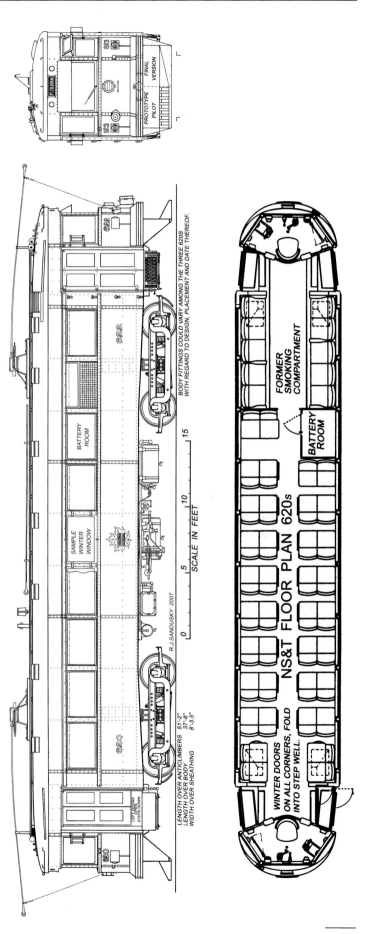

Drawings of cars 130, 327 and 620 series by R.J. Sandusky

171

COPY

Ottawa, Ont., Oct. 3, 1899.

J. A. Powers, Esq.,
    Troy, N. Y.

Dear Sir:-
        We have sent you under separate cover blue print showing seat-
ing arrangement for 38' car body measuring 48' over vestibules, and for
33' car body measuring 43' over all. We have also sent you a copy of
our general specifications for our standard 48' car body, this will not
cover your proposed car but will give you a general idea, you will note
on plan that we give you 2" wider passage at smoking compartment than
on your Troy cars, but it also gives you 5-1/2" wider smoking room.
        Price for 38' car body is two thousand dollars ($2,000) fob
Ottawa, for 33' car body one thousand eight hundred and fifteen dollars
($1815), this price does not include the following fittings: light fix-
tures, headlights, heaters, sand boxes, registers or register fittings.
All of the above fittings which are required we furnish at actual cost,
charging only for time necessary to attach them to cars.
        We make you the same price for car with baggage room as with-
out, as the extra cost of partitions will about cover what is saved in
seats. The style of smoking compartment you require necessitates extra
work, but in this case we will give you the price of our standard car,
as I am anxious to build a few cars with this style of smoker as I am
confident it is a considerable improvement on what we have been accustomed to. We figured on putting the same thickness of glass in partitions of smoker as in side lights of body, if bevel plate glass is
required there will be a slight extra cost.
        If you could arrange to come to Ottawa on Monday next the 9th
inst. I will meet you at the station and drive you to the shops, we
will have a car fitted up by that time and will have the Britannia cars
in stages which will enable you to see the construction, and have some
idea as regards the general appearance and finish. You will be able to
get through in plenty of time to catch the afternoon train back to Troy.
        I will be please to hear from you at an early date as if your
order is given at once we can put your cars through before the Quebec
order, which we will soon be ready to place on the floor.

                        Yours truly,
                        The Ottawa Car Company,
                            (signed) per W. W. Wylie,
                                Vice-Pres. and Man. Dir.

        The above offer is accepted for three 38 foot cars with
smoking and baggage compartments, subject to specifications as agreed,
upon this day, and all work to be subject to our inspection and approval. Copy of specification to follow and be part of this proposal and
acceptance. Two of these cars to be completed and delivered on cars
Ottawa in 60 days from date. The other two to be delivered in 95 days
from date.
                        Niagara St. Catharines & Toronto Ry. Co.
                            (signed) by J. A. Powers,
Ottawa, Ont.   Prest.
    Oct. 24th, 1899.

Top and Opposite: Copies of the memorandum of contract and
specifications for the first interurban cars, 1899.
(ONTARIO ELECTRIC RAILWAY HISTORICAL ASSOCIATION ARCHIVES)

LIST OF DETAILS

Cars to be built to our general specifications and according to our plan No. 65, combination passenger, smoker and baggage, 49 feet over all.

Steps to have three treads.

Material in curtains to be figured pantasote same as sample sent.

Car to have double floor, top floor to be laid diagonal and bottom floor laid level with bottom of sills.

veneer to be quartered oak.

Inside finish to be of mahogany. Extra cost of this not to exceed $100 per car.

Sash in vestibule to be stationary and made so as to be easily removed. Front sash to be made with top half to drop with small hinged light in center so as not to affect the view of a motor-man 5 ft. 8 in. tall.

Vestibule doors to be double hinged.

Front of vestibule to be covered with No. 14 steel plate extended around vestibule to the line of body and joint to be covered with suitable moulding.

Grab handles to be second growth hickory or white ash fitted into bronze sockets.

Seats in smoker to be covered with rattan and back to extend above sash rail, as shown in small car of Hull Electric Co. Seats in passenger compartment to be Walk-over No. 80-1/2 covered with figured plush as per sample which you are to send us. Inside casting to be the same as the one nearest aisle; this to allow for piping of heaters. Seat at baggag room partition and at bulks-head to be made about 1 foot longer and to seat three passengers.

Glass in top sash of side lights and in ventilator sash to be 32 oz., chipped centers with 3/4 inch clear border. Glass in bottom sash of side lights, vestibule sash, doors, smoker and baggage roompartitions to be 24 oz. If 32 oz glass is used the extra cost will be 11 ¢ per foot

Wiring for trolley to be either of two No. 4 rubber covered wires or one No. 2 and wired for hood switch in each vestibule. Light wire to be No. 14 rubber covered and to be wired in four circuits of five lights in each and arranged as per sketch given us, provision also to be made for attaching lights to trailers.
Foot gong to be 12 in.
Ball bearing ratchet brake handles.
Six parcel baskets to be used in passenger compartment. If any are required in smoker compartment please inform us. We will furnish you with the price of these baskets in a few days.
Car to be lettered "Niagara, St.Catharines & Toronto Ry." placed on side panels directly over the center of trucks. Style of lettering to be about 3-1/2 inch plain block letters. Car to be painted pullman car color and to be ornamented as shown in photograph which you intend sending us.

THE OTTAWA CAR CO., LTD.
W. W. Wylie,
V. P. & Man. Dir.

Non-Passenger Equipment

Number	Pre-1920 Number	Builder	Year	Seats	Length	Body Length	Width	Height	Weight	Motors	
II-1		NS&T	1927		28'6"						
1: Single-truck bonding car built using parts from Grand River Ry. open car.											
	18	Ruggles	1902		20'10"				28,000		
	19	Lewis & Fowler			22'9"				27,000		
20	I-1	NS&T	1918?		16'0"				18,000		
21	I-39										
22		NS&T	1920		44'9"	30'11"	7'5½"	13'3"	58,800	GE57	
22: Rebuilt with steel frame and trucks from 47 in 1947. To Oshawa 1960, scrapped 1965.											
23		McGuire-Cummings	1913		27'10"	24'1"	8'9"	11'6"	32,100	GE80	
I-24											
II-24		McGuire-Cummings	1913		27'10"	24'1"	8'9"	11'6"	32,100	GE80	
25					33'10"						
	I-30										
II-30	38	Russell	1918		41'10"		9'5½"	12'10"	56,000	GE216	
II-30: Tower added 1921. Arch-bar trucks replaced by Baldwins from 69 in 1940.											
I-31											
II-31		Russell	1911?		42'6"	36'8"	10'1½"	12'10"	63,300	GE216	
II-31: Possibly former No. 42 in Cleveland. Baldwin trucks from 66 in 1940.											

Top: Sweeper 23 in red paint, St. Catharines yard, c1948.
(R.T. VINCENT)

Opposite: Bonder No. 1, 1940s.
(CRHA, FONDS R.F. CORLEY)

Bottom: Line car 31 at work, Newman Hill, Niagara Falls.
(CRHA, FONDS LLOYD G. BAXTER)

Control	Truck	Truck Wheelbase	Truck Centres	Type	Disposition	Notes
				Bonder	Scr. 1950	Ret. 1940.
				Rotary	Scr. 1920	2 small rotors each end.
				Sweeper	Sold 1921	To St. Thomas Municpal Ry.
				Plow/Wrecker	Scr.	
				Plow	Scr. 1927	Cupola; flanger added 1920.
K-35	Taylor	6'0"	18'2½"	Sweeper		Rebuilt 1946. To Oshawa 1960.
K-10	Pedestal			Sweeper		ex Toronto Suburban 1924.
				Flat Car	Scr. 1928	
K-10	Pedestal			Sweeper	Scr. 6/1948	ex Toronto Suburban #3 1924.
				Plow	Scr. 1932	Probably ex Canadian Northern 1920.
				ST DE Plow	Scr. 1918	
K-35	Baldwin	6'6"	24'9½"	Plow/Line Car		Tower added 1921. Trucks ex #69 1940.
				Plow/Line Car	Scr. 1926	ex L&LE #52 1920; rebuilt.
K-35	Baldwin	6'0"	21'10"	Line Car		ex Cleveland & Eastern 1926, rebuilt.

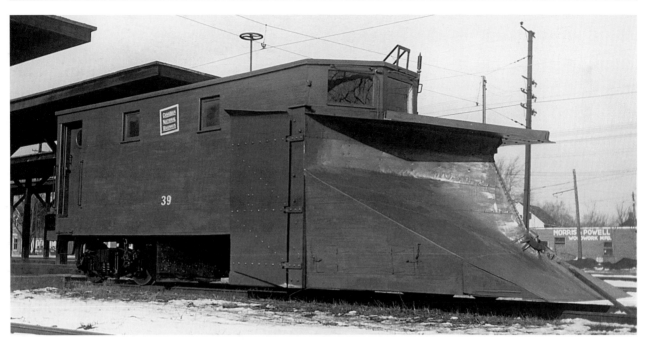

Top: Push snow plow 39, St. Catharines terminal 1945.
(J.D. KNOWLES)

Right: Express car 41 in green, St. Catharines yard, 1957.
(J.D. KNOWLES)

Number	Pre-1920 Number	Builder	Year	Seats	Length	Body Length	Width	Height	Weight	Motors
32		Reo	1920							
32: Body transferred from Reo to Leyland chassis 1924, put on rubber tires and sold 1928.										
33					28'2"					
36										
II-39		Russell	1911?							
39: Steel sheathed and wings added 1939.										
I-40		Kuhlman	1905?		39'0"					
II-40		Barney & Smith	1904		58'5"		8'7½"	13'4"	71,600	GE214
40: Wooden car with steel sheathing. Retired December 1954 account deteriorated sills.										
41		CP&A	1917?		58'6½"		8'6½"	13'2"	75,000	GE214
41: Wooden car with steel sheathing. Double-end but not symmetrical. Building data not definite. Much rebuilt on delivery from Cleveland.										
47										
47: Bought by Oshawa 1926 as No. 47, to NS&T 1939 and rebuilt. Trucks to 22 1946.										
	101		1899							
251		Preston	1920							

Top: Express car 40 before being steel sheathed, at St. Catharines yard May 20th 1932
(O.P. MAUS)

Bottom: NS&T centre cab flat motor plow 47 (ex Oshawa Railway 47 in 1939, previously Geneva, Seneca Falls & Auburn R.R.) at St. Catharines shops, April 12th 1941. Welding car no. 1 is on the right, uncompleted NS&T 83 on left.
(J.D. KNOWLES)

Control	Truck	Truck Wheelbase	Truck Centres	Type	Disposition	Notes
				Motor/Line Car	Sold 1930	
				ST Line Car	Scr. 1934	ex Toronto Suburban 1925.
				Bonder	Scr. 1920	Rebuilt from caboose.
				Plow		ex Cleveland & Eastern #41 or #44 1926.
				Express Car	Scr. 1919	Burnt 1916, rblt. 1918, not used.
HL	Baldwin	6'6"	33'10½"	Express Car	Scr. 1959	ex Cleveland & Eastern #55 1926.
HL	Baldwin	6'6"	35'4"	Express Car		ex Cleveland, Painesville & Ashtalbula #60 1927.
				Motor Plow	Scr. 10/1948	
				Motor Flat		Burnt 1902, rebuilt freight motor, ret. by 1919.
				Express Trailer	Scr. 12/1945	ex Toronto Suburban 1935 wrecker.

CHAPTER 14

Canadian National Transportation Ltd.

Note: This chapter is condensed from an article by Mr. John D. Knowles of Toronto as a history of Canadian National Transportation Ltd. road services. The NS&T was the first and most important component and provided major maintenance services for most CNT equipment. On account of the close relationship with the various operating territories, and frequent equipment exchanges, the NS&T should not be treated in isolation.

THE first operation of buses by the NS&T took place during track reconstruction in Niagara Falls when some old Toronto Transportation Commission vehicles were rented to provide a temporary substitute for street cars. NS&T entered the motor coach field on February 1st 1929 with a city bus route in St. Catharines, the Geneva-York loop. Two front-engine Yellow Coach buses were purchased and numbered 15 and 16. At the same time the opportunity was taken to enter the sightseeing and charter business, particularly between Port Dalhousie and Niagara Falls, with the purchase of highway coach 17, a British-built Leyland chassis and a body by Smith Brothers of Toronto. This coach was finished in the green and light cream uniform of the day and was lettered for Canadian National Electric Railways.

Eight further front-engine Yellow Coach vehicles were bought in 1930 and 1931 as bus operation expanded.

Highway Services

The first scheduled highway coach service commenced on January 16th 1931, replacing the Lake Shore Division. Leyland 17, the only highway coach at that time, was used when not in sightseeing or charter service. When it was not available, city-type Yellow coaches were used, though their smaller capacity necessitated double-heading rush-hour trips. In an effort to increase riding, all trips were routed via Virgil from August 27th 1931. However, the revenue amounted to about half the operating costs and the bus line was discontinued after April 30th 1932. Mr. F. I. Wherry operated a replacement service, and later sold the business to one of his drivers who adopted the name Niagara Coach Lines.

In 1931 Canadian National Transportation Ltd. was incorporated to operate highway truck and coach services for the CNR, and this name was eventually to appear on all NS&T coaches.

The next colour scheme adopted for the coaches was light red and yellowy cream, which was also used on local line streetcars and some interurbans. When the colours were again changed, a few buses and some trolleys of the 100, 129 and 301 groups were still in green and cream. The colours adopted in 1939 were red and desert sand. While the trolley colours were changed to CNR green in 1955, red and sand remained the CNT bus colours until the end.

Buses Replace Local Lines

The Victoria Lawn and Facer–Pelham bus routes in St. Catharines replaced streetcars on February 26th 1939 and also introduced the "transit type" bus to the NS&T in the form of Yellow Coach model 733, a small cab-over-engine design which was to remain popular with small bus systems long after production had ceased. Other similar units were added subsequently.

Oshawa's one streetcar route was abandoned and replaced by a comprehensive bus system covering the whole city on January 28th 1940. Nine Yellow Coach model TG2101s, an improved version of the 733, were purchased for this conversion. This model, being only seven feet wide, was well suited for operation on narrow residential

Opposite Top: Bus 16 at Niagara Falls terminal, 1946.
(R.T. VINCENT)

Right: 1930s NS&T help-wanted ad seeking bus drivers and brakemen.
(JOHN BURTNIAK COLLECTION, ST. CATHARINES MUSEUM)

Opposite Bottom: NS&T Thorold station with car 60 loading for Welland and Port Colborne in the distance and CNT 29 Yellow Coach leaving for Merritton and St. Catharines. June 19th 1943
(J.D. KNOWLES 20281)

streets, although it had only two-and-one seating. Before long, the NS&T was providing vehicles to bolster the Oshawa fleet, hard-pressed by wartime demands. The initial transfers were small Yellows and the Evans Autorailers, but exchanges of vehicles between the two properties were to continue as long as the Oshawa system remained in the Canadian National family.

CNT coach service was inaugurated between Victoriaville and Drummondville, Quebec on May 16th 1940 using new Ford cab-over-engine bus 101, which was to find its way to the NS&T in May 1942 when the service was discontinued.

Highway Operation Expands

A 170-mile coach route was introduced between Port Arthur and Geraldton, Ontario on September 9th 1940. This line traversed a wild, remote section of Northwestern Ontario noted mainly for gold and forest products. Although the route was 750 miles from St. Catharines by rail, the NS&T was closely associated with it over the years, both providing vehicles for, and obtaining vehicles from it. St. Catharines supplied the first two coaches, 27 and 32, while No. 36, ordered for the NS&T, was delivered new to the Lakehead in September 1940, and not shipped to St. Catharines until June 1943 when the Lakehead line was temporarily curtailed.

Conversion of the Main Line in the fall of 1940 caused the purchase of two new rear-engine highway coaches (nos. 37 and 38), and four 1929 Yellow coaches with Cadillac engines second-hand from Gray Coach Lines, Toronto. While not of modern design, the latter four were thoroughly reliable but rather small for GCL purposes. Five Yellow Coach model 739s, nos. 39-43, were considerably larger than other city-type Yellows purchased at this time

Top: Bus 33 meets car 82 at Niagara Falls, 1943. (R.T. VINCENT)

Opposite Top: CNR Evans Autorailer at Tower Inn Terminal, September 27th 1938. The General Brock Hotel forms the backdrop. (AL PATERSON COLLECTION)

Opposite Bottom: Car 82 at Thorold station on April 12th 1941 on run to Welland and Port Colborne, meets rented TTC bus 536 running to Merritton and St. Catharines. (J.D. KNOWLES 20596)

and were adequate to make Main Line runs when nos. 37 and 38 were not available. Nos. 39-43 were the first CNT buses to have a centre exit; the step well was employed on Main Line runs as a convenient location for express parcels. In February 1941, the immediate need for more buses resulted in the renting of TTC's 1930 Yellow Coaches Nos. 536, 539 and 546. These ran in St. Catharines with their TTC colours, numbers and insignia, but had CNT roll signs. Usual assignments were on St. Catharines local lines or Merritton–Thorold.

Wartime

Entry of the USA into World War II soon made the purchase of new buses difficult, and the small capacity of existing buses was inadequate to handle the growing ranks of war workers. Thus the streetcars, which had languished outside St. Catharines shops, soon found their way back into service, with shiny new paint jobs applied as time permitted. In mid-August 1941, the Dominion Government had announced appointment of a wartime Transit Controller, with very broad control over urban transit, interurban coach service, taxis, ferries, factories whose employees used such services, and over parking having any effect on the operation of these services or the movement

Top: CNT buses lined up at Port Dalhousie include Twin coaches 182, 180 and 181, CanCar-Brills 154 and 153 and unidentified 16? c1947. (ST. CATHARINES MUSEUM 4462)

Opposite: 1954 CNT timetable. (ADAM ZHELKA COLLECTION)

of war workers. In due course, the Transit Controller's office became greatly involved in the allotment of new and second-hand buses and street cars to operating companies. Of great concern was the conservation of tires, gasoline and vehicles, achieved by the elimination of bus services which duplicated or could be provided by the restoration of car lines, and elimination of all but a very few types of bus charter for purposes essential to the war effort, and which could not be provided by steam trains or trolley cars. Restoration of the Main Line, boat connection and St. Catharines local lines is discussed elsewhere.

For the duration of the war, American bus manufacturers ceased to paint new vehicles to customers' specifications, in order to simplify production, and because the purchaser was often designated by the Transit Controller after construction. Buses were turned out in a standard uniform, originally gloss khaki but later light grey and white, the latter being much easier to cover upon repaint.

Women appeared as bus drivers on the NS&T on September 3th 1943 and were also employed as garage mechanics' helpers.

New Coaches

With the cessation of hostilities in 1945, the system was still faced with a high level of ridership. In common with most other bus operators, the NS&T had to wait more than two years to obtain all the buses necessary for its immediate requirements. Thus most of the pre-war front-engine Yellows, including the original 1929 coaches 15 and 16, survived in service until 1947. In the immediate postwar period, bus operators often relieved the shortage of dependable highway coaches by sending late-model city buses out on the highway. Thus, CNT 70-series GM TG3608s went as far afield on charters as Toronto, with a spare wheel lashed in the exit stepwell for the occasion.

The Ford Motor Company continued in peacetime to produce its 27-passenger transit bus in the grey and white paint job only. Consequently, new Fords bought for Oshawa were sent to St. Catharines to be painted in CNT colours. The Twin Coach Company in 1945 announced introduction of a completely new line of buses, the body styling of which was quite advanced for this period. Torque-converter transmissions were employed at a time when other makers were still commonly providing "stick shifts" for city buses. Body construction was light by comparison with other makes. The NS&T eventually bought 12 units of various sizes. The first three were built in the Buffalo plant, but the remainder were assembled in Fort Erie, Ontario where Twin Coach for several years leased space in the Fleet Aircraft plant. Some of the these Twins eventually saw a period of service in Oshawa.

The postwar era saw the CNT numbering some buses in series by manufacturer, rather than the previous practice of numbering consecutively in order of purchase.

A prominent entrant into the Canadian bus business in 1945 was the Canadian Car & Foundry Company, which commenced manufacturing city and highway motor buses, as well as trolley coaches, in a plant at Fort William, Ontario as licensee for the designs of the J. G. Brill Company of Philadelphia. NS&T eventually bought fifteen model C-36 CanCar-Brills, numbered 150-164, the first four being manual shift and the rest automatic. In 1957, two similar vehicles were obtained second-hand for Oshawa, and ended up on the NS&T after service there.

CANADIAN NATIONAL BUS SERVICE
ST. CATHARINES — SANATORIUM — WELLAND — PORT COLBORNE

TIME TABLE — EFFECTIVE NOVEMBER 1st, 1954

Read Down   **Read Up**

Tues. Thurs. Sat. Sun.	Daily	Sun. Only	Daily Ex. Sun.	Daily Ex. Sun.	Eastern Standard Time	Daily Ex. Sun.	Daily Ex. Sun.	Daily	Tues. Thurs. Sat. Sun.	Sun. Only
p.m.	p.m.	p.m.	p.m.	a.m.		a.m.	p.m.	p.m.	p.m.	p.m.
....	....	....	....	....	Lv. St. Paul & William St. Ar.	....	....	....	....	....
....	....	....	....	....	Lv. James & St. Paul St. Ar.	....	....	....	....	....
8.00	6.51	5.38	3.00	8.25	Lv. Ontario & St. Paul St. Ar.	9.32	4.15	7.11	8.15	12.07
8.05	7.00	5.43	3.05	8 30	Lv. Sanatorium Ar.	9.27	4.10	7.00	8.10	12.02
....	....	6.03	3.25	8.50	Lv. Welland (Waterfields Ar.	9.07	3.47	....	....	11.42
....	....	6.07	3.29	8.54	Lv. Welland (King & 6th Ar.	9.00	3.40	....	....	11.35
....	....	6.23	....	....	Ar. Port Colborne Lv.	....	....	..	....	11.15
p.m.	p.m.	p.m.	p.m.	a.m.		a.m.	p.m.	p.m.	p.m.	p.m.

Bus tickets only may be purchased from operators, Geneva St., Terminal, St. Catharines C.N.R. Ticket Office and Waterfields Drug Store in Welland. Canada Coach Interline tickets will be honoured. Passengers should board buses in St. Catharines at Ontario & St. Paul St., in front of Goodrich Tire & Rubber Co. store.

TRAIN CONNECTIONS
CANADIAN NATIONAL BUS SERVICE
PORT COLBORNE — WELLAND — ST. CATHARINES — TORONTO

TIME TABLE — EFFECTIVE SEPTEMBER 26th, 1954

*Daily			Eastern Standard Time		†Daily Except Sunday	
North Bound—Read Down				South Bound—Read Up		
p.m. *	p.m. †	a.m. †		a.m. †	p.m. †	p.m. *
6.35	12.05	6.05	Lv. Port Colborne Ar.	11.15	5.10	11.15
6.49	12.19	6.19	Lv. Dain City Ar.	11.04	4.59	11.04
7.00	12.30	6.30	Lv. Welland Ar.	10.55	4.50	10.55
7.12	12.41	6.42	Lv. Turner's Corners Ar.	10.43	4.38	10.43
7.22	12.50	6.52	Lv. Sanatorium Ar.	10.35	4.30	10.35
....	....		Ont. & St. Paul Lv.	10.30	4.25	10.30
7.27	12.55	6.57	Lv. Glenridge Bridge	....	....	....
7.30	12.58	7.00	Ar. C.N.R. St. Catharines Lv.	10.20	4.15	10.20
7.40	1.17	7.09	Lv. C.N.R. St. Cath. (Rail) Ar.	10.20	4.10	10.17
8.45	2.05	7.55	Ar. Hamilton (Rail) Lv.	9.15	3.05	9.35
9.55	3.25	8.55	Ar. Toronto (Rail) Lv.	8.00	1.15	8.30
p.m.	p.m.	a.m.		a.m.	p.m.	p.m.

Rail Tickets may be purchased at C.N.R. Stations, Ticket Offices, or Sidey's Travel Bureau, Port Colborne

Additional trips are operated between St. Catharines, Sanatorium and Welland. For time table see reverse side. Secure time table from Ticket Agent or Bus Driver. Time tables are subject to change without notice.

Changes In Oshawa

The year 1951 saw replacement of Oshawa's original Yellow Coaches with new equipment. Many of the old buses were transferred to CNR maintenance-of-way service, painted dark blue and cream with their original numbers. These buses frequently appeared in St. Catharines shops in wintertime for overhaul. Thus began a trend which later saw several other NS&T buses transferred to the CNR for the same purpose.

Oshawa was then provided with the products of another US bus manufacturer which had set up a Canadian assembly plant, the Fitzjohn Coach Company of Muskegon, Michigan. This company from 1950 to its dissolution in 1958 had a large hangar building on the airport at

Top Left: CNT 126 CanCar-Brill model IC-37 at NS&T yards, St. Catharines, Ontario in 1954.
(R.T. VINCENT, ANDY DOUGLAS COLLECTION)

Top Right: Western Flyer "Standard" at the Royal Agricultural Winter Fair in Toronto on a charter on November 16th 1956.
(J.D. KNOWLES)

Brantford for its Canadian factory. The Fitzjohns, numbered 104-112, were never assigned to St. Catharines. These were rugged, dependable vehicles but being of cab-over-engine design, suffered from inconvenient front-vestibule arrangement. Fitzjohn later produced three sizes of a rear-engine model in Canada. NS&T ordered one such unit, No. 302, which was later transferred to Oshawa and eventually back to St. Catharines.

Another group of coaches purchased for Oshawa in 1951, Welles-Marmon-Herringtons 113-120, 400 and 401, were eventually well known in St. Catharines and Niagara Falls. This design had originally been produced by Ford, which decided to cease manufacturing city buses, and sold the business to the Marmon-Herrington Company of Indianapolis in 1950. The Welles Corporation of Windsor, which had already dealt in school buses, commenced operating the Canadian assembly business.

The year 1952 saw the arrival of the last "Cruiser" coaches bought new for NS&T, Nos. 255 and 256. These were Flxible-White "Visi-Coaches," a design originated by the Flxible [sic] Company of Loudonville, Ohio and distributed in Canada by the White Motor Company of Montreal from 1951 to 1954.

Equipment Shortages

No authorization for the purchase of further city buses was obtained from the CNR until 1957, when large GMC TDH4512s were obtained to eliminate rush-hour double-heading. In the meantime, the fleet of wartime and postwar Fords was gradually whittled down by sales, retirements and transfers to CNR track maintenance service. Since there was little hope of reducing bus requirements on either of the local line systems, the only method available was giving up relatively lucrative school bus contracts. This action served to permit the growth of competing Niagara Coach Lines.

The years 1953-56 saw the coming and going of various highway coaches, not only from the Lakehead, but from MacKenzie Thru Lines. The latter was a route from Boston to Nova Scotia's Cape Breton Island, operated in the tourist season. The former owners had become involved in a lawsuit brought by New Brunswick's principal highway coach operator due to the handling of local passengers, whereas MacKenzie's operating permit stipulated "closed-door" operation only. The owners sold out to the Maine

Central Railroad in 1951; CNR was designated as operator of the Canadian portion of the line and was later allowed to purchase it. Four 1949 Fitzjohn Duraliners came to the CNT with the line in November 1953, and all of them arrived at St. Catharines shops, 1050 miles from home, for overhaul. Such overhauls were always followed by a breaking-in period on NS&T routes. The Duraliners later at various times all served at the Lakehead. Three of them eventually returned to St. Catharines, and one of the three went on to Oshawa where the rest of the fleet consisted of city buses. Oshawa used it on school library charters. In the ensuing equipment shuffle, all four of the large Brill highway coaches originally purchased for the Lakehead spent time in St. Catharines.

Far-flung Operations

In December 1953, a 1951 Courier Model 50, which had been used to replace a mixed train on the Pacific coast, 2800 miles away, was received at St. Catharines. It was numbered 257 and was placed in service on the Port Colborne train connection. Two Courier 85s that CNR had purchased for MacKenzie Thru Lines came to St. Catharines for overhaul in January 1954. One entered service as 258, but before the other emerged from the shop, Mr. L.J. Henderson, Superintendent of Road Transport, gave orders that all new bus numbers were henceforth to be according to the year of construction. Thus 257 became 511. Mr. Henderson had been part owner of Western Ontario Motorways, a coach system centred on London, which had used this numbering system, also employed by numerous other bus systems.

MacKenzie Thru Lines got the three Couriers and Flxible 256 for the summers of 1954 and 1955. Two Duraliners went to the Lakehead between March and May 1954 in return for Brills 124-126 sent to the NS&T, but nos. 124 and 125 were later sent to the east coast along with 491 to replace a train between Charlottetown, Prince

Edward Island and Sackville, New Brunswick, commencing June 28th 1954. This was in effect for only one timetable and was never repeated, the buses being returned to St. Catharines in the fall.

In September 1955, Eastern Canadian Greyhound Lines Brill G1746 came to St. Catharines to be painted in CNR passenger train colours. CNR was discontinuing sending passenger cars from Windsor to Detroit via car ferry and Greyhound was to provide the replacement connection via tunnel.

Equipment Transfers

CNR discontinued the MacKenzie operation in 1956, selling out to Greyhound and thus reducing bus transfers. These movements had been made by rail, using large end-door boxcars of two CNR operations: Central Vermont 41000 series and Canadian National 589000 series. Only transfers to Oshawa had been made by road. NS&T was required to credit the MacKenzie operation with five cents per mile for all use made of their buses. As a result, strict orders were issued at St. Catharines against using them except as a last resort, or when charter customers requested them.

In the case of "permanent" bus transfers, capital and depreciation charges were transferred in lieu of levying a mileage rental fee. Superficially, these transfers appeared to make good use of vehicles in services of a seasonal nature, but in reality they created endless disputes over the condition of transferred vehicles, responsibility for defects, and the apportionment of costs for expensive repairs. Also, St. Catharines was on occasion ordered on short notice to send away coaches already booked for charters, and for which no substitutes were available.

In 1956, St. Catharines received three Western Flyer coaches formerly used on a 310-mile CNT line between Kamsack, Saskatchewan, The Pas and Flin Flon, Manitoba. They were numbered 531-533 by NS&T and used mainly in charter work. The Western Flyer and Motor Coach Industries (Courier) plants were both located in Winnipeg, Manitoba and specialized in building highway buses for unpaved western roads. Particular attention was given to strong frames, protection of the exhaust system from damage by flying stones, and prevention of the accumulation of clay mud under the body.

During 1957 and 1958, twelve GMC Model TDH4512 buses were delivered to St. Catharines, bringing about the only extensive use of diesel power on CNT's Ontario city operations. These were the last *city* buses bought new by CNT, although two MCI *highway* coaches for the Lakehead were the last actual buses purchased. In September 1958, highway Twin No. 254 was painted green, equipped with a small rear baggage compartment, and sent off permanently to Windsor to replace Greyhound Brill G1746 on the Detroit train connection.

When NS&T's last passenger rail service, Thorold–Welland–Port Colborne, was discontinued in March 1959,

Western Flyer coaches 531-533 were featured as the replacement. Actually, these coaches soon departed permanently for the CNR resort at Jasper, Alberta, with highway Twin 252 becoming the usual vehicle on the Port Colborne coach route. Later in 1959, CNT quietly bowed out of the charter business and the other highway coaches were disposed of.

City Operations Decline

When CNT announced its intention of withdrawing from Oshawa on December 31st 1959, a lengthy controversy resulted on the relative merits of private ownership, employee ownership or municipal ownership, with the latter winning out. The Oshawa Public Utilities Commission took over, buying CNT's nine Fitzjohns and twelve Marmon-Herrringtons. To give Oshawa this relatively standardized fleet, certain reassignments had been made, including the transfer of Brills 148-151 to the NS&T.

CNT also gave the required year's notice to withdraw from Niagara Falls effective September 1st 1960. The City of Niagara Falls and Stamford Township formed the Greater Niagara Transit Commission and ordered new buses, thus avoiding acquisition of any CNT vehicles. The actual changeover date was October 15th, the CNT providing the extra six weeks of service until the new operator was ready to take over. Equipment used in Niagara Falls had been quite a mixture of types, but CNT reduced its fleet by selling manual-shift Brills to Chambly Transport Limited of St. Lambert, Quebec; they were operated from a lot that had once been part of the right-of-way of the Montreal & Southern Counties Railway.

In the days of Niagara Falls streetcar operation, the few buses had been housed in a small garage near the CNR station. Now, with the conversion to all-bus operation, the carbarn opposite the end of Third Avenue, close to the Cyanamid plant, had been made into a bus garage; additional floor space was gained by removal of the equipment from the adjacent substation. Access was over a long driveway on the old Main Line right-of-way. The new Transit Commission, however, kept its buses at the Canada Coach Lines garage.

End of CNT Bus Operation

CNT services in the St. Catharines area were replaced by those of the St. Catharines Transit Commission on September 1st 1961. While the municipality had looked into the possibility of buying new vehicles, CNT offered an attractive price for the existing bus fleet. This had been standardized to twelve TDH4512s, eleven Brill "automatics" and twelve Twins, the oddments having been disposed of.

The long Fort William–Longlac line outlasted the other CNT bus operations, but was eventually sold to Greyhound, ending the bus operations of Canadian National Transportation Ltd. and leaving the company with only their extensive trucking network.

CHAPTER 15

Niagara Falls Park & River Railway (IRC)

THIS railway was incorporated in 1891 by E. B. Osler, Toronto, and R. B. Angus, Montreal. These men were connected with the Canadian Pacific Railway. It was, therefore, widely assumed to be a CPR promotion. Its charter rights extended from Fort Erie to Niagara-on-the-Lake, and included a water-level line at the bottom of the gorge on the Canadian side.

The whole Canadian bank of the Niagara River had been set aside in 1888 as a park under the jurisdiction of a body cumbersomely named the Queen Victoria Niagara Falls Parks Commissioners (since mercifully shortened to Niagara Parks Commission). The NFP&R line was to be largely on land owned by the Parks Commissioners and therefore, before construction was started, an agreement was made for operation of the railway for 40 years from September 1st 1892, the Commissioners to receive $10,000 annually as rental.

The line was opened on May 24th 1893 extending from Chippewa through Niagara Falls to Queenston. It was thus in a position to secure excursion traffic via steamers from both Toronto and Buffalo, as the two terminals were at the heads of navigation on the Niagara River from the respective cities. 56-lb. rails were used and 37 per cent of the original trackage was curved; sharp curves were protected by iron inner guard rails and outside wooden guard rails faced with angle iron. Minimum curve radius was 100 feet. Feeder and trolley wires were suspended from wooden poles except through the park where the feeder was underground and the wire was hung from ornamental iron poles with five lights in a cluster at the top. The earliest cars were built by Patterson & Corbin, though many later ones were built in the company shop.

Queenston

The tracks ran close to the edge of the Niagara Gorge between the Falls and Queenston Heights, giving an extremely fine view of the river. At Queenston it was necessary to descend the Niagara Escarpment to reach river level, a difference in level of 294 feet. The line therefore turned away from the river for 2,100 feet, falling on grades up to 5.7 per cent on a shelf cut into the rock face below Brock's Monument. It then reduced to single track and

Opposite Top: Car 584 decends Queenston grade, c1919. (NIAGARA FALLS (ONTARIO) PUBLIC LIBRARY D419951)

Opposite Bottom: NFP&R car 38 on the steel trestle crossing Bowman's Ravine at Thompson's Point by the Whirlpool on the Canadian side, c1900. Bridge replaced by fill 1903. (LIBRARY AND ARCHIVES CANADA E004665778)

made an abrupt reverse curve on a fill under which the highway passed. This fill was almost level, but the heavy downgrade then resumed, heading towards the river again. It ran through the village of Queenston on Queen and Dumfries streets, then, by making another U-turn on private right-of-way, ended close to the water at Queenston Dock. The first about-turn on the grade had a radius of only 115 feet. The total length of the line as originally built between Queenston Heights and the dock was 7,500 feet, though the two points are only 2,650 feet apart. Cars ascended the grade at a steady seven MPH pace.

From the beginning, close connections were made with steamers of the Niagara Navigation Company (after 1912 Canada Steamship Lines), and the railway could be called upon to transport up to 2,000 passengers in large groups four or five times a day, according to the sailing schedules. To handle these crowds, large open cars followed each other on the southbound trip up the grade at two-minute intervals, which meant that six or seven cars might be on the grade at any one time. A fifteen-minute base service was provided in the summer, but the line closed down in winter until 1895-96, when four daily trips were run.

Normal power demands were supplied by a pioneer hydraulic station at Niagara Falls, operating on a 62-foot head of water, containing three Thomson-Houston 200 kW generators. The tailrace, regarded as a notable engineering achievement at the time, was a 600-foot tunnel, 8'x10' in size, deep in the rock. The voltage was kept steady by the primitive method of diverting power through resistances when necessary.

A 300-HP steam "booster station" was located in Queenston to maintain voltage on the grade. It was used only between about June 1st and September 10th when the railway did 75 percent of its yearly business. This was a frame building, 100'x35' in size, housing two Wheelock reciprocating engines built by Goldie & McCulloch of Galt, Ontario driving two Canadian General Electric generators. Improved transmission techniques did away with the booster station after the turn of the century.

Early Prosperity

Business was good from the beginning. In the spring of 1894, the line was double-tracked from Chippewa to Dufferin Island and from the Whirlpool to Queenston. Track was also extended two miles south to Slater's Point. In 1898 the double track was extended from Dufferin Island to Table Rock, a total of twelve miles, leaving only short distances in Niagara Falls and Queenston where space did not permit doubling.

In 1892, the company purchased the Whirlpool Rapids Incline and two years later built the Clifton Incline, a cable-hauled incline railway on a fifty percent grade descending from Clifton House to the *Maid of the Mist* dock. These small craft have provided sightseeing cruises at the bottom of the gorge since 1846.

During 1895 almost exactly half a million passengers were carried, with receipts of $65,784 against expenses of $40,630. A correspondent for the *American Electrical Engineer* reported,

" ... The first thing that strikes an observer is the British solidity and massiveness of construction. The cars roll over the track as smoothly as billiard balls. A run was made last week from end to end — 11½ miles — in just over 29 minutes, a speed of 24 MPH. The rolling stock consists of four 28-foot ordinary box cars, ten open cars measuring 28 feet overall, and ten observation cars, all equipped with WP 50 HP motors. Besides the above motor cars, there are 18 open and closed trailer cars..... The track is built with 56-lb. CPR rails, with angle fish plates, laid on 8" x 6" cedar and tamarack ties spaced about 30" apart."

The "box cars" referred to were ordinary single-truck closed street cars.

The ten observation cars were described by a British visitor in 1895 as:

" .... specially constructed with two rows of seats, fitted lengthways of the car, one above the other and facing one way, so that everyone can get the view. The usual thing is to run one motor car and one trailer with over 150 people aboard".

Falls View Bridge

At this time, the only bridge for vehicular traffic was the Niagara–Clifton Suspension Bridge originally built in 1869 by the renowned Canadian engineer Samuel Keefer. It was the longest suspension bridge in the world (1268-foot span) but was only ten feet wide. It was widened and rebuilt with new main cables in 1888 but was severely damaged in a gale on January 10th 1889. A similar bridge was quickly built and opened on May 7th of the same year, but was dismantled in 1897 as it was not stiff enough to carry electric cars. It was replaced by the Falls View Bridge, also called the Upper Arch Bridge, by almost 300 feet the longest steel arch bridge on the world, having a clear span of 840 feet. The deck was 192 feet above the normal water level. The new span was opened on September 23rd 1897 when the mayors of the two towns of Niagara Falls met at the centre of the bridge for an impressive ceremony. The bridge company awarded an exclusive railway franchise to the NFP&R over spirited competition.

The bridge had double track, with overhead supported on ornamental iron centre poles. At first, the line was not connected to IRC rails on the American side owing to the refusal of the Commissioners of the State Reservation to approve the connecting route. Various problems prevented rail operation over the bridge until July 1st 1898 when a five-minute international service began, though a ceremonial trip had been made the previous evening.

In early days the NFP&R participated in low-priced through-excursion-fares offered by the Grand Trunk between points east of Grimsby to Niagara Falls, thence electric cars to Slater's Point and steamers to Buffalo.

Queenston Bridge

On July 21st 1899 the Queenston–Lewiston suspension bridge was opened. This was owned by the same interests as the Falls View Bridge and was 1,040 feet in span but the deck was only 65 feet above the water, so that the approaches were on a stiff grade. An earlier suspension bridge had been built at this location in 1852 but had been destroyed in a gale in February 1864 and never rebuilt. (Early suspension bridges were often destroyed in gales, since they would simply shake themselves apart until effective stiffening methods were developed.) The towers of the old bridge had been left in place with the useless cables spanning the gorge. Some of the tower masonry, including the cornerstones, was incorporated in the new towers, but the cables were those removed in 1897 from the Clifton bridge at Niagara Falls. Each cable was cut in half, doubled and reused, but in this form they were slightly too short, so that the final 75 feet at each end was constructed with a series of eye-bars. Despite this makeshift arrangement, the bridge proved to be quite sound and remained in use for motor traffic until 1963. The NFP&R built a new line from Queen Street via Kent Street and a short private right-of-way to the bridge approach.

The official opening was again the subject of formal celebrations by dignitaries of both countries, but those

Opposite Top: General view from Queenston Heights about 1899. NFP&R line to suspension bridge runs across bottom of picture: dock line emerges from Dumfries Street at centre left, crosses and reverses behind trees in right corner, then runs north along river. Steamer approaching the dock is probably the ferry *Ongiara*, while *Chippewa* is tied up at Lewiston, New York. Note the railway's "steam booster" station on the river bank.
(C. MARSH, COURTESY G. SEIBEL)

Opposite Bottom: NFP&R open cars at Queenston dock, about 1900. Note that most are trailers: only two motors are visible. *SS Chippewa* lasted on the Toronto–Queenston route until 1939.
(C. MARSH, COURTESY G. SEIBEL)

Top: An unusual view of four open cars at the short-lived Slater's Point dock, connecting with river steamer for Buffalo, 1900. The extension opened in 1898, closed c1902-03. Tracks were lifted 1905.
(STAMFORD KIWANIS, COURTESY G. SEIBEL)

Opposite Top: "Niagara Belt Line" car 681 on the US side at viewing platform across from the Whirlpool Rapids c1920. Cars operated in a clockwise direction, using equipment and trackage of the IRC (NFP&R Division) and the Niagara Gorge Railroad.
(ADAM ZHELKA COLLECTION)

Opposite Bottom: Niagara Gorge car No. 45, Niagara Falls, New York downtown 1932.
(JOHN BURTNIAK COLLECTION, ST. CATHARINES MUSEUM)

Circle Tours

Control of the NFP&R was acquired in April 1899 by the Buffalo Railway Company, which very soon was involved in the merger that produced the International Railway Company. The NFP&R became a wholly-owned subsidiary in 1901 and thereafter its former name was not generally used, though it continued to be referred to as the "Park & River" Division of the IRC.

Upon completion of the two bridges, a long-standing and very popular belt line excursion service was started in co-operation with the Niagara Gorge Railroad Company, whose line was located almost at water level from Lewiston to Niagara Falls, New York. Cars ran from Niagara Falls north atop the cliffs on the Canadian side to Queenston, then at the bottom of the gorge back to Niagara Falls again. Through tickets, and occasionally through cars, were provided from Buffalo via the IRC interurban line.

An operating agreement in 1900 allowed NS&T excursion trains to run from the foot of Bridge Street to Niagara Falls, New York over NFP&R rails. Regular NS&T services terminated on Bridge Street, however, and in 1906 a regular IRC shuttle service was inaugurated between that point and the American side.

In the early days some freight service was provided (the company reported over 38,000 tons in 1903) but this business had disappeared by 1908. Passenger business was the mainstay of the NFP&R, which increased as the Parks Commissioners and commercial interests improved the attractions in the Niagara Falls area. In 1904, the company posted the best operating ratio for Canadian electric railways. Its fleet that year comprised 41 passenger cars and three express/freight cars.

The Niagara Falls power plant was enlarged in 1904 and it may have been at this time that the "booster station" was closed. Headrace capacity was increased and the old turbines were overhauled. These had been installed in 1893 by William Kennedy & Sons of Owen Sound, Ontario. A new turbine by Jenckes Machine Company of Sherbrooke, Quebec, was installed, driving a 1,500 kW CGE generator.

from the Canadian side might have been excused for taking a "dim view" of the extravagant decorations, the chief component of which was a so-called "Annexation Arch" indicating the prevailing misapprehension (or hope) in the USA that Canada would before long become part of the United States of America.

The NFP&R at that time operated 13.7 miles of line, of which 11.4 miles was double track. The two miles between Chippewa and Slater's Point were intended only to connect with Buffalo steamers, but this business was lost on completion of a Buffalo–Niagara Falls interurban. The extension was not operated in some seasons and was torn up about 1905.

On February 12th 1906 the car barn, a short distance north of the Lower Arch Bridge, was burnt destroying thirteen open cars, fourteen closed cars and a snow plow. As this was most of the rolling stock owned by the line, cars had to be obtained from parent IRC, a situation that remained in effect until the end. Unfortunately, no even remotely modern cars were ever provided. A small sheet iron shed and an open yard replaced the burnt structure.

Queenston Disaster

On Wednesday July 7th 1915 occurred one of the worst electric railway accidents in Canadian history. A sudden shower had sent the participants in a Queenston Heights picnic, sponsored by two Toronto churches, running for the first car back to the Queenston dock shelter. Open car 685, grossly overloaded with 157 passengers crowded aboard, ran out of control on the Queenston grade and smashed off the line at a curve, killing fifteen and injuring many others. The motorman of the car and the General Manager of the IRC were charged with "slack observance of the rules" and arrested on August 4th but the charges were eventually dismissed.

More usefully, the Ontario Railway & Municipal Board conducted a thorough investigation of the line, and its findings were not very flattering to the management. It found that many spikes were loose or missing, rail on curves was badly worn and in some cases lacked guard rails, drainage was faulty and many ties were rotten. The precise cause of the accident was found to be a broken brake rod, rendering the brakes useless. To reduce the chance of another acci-

Top: Niagara Gorge Railroad private car "Rapids" on Canadian side at Table Rock, August 8th 1927.
(TED WICKSON COLLECTION)

Opposite Top: NFP&R car, upgrade from Queenston Dock, over new trackage. Excavation on left is for Power Plant line to MCRR, built during the summer of 1920.
(ONTARIO HYDRO ELECTRIC POWER COMMISSION)

Opposite Bottom: IRC "Niagara Belt Line" open car 685 on River Road at Tower Inn Terminal c1928.
(AL PATERSON COLLECTION)

dent, the Board ordered many changes to the railway and its equipment. The aforementioned deficiencies were to be corrected; an annual inspection of the rock was to be made where the line ran close to the edge; the Queenston grade was to be reduced to a maximum of 4.5 per cent (previously this had been the *average* figure); the sharp curve was to be eased and safety switches installed. Only four-motor cars were to be allowed on the grade, and specially-strengthened brake rods were to be installed. Standees were restricted to ten percent in excess of seating capacity in open cars and thirty percent in closed cars.

An inspection made in August 1916 showed that the 5.7 per cent grade had been reduced to 4.2 per cent and the sharp curve widened to 145-foot radius. A car was set running free down the grade without brakes, and it rounded the curve safely. Improvement in the mechanical equipment was shown when a car was slowed to a walking pace on the grade using motor resistance only.

INTERNATIONAL RAILWAY CO.
ONE CROSSING OVER
UPPER STEEL ARCH BRIDGE or
LEWISTON & QUEENSTON SUSPENSION BRIDGE.
A 84509 | 38 | VOID IF DETACHED.

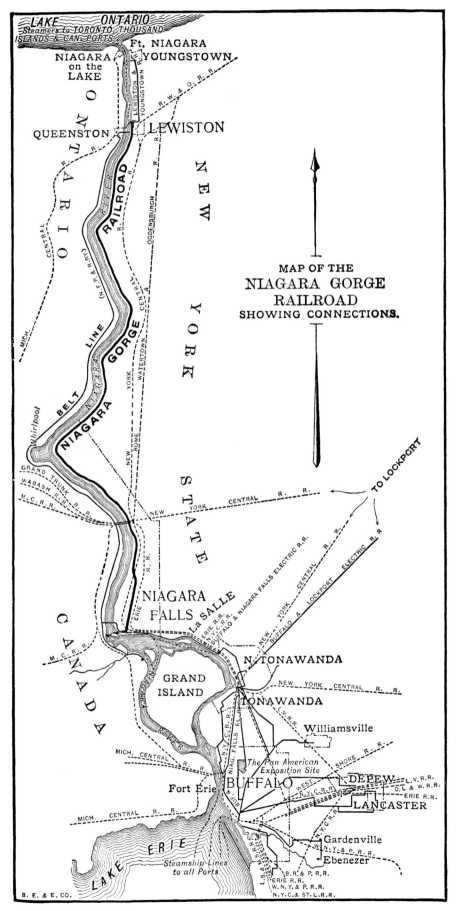

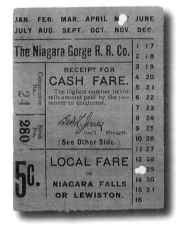

Opposite: NS&T car 65, one of two cars used in shuttle service over the Falls View Bridge between 1929 and 1932, photographed at Tower Inn Terminal circa 1930. Note "Canadian National Electric Railways" markings. Car also featured rare pinstriping as part of its neat appearance, in keeping with its special route assignment. (H.E. BATTEL COLLECTION)

Left: Figure 15.1 — Map of Niagara Gorge Railroad, showing "Belt Line" operated in conjunction with NFP&R, 1902. (TED WICKSON COLLECTION)

Dock Access

In 1920, the Hydro Electric Power Commission was building the first of its huge power developments in the Niagara area. This involved a large canal with its intake near Chippewa, swinging around the city of Niagara Falls and ending at the generating station near Queenston. The HEPC and the NFP&R co-operated in building an improved line to the Queenston dock, over part of which the Hydro had trackage rights for construction trains running from the Michigan Central to the new powerhouse at the bottom of the gorge south of the suspension bridge. The new line, instead of turning east into Dumfries Street, continued along Queen Street to the north end of the village, then made a comparatively easy half-circle on private right-of-way shared with the Hydro trains.

On June 24th 1928 the first one-man car was quietly put in service on the shuttle run (NS&T connection). Official permission had not been obtained, and the employees took the case to the Municipal Board, making the tiresomely familiar plea that one-man operation was unsafe. The Board observed that the one-man cars had been running for some time when the hearing was held, without ill effect, and granted permission for them to continue.

The End Approaches

Passenger traffic developed rapidly at first, increasing between 1903 and 1908 about 400 percent, to a total of 1,440,000 annually. Unfortunately, it never developed much beyond this figure, though a peak of about two million was briefly reached around 1923. Owing to the peculiar nature of the business, operating costs could not be reduced beyond a certain figure, so that deficits made their unwelcome appearance as early as 1918. This trend was linked to a drastic decline in business a little later, as shown by these figures: *1923*, 1,951,000 passengers; *1928*, 931,000; *1930*, 731,000; *1931*, 486,000; *1932 (9 months)*, 230,000. The highly seasonal nature of the traffic, the "peaks" inseparable from steamer sailings, and the complete lack of freight business meant that under modern conditions the railway was most unlikely ever to make expenses; in the last 2½ years the deficit totalled about $150,000. It must be said, however, that the cars were outmoded and unattractive, and IRC policies in the 1930s were emphatically not aimed at stimulating passenger business.

Whatever the cause, the railway notified the Niagara Parks Commission that it would not seek a renewal of the 1892 franchise, meaning that the operation would be giv-

en up on August 31st 1932. Later negotiations continued the service until the end of the summer peak period, but on September 11th the line ceased running and a separate bus service took over.

The 1892 agreement provided that the company would be bought out at the end of the term. The Commissioners offered $179,104 representing scrap value of the assets. This was refused, and the case was fought through the courts until it reached the Judicial Committee of the Privy Council (London), which decided that the company should be paid not on the basis of present value, but of replacement value less depreciation. Those who knew the line in its last years might have thought that the assets were one-hundred percent depreciated; nevertheless the IRC finally received $1,047,807.

So long did this process take that not until June 1935 could tenders be invited for dismantling the line.

Apart from the immediate area of the Falls, the right-of-way is now a well-maintained bicycle path, suggesting very well the excellent scenery to be seen from the electric cars. The Niagara Falls powerhouse, a handsome stone structure, is still in use by the Niagara Parks Commission, though not for power generation.

The Niagara Parks Commission assumed ownership of both incline railways formerly operated by the IRC. The Whirlpool Rapids Incline was closed in May 1934, following a serious fire. It was soon replaced by a bank of elevators known as the "Great Gorge Trip," which was renamed "Great Gorge Adventure" in 1989.

Equipment Assigned to the Park & River Division

Number	Seats	Control	Motors	Weight	Type
500-502, 504-505	57	B29	4-GE57	44,000	Closed
500s were rebuilt from 600s, as closed Pay-As-You Enter cars in 1912					
650-653, 655-656, 659, 668, 670, 673, 677-679, 682, 686-687	70	B8	4-GE57	37,000	Open
600s were part of a group of 50 built by Brill in 1900.					
684, 685	50?	B29	4-GE57	37,000	Open
722, 732	40	K6	4-GE67	42,460	Closed
737, 741, 746	40	K6	4-GE67	44,120	Closed
700s were probably built in the late 1890s.					
32	—	K14	4-GE57	44,650	Line Car

Top: Great Gorge car at entrance to
Upper Arch (Honeymoon) Bridge c1910.
(JOHN BURTNIAK COLLECTION, ST. CATHARINES MUSEUM)

Opposite: Niagara Belt Line car 647 poses with crew and passengers.
(LIBRARY AND ARCHIVES CANADA E004665777)

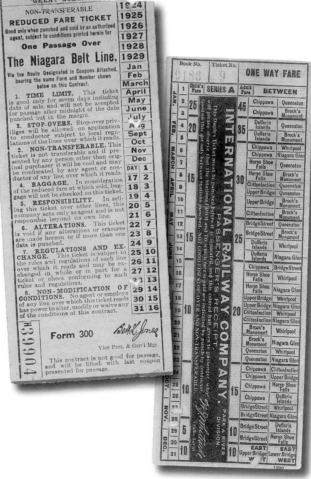

The Clifton Incline was renamed "Maid of the Mist Incline" in 1973. However, its small twelve-passenger cars could not handle the increased traffic that resulted from larger new vessels added to the *Maids of the Mist* fleet. At the close of the 1976 season, the incline was dismantled and a new incline constructed roughly on the same alignment. On May 14th 1977, the second Maid of the Mist Incline was inaugurated, with cars carrying 24 passengers and a trip time of just 45 seconds down to water level. However, this new incline railway still could not keep pace with the increased customer patronage resulting from newly-introduced sightseeing vessels *Maids of the Mist VI* and *VII*. Thus, after just fifteen seasons of operation, the last incline to carry passengers to the bottom of the gorge was abandoned in October 1990 (its remains partly visible today through the undergrowth). A high-capacity elevator service took over.

Niagara Falls today boasts one surviving funicular railway, the Falls Incline Railway (originally named the Horseshoe Falls Incline Railway), opened by the Niagara Parks Commission in 1966. It rises 100 feet, providing a direct link from Victoria Park to the commercial district on the heights of Table Rock.

CHAPTER 16

Niagara, Welland & Lake Erie Railway

THIS tiny railway, operating entirely in the town of Welland, has been almost unnoticed and information available is very scanty. It was the only section ever built of an interurban line that would have run from Niagara Falls through Welland and Port Colborne to Fort Erie. It would thus have been directly competitive with the NS&T then being built through the same territory. Why such duplication was considered at all is hard to understand.

The Welland section of the interurban was built first in order to secure rights in the town, since several other nebulous companies were being promoted at the time. The first spike was driven by the mayor on October 4th 1911 and service began the following January on 1.74 miles of track. This extended from the Grand Trunk station via East Main Street and South Main Street (later renamed King Street) to the Michigan Central crossing. Three cars were operated, the origin of which is unknown.

In 1913 the streets on which the line ran were paved with brick and the company agreed to pay the town $3,000 per year for twenty years, being the estimated interest on money borrowed by the town to pay the company's share of the paving costs. This payment was in lieu of all municipal taxes except, for some reason, the school tax.

During 1912 and 1913, track was laid on West Main Street and on North Main Street (later Niagara Street) to Elm Street in Parkway Heights. This was not operated, however, owing to a severe weight restriction on the Alexandra Swing Bridge over the Welland Canal. It was not until 1915 that permission was obtained to cross the bridge. Even then, those rights were granted only on condition that lighter cars were to be obtained. Wartime conditions prevented any action being taken.

In the year ending June 30th 1913, the company reported it had carried 377,177 passengers and earned $4,084; in the following year it carried 458,450 and earned $7,223. As of June 30th 1915, its reported mileage increased from 1.74 to 1.87 miles operated, but where the new track was located is unknown.

Futile Extensions

The track connection across the bridge was completed in 1922 and the West Main and Parkway Heights branches operated for the first time, using two new and lighter cars from an unknown source. One car made alternate trips on the two lines, giving approximately half-hourly service on each. Track mileage increased to 2.9.

These long-awaited extensions proved a sad disappointment, however, since they were so short that prospective passengers would walk rather than wait for the next car. The new lines were discontinued after only six months, though the tracks continued to be listed as operated in statistical reports until 1925. The rails were never removed, and much of the track was visible in the streets many decades later.

The original line, amounting to about 1½ miles, continued in operation largely for the benefit of employees of Page Hersey Tubes Limited, owners of the line, whose large plant was located near the southern terminus. Despite its small size, the railway managed to make ends meet for most of its life (as late as 1928 it reported a surplus of $2,296.19) though it is likely that Page Hersey underwrote some of the expenses. The end of the franchise period was approaching, however, and as the town was unwilling to take over the company, service ended the day the franchise expired, July 4th 1930.

Right: Niagara, Welland & Lake Erie Railway No. 50 (LIBRARY AND ARCHIVES CANADA E004465768)

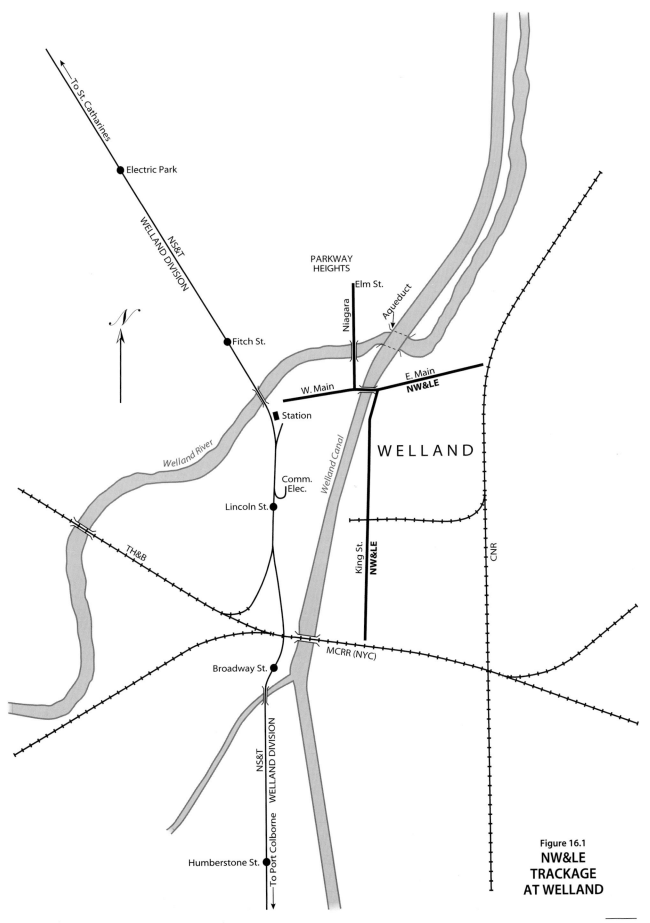

Figure 16.1
NW&LE TRACKAGE AT WELLAND

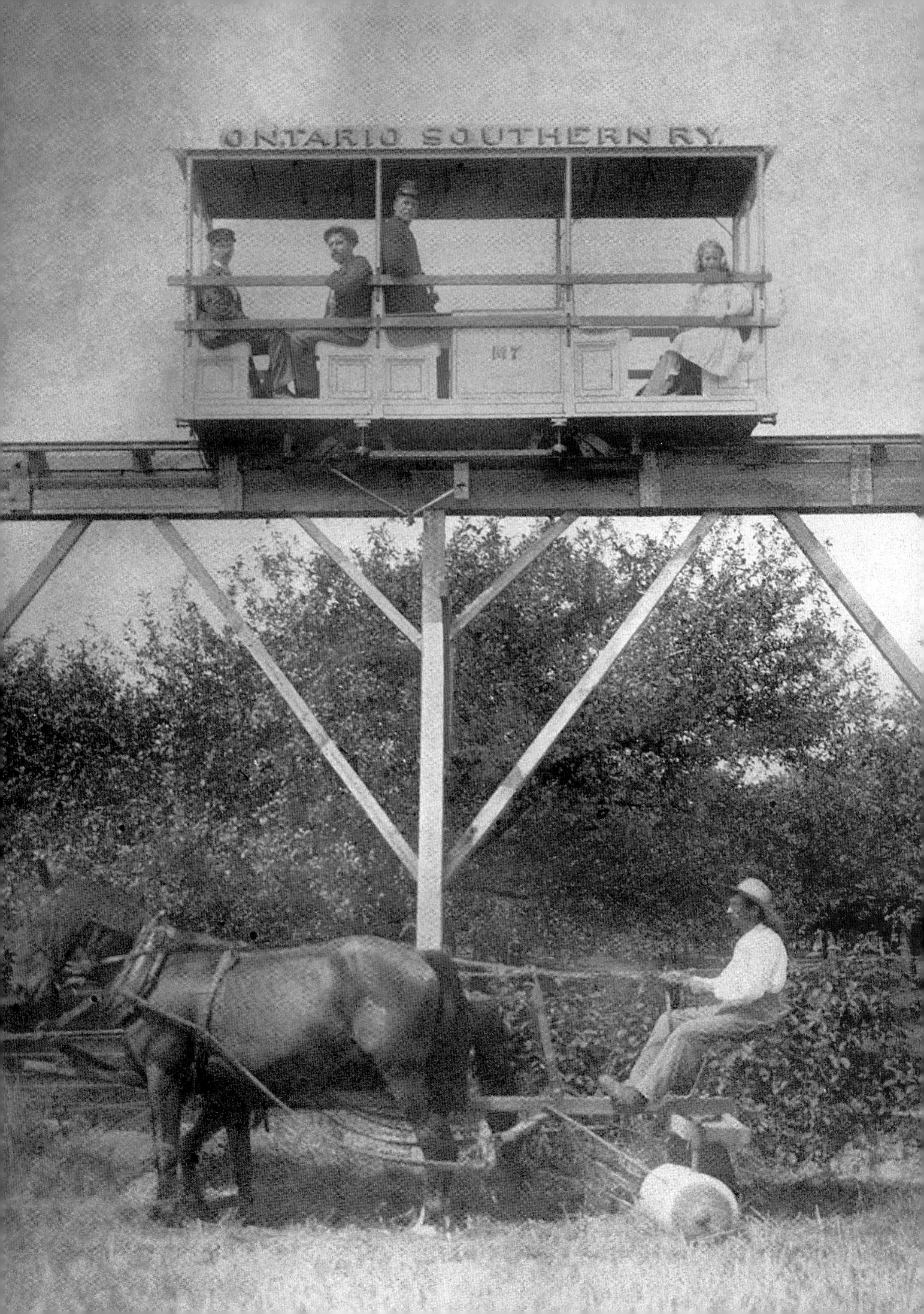
ONTARIO SOUTHERN RY.
117

CHAPTER 17

Ontario Southern Railway

THIS peculiar little line operated for only three seasons over a 1½ mile route between a railway connection at Ridgeway, Ontario and the popular Lake Erie amusement park at Crystal Beach. The promoter was Lina Beecher of Albion, New York who was said to be a high-pressure salesman pitching to gullible farmers. Beecher had promoted the "Waterport Electric Power & Railway Company" to build a single-rail line of his own design from Waterport to Lakeside, New York, some 4½ miles. A short experimental section was built in 1894 but nothing else resulted.

The Ontario Southern structure consisted of a single rail laid on a heavy wooden stringer mounted on eight-inch square posts, earning it the nickname "Peg Leg Railway." The height varied from ten to thirty feet above the ground, chosen so that farmers' carts could pass under the structure, since the line ran across farmlands and had no right-of-way. A heavy centre rail was flanked by lighter stabilizing guides (common angle iron) about eighteen inches to each side of the main rail, the under-side of which was contacted by small vertical guide wheels. The two cars, fifteen feet long and five feet wide, were little more than platforms supporting six three-passenger benches placed back-to-back in pairs, surmounted by a lightly-built roof. The power car had one five-HP motor driving a large drive wheel and carried a 55-cell battery slung below the body as a balancing aid. The line's only fatality was a cow that was killed when hit on the head by the battery cases.

The unusual railway began behind the Grand Trunk freight shed at Ridgeway and ended at the corner of Derby and Erie Streets, Crystal Beach. There was a wooden loading platform at the mid-point of the line. The highest structure was where the line crossed Beachville Road not far from Ridgeway. There was a short tunnel under the main highway and a ridge of land just outside the town.

The cars, said to weigh about 3,000 lbs. exclusive of electrical equipment, were built by Stuart & Felker of Thorold, who also built the fence-track. Top speed was about 25 MPH, when the cars would balance on the centre rail alone without help from the side wheels. Batteries were charged by an eight-HP steam-operated generator at the Beach, and the total electrical installation (probably transferred from Waterport) was designed by M. H. Johnson of Utica, New York.

Service started about July 15th 1896 on a rather haphazard basis. When all went well, a fifteen-minute service was provided for a nickel fare. "The Only Road of its Kind on Earth," exclaimed the handbills. "The Perfection of Safe Rapid Transit!" "Elegant Views of the Lake, Buffalo and surrounding Country. The quickest, cheapest, best and only way to the pretty village of Ridgeway in Comfort!" And so on. Departures from the Beach were heralded by whistle blasts from the generating plant.

Unfortunately, the batteries proved only marginally capable of hauling a loaded train up the hill northbound; after every heavy rain the oak uprights would sway in the softened earth and frost-heaving played havoc with alignments in the spring. A ride on this line was not for the faint-hearted, though no serious accident was ever reported. Nevertheless, many people took a single trial ride and no more.

At the end of the first season the line was declared (by the engineering press), "a failure, on account of inadequate construction and unfortunate designing," and management was taken over by E. Cutler of Ridgeway who had provided the lumber for the "fence-track." Apparently he had retained title to the timber, as he paid the former owners only $600 covering the generating plant and the cars.

Mr. Cutler operated the line in 1897 and, deciding that the batteries were more of a hindrance than a help, erected a trolley wire for the 1898 season. The battery charger was used to energize the wire, and the same five-HP motor drove the car. However, since most visitors came to Crystal Beach by steamer from Buffalo, nothing could remedy the basic problem — lack of passengers — so the line was closed down and dismantled after the 1898 season.

Opposite: Peg Leg Railway, 1896.
(FORT ERIE PUBLIC LIBRARY)

Top: Canada Customs, Crystal Beach, Fort Erie, c1925.
(NIAGARA FALLS (ONTARIO) PUBLIC LIBRARY D413793)

Bottom: Crystal Beach, *Canadiana* in the background, c1925.
(NIAGARA FALLS (ONTARIO) PUBLIC LIBRARY D12836)

Top: Ontario Southern Railway, Ridgeway and Crystal Beach, 1895.

Bottom: Crystal Beach — The Great White Way (walkway) and Dexter's Imperial Roller Skating Rink, c1920.

CHAPTER 18

Queenston Power Canal Construction Ry. (Hydro-Electric Power Commission)

WHILE industrial and similar lines that are not common carriers are outside the scope of this book, mention should be made of the extensive but short-lived electric railway operated by the Hydro-Electric Power Commission of Ontario in connection with power canal construction. During World War I, the Hydro Commission started the first of its developments at Niagara Falls. In order to obtain the maximum head of water, the generating station was located at Queenston, while the intake was obtained by reversing the flow of the Welland River above the Falls, and building a wide canal to Queenston. This gave a head of about 305 feet at the power house, enough to give a potential capacity estimated at about one million horsepower.

The canal is 8½ miles long. Its construction involved removal and dispersal of nine million cubic yards of earth and four million yards of rock, much of which was limestone and was crushed for use as concrete aggregate. The entire line of the canal was paralleled by a double-track electric railway 175 feet west of the centre line, on which an eventual fleet of 24 electric and seven steam locomo-

Opposite Top: HEPC locomotive E-1 and six dump cars, February 6th 1919.
(LIBRARY AND ARCHIVES CANADA E004666258)

Opposite Bottom: HEPC locomotive E-9 in service, November 6th 1919.
(LIBRARY AND ARCHIVES CANADA E004665765)

tives hauled trains continuously through two ten-hour daily shifts. Work started in 1918 and, when it was at its height, about 250 dump cars were run in trains of eight to ten cars. The first cut in earth to bedrock was made by track-mounted equipment, after which huge electrically-powered shovels, lifting eight yards in a single "bite," travelled along the exposed rock surface, dumping the crushed rock into a continuous procession of trains which took the spoil to a dispersal area northwest of Stamford. The 2½ mile branch leading to this area was one of the busiest railways in Canada, regularly carrying between 180 and 200 trains a day. The "main line" at its peak had about 65 miles of track (sidings included). Maximum grade was one per cent against loaded trains. The trolley wire was offset seven feet to clear crane booms and to permit the spoil to be dumped directly into the cars; it was supported in the dispersal area by square wooden towers that could be moved readily as the track was shifted.

There was a second separate line, which could be reached only by using the Michigan Central. This section extended almost to water level at Queenston and served the site of the generating station at the bottom of the gorge. The Hydro shared some trackage with the NF&R in this area. (See Chapter 15).

The Queenston plant was officially opened on December 28th 1921 and the railway was dismantled and the equipment dispersed. Most of the electric locomotives were sold to other Canadian electric lines.

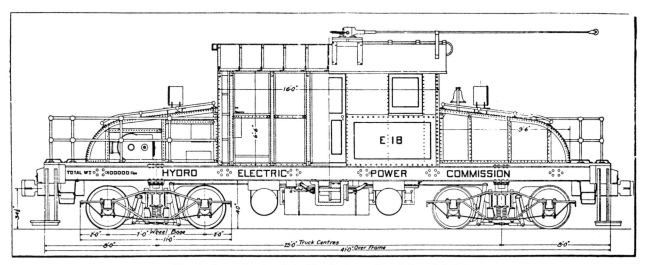

Electric Locomotive for Hydro-Electric Power Commission of Ontario.

Notes on the Locomotives

Series	Builder	Year	Weight Tons	Length Feet	Notes
E-1 to E-12	National Steel Car Co., Hamilton	1918	50	35	Arch-bar trucks. Multiple-unit control, six by Westinghouse, six by General Electric
E-13 to E-18	Canadian Car & Foundry Co., Montreal	1919	50	41	Arch-bar trucks. General Electric "M" control.
E-19 to E-20	National Steel Car Co., Hamilton	1919			Details lacking but very similar to E-13 series.
E-21	Baldwin-Westinghouse				Standard Baldwin-Westinghouse locomotive second-hand from Auburn & Syracuse Railway in 1919.
E-22 to E-24	Canadian Car & Foundry Co., Montreal	1920			Details lacking but virtually identical to E-13 series.

There is a record of five or six locomotives being purchased second-hand through a U.S. equipment dealer in 1917. They do not appear to have been used by HEPC and their electrical and other components may have been used in building some of the 1918 engines. All (except E-21) were assembled and finished off by HEPC from body shells provided by builders.

All locomotives had four trolley poles owing to the off-centre wire, and were equipped with extra air-compressor capacity for operation of air-operated dump cars as well as brakes. All were black with yellow striping and lettering.

There were in addition at various times a total of 22 steam engines, mostly 0-4-0 of both tank and tender types. Non-typical were ancient 4-4-0 no. 38 used on workers' trains, and a Whitcomb gasoline locomotive which was retained for use on the non-electrified low-level Queenston section. This part of the system remaining in place for over 25 years, though latterly disused. Additional equipment eventually included 319 dump cars, 26 flat cars, 16 box cars, 4 gondolas, 3 old coaches, 3 street cars, 11 speeders, 8 cranes and a plow. Shops and storage yards were at Whirlpool Yards, just south of the wye leading to the main disposal area.

Left: Cab interior of HEPC locomotive E-12, 1919. (R.J. SANDUSKY COLLECTION)

Disposition of Electric Locomotives

E-7, E-12 to E-17	To International Nickel Co., Sudbury, Ont. 1926 — Nos. 101-107
E-11	To Chatham, Wallaceburg & Lake Erie Ry. 1926 as No. 11; to INCo, Sudbury 1930 as No. 108
E-19 & E-20	To Shawinigan Falls Terminal Ry. as Nos. 3 & 6; No. 3 later to Quebec Railway Light & Power Co. as No. 33
E-21	To Toronto & York Radial Rys. as No. 2; to NS&T 1927 as No. 18
7 engines	To Steel Co. of Canada, Hamilton 1926 and most rebuilt for other uses
2 engines	To Quebec Railway Light & Power Co. 1924 as Nos. 31 and 32
1 engine	To Montreal & Southern Counties 1926 as No. 326; later Oshawa Ry. No. 326
2 engines	To Niagara, St. Catharines & Toronto 1926 as Nos. 16 and 17
1 engine	Not accounted for

Disposition data from Ray Corley

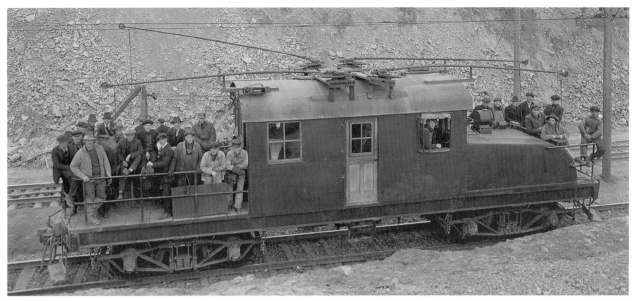

Left: Workers crowd HEPC locomotive E-16 on May 4th 1921.
(R.J. SANDUSKY COLLECTION)

Figure 18.1
HEPC TRACKAGE AT NIAGARA FALLS

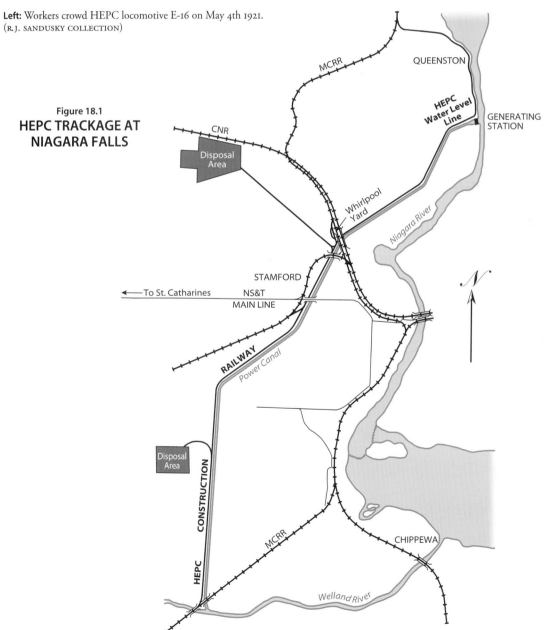

Top: 320 series car loads passengers at Port Dalhousie dock for a late afternoon inbound trip to St. Catharines, c1945.
(BRO. BERNARD POLINAK, S.J., COLLECTION OF RICHARD A. KRISAK)

Bottom: This same car, with its passenger complement, leaves Port Dalhousie dock and heads up the grade to the town's commercial district, en route to St. Catharines, c1945.
(BRO. BERNARD POLINAK, S.J., COLLECTION OF RICHARD A. KRISAK)

Top: Car 83 northbound approaching Welland.
(WILLIAM PHAROAH)

Bottom: Car 82 at Thorold station layover siding c1953.
(BILL VOLKMER)

Top: Cars 309 & 306 at St. Catharines shops, July 24th 1948. (J.W. HOOD)

Bottom: Cars 327 and 303 inbound on the Port Dalhousie line at Canning Siding, July 24th 1948. (J.W. HOOD)

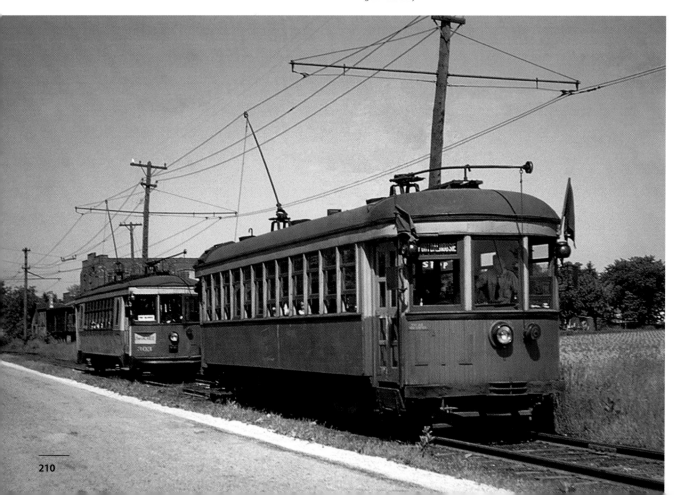

Top: Car 623 on regular run northbound on Welland Division, crossing Rice Road, just north of Fonthill, March 3rd 1956. (R.J. SANDUSKY)

Bottom: Chartered car 83 turning off Welland Avenue onto Geneva Street, July 29th 1956. Former terminal building is directly behind the car. (R.J. SANDUSKY)

NIAGARA FALLS PARK & RIVER RY.

THERE IS BUT

One way of seeing the Niagara River

With all its points of interest, thoroughly, cheaply, and quickly, and that is from the

Electric Cars of the Niagara Falls Park and River Railway

which skirts the edge of the Canadian bank from Queenston to Chippawa, a distance of thirteen and a half miles, following the route taken by Father Hennepin in 1678.

This road affords the only means of access to every point of interest on the river.

In its construction nothing was left undone that could in any way add to its safety or its convenience.; it is double tracked; the ballast is of broken stone; the ties are large; the rails are heavy and of the very best steel; the bridges are of steel, resting on abutments and pedestals of the finest masonry; all curves are thoroughly protected with guard rails and rail braces; in short, everything has been done to make it a model road. The cars are unusually strong and convenient; the trucks have solid steel wheels thirty-three inches in diameter, and extra large steel axles. Specially-designed observation cars are used, with three tiers of seats running longitudinally, from which passengers can view the scenery without rising from their seats, while for parties desiring a private car, the Company will provide one upon application being made in advance.

Description of the Route

On leaving the steamboat wharf at Queenston, we are carried along the edge of the river a short distance until we arrive opposite the Company's Queenston Power House, which was built to supply the electricity necessary for operating the long grade up the mountain. This grade is nearly a mile and a half long, and rises five feet in a hundred, the total height of the mountain being about three hundred and fifty feet.

—2—

NIAGARA FALLS PARK & RIVER RY.

We then turn away from the river and pass through the picturesque and historic village of

QUEENSTON

in which many an interesting tale of deeds done in days gone by can be gathered from the older residents. There are only about three hundred inhabitants now, although at one time it was a busy and prosperous town, being one end of the old Portage from Chippawa to Queenston, but the building of the Erie and Welland canals took most of its trade away.

Leaving the village, the road passes within a few feet of where General Brock was killed in the war of 1812; a stone erected by the Prince of Wales in 1860, marks the exact spot.

We are now passing over the famous battlefield of Queenston Heights.

As the car ascends the mountain side, a superb view is caught of the country below; seven miles away is Lake Ontario; on either side as far as the eye can reach lies the

Fruit Garden of Canada

while old Niagara, no longer a mad, seething torrent, slowly and majestically, as though wearied with its struggle for liberty, winds its way to the lake.

To the right of the track, as we ascend, on top of the heights, stands

BROCK'S MONUMENT

This was first erected in 1826, but destroye
1840. The present structure, built in 1853,
eighty-five feet high, standing on a base
The top is reached by a spiral stairway o
here one has a splendid view of the surrou
points of the compass, and on a clear day
is plainly distinguishable in the distance
Monument is a beautiful Park, in which
old Forts used in 1812, one of them being
state of preservation.

From here the railway keeps close to
the cars splendid views of the river and lov

Then comes the world-renowned

WHIRLPO

Here the river, taking an abrupt turn,
angle, and the tremendous force of the wa
opposite shore has worn a huge basin, the
pendicularly to a height of two hundred

—3—

NIAGARA FALLS PARK & RIVER RY.

and around this basin the current flows in great swirling eddies, and stumps and trees have been known to remain in the "Pool" for days, vainly seeking an outlet.

Leaving the water's edge, we find ourselves, in a few minutes on the Viaduct over the Whirlpool Ravine, from the centre of which we have a good view of the

Whirlpool Rapids

with the Suspension and Cantilever bridges, and the town of Niagara Falls in the distance. This Viaduct, built of steel, is 500 feet long and 135 feet high.

A few minutes more and we are back at the Whirlpool, looking across to where we were before, apparently only a stone's throw, but, in reality, half a mile away.

From there to the Company's Inclined Railway, the famous Whirlpool Rapids are in view all the way. No one should miss the opportunity of a trip down to the water's edge by the

INCLINED RAILWAY

as the view from the top, although very fine, is nothing in comparison with its impressive grandeur when seen from below. The channel here, being very narrow, causes the water to churn itself up into a boiling, leaping mass of foam, in its mad rush to escape.

Next comes the

Railway Suspension Bridge

This was first built of wood, with stone towers, in 1852, but
... and a steel structure built in its place.

NIAGARA FALLS

PARK & RIVER Railway

The Finest Electric Railway in the World.

NIAGARA FALLS PARK & RIVER RY.

Don't Fail To Take a Trip Over

The Whirlpool Route

The Best Equipped Electric Line On The Continent

Rock Ballast
No Dust....
No Smoke..
No Cinders..

THIS LINE affords the only satisfactory means of seeing every point of interest on the Canadian side, thoroughly, cheaply, and quickly, as it skirts the bank of the river the entire distance from Queenston to Chippawa, and stops at every point of interest on the way.

For rates or other information apply to
ROSS MACKENZIE, Manager
NIAGARA FALLS, ONT.

Top, Bottom and Right: Niagara Falls Park & River Railway brochure c1900.
(JOHN BURTNIAK COLLECTION, ST. CATHARINES MUSEUM)

NIAGARA FALLS PARK & RIVER RY.

From these bridges to the Falls proper, the water is smooth and unbroken, and of a beautiful emerald green.

Just before arriving at the Falls we pass the

New Foot and Carriage Suspension Bridge

This was first built, in 1869, of wood, but was rebuilt in 1889, entirely of steel; the span is twelve hundred and sixty-eight feet from centre to centre of towers.

Leaving the New Suspension Bridge, the car glides past the Clifton House, the best hotel on the Canadian side, and enters the

Queen Victoria Niagara Falls Park

which was established in accordance with an Act passed by the Legislature of Ontario, in 1885, in commemoration of Her Majesty's Jubilee. The commissioners appointed to carry out the work were Col. Sir Casimir S. Gzowski, A.D.C., and Messrs. J. W. Langmuir, J. Grant Macdonald, and J. A. Orchard, and through their efforts the Park has become what it is to-day,

The Very Embodiment of Loveliness

From it the tourist can view to the best possible advantage both the American and Canadian, or Horseshoe Falls.

The American Fall

exactly opposite, is 1000 feet wide, with a fall of approximately 160 feet.

The Horseshoe Fall

was so named on account of its shape at the time of christening, but since then its crest line has changed considerably; the contour is 2,600 feet in length, and its height is 158 feet. Within the confines of the park an

INCLINED RAILWAY

descends the bank to the landing of the Steamer

"MAID OF THE MIST"

and from its deck the most comprehensive view of both Falls may be had.

Directly opposite the Falls, in the Old Museum Building, Mr. S. Barnett, of the Board of Trade Restaurant, Toronto and House of Commons Restaurant, Ottawa, has established a

RESTAURANT

named the "Dufferin Cafe" which will be found to be first-class in every respect and the charge moderate. Special rates to excursion parties can be arranged by applying in advance to Mr. Barnett.

—[illegible]—

NIAGARA FALLS

Close to the edge of the Fa
House, which has a capacity
struction many difficulties wer
come. The water is taken fro
by a flume 200 feet long to th
of 62 feet on to the turbines
by a tunnel 600 feet long, discha
The power is conveyed by the proper shafting and belting to the dynamos in such a manner that any required number of these machines may be used as necessity demands.

At Table Rock House

close by, you may procure a rubber suit to go underneath the Falls by the elevator and tunnel constructed for that purpose. Here alone, at the foot of the

Great Cataract

can you begin to realize the stupendous volume and force of the water as it dashes itself into foam at your feet. Standing for a few moments, with that awful roar penetrating your whole being, and the angry gusts causing you to cling to the handrail for support, you begin to feel infinitely small and powerless in comparison with this great work of Nature.

From the Falls to the Islands, we skirt the edge of those beautiful rapids above, of which Nathaniel Parker Willis has said: "No one who has not seen this spectacle of turbulent grandeur can conceive with what force the swift and overwhelming waters are flung upwards. The rocks, whose soaring points show above the surface, seem tormented with supernatural agony, and fling off the wild and hurried waters as with the force of a giant's arm. Nearer the plunge of the fall the rapids become still more agitated, and it is impossible for the spectator to rid himself of the idea that they are conscious of the abyss to which they are hurrying, and struggle back in the very extremity of horror."

The car passes on to the

Dufferin Islands

which abound in shady pathways and quiet corners with such romantic names as **Lovers' Retreat, Ramblers' Rest, Lovers' Walk,** etc. **The Old Burning Spring** is but a few minutes' walk from these Islands.

We leave the Islands by a steel bridge of 400 feet span, and, crossing on our way the

Famous Battlefield

of Chippawa Creek, arrive at the flourishing village of Chippawa, which, like Queenston, was once a thriving town, but of late years its business has considerably fallen off. Chippawa is an

—6—

which plies between that point and ...

LUNDY'S LANE

This battlefield, the scene of one of the most decisive engagements of the war of 1812, is within easy reach of the railway, being about a mile west of the Falls. The battle ground is to be seen with its long trenches, and a few headstones to mark as many names of the slain. An Historical Society has been formed for the purpose of erecting a monument worthy of the occasion.

ALL OF THE FOLLOWING

Points of Interest

can be seen from the cars of the Niagara Falls Park and River Railway **without any charge other than the railway fare:**

American Falls (front view), Horseshoe Falls (front and side views), The Rapids above the Falls, The Queen Victoria Niagara Falls Park, Cedar Island, The Dufferin Islands, The Town and Battlefield of Chippawa, The Suspension and Cantilever Bridges, The Whirlpool Rapids, The Whirlpool, The Rapids below the Whirlpool, The Gorge, The View from the top of Queenston Heights of the River from Queenston to Lake Ontario, Brock's Monument, The Battlefield of Queenston Heights, The Stone erected by the Prince of Wales, marking the spot where General Brock fell.

Points of Interest

along the route where a small charge is made:

Brock's Monument	25 cents
Whirlpool Rapids Inclined Railway	25 cents
Railway Suspension Bridge	10 cents
New Suspension Bridge	25 cents
Clifton Inclined Railway	10 cents
Str. "Maid of the Mist" and Inclined Railway	50 cents
Table Rock House—Rubber Suit to go under the Falls	40 cents
Old Burning Spring	25 cents

NOTE.—At the Whirlpool Rapids Inclined Railway—the Old Burning-Spring—and for Guide and Rubber Suit for going under the Falls, the usual charge is 50 cents, but the Company's passengers are taken at the above reduced rates if tickets are purchased from agents or conductors.

Points of Connection

with other railways and steamboat lines:

AT QUEENSTON—Niagara Navigation Company's Steamboat Line to and from Toronto.
NIAGARA FALLS, ONT.—Grand Trunk, Erie and Michigan Central Railways.
CHIPPAWA—Michigan Central Railway.
R. & O. N. Company's Steamer "Columbian" to and from Buffalo.

NOTE.—Passengers arriving at Niagara Falls, New York, have only to walk across either of the Suspension Bridges, at the ends of which all the Company's trains stop.

—7—

Top and Left: Niagara Gorge Railroad Co. brochure c1927.
(JOHN BURTNIAK COLLECTION, ST. CATHARINES MUSEUM)

WHY NOT GO BY BOAT TO
TORONTO
TAKING ADVANTAGE OF A TRIP THROUGH THE GORGE
WHERE A CLOSEUP VIEW IS OBTAINED OF
THE WHIRLPOOL RAPIDS
No Automobile through the Gorge

Schedule via Niagara Gray Bus Line, Inc.—International Bus Corporation—Canada S. S. Lines, Ltd.
Between BUFFALO, N. Y., NIAGARA FALLS, N. Y., LEWISTON, N. Y., and TORONTO, ONT.

NORTHBOUND—Read Down / SOUTHBOUND—Read Up

May 31 Sept. 21 Daily	May 17 Oct. 4 Daily	May 18 Sept. 21 Daily	May 17 Oct. 5 Sun.only	May 17 Oct. 5 Ex. Sun.	Opening and Closing Dates of Service — EASTERN STANDARD TIME	May 17 Oct. 4 Ex. Sun.	May 17 Oct. 5 Sun.only	May 31 Sept. 21 Daily	May 17 Oct. 5 Daily	May 31 Sept. 21 Sun.only	May 31 Sept. 20 Ex. Sun.
PM 5.25 6.45	PM 3.45 5.05	AM 10.20 11.40	AM 8.20 9.40	AM 7.50 9.10	Lv........Buffalo, Terrace......Ar. Ar...Niagara Falls, Gorge Terminal..Lv.	AM 11.25 10.00	AM 11.55 10.30	PM 12.55 11.30	PM 6.10 4.45	PM 8.25 7.00	PM 9.00 7.35
6.50 6.52 7.15	5.10 5.12 5.35	11.45 11.47 12.10	9.45 9.47 10.15	9.15 9.17 9.40	Lv..Niagara Falls, Gorge Terminal..Ar. Lv..Niagara Falls, N. Y. C. Station..Ar. Ar........Lewiston, Gray Bus......Lv.	10.00 9.57 9.35	10.30 10.27 10.05	11.30 11.27 11.05	4.45 4.42 4.20	7.00 6.58 6.35	7.35 7.32 7.10
7.15 10.00 PM	5.35 8.30 PM	12.10 * 2.45 PM	10.15 12.40 PM	9.40 12.40 PM	Lv....Lewiston, Canada SS. Lines....Ar. Ar....Toronto, Canada SS. Lines....Lv.	9.30 6.45 AM	10.00 7.15 AM	11.00 8.15 AM	4.15 1.15 PM	6.30 3.30 PM	7.05 4.40 PM

* Connects with Montreal Steamer.
In Niagara Falls, busses arrive and depart from Great Gorge Route Terminal, making connections with N. Y. C. R. R., International High Speed Cars and International Bus Line to and from Buffalo.
No local passengers carried within City of Niagara Falls.

Schedule between BUFFALO and TORONTO via Niagara Falls and the International Railway Co.
NORTHBOUND—Read Down / SOUTHBOUND—Read Up

May 31 Sept. 21 Daily	May 17 Oct. 5 Daily	May 18 Sept. 22 Daily	May 17 Oct. 5 Sun.only	May 17 Oct. 4 Ex. Sun.	Opening and Closing Dates of Service — EASTERN STANDARD TIME	May 17 Oct. 4 Ex. Sun.	May 17 Oct. 5 Sun.only	May 31 Sept. 21 Daily	May 17 Oct. 5 Daily	June 1 Sept. 21 Sun.only	May 31 Sept. 20 Ex. Sun.
PM 5.20 6.30	PM 3.20 4.30	AM 9.50 11.00	AM 8.00 9.00	AM 7.20 8.20	Lv......Buffalo, I. R. C. Terminal....Ar. Ar...Niagara Falls, I. R. C. Terminal...Lv.	AM 11.28 10.20	PM 12.23 11.20	PM 12.58 11.50	PM 6.30 5.20	PM 8.23 7.20	PM 9.03 7.50
6.30 7.10	4.52 5.30	11.25 12.05	9.30 10.10	8.55 9.35	Lv....Niagara Falls, Gorge Route....Ar. Ar.......Lewiston, Gorge Route......Lv.	10.15 9.35	10.45 10.05	11.45 11.05	5.00 4.20	7.05 6.25	7.50 7.10
7.15 10.00 PM	5.35 8.30 PM	12.10 * 2.45 PM	10.15 12.40 PM	9.40 12.40 PM	Lv....Lewiston, Canada SS. Lines....Ar. Ar....Toronto, Canada SS. Lines....Lv.	9.30 6.45 AM	10.00 7.15 AM	11.00 8.15 AM	4.15 1.15 PM	6.20 3.30 PM	7.05 4.40 PM

* Connects with Montreal Boat.

Schedule between BUFFALO and TORONTO via Niagara Falls and the New York Central R. R.
NORTHBOUND—Read Down / SOUTHBOUND—Read Up

May 31 Sept. 21 Daily	May 17 Oct. 5 Daily	May 31 Sept. 22 Daily	May 17 Oct. 5 Sun.only	May 17 Oct. 4 Ex. Sun.	Opening and Closing Dates of Service — EASTERN STANDARD TIME	May 17 Oct. 4 Ex. Sun.	May 18 Oct. 5 Sun.only	May 31 Sept. 21 Daily	May 17 Oct. 5 Daily	June 1 Sept. 21 Sun.only	May 31 Sept. 20 Ex. Sun.
PM 5.25 6.23	PM 2.30 3.30	AM 10.20 11.20	AM 8.20 9.20	AM 7.15 8.05	Lv......Buffalo, N. Y. C. Station......Ar. Ar....Niagara Falls, N. Y. C. Station....Lv.	AM 11.52 10.15	PM 12.35 11.35	PM 2.20 1.25	PM 6.13 5.15	PM 9.23 8.25	PM 9.23 8.25
6.30 7.10	4.50 5.30	11.25 12.05	9.30 10.10	8.55 9.35	Lv....Niagara Falls, Gorge Route....Ar. Ar.......Lewiston, Gorge Route......Lv.	10.15 9.35	10.45 10.05	11.45 11.05	5.00 4.20	7.05 6.25	7.50 7.10
7.15 10.00 PM	5.35 8.30 PM	12.10 * 2.45 PM	10.15 12.40 PM	9.40 12.40 PM	Lv....Lewiston, Canada SS. Lines....Ar. Ar....Toronto, Canada SS. Lines....Lv.	9.30 6.45 AM	10.00 7.15 AM	11.00 8.15 AM	4.15 1.15 PM	6.20 3.30 PM	7.05 4.40 PM

* Connects with Montreal Boat.

The Niagara Gorge Railroad Company is not responsible for errors in time tables, inconvenience or damage resulting from delayed trains or boats, or failure to make connections, but in so far as possible, connections will be protected. Schedules herein are subject to change without notice.

For tickets or further information apply to any railroad or tourist agent, or
BUFFALO—Canada Steamship Lines, Stock Exchange Building, Consolidated Ticket Office, 156 Pearl Street; International Railway Co., 7 Terrace; New York Central Stations.
NIAGARA FALLS—Great Gorge Route Terminal, Foot of Falls Street.
TORONTO—Canada Steamship Lines, Yonge Street or Dock.
GEO. H. STAGG, *Gen. Pass. Agt.*, The Niagara Gorge R. R. Co., Niagara Falls, N. Y.

The fares from Niagara Falls to Toronto are so reasonable that they are within the reach of all:
One way $1.95
Two-day round trip . 3.00
Thirty-day round trip, 3.60
Children between the ages of 5 and 12 one-half fare.

1   2

Souvenir ribbons given to employees
attending 1902 and 1914 annual summer
picnics at Lakeside Park, during the time
of Canadian Northern Railway ownership.
(ST. CATHARINES MUSEUM COLLECTION)

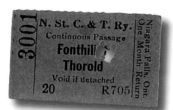

Ticket.
(ADAM ZHELKA COLLECTION)

IRC Ticket.
(ADAM ZHELKA COLLECTION)

Employee pass, front and back.
(ADAM ZHELKA COLLECTION)

Receipt.
(ADAM ZHELKA COLLECTION)

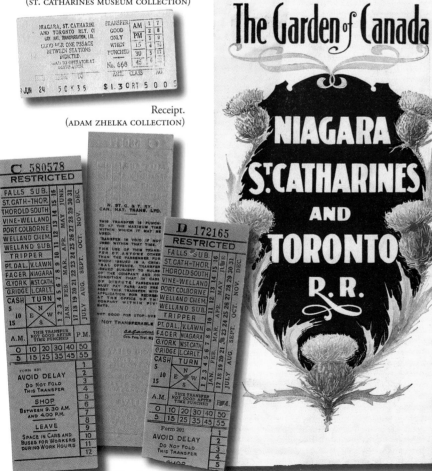

Transfers.
(J.M. MILLS AND
ADAM ZHELKA COLLECTIONS)

Pamphlet cover.
(R.J. SANDUSKY COLLECTION)

Printer's proof of 12-trip ticket.
(PUBLISHER'S COLLECTION)

SEE!
NIAGARA FALLS
"SCENIC HISTORIC"
CARS LEAVE HERE EVERY
HOUR AT 35 MINUTES
AFTER THE HOUR
ADULTS RETURN 65¢
CHILDREN RETURN 35¢
PURCHASE TICKETS AT OFFICE

INSPECTOR

Clockwise from top left: "Toronto" type farebox (possibly surplus from TTC buses leased during WWII); fare sign; inspector's embroidered cloth shoulder patch c1940; farebox manufactured by Canadian Cleveland Farebox Co. of Preston, Ontario c1914 and initially used on new 130-series interurban cars built locally; transfer cutter used on local lines (probably streetcars and buses) c1940; coin changer used by conductors or motormen on one-man cars c1940; CNR uniform button c1940; and "coffee pot" farebox, a hand-me-down from the Toronto Railway Company or other CNoR subsidiary electric railway, last used to collect tickets for rides at Lakeside Park.
(TED WICKSON,
ARTIFACTS COURTESY OF
ST. CATHARINES MUSEUM)

Left: Model of car no. 3 with original Van Depoele current collection system. Scratchbuilt by David Haire for Philip Spencer, subsequently donated to St. Catharines Museum.
(TED WICKSON,
ARTIFACTS COURTESY OF
ST. CATHARINES MUSEUM)

CHAPTER 19

Rail Enthusiasts and the NS&T

For two decades, commencing in 1940, the NS&T played host to many railfan excursions over its lines. Management was usually very accommodating towards routing and equipment requests made by enthusiast groups. The diversity of rolling stock (especially "boomer" cars), livery and unique physical plant appealed to many traction fans who also made many independent trips to ride and photograph regular service on the NS&T. Its lake boats also did not escape the attention of marine enthusiasts. Photographs appearing in this chapter were taken on some of these fantrips. Other views of these special movements may be found in earlier chapters.

The two most frequent charter customers were the National Railroad Historical Society (Buffalo Chapter) and the Upper Canada Railway Society (based in Toronto). Often, the two clubs collaborated on joint excursions. The following is a detailed account of the first NS&T charter by the UCRS on June 13th 1943, as reported on its 20th anniversary in the Society's *Newsletter* of June 1963. An excursion photographer captured the event as seen on page 222.

Fantrips!
A 20th ANNIVERSARY OF ONE

By J. William Hood and Stuart I. Westland
All Photos by J. W. Hood

Exactly 20 years ago this month, on June 13th 1943, the Upper Canada Railway Society, then less than two years old, sponsored its first charter fantrip. The trip, co-sponsored with the Buffalo Chapter of the National Railway Historical Society, consisted of a seven hour tour of the lines of the Niagara, St. Catharines and Toronto Railway, and used newly-refurbished car 83, which was making its first revenue run in almost 12 years.

The events leading up to this excursion are very interesting to relate. In 1924 and 1925, the St. Catharines shops of the NS&T built two new cars for the Toronto Suburban Railway, another Canadian National Electric Railways property. These two cars, #107, which was a straight coach, and #108, a combination baggage-passenger car, provided most of the base

service on the TSR up until the time of the line's abandonment on August 15th 1931. Following abandonment, 107 and 108 were placed in storage at the Lambton Carhouse, along with the other equipment of the railway. In 1935, when all the legal aspects of the abandonment had been disposed of, some of the cars were scrapped, while others were transferred to other CNER lines. Nos. 107 and 108 came to the NS&T, where it was planned to rebuild them and place them in service as 83 and 84, respectively. During the late thirties, some work was done on 107, but following the discontinuance of service on the Niagara Falls Subdivision, and the resulting surplus of cars, no further work was done, and both cars were shoved out into the boneyard to rust away. In 1942, the Montreal & Southern Counties Railway, again another CNER property, decided that they had a need for a new snowplow, so car 108 was shipped to Montreal and rebuilt as M&SC 300, and saw many years of service in this guise. Meanwhile, in St. Catharines, the NS&T had been ordered by the Department of Transport to restore interurban service on the Niagara Falls line because of the war. The increased traffic thus generated brought on a shortage of cars, and the management's eyes turned again to the hulk of 107 sitting in the corner. The final stages of the rebuilding of the car were completed about the middle of May 1943, and 107 emerged from the shops, resplendent in red and grey livery, as NS&T no. 83. It was then that the Upper Canada Railway Society and the National Railway Historical Society approached the railway and arranged for the chartering of the car before it entered regular service.

It is believed that this was the first charter excursion operated by a Canadian railway enthusiasts' group. It was not the first such operation in Canada, however, as this honour apparently falls to a trip operated on the London & Port Stanley Railway in 1941 by the Railroad Enthusiasts of Rochester, New York.

Present day members of the Society, used to an abundance of railway charter excursions of all types, will probably find it difficult to imagine what a rare event a fantrip was in 1943. This was during the height of World War II and railway enthusiast activities, which had begun to flourish in the United States and to a lesser degree in Canada during the late 1930s, had been dealt a body blow during 1940 and 1941. Not only were excursions just not possible on most railways during the war because of security restrictions and the shortage of equipment, but in addition the loss of members of the railway societies to the armed forces depleted numbers to the point where many such groups found it difficult to carry on. At one point during 1943 there were only twelve resident members of the UCRS in the City of Toronto.

Opposite Top: Car 82 at Thorold, July 1955.
(KENNETH F. CHIVERS, C. ROBERT CRAIG MEMORIAL LIBRARY, CI-CSI399)

Opposite Bottom: NS&T regular run car 623 laying over at Thorold station (Main Street), March 14th 1959.
(R.J. SANDUSKY)

It was under these unfavourable circumstances that the Directors of the UCRS resolved to operate a charter trip, as the return to service of the historic car 107 of the Toronto Suburban Railway as NS&T 83 was an event worth taking a long chance on. While the degree of financial involvement was small in contrast to that of today's excursions, it looked large in those days. There was no mailing list, no known "fan-trip clientele", and no way of obtaining newspaper or radio advertising. Intention of the Society to operate the trip was circulated by word of mouth among the Toronto members and presumably much the same was done in Buffalo. Individual hand-written letters were sent to Associate members resident elsewhere in Ontario urging them to attend the excursion.

Somehow, by dint of hard work and enthusiasm on the part of the UCRS members who arranged the trip, a total of 76 persons turned up at Bridge Street, Niagara Falls on the morning of June 13th, 1943 to await the arrival of the resplendent car 83. This would be a respectable total for an electric trip today, but at the time it was nothing short of phenomenal.

Such are the events leading up to the excursion. Now for the trip itself. The fans from Toronto arrived at the CNR Bridge Street station in Niagara Falls on train 101, while the Buffalo group travelled by the New York Central to the Suspension Bridge and crossed over there. Promptly at 11:00 AM, 83 came rolling down Bridge Street to pick up the two groups, and the trip began. A fast run was made over the main line to St. Catharines, where the car switched over to the Port Dalhousie line for the trip to Lakeside Park at Port Dalhousie. Here the railfans had lunch at the Lakeside Inn, and many photos were taken of the new car, the regular service cars, and the two boats bringing crowds of picnickers from Toronto for a day's outing at the Falls.

Following the lunch period, the excursion made its way back to St. Catharines for a two-hour tour of the railway's shops. Here the fans lost no time in photographing the many various and interesting types of cars in the yards. After the tour was completed, car 83 was exchanged for one of the classic arch-windowed wooden interurbans which were so popular on the NS&T, No. 130. Leaving the shops, 130 traversed the main line to Substation Junction, at Thorold, where the Welland Subdivision branched off to Port Colborne. An interesting sidelight at Substation Junction was seeing car 82 sitting in the siding, with its pilot, front steps and anti-climber damaged, and the front pole missing. Investigation revealed that the car had just been involved in a level crossing accident, and was on its way to the shops.

Opposite Top: Cars 135 and 134 at Port Colborne station, looking east. July 28th 1940.
(ADDISON LAKE COLLECTION, COURTESY FRED ANGUS)

Opposite Bottom: Car 80 on Port Weller line meets "Bessy" the cow, November 2nd 1952.
(J.M. MILLS)

An uneventful run was made over the Welland Subdivision, destined to be the last strong-hold of passenger service on the NS&T, and Port Colborne was soon reached. The return trip to Substation Junction was made, and 130 swung onto the rails of the Falls Subdivision again for the final leg of the excursion to Niagara Falls. While winding its way through the city streets to the CNR station, 130 dug its pilot into the roadway at the corner of Queen and Erie streets, breaking the braces. From here the car limped down to Bridge Street with the pilot digging a rut in the asphalt.

Upon arriving at the end of the line, the two groups bade farewell to the NS&T, and departed for their respective cities, well satisfied with a very enjoyable day's travel.

The following is the timetable used on the June 13th, 1943, trip:

TORONTO GROUP

8:00 AM: Leave Toronto on CNR train #101-102.

10:50 AM: Arrive Niagara Falls, Ontario (Bridge Street).

BUFFALO GROUP

9:15 AM: Leave Buffalo on New York Central train #211.

10:31 AM: Arrive Suspension Bridge, New York.

11:00 AM: Party will board NS&TRy car #83 at the Canadian end of the Whirlpool Rapids Bridge, Niagara Falls.

11:17 AM: Leave Bridge and Victoria Streets as a section of Falls Subdivision train #890.

11:50 AM: Arrive St. Catharines station.

12:05 PM: Leave St. Catharines as 2nd section of Port Dalhousie Subdivision train #27.

12:28 PM: Arrive Port Dalhousie.

12:30 to 1:30 PM: DINNER AT LAKESIDE INN.

1:32 PM: Leave Port Dalhousie as section of Port Dalhousie Subdivision train #32.

1:55 PM: Arrive St. Catharines Shops for tour of inspection. CHANGE TO CAR #130.

3:11 PM: Leave St. Catharines for Substation Junction as a section of Falls Subdivision train #98.

3:30 PM: Leave Substation Junction and run extra on Welland Subdivision to Port Colborne.

4:24 PM: Arrive Port Colborne.

4:31 PM: Leave Port Colborne as a section of Welland Subdivision train #141.

5:20 PM: Arrive Substation Junction.

5:30 PM: Leave Substation Junction as a section of Falls Subdivision train #102.

5:45 PM: Arrive Bridge and Victoria streets, Niagara Falls.

TORONTO GROUP

7:00 PM: Leave Bridge Street station on CNR train #107-108.

BUFFALO GROUP

8:05 PM: Leave Suspension Bridge on NYC train #246.

Opposite Top: Car 620 returning from Port Weller on Martindale Road near the QEW, October 9th 1955. Note spoked pilot, soon replaced by metal plate.
(AL PATERSON COLLECTION)

Opposite Bottom: Car 130 at Port Weller with canal bridge in the background, July 1940.
(J.W. HOOD)

Top: Car 131 at Substation Junction in 1946.
(R.J. SANDUSKY)

Bottom: Car 135 and train looking southwest at Port Colborne in 1946.
(R.J. SANDUSKY)

Top: Freshly outshopped car 83 on Victoria Avenue, Niagara Falls, on a rail enthusiasts' excursion June 13th 1943. See text, page 217. (B. SCHUFF COLLECTION)

Bottom: Car 83, on enthusiasts' charter, crosses Martindale trestle, September 8th 1957. (R.J. SANDUSKY)

Opposite Top: Car 80 on the Fonthill Cannery spur, running beside Hurricane Road, November 2nd 1952. (R.J. SANDUSKY)

Opposite Bottom: Car 130 at end of the Pine Street Spur, November 1st 1953. (J.M. MILLS)

APPENDIX A
Mileage/Altitude Charts

MAIN LINE:

0.00	Street Catharines Terminal	Stop 50
0.29	Page Avenue (platform)	
0.44	Grantham Div. crossover	
0.49	Freight yard east switch	
0.70	Berryman Avenue (shelter)	
1.10	Queenston Street bridge	
1.63	Lincoln Avenue (shelter)	
1.78	Garden City siding	
2.12	Lincoln Junction	
2.39	Thorold Road (platform)	
3.00	CNR overpass	
3.02	Merritton (shelter & siding)	Stop 51
3.93	Interlake Tissue Mills Spur (3787 ft.)	
3.96	Nihan's or Ball's (shelter)	Stop 52
4.84	Thorold (station)	Stop 60
5.01	Scale siding	
5.14	Lynden Street (shelter & siding, formerly Martin's)	
5.35	Old Canal swing bridge	
5.45	New canal swing bridge	
5.59	Walker's Quarry spur (7922 ft.)	
5.69	Shriner's siding	
5.89	Shriner's stop (shelter)	
6.52	Town Line (shelter)	Stop 61
7.70	Lobb's siding	
7.80	Lobb's stop (shelter)	Stop 62
8.45	Kaler's (shelter)	Stop 63
9.09	Hutt's (shelter)	Stop 64
9.32	Queen Elizabeth Way	
9.74	Wright's stop (shelter)	Stop 65
9.88	Wright's siding	
10.45	Stamford (station)	Stop 66
10.67	CNR diamond	
11.05	Stanley Street (shelter)	Stop 67
11.40	Fourth Avenue (shelter)	Stop 68
11.51	Car barn	
11.78	Bridge Street	Stop 69
11.93	Queen Street	
12.60	Victoria Avenue — Newman Hill	
13.04	Tower Inn Terminal	Stop 70
13.08	IRC switch	
13.58	IRC Terminal, Niagara Falls, NY	

NIAGARA FALLS LOCAL LINES:

0.00	River Road	
0.27	MCRR diamont	
0.42	Queen Street siding	
0.80	Victoria Avenue — Queen Street	
1.49	Newman Hill	
1.94	MCRR spur diamond	
2.11	Rink Siding (later Centre Siding)	
2.41	Stanley Street wye	
2.75	Perry Street siding	
2.79	Main and Ferry streets Junction	
3.26	Murray Street siding	
3.90	Falls View siding	
4.50	Montrose	

WELLAND DIVISION:

0.00	Substation Junction	
0.22	Siding	
0.29	Pine Street	Stop 1
0.36	Pine Street spur (3937 ft.)	
0.57	shelter	Stop 2
1.16	Beamer's	Stop 3
1.49	Beaver Dams (shelter)	Stop 4
2.20	Summer's (shelter)	Stop 5
2.68	Dixon's siding	

2.81	Dixon's stop (shelter)	Stop 6
3.64	Hansler's (shelter)	Stop 7
4.03	Moore's	Stop 8
4.38	Seburn's	Stop 9
4.86	Merrittville Highway	Stop 10
5.25	Miller's	Stop 11
5.43	Hillrust siding	
5.50	Hillrust stop (shelter)	Stop 12
6.39	McNeil's	Stop 13
6.72	Fonthill (station)	Stop 14
6.79	Cannery spur (2474 ft.)	
7.23	Emmett's (shelter)	Stop 15
7.87	Mark's	Stop 16
8.51	Scanlan's stop (shelter)	Stop 17
8.59	Scanlan's siding	
9.15	Rice's	Stop 18
9.79	Electric Park siding	
9.89	Electric Park (shelter)	Stop 19
10.66	Fitch Street	Stop 20
11.02	Welland (station)	Stop 21
11.41	Commonwealth Electric Co. spur	
11.45	Lincoln Street	Stop 22
11.53	TH&B Transfer	
11.93	MCRR diamond	
12.11	Broadway Street	Stop 23
12.96	Humberstone Street	Stop 24
13.90	CNR diamond	
14.02	Dainsville (shelter)	Stop 25
14.12	Dainsville siding	
14.65	Nugent's	Stop 26
16.03	Uptergrove's siding	Stop 27
16.56	Barrick's	Stop 28
17.21	Omer Street, Humberstone	Stop 29
17.34	West Main Street, Humberstone	Stop 30
17.40	Humberstone (shelter)	
17.84	Killaly Street (Main Street)	Stop 31
17.93	Canada Cement Co. Ry. diamond	
18.32	CNR station, Port Colborne	Stop 35

Pre-1926

18.2	CNR diamond	
18.5	NS&T station, Port Colborne	Stop 35

LAKE SHORE DIVISION:

—	Street Catharines Terminal	Stop 50
0.00	Lake Shore Junction	
0.76	Niagara Street siding	
1.21	Grantham Avenue	Stop 42
1.33	Facer Street siding	
1.77	Carlton Street (shelter)	Stop 43
2.44	Scott Street (siding, shelter)	Stop 44
3.09	Church Street	Stop 45
4.16	Welland Canal drawbridge	
4.20	Port Weller (shelter)	Stop 46
4.61	End of Track (after 1931)	
4.64	Lake Shore siding	
6.01	McNab	
7.32	Coleman's siding	
8.76	Chaplin's	
11.54	Freight House	
12.12	Niagara-on-the-Lake	

PORT DALHOUSIE LINE:

0.00	Lakeside Park	
0.99	Corbett's (Canning Factory siding)	
1.26	Reid's	
1.41	Fruit Station spur	
1.42	Lake Shore Road	
1.81	Blair's	

2.16	Martindale (shelter)	
2.46	Barnesdale siding	
2.53	Queen Elizabeth Way	
2.70	Barnesdale stop	
2.95	Houtby's stop	
3.19	Houtby's siding	
3.31	Welland Vale spur (4977 ft.)	
3.33	Old Welland Canal bridge	
3.88	Ontario Street diamond	
3.95	Woodruff's siding	
4.33	Lake and Louisa streets	
4.71	Welland Avenue	

"LOW LINE":

0.00	CNR station, St. Catharines	
0.44	Henrietta Street siding	
0.79	Ontario Street	
1.35	Geneva Street	
1.74	Thorold Road siding	
1.76	Hennessey's Corner	
2.42	Knife Works siding	
2.69	Lincoln Avenue	
2.78	Turner Street siding	
3.20	Carbide siding	
4.15	Main Line diamond	
4.28	Merritton siding	
4.56	Merritt Street siding	
4.88	Merritton–Thorold town line	
5.46	Ormond and Regent streets	
5.65	Thorold station	

GRANTHAM DIVISION:

0.00	Port Dalhousie East	
1.71	Old Welland Canal swing bridge	
2.12	Queen Elizabeth Way	
2.90	Geneva Street	
2.93	St. Catharines Terminal	
3.05	Main Line crossover	
3.05	Lake Shore Junction	
3.40	Main Line crossover	
3.62	Freight Yard switch	
4.06	Queenston Street	
4.80	Garden City Junction	
5.56	CNR Merritton station	

ST. CATHARINES LOCAL LINE:

0.00	McKinnon's, Carlton Street	
0.26	Port Dalhousie line diamond	
0.51	Welland Avenue siding	
1.02	King Street	
1.19	St. Paul and Ontario streets	
1.38	James Street	
1.72	Geneva Street	
1.91	Phelps Street spur	
2.11	Thorold Road siding	
2.13	Hennessey's corner	
2.62	Clayburn siding	
2.74	Main Line bridge	
3.52	Victoria Lawn cemetery	

NIAGARA FALLS PARK & RIVER RAILWAY:

	(1913)	Altitude
0.0	End of track, MCR	570
0.3	Chippewa	572
1.5	N. Falls, Queen Victoria House	566
2.6	N. Falls, Table Rock House	515
3.4	N. Falls, Falls View Bridge	529
4.8	N. Falls, Whirlpool Rapids Bridge	557
6.4	Bowman Ravine Bridge	587
7.7	Wintergreen Flat Road	581

9.3	Smeaton crossing	570
10.3	Niagara Falls Road	537
10.6	St. David's Road	427
10.9	Queen Street, Queenston	363
11.0	Dumfries Street, Queenston	328
11.4	Queenston Dock	259

PROJECTED LINES (1913):

0.0	Toronto, Yonge Street	418
3.0	Davenport Road bridge	435
3.1	GTR crossing	GTR 416; NS&T 440
3.9	GTR and CPR crossing	GTR 407; NS&T 431
5.9	CPR crossing	CPR 399; NS&T 375
6.1	Humber River bridge	354
7.3	Mimico Creek bridge	400
7.9	Islington station	400
10.0	Summerville station	386
11.0	Etobicoke Creek	366
13.9	Cooksville Creek	330
14.0	Cooksville station	328
15.2	Credit River	317
17.0	Lorne Park station	329
23.1	Oakville station	329
23.3	Sixteen Mile Creek bridge	334
24.1	summit	347
27.8	Bronte Creek	343
28.0	Crossing, main line G.	348
28.2	Appleby station	348
33.0	Burlington station	336
33.3	GTR crossing (N&NW)	336
36.9	Waterdown station	356
38.8	Desjardins canal	332
39.4	CPR crossing	CPR 296; NS&T 326
40.9	Hamilton, Caroline Street	302
41.2	GTR crossing	GTR 266; NS&T 299
41.9	GTR crossing	GTR 254; NS&T 282
42.8	HRER crossing	HRER 248; NS&T 265
43.1	TH&B level crossing	257
47.2	GTR level crossing	275
58.1	Grimsby station	342
63.1	Beamsville station	408
65.6	Vineland station	423
68.2	Jordan Creek bridge	419
69.0	Jordan station	405
71.8	Fifteen Mile Creek bridge	401
75.0	Brook	474
75.8	DeCew Falls power house	505
78.6	Thorold station	578
79.3	Old Welland Canal bridge	587
79.6	Thorold Junction	595

0.0	Fonthill Junction (6.0 from Substation Junction)	605
3.9	Creek	618
4.5	Summit	626
7.7	Depression	578
12.2	TH&B crossing	596
27.9	Buckhorn Creek	617
35.5	GTR crossing	643
35.8	Caledonia station	649
39.6	Little Creek	639
46.8	Fairchild Creek	644
49.6	TH&B crossing	714
49.7	Cainsville	715
49.9	B&HE Ry. crossing	716
49.9	GTR crossing	717
50.9	Brantford, Echo Place	724

SAFETY FIRST

Niagara, St. Catharines & Toronto Railway

Employees

Time **52** Table

For the Government and Information of Employees Only

EFFECTIVE

Sunday, April 3rd
1938

at 4.00 o'clock a.m.

DESTROY ALL FORMER TIME-TABLES

Trains are run on Eastern Standard Time unless otherwise indicated

---

Every employee concerned in the operation of trains MUST have a copy of this
Time Table in his possession while on duty, and must be fully
conversant with its contents.

Time of Trains at Meeting Points is Shown in Underscored Bold Face Type

W. A. KINGSLAND,	E. B. WALKER,	J. R. EMPRINGHAM,
Vice-President	General Superintendent	Superintendent

COURTESY—SAFETY—SERVICE

Precautions at Railway Crossings

(Extract from the Railway Act, Chapter 68, Section 306, 1919)

(1) No train or engine or electric car shall pass over any crossing where two main lines of railway, or the main tracks of any branch lines, cross each other at rail level, whether they are owned by different companies or the same company, until a proper signal has been received by the conductor or engineer in charge of such train or engine from a competent person or watchman in charge of such crossing that the way is clear.

(2) In the case of an electric car crossing any railway track at rail level, if there is no competent person or watchman in charge of the crossing, it shall be the duty of the conductor, before crossing and before giving the signal to the motorman that the way is clear and to proceed, to go forward and see that the track to be crossed is clear.

Special Notice—For One-Man Car Operation, see special instructions under each division.

In Case of Accident

When employees are injured, and medical attention is required, a Medical Warrant (Form 45) should be obtained from the supervisory officer, and it will constitute authority to the physician named, to give attention to the injured employee. In cases of serious injury, when it is not possible or advisable, to take necessary time to secure a Medical Warrant, the Warrant will afterwards be forwarded by the supervisory officer to the physician consulted.

In all cases requiring medical attention employees should first endeavour to secure the services of the Company's authorized physician. If his services be not available, and the case is urgent, call any doctor whose services can be had.

In assisting in providing medical relief for persons—other than employees—injured, the Company has in view humanitarian considerations and the general welfare of the service; but any such action is not to be regarded as an admission or evidence of liability.

In the performance of this humanitarian duty in cases of injury to persons other than passengers or employees, while upon the Company's premises, the assistance is to be limited to rendering first aid only. "First Aid" means such medical and surgical services as are known to relieve the immediate danger or suffering of the injured person, and to make it safe and comfortable for such person to be removed from the scene of the accident. Under no circumstances shall it mean the performance of surgical operations or elaborate surgical dressings such as setting fractures, etc.

Employees of the Company, whether authorized to do so or not, when calling for the services of a physician should notify said physician that the call is for first aid only and will not include services rendered subsequent to the first dressing on the Company's premises or adjacent thereto.

The following is a list of the Company's authorized physicians:

St. Catharines		Dr. G. T. Zumstein	Tel. 349
" "		Dr. R. M. Calder	Tel. 330
Port Dalhousie		Dr. A. R. MacDonald	Tel. 25
Thorold		Dr. J. Herod	Tel. 98
Niagara Falls, Ont.		Dr. E. T. Kellam	Tel. 14
Welland		Dr. H. D. Cowper	Tel. 984
Port Colborne		Dr. E. A. MacKenzie	Tel. 17

Operating Officers

At St. Catharines, Ont.
{
J. R. Empringham, Superintendent
T. Marriott, Inspector, St. Catharines
H. M. Palmer, Supervisor of Freight Train Service
G. S. Hallett, Dispatcher
H. J. McIntyre, Dispatcher
F. A. Hall, Dispatcher
F. Oakley, Relief Dispatcher
A. N. Caughill, Relief Dispatcher
}

At Niagara Falls, Ont.
{
M. Howarth, Timekeeper and Inspector
W. V. Bray, Inspector
Niagara Falls, Ont.
}

Abbreviations

(Ar) Arrive   (Lv) Leave   (Sid) Siding   (Tel) Dispatcher's Telephone

Dispatcher's Telephones

At Terminal, Geneva Street	3000
At Terminal, Geneva Street, on Sundays, Holidays and after Regular Office Hours	3010 and 3016

Runs and Time Allowed

WEEK DAY TIME	SUNDAY TIME

Main Line Division

WEEK DAY TIME	SUNDAY TIME
No. 1......5.35 am to 3.05 pm...... 9½ hrs	No. 1......7.35 am to 4.05 pm...... 8½ hrs
No. 2......3.05 pm to 1.05 am......10 hrs	No. 2......3.05 pm to 1.05 am......10 hrs
No. 3......6.35 am to 4.05 pm...... 9½ hrs	No. 3......6.35 am to 3.05 pm...... 8½ hrs
No. 4......4.05 pm to 2.05 am......10 hrs	No. 4......4.05 pm to 2.05 am......10 hrs

Crews on Runs No. 1 and No. 3 change at Lobb's Siding at 9.28 a.m.

Welland Division

WEEK DAY TIME	SUNDAY TIME
No. 1......5.30 am to 2.48 pm...... 9¼ hrs	No. 1......8.00 am to 2.48 pm...... 6¾ hrs
No. 2......2.05 pm to 12.50 am......10¾ hrs	No. 2......2.05 pm to 12.50 am......10¾ hrs
No. 3......5.57 am to 2.24 pm...... 8½ hrs	No. 3......8.16 am to 2.24 pm...... 6¼ hrs
No. 4......2.24 pm to 12.39 am......10¼ hrs	No. 4......2.24 pm to 12.39 am......10¼ hrs

Port Dalhousie Division

WEEK DAY TIME	SUNDAY TIME
No. 1......6.20 am to 3.56 pm...... 9½ hrs	No. 1......7.41 am to 3.56 pm...... 8¼ hrs
No. 2......3.56 pm to 1.11 am...... 9¼ hrs	No. 2......3.56 pm to 1.11 am...... 9¼ hrs
No. 3......12.11 pm to 9.41 pm...... 9½ hrs	No. 3......12.11 pm to 9.41 pm...... 9½ hrs

St. Catharines-Thorold Coach Route

WEEK DAY TIME	SUNDAY TIME
No. 1......5.39 am to 2.37 pm...... 9 hrs	No. 1......9.35 am to 2.37 pm...... 5 hrs
No. 2......2.37 pm to 11.58 pm...... 9¼ hrs	No. 2......2.37 pm to 11.58 pm...... 9¼ hrs
No. 3......5.59 am to 2.57 pm...... 9 hrs	No. 3......9.55 am to 2.57 pm...... 5 hrs
No. 4......2.57 pm to 12.18 am...... 9¼ hrs	No. 4......2.57 pm to 12.18 am...... 9¼ hrs
No. 5......6.19 am to 3.17 pm...... 9 hrs	No. 5......10.15 am to 3.17 pm...... 5 hrs
No. 6......3.17 pm to 12.38 am...... 9¼ hrs	No. 6......3.17 pm to 12.38 am...... 9¼ hrs

Victoria Lawn Cemetery Division

WEEK DAY TIME	SUNDAY TIME
No. 1......5.41 am to 2.57 pm...... 9¼ hrs	No. 1......9.41 am to 2.57 pm...... 5¼ hrs
No. 2......2.57 pm to 12.11 am...... 9¼ hrs	No. 2......2.57 pm to 12.11 am...... 9¼ hrs
No. 3......5.48 am to 2.59 pm...... 9¼ hrs	No. 3......9.48 am to 2.59 pm...... 5¼ hrs
No. 4......2.59 pm to 12.15 am...... 9¼ hrs	No. 4......2.59 pm to 12.15 am...... 9¼ hrs

Facer Street Division

WEEK DAY TIME	SUNDAY TIME
No. 1......5.46 am to 2.41 pm...... 9 hrs	No. 1......9.46 am to 2.41 pm...... 5 hrs
No. 2......2.41 pm to 11.55 pm...... 9¼ hrs	No. 2......2.41 pm to 11.55 pm...... 9¼ hrs
No. 3......5.40 am to 3.01 pm...... 9¼ hrs	No. 3......9.40 am to 3.01 pm...... 5¼ hrs
No. 4......3.01 pm to 12.15 am...... 9¼ hrs	No. 4......3.01 pm to 12.15 am...... 9¼ hrs

Geneva-York Coach Route

WEEK DAY TIME	SUNDAY TIME
No. 1......6.07 am to 3.02 pm...... 9 hrs	No. 1......10.07 am to 3.02 pm...... 5 hrs
No. 2......3.02 pm to 12.03 am...... 9 hrs	No. 2......3.02 pm to 12.03 am...... 9 hrs

Niagara-York Coach Route

WEEK DAY TIME	SUNDAY TIME
No. 1......6.49 am to 2.50 pm...... 8 hrs	No Service
No. 2......2.50 pm to 11.13 pm...... 8½ hrs	

NIAGARA FALLS LOCAL DIVISION

MONTROSE

Week Days	Sundays
No. 1......5.17 am to 2.50 pm...... 9½ hrs	No. 1......5.51 am to 2.47 pm...... 9 hrs
No. 2......2.50 pm to 12.32 am...... 9¾ hrs	No. 2......2.47 pm to 12.17 am...... 9½ hrs
No. 3......5.26 am to 3.02 pm...... 9½ hrs	No. 3......6.21 am to 3.02 pm...... 8¾ hrs
No. 4......3.02 pm to 12.44 am...... 9¾ hrs	No. 4......3.02 pm to 12.36 am...... 9½ hrs
No. 5......5.38 am to 3.14 pm...... 9½ hrs	No. 5......9.36 am to 3.48 pm...... 6¼ hrs
No. 6......3.14 pm to 12.56 am...... 9¾ hrs	No. 6......3.48 pm to 1.06 am...... 9¼ hrs
No. 7......5.50 am to 3.26 pm...... 9½ hrs	Runs Nos. 7 and 8 do not operate on Sundays.
No. 8......3.26 pm to 1.08 am...... 9¾ hrs	

Week Days
Runs Nos. 2 and 8 change at Queen and Victoria Junction at 10.53 p.m.
Runs Nos. 4 and 8 change at Murray Street Siding at 11.30 p.m.
Runs Nos. 6 and 8 change at Queen and Victoria Junction at 12.05 a.m.
Week days and Sundays all runs relieve at Victoria Junction.

Sundays
Runs Nos. 2 and 4 change at Main and Ferry Junction at 11.26 p.m.

LUNDY'S LANE

Week Days	Sundays
No. 1......5.32 am to 3.08 pm...... 9½ hrs	No. 1......9.47 am to 3.11 pm...... 5½ hrs
No. 2......3.08 pm to 12.02 am...... 9 hrs	No. 2......3.09 pm to 12.06 am...... 9 hrs

COACH SERVICE

Week Days	Sundays
No. 1......6.13 am to 3.41 pm...... 9½ hrs	No. 1......7.13 am to 3.41 pm...... 8½ hrs
No. 2......3.41 pm to 1.43 am......10 hrs	No. 2......3.41 pm to 1.43 am......10 hrs

MAIN LINE DIVISION—East Bound

Time Table No. 52

Effective April 3rd, 1938, at 4.00 a.m.

	STATIONS	Daily ex Sun	Daily ex Sun	Daily ex Sun	Daily	Daily	Daily	Daily	Daily	Daily	Daily	Daily	Daily	Daily	Daily	Daily	Daily	Daily	Daily	Daily	Daily	Daily
		120	**2**	**48**	**4**	**6**	**8**	**10**	**12**	**14**	**16**	**18**	**20**	**22**	**24**	**26**	**28**	**30**	**32**	**34**	**36**	**38**
Miles		am	am	am	am	am	am	am	am	am	pm	pm	pm	pm	pm	pm	pm	pm	pm	pm	pm	pm
0.00	Port Dalhousie East.......Tel..Sid...	....	....	....	....	....	....	....	....	....	....	....	....	....	....	....	....	....	....	....	....	....
2.93	St. Catharines Terminal....Tel..Sid...	....	....	....	....	....	....	....	....	....	....	....	....	....	....	....	....	....	....	....	....	....
0.00	St. Paul and James........Tel..Sid.Lv	....	5 55	....	6 55	7 55	8 55	9 55	10 55	11 55	12 55	1 55	2 55	3 55	4 55	5 55	6 55	7 55	8 55	9 55	10 55	11 55
0.89	St. Catharines Terminal....Tel..Sid.Ar	....	6 00	....	7 00	8 00	9 00	10 00	11 00	12 00	1 00	2 00	3 00	4 00	5 00	6 00	7 00	8 00	9 00	10 00	11 00	12 00
0.00	St. Catharines Terminal....Tel..Sid.Lv	5 45	6 05	6 37	7 05	8 05	9 05	10 05	11 05	12 05	1 05	2 05	3 05	4 05	5 05	6 05	7 05	8 05	9 05	10 05	11 05	12 05
1.78	Garden City..............Tel..Sid...	5 50	6 10	6 42	7 10	8 10	9 10	10 10	11 10	12 10	1 10	2 10	3 10	4 10	5 10	6 10	7 10	8 10	9 10	10 10	11 10	12 10
2.12	Lincoln Junction..........Tel..Sid...	5 51	6 11	6 43	7 11	8 11	9 11	10 11	11 11	12 11	1 11	2 11	3 11	4 11	5 11	6 11	7 11	8 11	9 11	10 11	11 11	12 11
3.02	Merritton.................Tel..Sid...	5 54	6 13	6 46	**7 13**	8 13	9 13	10 13	11 13	12 13	1 13	2 13	3 13	4 13	5 13	6 13	7 13	8 13	9 13	10 13	11 13	12 13
					121																	
3.96	Nihan's...................Tel..Sid...	5 56	6 15	6 48	7 15	8 15	9 15	10 15	11 15	12 15	1 15	2 15	3 15	4 15	5 15	6 15	7 15	8 15	9 15	10 15	11 15	12 15
4.84	Thorold...................Tel..Sid...	5 58	6 18	6 50	7 18	8 18	9 18	10 18	11 18	12 18	1 18	2 18	3 18	4 18	5 18	6 18	7 18	8 18	9 18	10 18	11 18	12 18
5.11	Substation Junction.......Tel..Sid...	....	6 21	....	7 21	**8 21**	**9 21**	**10 21**	**11 21**	**12 21**	**1 21**	**2 21**	**3 21**	**4 21**	**5 21**	**6 21**	**7 21**	**8 21**	**9 21**	**10 21**	**11 21**	**12 21**
						123	**125**	**127**	**129**	**131**	**133**	**135**	**137**	**139**	**141**	**143**	**145**	**147**	**149**	**151**	**153**	**155**
5.69	Shriner's.................Tel..Sid...	....	6 24	....	7 24	8 24	9 24	10 24	11 24	12 24	1 24	2 24	3 24	4 24	5 24	6 24	7 24	8 24	9 24	10 24	11 24	12 24
7.70	Lobb's....................Tel..Sid...	....	6 28	....	**7 28**	**8 28**	**9 28**	**10 28**	**11 28**	**12 28**	**1 28**	**2 28**	**3 28**	**4 28**	**5 28**	**6 28**	**7 28**	**8 28**	**9 28**	**10 28**	**11 28**	**12 28**
					3	**5**	**7**	**9**	**11**	**13**	**15**	**17**	**19**	**21**	**23**	**25**	**27**	**29**	**31**	**33**	**35**	**37**
9.87	Wright's..................Tel..Sid...	....	6 32	....	7 32	8 32	9 32	10 32	11 32	12 32	1 32	2 32	3 32	4 32	5 32	6 32	7 32	8 32	9 32	10 32	11 32	12 32
10.49	Stamford.....................	....	6 33	....	7 33	8 33	9 33	10 33	11 33	12 33	1 33	2 33	3 33	4 33	5 33	6 33	7 33	8 33	9 33	10 33	11 33	12 33
11.51	Car Barn..................Tel..Sid...	....	6 36	....	7 36	8 36	9 36	10 36	11 36	12 36	1 36	2 36	3 36	4 36	5 36	6 36	7 36	8 36	9 36	10 36	11 36	12 36
11.75	Double Track Begins..........	....	6 37	....	7 37	8 37	9 37	10 37	11 37	12 37	1 37	2 37	3 37	4 37	5 37	6 37	7 37	8 37	9 37	10 37	11 37	12 37
11.91	Queen Street Junction.....Tel........	....	6 38	....	7 38	8 38	9 38	10 38	11 38	12 38	1 38	2 38	3 38	4 38	5 38	6 38	7 38	8 38	9 38	10 38	11 38	12 38
12.60	Victoria Avenue Junction.........	....	6 41	....	7 41	8 41	9 41	10 41	11 41	12 41	1 41	2 41	3 41	4 41	5 41	6 41	7 41	8 41	9 41	10 41	11 41	12 41
13.05	Niagara Falls Terminal....Tel..Sid.Ar	....	6 43	....	7 43	8 43	9 43	10 43	11 43	12 43	1 43	2 43	3 43	4 43	5 43	6 43	7 43	8 43	9 43	10 43	11 43	12 43
	Bus to Niagara Falls, N.Y.																					
0.00	Queen and Victoria Jct..............Lv	....	6 41	....	7 41	8 41	9 41	10 41	11 41	12 41	1 41	2 41	3 41	4 41	5 41	6 41	7 41	8 41	9 41	10 41	11 41	12 41
2.90	Int. Ry. Terminal, Niagara Falls N.Y.. Ar	....	6 57	....	7 57	8 57	9 57	10 57	11 57	12 57	1 57	2 57	3 57	4 57	5 57	6 57	7 57	8 57	9 57	10 57	11 57	12 57

All trains operating beyond Queen St. and Victoria Avenue, Niagara Falls, and not destined to Tower Inn Terminal must report to Dispatcher at Queen and Victoria.

SPEED RESTRICTIONS

Miles Per Hour

Eastbound

St. Catharines—Over Crossings at Page St., Haynes Ave: and Vine St..........10
Over Westchester Ave....................................10
Merritton—Over Main Street (Merritt St.)...............................10
Over Bridge Crossing C.N.R. Main Line Tracks....................10
Thorold—Ormond Street, First Crossing East of Thorold Station............10

Westbound

Thorold—Ormond Street, First Crossing East of Thorold Station.............10
Merritton—Over Main Street (Merritt Street)............................10
Over Bessey Street....................................10
Over Bridge Crossing C.N.R. Main Line Tracks................10
St. Catharines—Over Haynes Ave...................................10
Over Westchester Ave.................................10

RAILWAY CROSSINGS AT GRADE

C.N.R. (Wabash) Stamford—Interlocked ....Mileage 10.67

PASSENGER TRANSFER POINTS

Eastbound—Welland Division Northbound at Substation Junction, Thorold.
Niagara Falls Local to Lower Bridge at Queen and Victoria Streets.
Bridge Coach at " " " "

Westbound—Bridge Coach at " " " "
Niagara Falls Local from Lower Bridge at Queen and Victoria Sts.
Welland Division Southbound at Thorold Station.
Niagara-York Coach at Niagara Street.
Port Dalhousie Division; Facer Street Division Westbound; and Geneva-York Coach at St. Catharines Terminal Station.
Victoria Lawn Westbound and Thorold Coach Westbound at St. Paul and James Streets.

SPRING SWITCHES

Lincoln Junction.
Thorold Station—Short track where Welland Division cars stand.
West Wye Switch to Welland Division.
Shriner's Siding—Both ends.
Lobb's Siding—Both ends.
Niagara Falls Terminal Yard—End of Double track.

See Special Instructions on Pages 6, 7 and 8

Main Line trains will take siding on Welland Avenue opposite St. Catharines Terminal. Siding is equipped with street switch on west end, and spring switch on east end. Freight trains must not use this siding.

MAIN LINE DIVISION — Westbound

Time Table No. 52

Effective April 3rd, 1938, at 4.00 a.m.

	STATIONS	Daily ex Sun	Daily ex Sun	Daily	Daily	Daily	Daily	Daily	Daily	Daily	Daily	Daily	Daily	Daily	Daily	Daily	Daily	Daily	Daily	Daily	Daily	Daily
		121	**3**	**5**	**7**	**9**	**11**	**13**	**15**	**17**	**19**	**21**	**23**	**25**	**27**	**29**	**31**	**33**	**35**	**155**	**37**	**39**
M es	Bus from Niagara Falls, N.Y.		am	am	am	am	am	am	pm	pm	pm	pm	pm	pm	pm	pm	pm	pm	pm	am	pm	am
0.00	International Ry. Term'l, Niagara Falls,N.Y	....	6 58	7 58	8 58	9 58	10 58	11 58	12 58	1 58	2 58	3 58	4 58	5 58	6 58	7 58	8 58	9 58	10 58	.....	11 58	12 58
3.10	Queen and Victoria Jct. ....Ar	....	7 15	8 15	9 15	10 15	11 15	12 15	1 15	2 15	3 15	4 15	5 15	6 15	7 15	8 15	9 15	10 15	11 15	.....	12 15	1 15
0.00	Niagara Falls Terminal, Ont..Tel..Sid..Lv	....	7 11	8 11	9 11	10 11	11 11	12 11	1 11	2 11	3 11	4 11	5 11	6 11	7 11	8 11	9 11	10 11	11 11	.....	12 11	1 11
0.45	Victoria Avenue Junction................	....	7 13	8 13	9 13	10 13	11 13	12 13	1 13	2 13	3 13	4 13	5 13	6 13	7 13	8 13	9 13	10 13	11 13	.....	12 13	1 13
1.11	Queen Street Junction.......Tel..........	....	7 17	8 17	9 17	10 17	11 17	12 17	1 17	2 17	3 17	4 17	5 17	6 17	7 17	8 17	9 17	10 17	11 17	.....	12 17	1 17
1.30	Double Track Ends..........................	....	7 18	8 18	9 18	10 18	11 18	12 18	1 18	2 18	3 18	4 18	5 18	6 18	7 18	8 18	9 18	10 18	11 18	.....	12 18	1 18
1.54	Car Barn.................Tel..Sid.......	....	7 19	8 19	9 19	10 19	11 19	12 19	1 19	2 19	3 19	4 19	5 19	6 19	7 19	8 19	9 19	10 19	11 19	.....	12 19	1 19
2.56	Stamford...............................	....	7 22	8 22	9 22	10 22	11 22	12 22	1 22	2 22	3 22	4 22	5 22	6 22	7 22	8 22	9 22	10 22	11 22	.....	12 22	1 22
3.18	Wright's.................Tel..Sid.......	....	7 24	8 24	9 24	10 24	11 24	12 24	1 24	2 24	3 24	4 24	5 24	6 24	7 24	8 24	9 24	10 24	11 24	.....	12 24	1 24
5.35	Lobb's...................Tel..Sid.......	....	**7 28**	**8 28**	**9 28**	**10 28**	**11 28**	**12 28**	**1 28**	**2 28**	**3 28**	**4 28**	**5 28**	**6 28**	**7 28**	**8 28**	**9 28**	**10 28**	**11 28**	.....	**12 28**	1 28
			4	**6**	**8**	**10**	**12**	**14**	**16**	**18**	**20**	**22**	**24**	**26**	**28**	**30**	**32**	**34**	**36**		**38**	
7.36	Shriner's................Tel..Sid.......	....	7 31	8 31	9 31	10 31	11 31	12 31	1 31	2 31	3 31	4 31	5 31	6 31	7 31	8 31	9 31	10 31	11 31	.....	12 31	1 31
7.94	Substation Junction........Tel..Sid.......	....	7 33	8 33	9 33	10 33	11 33	12 33	1 33	2 33	3 33	4 33	5 33	6 33	7 33	8 33	9 33	10 33	11 33	.....	12 34	1 34
8.21	Thorold..................Tel..Sid{Ar..	....	7 35	8 35	9 35	10 35	11 35	12 35	1 35	2 35	3 35	4 35	5 35	6 35	7 35	8 35	9 35	10 35	11 35	.....	12 35	1 35
	{Lv..	7 07	7 36	8 36	9 36	10 36	11 36	12 36	1 36	2 36	3 36	4 36	5 36	6 36	7 36	8 36	9 36	10 36	11 36	12 23	12 36	1 36
9.09	Nihan's..................Tel..Sid.......	7 09	7 38	8 38	9 38	10 38	11 38	12 38	1 38	2 38	3 38	4 38	5 38	6 38	7 38	8 38	9 38	10 38	11 38	12 25	12 38	1 38
10.03	Merritton................Tel..Sid.......	**7 11**	7 40	8 40	9 40	10 40	11 40	12 40	1 40	2 40	3 40	4 40	5 40	6 40	7 40	8 40	9 40	10 40	11 40	12 27	12 40	1 40
		4																				
10.93	Lincoln Junction..........Tel..Sid.....	7 15	7 42	8 42	9 42	10 42	11 42	12 42	1 42	2 42	3 42	4 42	5 42	6 42	7 42	8 42	9 42	10 42	11 42	12 29	12 42	1 42
11.27	Garden City..............Tel..Sid.....	7 16	7 43	8 43	9 43	10 43	11 43	12 43	1 43	2 43	3 43	4 43	5 43	6 43	7 43	8 43	9 43	10 43	11 43	12 30	12 43	1 43
13.05	St. Catharines Terminal.....Tel..Sid.Ar..	7 21	7 48	8 48	9· 48	10 48	11 48	12 48	1 48	2 48	3 48	4 48	5 48	6 48	7 48	8 48	9 48	10 48	11 48	12 35	12 48	1 48
.00	St. Catharines Terminal.....Tel..Sid..Lv	7 21	7 50	8 50	9 50	10 50	11 50	12 50	1 50	2 50	3 50	4 50	5 50	6 50	7 50	8 50	9 50	10 50	11 50	Via S	t.Paul	l and
0.65	St. Paul and James..................	7 26	7 55	8 55	9 55	10 55	11 55	12 55	1 55	2 55	3 55	4 55	5 55	6 55	7 55	8 55	9 55	10 55	11 55	Jam	es to	Barn.

NOTE—Extra trains between Lincoln Junction and C.N.R. Merritton Station report to Dispatcher on arrival at Lincoln Junction and Register.

TROLLEY BREAKERS—SHUT OFF CONTROLLERS

Port Dalhousie—Opposite Passenger Shelter.
St. Catharines—Between Maple and Geneva Streets, 465 feet west of Geneva St.
On Welland Avenue, 155 feet east of Geneva Street.
Between Vine Street and Berryman Avenue, 305 feet east of Vine Street.
Merritton—At Lincoln Junction, centre of crossover track between Main Line and Grantham Divisions.
Niagara Falls—In Yards, near Bridge Street, 500 feet west of Double Track.

TROLLEY CUT-OUT SWITCHES

Port Dalhousie—Opposite Passenger Shelter.
St. Catharines—On Imperial Oil Company's Siding.
On English Electric Company's Siding.
On Shell Oil Company's Siding.
On Domestic Storage Siding.
Merritton—On Carbide and Hayes Steel Siding.
On Town Line Industrial Siding.
Thorold On Walker's Quarry Siding (two).
Niagara Falls—Morris Crane Siding.
Niagara Falls Car Shop.

YARD LIMITS

Port Dalhousie—From Port Dalhousie Station to 350 ft. south of Johnston's Spur.
Tracks at Port Dalhousie East will be numbered as follows:
No. 1—Old Main Line Track (most easterly).
No. 2—Passing Track.
No. 3—Passenger Track.
No. 4—Passenger Track (next to dock).
The permanent position of switch controlling the yard is for No. 1 Track.
St. Catharines—From 200 feet north of Imperial Oil Company's Spur, near Carleton Street, to Queenston Street Bridge.
Lincoln Junction—800 feet east and west.
Merritton—From 400 feet west of Merritton Siding to 700 feet east of Merritton Siding.
Thorold—From west end of bridge over Front Street to west switch of Shriner's Siding.
Niagara Falls—From Fourth Avenue to Tower Inn Terminal.

SWING AND LIFT BRIDGES—(From St. Catharines)

Welland Ship Canal at Thorold............................Mileage 5.35
Third Welland Canal at Thorold (closed until further notice).....Mileage 5.45

See Special Instructions on Pages, 6, 7 and 8

Page 6

Instructions on Operations Between Wright's and Lobb's Sidings and Lobb's and Shriner's Sidings

AUTOMATIC BLOCK SIGNALS control the use of track between Wright's Siding and Lobb's Siding; and Lobb's Siding and Shriner's Siding. Nachod type of block signals are located on poles at the east and west entrance to main track between Wright's Siding and Lobb's Siding; and Shriner's Siding and Lobb's Siding. They are actuated by contactors located overhead under the trolley wire at the west end of Wright's Siding and east end of Lobb's Siding; and west end of Lobb's Siding, and east end of Shriner's Siding. Signal Indications:

" Disks for day indication; Lights for night indication"

The signal indication before train passes the contactor, shows the condition of the block; the indication after passing the contactor shows that the desired change has taken place.

STOP SIGNAL—RED LIGHT, RED DISK, indicates DANGER, that the block is occupied by one or more trains approaching from the opposite direction. The block thus occupied must not be entered. Trains must wait behind the contactor until the STOP SIGNAL is changed to NEUTRAL.

NEUTRAL SIGNAL—NO LIGHT, NO DISK, indicates clear track, and that train may proceed under the contactor. As soon as the train passes the contactor, the PERMISSIVE SIGNAL will be displayed, which indicates that the STOP SIGNAL is displayed at the other end of the block. The appearance of the PERMISSIVE SIGNAL authorizes the train to proceed through the block. If, for any reason, the signal fails to change from NEUTRAL to PERMISSIVE when entering block, the STOP SIGNAL will not have been set at the other end. In such a case, the train will back, coasting under the contactor with trolley pole pulled down, and will move forward again with pole on wire. If the signal still fails to work properly, such signal failure must be reported to the Dispatcher immediately, and train movements controlled by Dispatcher.

When two trains entering a block from opposite ends, pass under the contactors at exactly the same instant, both signals will still indicate NEUTRAL. A NEUTRAL SIGNAL that continues after the contactor is passed, is to be taken in the most restrictive indication as a STOP SIGNAL.

PERMISSIVE SIGNAL—WHITE LIGHT, WHITE DISK. The PERMISSIVE SIGNAL, in addition to indicating that STOP SIGNAL is displayed at the other end of the block, also indicates to trains following that there are one or more trains in the block travelling in the same direction. Sections, or other trains following, are authorized by this signal to enter the block, with the knowledge that there is at least one train ahead. As trolley wheel of the following train passes under the contactor when the PERMISSIVE SIGNAL is showing, the white light will momentarily disappear and immediately re-appear, showing that the following train is properly counted in. IT IS VERY IMPORTANT THAT THIS EXTINGUISHING OF THE LIGHT BE OBSERVED. If, on entering a block upon a PERMISSIVE SIGNAL, the white light should fail to blink, the train will at once back, coasting under the contactor with the pole pulled down, and again move forward under the contactor with pole on wire. If the signal fails to blink, report to Dispatcher immediately, for movement only by Dispatcher's instructions. Any number of trains, up to 15, or the equivalent in cars in a train, with trolley poles on wire, may enter the block under the PERMISSIVE SIGNAL and occupy it at one time. It is necessary that the same number of cars shall pass out at either, or both ends of the block before signals will again indicate a clear track—NEUTRAL SIGNAL indication.

When power is off the line, trains must not be permitted to drift under a contactor, as the signals will not be changed thereby.

CAUTION—Trains should not be stopped, nor the pole replaced with the wheel under the contactor. If, for any reason, a motorman runs under a contactor against a STOP SIGNAL, his passage will be "recorded" though there will be no visible change in the signal. Train must back out again under either contactor at that end of the block, when the record of the passage will be cancelled. CREWS WILL REPORT ANY CASE OF RUNNING AGAINST A STOP SIGNAL, AVOIDABLY OR NOT. Crews will report any failure to obtain a PERMISSIVE SIGNAL, or absence or burning out of any signal lights. Promptly report if trolley pole has thrown at frog trolley pan.

These automatic block signals, unless otherwise provided, do not supersede the superiority of trains or dispense with the use or observance of other signals whenever or wherever required; or relieve trainmen from observance of proper rear-end or front-end protection when required.

REGULAR TRAINS, either direction, having meeting points at Lobb's Siding as shown in Time Table may use main track, either direction, under protection of automatic block signals.

EXTRA TRAINS, either direction, with train order for movenemt over tracks controlled by block signals may use main track, either direction, under protection of automatic block signals.

When meets are arranged by train order, Dispatcher will use Lobb's Siding in the train order when automatic block signals are operative at both Shriner's and Wright's Siding, and trains, either direction, with meet at Lobb's Siding, may use main track between Wright's Siding and Lobb's Siding; and Lobb's Siding and Shriner's Siding, under protection of automatic block signals.

When signal failure occurs or block signal is not working, train movement between sidings in which block is out of order will be controlled by train order.

Should meeting point or "hold order" be necessary at siding at either end of the block signal which is not working, the specific siding—i. e., Wright's, Lobb's or Shriner's—will be named in the train order.

Traffic Signal, Bridge St., Niagara Falls

Traffic Actuated Automatic Signals are installed at the intersection of Bridge Street and Victoria Avenue, Niagara Falls. Signals are controlled by detectors set in the pavement for vehicular traffic, detectors set in the trolley wire for our train movements, and hand operated controls for Michigan Central Railroad train movements. Passenger cars should be stopped to take on and let off passengers before the trolley wheel passes the detector. When the trolley wheel passes under the detector, the controller should be on two or three notches and the brakes slightly applied, in order to supply sufficient current to actuate the signals. When lights show permissive proceed signal, Bridge Street should be crossed promptly as indication will likely hold only for sufficient time required to make crossing. In the event of detector failing to work, Operator should back under it and have trolley wheel pass over it again or car may wait for a vehicle on the street to change direction of signal.

(Signal Protection Between Lobb's and Shriner's Sidings Approved by Order of the Board of Railway Commissioners No. 42976)

MAIN LINE DIVISION — Special Instructions

1. Conductors or operators of first and last sections of all trains must report to Dispatcher before leaving Thorold.
   On two-man cars or trains, conductors on first and last sections before leaving Thorold will notify their motormen if there are no orders, and motormen will not proceed until such instructions have been received from conductor.

2. Eastbound trains are superior. Trains operating in the inferior direction will take siding at crossing points, unless otherwise ordered.

3. Within the limits of the City of St. Catharines, the sounding of whistles is prohibited except to give such signals as are necessary to train operation only, or except when necessary or advisable to prevent possible accident (B. R. C. Order No. 46708). The boundary line between Merritton and St. Catharines is Lincoln Avenue.

4. St. Catharines Terminal—All tracks are controlled by Operator in Tower at Niagara Street. Main Line signal to Tower Operator is ONE long whistle.
   Dwarf signals controlling switches on tracks in St. Catharines Terminal Yards are operated from Signal Tower situated at Niagara Street, and motormen entering this area must make sure before passing these signals that they are set for "Proceed". Colour signal indications at night are: Red—"STOP"; Yellow—"PROCEED".

5. St. Catharines Terminal Yards—Freight cars must be placed so that all street intersections are left clear. They must not be placed nearer than forty (40) feet to the street line at John and Page Streets, in accordance with B. R. C. Orders Nos. 33066 and 33106.

6. Cars westbound on St. Paul Street, St. Catharines, may proceed from St. Paul Street to regular stop on James Street with or against the traffic signal if other traffic is clear.

7. Hayes Steel Products Ltd., Industrial Spur—
   Operate up to the entrance of building but not beyond that point. (B.R.C. Order No. 43512).

8. Distant Semaphore at Nihan's Cut (Ball's Crossing) protects eastbound movements. Control levers are located adjacent to switch to Interlake Siding and are operated by freight crews when switching Interlake Siding and Thorold Pulp Co. siding. Signal shows a "red" light when arm is in horizontal position.

9. Interlake Siding—Hand derail is installed on lead to this siding, just clear of Town Line Roadway. Freight Trainmen when working in this siding will see that main track is properly protected.

10. Welland Ship Canal Bridge at Thorold—Trains may be operated over this bridge without first coming to a stop, provided that the rate of speed shall not exceed fifteen miles per hour and that the signals are in the "PROCEED" position during that portion of the year when the canal is open for navigation. In winter months, when canal is closed and bridge permanently locked, colored light signals are discontinued.
    When canal is open for navigation, eastbound and westbound movements on main track approaching Ship Canal Bridge are governed by "Color Light" distant and home signals; also "Color Light" dwarf signal on passing-siding for eastbound movements.

Distant Signal "Color Light" by Day and by Night
Aspect, Indication—Green—Proceed.
   "   "   —Yellow—Proceed with caution, prepared to stop at next signal.
Home Signal Color" Light" by Day and by Night
Aspect, Indication—Green—Proceed.
   "   "   —Red—Stop.
Dwarf Signal "Color Light" by Day and by Night
Aspect, Indication—Yellow—Indicates that east switch to Main Track is set and lined for movement from siding to Main Track. Proceed with caution, bridge closed.

Aspect, Indication—Red—Stop—Can be changed to yellow by Bridge Operator, only when bridge closed and east switch of siding set and lined for movement from siding to main track.
Absence of "Color Light" signal is to be taken as the most restrictive indication.

11. Old Canal Bridge, Thorold—Derails and semaphores are disconnected. Bridge is not regularly in use. When bridge is opened for emergency purposes, protection will be entirely by hand signals from flagmen to be sent out in advance at each end of bridge. Motormen and operators will observe extreme caution approaching this old canal bridge.

12. Walker's Quarry Siding—Freight Crews when operating into this siding at Thorold will not close second trolley cut-out switch until whistle signal has been given and answered by employees of quarry, indicating that all is clear.

13. C.N.R. (Wabash) Crossing, Stamford—Movements governed by distant and home semaphores and derails.

14. Niagara Falls Terminal Grade—All trains must descend grade under complete control. All eastbound trains must stop before crossing Bender Avenue. All westbound trains will use extra precaution entering Victoria Avenue.

15. Niagara Falls Terminal—Main Line cars will be placed on Track No. 4, next to station platform.

interchange Tracks

16. With C.N.R. at Thorold—N.St.C.& T. Railway will deliver cars to C.N.R. on right hand track. C.N.R. will make delivery of cars to N. St. C. & T. Railway on left hand track. Leads must be left clear at all times and derails placed on both tracks.
    With M.C.R. at Niagara Falls—N.St.C.& T. Railway will deliver and receive cars on either of two tracks between N.St.C.& T. Railway main track and M.C.R. main track.
    With Wabash and C.N.R. at Stamford—Interchange track is siding running off Main Line Division in southerly direction, slightly east of diamond at Stamford and connected with Wabash Main Line. Switch to interchange with Wabash is controlled by Tower Operator. Movements are governed by dwarf signal at switch. Signal to Tower Operator for entering interchange switch is FOUR short whistles. Cars for interchange must be left clear of detector bars of the interlocking plant, which are located at both ends of siding.

Level Crossing Protection at Niagara Street, St. Catharines:

17. Gate protection at Niagara Street Crossing, St. Catharines—Gates are operated by Towerman on duty in Tower. Motormen or Operators will look for indication light hung from span wire opposite the Tower which, when showing "WHITE" indicates that gates have been lowered. When gates have not been lowered, Motormen or Operators will stop on near side of crossing before proceeding.

Automatic Wig-Wag Protection Device at Stanley Street Level Crossing on Main Line, Niagara Falls:

18. The Wig-Wag is set in operation by trolley wheel contact on the trolley wire at two points about 1,800 feet east and west of the crossing. Motormen will look for indication light 1,100 feet each side of the crossing which, when showing pale white light, indicates that the wig-wag is in operation. When the wig-wag is not in operation Motormen will stop on near side of crossing and proceed cautiously.
    The contactors are car counting. For each car passing and actuating contactor, an equal number of cars must pass the cut-out contactor at crossing, otherwise the wig-wag will continue to operate.

(Continued on Page 8)

Page 8

MAIN LINE DIVISION — Special Instructions

(Continued from Page 7)

Train or car movements will occur in which actual crossing of Stanley Street is not made after trolley contact has set the wig-wag in motion. The following procedure is necessary in order to count out the car or engine and stop the wig-wag, when no crossing is to be made:

(a) When an eastbound train is about to back into Wabash Transfer after passing contact on Main Line, conductor will press button in box just west of Wabash Switch. Then, when movement is to be made out of Wabash Transfer on to Main Line, contact is made in trolley and wig-wag commences operation. If movement is not to pass over Stanley Street, same procedure is to be followed and conductor will again press button in box.

(b) At east end, near Fourth Avenue, trolley contact is made for westbound movements. If, after passing trolley contact and starting wig-wag, Stanley Street is not to be crossed, conductor will press button in box near Fourth Avenue to stop wig-wag.

(c) When movements are made up to Stanley Street but street not crossed by car or engine, conductor will proceed to box just east of Stanley Street and press button marked "Stop" which will stop the wig-wag. For movement eastbound into Morris Crane Spur, conductor will press button marked "Stop" after crossing has been cleared.

Should an eastbound passenger car or engine stop after crossing Stanley Street and change ends to proceed westbound, the conductor will first restart wig-wag by pressing button marked "Start".

When freight movement is to be made out of Morris Crane Spur, and Stanley Street is to be crossed, conductor will start wig-wag by pressing button marked "Start" and after crossing has been cleared will press button marked "Stop," unless Stanley Street is again to be crossed.

The boxes referred to are under the protection of standard switch locks and conductor using same is solely responsible for seeing that they are properly locked after use.

When wig-wag or its control devices are noted to be out of order an immediate report must be made to the Dispatcher.

SIDINGS AND TURN-OUTS (From St. Catharines)

Laughlin Siding	Mileage	0.01
Freight Yard Connection	"	0.02
Passenger Car Storage	"	0.05
Passenger Track No. 1	"	0.06
Passenger Track No. 2	"	0.07
Passenger Tracks No. 3 and 4	"	0.09
Grantham Division Connection	"	0.10
Freight Yard Connection	"	0.11
Freight Yard Connection	"	0.43
Cross-over to Grantham Division	"	0.44
Freight Yard Connection (Cold Storage Siding)	"	0.49
Cross-over to Grantham Division	"	0.51
Sterling Electric Siding	"	0.62
Davis Lumber Company Siding	"	0.68
Freight Classification Yard	"	0.71
Wise Lumber Co. and Crown Dominion Oil Siding	"	0.84
Freight Classification Yard	"	0.95
Imperial Oil Company	"	1.09
City of St. Catharines	"	1.56
Material Yard	"	1.60
Garden City Passing Siding—(550 ft. long) Switches	"	{ 1.73 / 1.83
	"	1.90
Garden City Paper Co.	"	2.08
Hayes Steel Products, Ltd.		
Connection to Grantham Division (1,225 ft. long)	"	2.12

Merritton Interlake Tissue Mills Siding— (873 feet long) Switches	Mileage	{ 2.88 / 3.05
(Siding to W. R. Savigny)		
Alliance (Lybster) Paper Mill Siding	"	2.94
Material Siding	"	2.95
Material Yard and Macoretta & Aldo Siding	"	3.07
Interlake Tissue Mills Siding	"	3.93
Storage Siding	"	3.96
Storage Siding	"	3.98
Davy Paper Company Siding	"	4.78
Thorold Passing Siding—(345 feet long) Switches	"	{ 4.81 / 4.88
Passenger Car Storage	"	4.89
Thorold Scale Siding—(452 ft. long) Switches	"	{ 4.95 / 5.04
Freight Yard and A. Martin & Son Siding	"	5.05
Welland Division Junction Wye	"	5.11
Passing Siding—(861 feet long) Switches (Moore-McCleary Siding)	"	{ 5.12 / 5.28
Welland Division Junction Wye	"	5.19
C. N. R. Interchange	"	5.19
Walker Brothers Quarry Siding	"	5.59
Shriner's Passing Siding—(805 ft. long) Switches	"	{ 5.61 / 5.77
Lobb's Passing Siding—(915 ft. long) Switches	"	{ 7.61 / 7.79 / 9.80
Wright's Passing Siding—(773 ft. long) Switches	"	{ 9.95 / 10.51
Canadian Ramapo Iron Works Siding	"	
C. N. R.—Wabash Interchange	"	10.75
Herbert Morris Crane & Hoist Siding	"	11.03
Storage Siding	"	11.06
Reid Bros. Siding	"	11.50
Niagara Falls Car Shops	"	11.51
M. C. R. Interchange, West End Switch	"	{ 11.51 / 11.66
M. C. R. Interchange, East End Switch	"	11.61
Team Track	"	11.75
Beginning of Double Track	"	
Victoria and Queen Switches (Crossovers and Wyes)	"	{ 11.89 / 11.91 / 11.91 / 11.94 / 11.94 / 11.96 / 11.59
Victoria Avenue and Newman Hill	"	{ 11.60 / 11.60
South Wye Switch	"	12.66
Crossover Switches	"	{ 12.66 / 12.68
End of Double Track	"	12.98
Passenger Tracks No. 6 and 7	"	12.98
Passenger Tracks No. 1 and 2	"	12.99
Passenger Track No. 5	"	13.00
Passenger Track No. 3	"	13.00

SIDINGS AND TURN-OUTS (From Port Dalhousie)

Graham & Son Coal Company	Mileage	0.04
Yard Switch	"	0.13
Johnston Coal Company Siding	"	0.20
Dominion Canners Siding	"	0.63
Lake Street Team Track	"	1.02
Imperial Oil Company Siding	"	2.21
Lincoln Canning Company Siding	"	2.23
Cloney & Winton Siding	"	2.33
J. H. Wethey's Siding	"	2.38
English Electric Company Siding	"	2.64
E. F. McCordick and Canadian Canners Sid'g	"	2.66
A. E. Bracken Coal Company Siding	"	2.81

GRANTHAM DIVISION

Time Table No. 52   Effective April 3rd, 1938, at 4.00 a.m.

		EASTBOUND					WESTBOUND	
Mls		STATIONS			Mls		STATIONS	
0.00	St Catharines Terminal....Tel..Sid		**No Regular Service**		0.00	Merritton C.N.R. Station..Tel....Sid		**No Regular Service**
0.12	Lake Shore Junction........Tel......				0.76	Garden City Junction.......Tel......		
0.47	Vine Street Crossover...............				2.16	Vine Street Crossover...............		
1.87	Garden City Junction......Tel......				2.51	Lake Shore Junction.......Tel......		
2.63	Merritton C.N.R. Station..Tel....Sid				2.63	St. Catharines Terminal....Tel.Sid		

Grantham Division — Special Instructions

1. Within the limits of the City of St. Catharines, the sounding of whistles is prohibited except to give such signals as are necessary to train operation only, or except when necessary or advisable to prevent possible accident. (B.R.C. Order No. 46708). The boundary line between Merritton and St. Catharines is Lincoln Avenue.

2. St. Catharines Terminal Yards—Dwarf Signals controlling switches are operated from Signal Tower at Niagara Street. Motormen entering this area must make sure, before passing these signals, that they are set for "Proceed". Color Signal indications at night are: Red—"STOP"; Yellow—"PROCEED". Grantham Division signal to Tower Operator is TWO long whistles.

3. Freight cars must be placed clear of all street intersections. They must not be placed nearer than forty (40) feet to the street line at John and Page Streets.

4. Lake Shore Junction switch is normally set for Lake Shore Division.

5. Gates at Niagara Street Crossing, St. Catharines, are operated from Signal Tower. Indication Light, hung from span wire opposite tower, showing "WHITE" light indicates that gates have been lowered. When gates have not been lowered, motorman will stop on near side of crossing before proceeding.

6. When cars are being moved ahead of engine in switching movements over crossings of Berryman Avenue, Vine Street, Haynes Avenue, John Street, and Welland Avenue, a member of train crew shall act as flagman to protect public.

7. Switch at Garden City Junction must be left set for Grantham Division.

8. Derail situate 800 feet west of Lincoln Paper Co. Spur must be left open when crews are working west or east of same.

9. Merritton Transfer—Tracks are designated as follows:
   (a) Team Track (not to be used by N. St. C. & T. Ry. crews, except in cases of emergency.)
   (b) Tracks Nos. 1, 2, 3, and 4. Track No 1 is to be left clear, and used as a run-around track.
   Switches are to be left set for Track No. 1.

10. Limit for C.N.R: Trains—The limit for operation of C.N.R. trains is marked by a board, situate slightly east of Hartzel Road, Merritton.

SPEED RESTRICTIONS
St. Catharines—At Crossings of Berryman Avenue, Vine Street, John Street, Haynes Avenue and Welland Avenue........Miles Per Hour 10
Merritton—At Crossing of Hartzel Road ....Miles Per Hour 10

SPRING SWITCHES—Garden City Junction.

SIDINGS AND TURN-OUTS   Mls
East End of Through Siding (Rogers Coal Siding) 0.11
Main Line Division Connection..................................... 0.12
Lake Shore Division Junction..................................... 0.12
Wilson Lumber Co. Siding... 0.28
Jones & Lockhart Siding.. 0.32
Canadian Canners Siding.. 0.41
Main Line Division Connection..................................... 0.47
Main Line Division Connection..................................... 0.47
Yale & Towne Siding.. 0.49
Classification Yard Tracks.. 0.69
Industrial Area Spur... 0.74
Imperial Iron Siding... 0.90
Classification Yard Tracks.. 0.97
Foster-Wheeler Siding.. 0.98
British American Siding.. 1.14
Lincoln Oil Siding... 1.37
Canadian Vegetable Parchment Siding.............................. 1.87
Garden City Junction... 1.87
Derail Switch.. 1.97
Alliance Paper Mills Siding....................................... 2.12
Perfection Petroleum Siding....................................... 2.22
West End of Scale Siding.. 2.38
No. 4 Track.. 2.44
East End of Scale Siding.. 2.49
No. 3 Track.. 2.49
No. 2 Track.. 2.52
Connection to Platform Track...................................... 2.56

TROLLEY CUT-OUT SWITCHES
On Lord & Burnham Siding.
On Imperial Iron Corporation Limited Siding (Two).
On Foster-Wheeler Co's Siding, at Switch.
On British American Oil Co's Siding, Queenston Street.
On Lincoln Oil Co's Siding.
On Alliance Paper Mills Siding.
On Perfection Petroleum Siding.

YARD LIMITS
St. Catharines—From Terminal Station to Queenston Street Bridge.
Merritton—From 800 feet west of Garden City Junction to Merritton Transfer.

TROLLEY BREAKERS—SHUT-OFF CONTROLLERS
305 feet east of Vine Street.

WELLAND DIVISION — Southbound

Time Table No. 52   Effective February 20th, 1938, at 4.00 a.m.

Miles	STATIONS	Daily ex Sun 120	Daily ex Sun 122	Daily ex Sun 124	Daily 126	Daily 128	Daily 130	Daily 132	Daily 134	Daily 136	Daily 138	Daily 140	Daily 142	Daily 144	Daily 146	Daily 148	Daily 150	Daily 152	Daily 154
		am	am	am	am	am	am	pm	pm	pm	pm	pm	pm	pm	pm	pm	pm	pm	pm
0.00	Thorold............Tel..Sid Lv	6 00	7 36	8 36	9 36	10 36	11 36	12 36	1 36	2 36	3 36	4 36	5 36	6 36	7 36	8 36	9 36	10 36	11 36
0.27	Substation Junction.....Tel..Sid	6 02	7 37	8 37	9 37	10 37	11 37	12 37	1 37	2 37	3 37	4 37	5 37	6 37	7 37	8 37	9 37	10 37	11 37
2.94	Dixon's............Tel..Sid	6 09	7 43	8 43	9 43	10 43	11 43	12 43	1 43	2 43	3 43	4 43	5 43	6 43	7 43	8 43	9 43	10 43	11 43
4.72	Stop 9............Tel..Sid	6 13	7 46	8 46	9 46	10 46	11 46	12 46	1 46	2 46	3 46	4 46	5 46	6 46	7 46	8 46	9 46	10 46	11 46
5.70	Stop 12............Tel..Sid	6 15	7 48	8 48	9 48	10 48	11 48	12 48	1 48	2 48	3 48	4 48	5 48	6 48	7 48	8 48	9 48	10 48	11 48
6.99	Fonthill............Tel..Sid	6 18	7 51	8 51	9 51	10 51	11 51	12 51	1 51	2 51	3 51	4 51	5 51	6 51	7 51	8 51	9 51	10 51	11 51
8.84	Stop 17............Tel..Sid	6 23	7 55	8 55	9 55	10 55	11 55	12 55	1 55	2 55	3 55	4 55	5 55	6 55	7 55	8 55	9 55	10 55	11 55
10.06	Stop 19............Tel..Sid	6 26	7 58	8 58	9 58	10 58	11 58	12 58	1 58	2 58	3 58	4 58	5 58	6 58	7 58	8 58	9 58	10 58	11 58

Miles	STATIONS	123	125	127	129	131	133	135	137	139	141	143	145	147	149	151	153	155
11.29	Welland............Tel..Sid	6 30	8 02	9 02	10 02	11 02	12 02	1 02	2 02	3 02	4 02	5 02	6 02	7 02	8 02	9 02	10 02	11 02	12 02
11.80	T. H. & B. Transfer.....Tel..Sid	6 32	8 04	9 04	10 04	11 04	12 04	1 04	2 04	3 04	4 04	5 04	6 04	7 04	8 04	9 04	10 04	11 04	12 04

Miles	STATIONS	121																
12.63	Chemical Spur............Sid	6 35	8 07	9 07	10 07	11 07	12 07	1 07	2 07	3 07	4 07	5 07	6 07	7 07	8 07	9 07	10 07	11 07	12 07
14.39	Dainsville............Tel..Sid	6 41	8 14	9 14	10 14	11 14	12 14	1 14	2 14	3 14	4 14	5 14	6 14	7 14	8 14	9 14	10 14	11 14	12 14
16.30	Mile 16............Tel..Sid	6 45	8 18	9 18	10 18	11 18	12 18	1 18	2 18	3 18	4 18	5 18	6 18	7 18	8 18	9 18	10 18	11 18	12 18
17.67	Humberstone............Tel..Sid	6 48	8 21	9 21	10 21	11 21	12 21	1 21	2 21	3 21	4 21	5 21	6 21	7 21	8 21	9 21	10 21	11 21	12 21
18.59	Port Colborne............Tel..Sid Ar	6 51	8 24	9 24	10 24	11 24	12 24	1 24	2 24	3 24	4 24	5 24	6 24	7 24	8 24	9 24	10 24	11 24	12 24

SPEED RESTRICTIONS
Southbound   Miles Per Hour

Thorold—Crossing of Ormond Street, first crossing south of Thorold Station....................10

Mile 10.06—Crossing of Highway, Stop 19........Stop

Humberstone—Main and Cranberry Streets..........10

Port Colborne—Crossing of King Street..........Stop

PASSENGER TRANSFER POINTS
Southbound

Main Line Westbound at Thorold Station.

YARD LIMITS
Thorold—From Main Line Switch at Thorold Substation to south switch at Exolon Siding.
Fonthill—From 775 feet north of Station to Stop 15.
Welland—From Welland Station to south of switch leading to T. H. & B. Ry. Interchange, and to fifty feet west of the west end switch of interchange tracks.
Humberstone and Port Colborne—From end of private right-of way north of Humberstone, to end of track at C.N.R. Station, Port Colborne.

TROLLEY BREAKERS—Shut-off Controllers
100 feet south of Bridge over Old Welland Canal, Thorold.
100 feet north of Welland Substation.

See Special Instructions on Page 12

WELLAND DIVISION — Northbound

Time Table No. 52 Effective April 3rd, 1938, at 4.00 a.m.

Miles	STATIONS	Daily ex Sun	Daily ex Sun	Daily	Daily	Daily	Daily	Daily	Daily	Daily	Daily	Daily	Daily	Daily	Daily	Daily	Daily	Daily	Daily
		121	**123**	**125**	**127**	**129**	**131**	**133**	**135**	**137**	**139**	**141**	**143**	**145**	**147**	**149**	**151**	**153**	**155**
		am	am	am	am	am	am	pm	pm	pm	pm	pm	pm	pm	pm	pm	pm	pm	pm
0.00	Port Colborne..........Tel...Sid.. Lv	6 12	7 31	8 31	9 31	10 31	11 31	12 31	1 31	2 31	3 31	4 31	5 31	6 31	7 31	8 31	9 31	10 31	11 31
0.92	Humberstone..........Tel...Sid.....	6 15	7 34	8 34	9 34	10 34	11 34	12 34	1 34	2 34	3 34	4 34	5 34	6 34	7 34	8 34	9 34	10 34	11 34
2.29	Mile 16................Tel...Sid.....	6 18	7 37	8 37	9 37	10 37	11 37	12 37	1 37	2 37	3 37	4 37	5 37	6 37	7 37	8 37	9 37	10 37	11 37
4.20	Dainsville..............Tel...Sid.....	6 22	7 41	8 41	9 41	10 41	11 41	12 41	1 41	2 41	3 41	4 41	5 41	6 41	7 41	8 41	9 41	10 41	11 41
5.96	Chemical Spur...............Sid.....	6 29	7 48	8 48	9 48	10 48	11 48	12 48	1 48	2 48	3 48	4 48	5 48	6 48	7 48	8 48	9 48	10 48	11 48
6.79	T. H. & B. Transfer.....Tel...Sid.....	**6 32**	7 51	8 51	9 51	10 51	11 51	12 51	1 51	2 51	3 51	4 51	5 51	6 51	7 51	8 51	9 51	10 51	11 51
		120																	
7.30	Welland................Tel...Sid.....	6 35	7 54	8 54	9 54	10 54	11 54	12 54	1 54	2 54	3 54	4 54	5 54	6 54	7 54	8 54	9 54	10 54	11 54
8.53	Stop 19................Tel...Sid.....	6 38	**7 58**	**8 58**	**9 58**	**10 58**	**11 58**	**12 58**	**1 58**	**2 58**	**3 58**	**4 58**	**5 58**	**6 58**	**7 58**	**8 58**	**9 58**	**10 58**	**11 58**
			122	**124**	**126**	**128**	**130**	**132**	**134**	**136**	**138**	**140**	**142**	**144**	**146**	**148**	**150**	**152**	**154**
9.75	Stop 17................Tel...Sid.....	6 41	8 01	9 01	10 01	11 01	12 01	1 01	2 01	3 01	4 01	5 01	6 01	7 01	8 01	9 01	10 01	11 01	12 01
11.60	Fonthill................Tel...Sid.....	6 45	8 05	9 05	10 05	11 05	12 05	1 05	2 05	3 05	4 05	5 05	6 05	7 05	8 05	9 05	10 05	11 05	12 05
12.89	Stop 12................Tel...Sid.....	6 48	8 08	9 08	10 08	11 08	12 08	1 08	2 08	3 08	4 08	5 08	6 08	7 08	8 08	9 08	10 08	11 08	12 08
13.87	Stop 9..................Tel...Sid.....	6 50	8 10	9 10	10 10	11 10	12 10	1 10	2 10	3 10	4 10	5 10	6 10	7 10	8 10	9 10	10 10	11 10	12 10
15.65	Dixon's................Tel...Sid.....	6 54	8 14	9 14	10 14	11 14	12 14	1 14	2 14	3 14	4 14	5 14	6 14	7 14	8 14	9 14	10 14	11 14	12 14
18.32	Substation Junction.....Tel...Sid.....	7 00	**8 21**	**9 21**	**10 21**	**11 21**	**12 21**	**1 21**	**2 21**	**3 21**	**4 21**	**5 21**	**6 21**	**7 21**	**8 21**	**9 21**	**10 21**	**11 21**	**12 21**
			6	**8**	**10**	**12**	**14**	**16**	**18**	**20**	**22**	**24**	**26**	**28**	**30**	**32**	**34**	**36**	**38**
18.59	Thorold................Tel...Sid...Ar	7 02	8 23	9 23	10 23	11 23	12 23	1 23	2 23	3 23	4 23	5 23	6 23	7 23	8 23	9 23	10 23	11 23	12 23

SPEED RESTRICTIONS

Northbound — Miles Per Hour

Port Colborne—Crossing of King Street..........Stop
Humberstone—Main and Cranberry Streets.........10
Mile 6.31—Crossing of Highway, Stop 23...........10
Mile 8.53—Crossing of Highway, Stop 19............6
Thorold—Crossing of Ormond Street..............10

PASSENGER TRANSFER POINTS

Northbound

Main Line Eastbound at Substation Junction, Thorold.

SPRING SWITCHES

Thorold Station—Short Track where Welland Division cars stand.
Substation Junction—North Wye Switch to Welland Division.
Siding at Stop 19—Both ends.

TROLLEY CUT-OUT SWITCHES

On Pine Street, Thorold.
On Exolon Sidings.
On Gravel Pit Siding, Fonthill.
On British American Oil Spur, Welland.
On Imperial Oil Spur, Welland.
On Commonwealth Electric Spur, Welland.
On T. H. & B. Ry. Interchange, Welland.
On Canada Cement Co's Siding, Port Colborne, near switch.

RAILWAY CROSSINGS AT GRADE

T. H. & B. Ry. } At Welland, Interlocked { Mileage 12.19
M. C. R.......} { Mileage 12.20
C. N. R. (Wabash) at Dainsville, Half-Interlocked ....Mileage 14.17
Canada Cement Co. Industrial Spur, Humberstone, Not Interlocked......................Mileage 18.19

See Special Instructions on Page 12

VICTORIA LAWN CEMETERY DIVISION

Time Table No. 52 **EASTBOUND** Effective April 3rd, 1938, at 4.00 a.m.

Miles	STATIONS	Daily ex Sun	Daily ex Sun	Daily ex Sun	Daily ex Sun	Daily ex Sun	Daily ex Sun	Daily ex Sun	Daily ex Sun	Daily ex Sun	Daily ex Sun	Daily ex Sun	Daily ex Sun	Daily ex Sun	Sun Only	Daily	Daily	Daily		Daily	Daily	Daily
		am	am	am	am	am	am	am	am	am	am	am	am	am	am	am	am	am		pm	pm	pm
0.00	McKinnon's............Lv	....	6 08	6 28	6 48	7 08	7 28	7 48	8 08	8 28	8 48	9 08	9 28	9 48	.....	10 08	10 28	10 48	And	11 08	11 28	11 48
1.02	Ontario and King..........	....	6 13	6 33	6 53	7 13	7 33	7 53	8 13	8 33	8 53	9 13	9 33	9 53	.....	10 13	10 33	10 53	Every	11 13	11 33	11 53
1.20	William and St. Paul.........	....	6 14	6 34	6 54	7 14	7 34	7 54	8 14	8 34	8 54	9 14	9 34	9 54	.....	10 14	10 34	10 54	Twenty	11 14	11 34	11 54
1.36	St. Paul and James.....Tel.	5 56	6 16	6 36	6 56	7 16	7 36	7 56	8 16	8 36	8 56	9 16	9 36	9 56	9 56	10 16	10 36	10 56	Minutes	11 16	11 36	11 56
1.71	St. Paul and Geneva........	5 59	6 19	6 39	6 59	7 19	7 39	7 59	8 19	8 39	8 59	9 19	9 39	9 59	9 59	10 19	10 39	10 59	To	11 19	11 39	Barn
2.12	Queenston & Thorold Rd.Tel.	6 01	6 21	6 41	7 01	7 21	7 41	8 01	8 21	8 41	9 01	9 21	9 41	10 01	10 01	10 21	10 41	11 01		11 21	11 41	
3.51	Victoria Lawn...........Ar	6 08	6 28	6 48	7 08	7 28	7 48	8 08	8 28	8 48	9 08	9 28	9 48	10 08	10 08	10 28	10 48	11 08		11 28	11 48	

PASSENGER TRANSFER POINTS

Eastbound
- Port Dalhousie Division, Southbound, at Diamond.
- Facer Street, Thorold Coach and Geneva-York Coach, Eastbound, at William and St. Paul Streets·
- Port Dalhousie Division, Northbound, at Geneva and St. Paul Streets.
- Facer Street and Thorold Coach, Westbound, at Geneva and St. Paul Streets.

WESTBOUND

Miles	STATIONS	Daily ex Sun	Daily ex Sun	Daily ex Sun	Daily ex Sun	Daily ex Sun	Daily ex Sun	Daily ex Sun	Daily ex Sun	Daily ex Sun	Daily ex Sun	Daily ex Sun	Daily ex Sun	Daily ex Sun	Sun Only	Daily	Daily	Daily		Daily	Daily	Daily
		am	am	am	am	am	am	am	am	am	am	am	am	am	am	am	am	am		pm	pm	pm
0.00	Victoria Lawn...........Lv	....	6 08	6 28	6 48	7 08	7 28	7 48	8 08	8 28	8 48	9 08	9 28	9 48	.....	10 08	10 28	10 48	And	11 08	11 28	11 48
1.39	Queenston & Thorold Rd.Tel.	....	6 15	6 35	6 55	7 15	7 35	7 55	8 15	8 35	8 55	9 15	9 35	9 55	.....	10 15	10 35	10 55	Every	11 15	11 35	11 55
1.80	St. Paul and Geneva........	....	6 17	6 37	6 57	7 17	7 37	7 57	8 17	8 37	8 57	9 17	9 37	9 57	.....	10 17	10 37	10 57	Twenty	11 17	11 37	11 57
2.14	St. Paul and James......Tel.	....	6 20	6 40	7 00	7 20	7 40	8 00	8 20	8 40	9 00	9 20	9 40	10 00	.....	10 20	10 40	11 00	Minutes	11 20	11 40	12 00
2.46	Ontario and King..........	6 03	6 23	6 43	7 03	7 23	7 43	8 03	8 23	8 43	9 03	9 23	9 43	10 03	10 03	10 23	10 43	11 03	To	11 23	11 43	Barn
3.50	McKinnon's............Ar	6 08	6 28	6 48	7 08	7 28	7 48	8 08	8 28	8 48	9 08	9 28	9 48	10 08	10 08	10 28	10 48	11 08		11 28	11 48	

PASSENGER TRANSFER POINTS

Westbound
- Facer Street, Westbound, Ontario and King Streets.
- Port Dalhousie Division, Northbound, at James and King Streets.

Victoria Lawn Cemetery Division — Special Instructions

1. All sidings and turn-outs other than those mentioned below are shown in column headed "Stations".
2. Block Signals—On Queenston Street near Geneva Street, Red Light indicates a car on Queenston Street between Geneva Street and end of line—Victoria Lawn. Green Light indicates no car between Geneva Street and end of line—Victoria Lawn. Absence of light indicates signal out of order. Freight Crews operating via Geneva Street and Queenston Street in and out of Guaranty Silk Dye Co. Siding will avoid actuating contactor on trolley controlling red light.

   On Ontario Street, near King Street, Red Light indicates car on Ontario Street between King Street and end of line—McKinnon's. Green Light indicates no car on Ontario Street between King Street and end of line—McKinnon's. Absence of light indicates signal out of order.
3. Automatic Traffic Control Signals, St. Paul and James Streets—Westbound cars may proceed from St. Paul Street to stop on James Street with or against signal when other traffic is clear; Eastbound cars are governed entirely by automatic signals.
4. Ontario Street Diamond—Stop before crossing. Operators of one-man cars will proceed cautiously after making sure that crossing is clear. Port Dalhousie Division trains have right of way.

TROLLEY BREAKERS—Shut Off Controllers

On Ontario Street, 100 feet North of Woodruff Avenue.

TROLLEY CUT-OUT SWITCHES

On Canadian Oil Company's Siding (Canadian Warren Pink, Ltd. Siding).

SIDINGS AND TURN-OUTS

Canadian Warren Pink, Ltd., Siding..................Mileage 0.00
McKinnon Industries (General Motors)............... " 0.02
Port Dalhousie Division Switch...................... " 0.28
Welland Vale and Guaranty Silk Dye Co.............. " 1.78

Page 12

WELLAND DIVISION

Instructions on Operations between Stop 17 and Stop 19 Sidings

AUTOMATIC BLOCK SIGNALS control the use of track between Stop 17 Siding and Stop 19 Siding. Nachod type of block signals are located on poles at the north and south entrance to main track between Stop 17 Siding and Stop 19 Siding. They are actuated by contactors located overhead under the trolley wire at the south end of Stop 17 Siding, and the north end of Stop 19 Siding. Signal indications:

"Disks for day indication; Lights for night indication."
The signal indication before train passes the contactor, shows the condition of the block; the indication after passing contactor shows that the desired change has taken place.

STOP SIGNAL—RED LIGHT, RED DISK, indicates DANGER, that the block is occupied by one or more trains approaching from the opposite direction. The block thus occupied must not be entered. Trains must wait behind the contactor until the STOP SIGNAL is changed to NEUTRAL.

NEUTRAL SIGNAL—NO LIGHT, NO DISK, indicates clear track, and that train may proceed under the contactor. As soon as the train passes the contactor, the PERMISSIVE SIGNAL will be displayed, which indicates that the STOP SIGNAL is displayed at the other end of the block. The appearance of the PERMISSIVE SIGNAL authorizes the train to proceed through the block. If, for any reason, the signal fails to change from NEUTRAL to PERMISSIVE when entering block, the STOP SIGNAL will not have been set at the other end. In such a case, the train will back, coasting under the contactor with trolley pole pulled down, and will move forward again with pole on wire. If the signal still fails to work properly, such signal failure must be reported to the Dispatcher immediately, and train movements controlled by Dispatcher.

When two trains entering a block from opposite ends, pass under the contactors at exactly the same instant, both signals will still indicate NEUTRAL. A NEUTRAL SIGNAL that continues after the contactor is passed, is to be taken in the most restrictive indication as a STOP SIGNAL.

PERMISSIVE SIGNAL—WHITE LIGHT, WHITE DISK. The PERMISSIVE SIGNAL, in addition to indicating that STOP SIGNAL is displayed at the other end of the block, also indicates to trains following that there are one or more trains travelling in the block in the same direction. Sections, or other trains following, are authorized by this signal to enter the block, with the knowledge that there is at least one train ahead. As trolley wheel of the following train passes under the contactor when the PERMISSIVE SIGNAL is showing, the white light will momentarily disappear and immediately re-appear, showing that the following train is properly counted in. IT IS VERY IMPORTANT THAT THIS EXTINGUISHING OF THE LIGHT BE OBSERVED. If, on entering a block upon a PERMISSIVE SIGNAL, the white light should fail to blink, the train will at once back, coasting under the contactor with the pole pulled down, and again move forward under the contactor with pole on wire. If the signal fails to blink, report to Dispatcher immediately, for movement only by Dispatcher's instructions. Any number of trains, up to 15, or the equivalent in cars in a train, with trolley poles on wire, may enter the block under the PERMISSIVE SIGNAL and occupy it at one time. It is necessary that the same number of cars shall pass out at either or both ends of the block before signals will again indicate a clear track—NEUTRAL SIGNAL indication.

When power is off the line, trains must not be permitted to drift under a contactor, as the signals will not be changed thereby.

CAUTION—Trains should not be stopped, or the pole replaced with the wheel under the contactor. If, for any reason, a motorman runs under a contactor against a STOP SIGNAL, his passage will be "recorded" though there will be no visible change in the signal. Train must back out again under either contactor at that end of the block, when the record of the passage will be cancelled. CREWS WILL REPORT ANY CASE OF RUNNING AGAINST A STOP SIGNAL, AVOIDABLY OR NOT. Crews will report any failure to obtain a PERMISSIVE SIGNAL, or absence or burning out of any signal lights. Promptly report if trolley pole has thrown at frog trolley pan.

These automatic block signals, unless otherwise provided, do not supersede the superiority of trains or dispense with the use or observance of other signals whenever or wherever required; or relieve trainmen from observance of proper rear-end or front-end protection when required.

REGULAR TRAINS, either direction, having meeting points at Stop 19 Siding as shown in time table may use the main track, either direction, under protection of automatic block signals. EXTRA TRAINS, either direction, with train order for movement over tracks controlled by block signals may use main track, either direction, under protection of automatic block signals.

When meets are arranged by train order, Dispatcher will use Stop 19 Siding in the train order when automatic block signals are operative and trains either direction with meet at Stop 19 may use main track between Stop 17 Siding and Stop 19 Siding under the protection of Automatic Block Signals. When signal failure occurs or block signal is not working, train movement between sidings will be controlled by train order.

Should meeting point or "hold order" be necessary at siding at either end of the block signal when it is not working, the specific siding will be named in the train order.

WELLAND DIVISION — Special Instructions

1. Southbound trains are superior—Trains operating in the inferior direction will take siding at crossing points, unless otherwise ordered (Stop 19 Siding excepted)

2. Conductors or Operators of first and last sections of all trains will report to Dispatcher before leaving Welland.

3. Within the limits of the Town of Port Colborne, the sounding of the whistle is prohibited, except to give such signals as are necessary to train operation only, or except when necessary or advisable to prevent possible accident. (B.R.C. Order No. 45316). The boundary line between Port Colborne and Humberstone is Killallay Street.

4. At the North wye switch to Welland Division from Main Line Division, not necessary to re-throw switch after it has been used by Southbound Welland Division trains.

5. Thorold Yards—On siding crossing Cunningham Street, posts have been placed approximately fifty (50) feet back from street lines on both sides and cars must not be placed between these posts. (B. R. C. Order No. 37527).

6. M. C. R. Crossing, Welland—Movements governed by home semaphore and derail. Controlled by Operator at Swing Bridge on M. C. R.

7. C.N.R. (Wabash) Crossing, Dainsville—Movements on N.St.C. & T. Railway governed by home semaphores and derail, and on C.N.R. (Wabash) by home semaphores, operated from signal cabin at diamond. Normal setting of signals is clear for train movements on the C.N.R. (Wabash), and against train movements on the N. St. C. & T. Railway. Signals will be operated by trainmen or signalmen of the N. St. C. & T. Railway. Signals may be set against C.N.R. (Wabash) movements only when no train is to be seen approaching on that track or when it is certain that a train approaching on that track can be brought to a stop without difficulty before reaching the home semaphore on its side of the diamond crossing. Signals may be set to allow passage over diamond crossing by N. St. C. & T. Railway trains only when C. N. R. (Wabash) track is clear so that passage may be made in safety.

   Four levers in the signal cabin are numbered in order from west to east, the operator facing them toward the north. Nos. 1 and 4 operate signals on the C. N. R. (Wabash), and Nos. 2 and 3 operate derails and signals (together) on the N.St.C. & T. Railway, No. 2 the northerly and No. 3 the southerly. Lever No. 1 has an electric-lock control tieing in with C. N. R. (Wabash) signal plant governing movements over Welland Ship Canal, which will not allow semaphore to be set against eastbound movements if it has been set in a vertical position from the bridge nor allow it to be cleared from the bridge after being set against eastbound movements. Lever No. 4 has a time-lock on it which provides a safety interval of one minute between setting signals against C. N. R. (Wabash) movements and setting derails and signals to allow movement by N.St.C.& T. Railway trains over diamond crossing. To change routing of movements from normal to permissive on N. St. C. & T. Railway; first push lever No. 1 half its full travel to the north, wait a few seconds until a click is heard from the electric lock (indicating that the arm on the west semaphore has reached the horizontal position), then push No. 1 lever to its full forward or north position. Until the west semaphore arm has completed its full travel, the electric lock holds up the latch on No. 1 lever, and mechanism is damaged by trying to force or hurry the operation of this lever and latch. When this movement is complete push lever No. 4 to the north, then pull the other two levers singly to the south, giving priority to the signal and derail on the side of the diamond crossing opposite to that of the car. After train has cleared the diamond crossing and derails, signals will be returned to normal by reversing order and directions of previous lever movements. A manipulation chart is mounted on the wall inside the signal cabin.

   Levers must not be pushed nor pulled violently, nor allowed to drop into desired positions when a signal arm is being lowered. Door of signal cabin must be closed and locked when not in use.

When schedule is operated by one-man cars, signalman will be on duty, daily, at times regular trains are scheduled for this crossing. After operating interlocking plant, signalman will ride one-man trains that will next be using crossing, and when riding will assist operator with baggage, trolley pole, etc., and changing ends of car at end of line. Should signalman be absent from interlocking plant, one-man car operator will comply with Special Instructions contained in above.

8. Canada Cement Co. Industrial Spur Crossing—Stop before crossing. Proceed signal to be given by conductor from diamond.

   Operators of One-Man Cars—Stop before crossing and proceed cautiously after making sure crossing is clear.

9. Passenger cars left standing at Port Colborne over night are to be placed on spur track near King Street. Red hand lanterns are to be left lit and attached in holder clip provided at each end of car. Portable telephone, can containing fusees, torpedos and flags are to be removed and locked in telephone box opposite station.

SIDINGS AND TURN-OUTS

		Mileage
South End Thorold Siding	"	0.04
Passenger Car Storage	"	0.05
Scale Siding—(452 feet long) Switches	"	{ 0.11
		0.20
Freight Yard and A. Martin & Son	"	0.21
North Y Switch	"	0.27
Switch for Y and Shell Oil Co.	"	0.33
Passing Siding—(626 feet long) Switches	"	{ 0.43
		0.55
Pine Street Spur	"	0.63
Exolon Sidings—(1,082 feet long) Switches	"	{ 0.77
		0.98
Dixon's Sidings—(991 feet long) Switches	"	{ 2.85
		3.04
Loading Spur	"	4.72
Passing Siding—(730 feet long) Switches	"	{ 5.63
		5.77
Fonthill Station Siding(585 ft. long)Switches	"	{ 6.92
		7.03
Fonthill Spur (Canadian Canners)	"	7.06
Freight Siding—(1,664 feet long) Switches	"	{ 7.11
		7.43
Passing Siding—(759 feet long) Switches	"	{ 8.78
		8.93
Passing Siding—(954 feet long) Switches	"	{ 9.97
		10.15
Loading Spur	"	10.32
Freight Spurs	"	{ 11.37
		11.40
Crowland Ice and Coal Spur	"	11.46
British American Oil Spur	"	11.64
Clemens & Miller Spur	"	11.67
Commonwealth Electric & Imperial Oil Spur	"	11.68
T. H. & B. Ry. Transfer	"	11.80
Loading Spur	"	12.39
Metals Chemical Spur	"	12.63
Dainsville Siding—(962 feet long) Switches	"	{ 14.30
		14.48
Passing Siding—(1,087 feet long) Switches	"	{ 16.20
		16.40
Herron's Spur	"	17.46
Freight and Team Track	"	17.71
E. T. White Co. Spur	"	18.12
Canada Cement Spur	"	18.14
South Switch of Y—Canada Cement Co.	"	18.24
Spur	"	18.36
C. N. R. Cross-over	"	18.56

INTERCHANGE TRACKS

With T. H. & B. Ry. at Welland—The N. St. C. & T. Ry. will deliver cars to the T. H. & B. Ry. on the right hand, or northerly track, and the T. H. & B. Ry. will deliver cars to the N. St. C. & T. Ry. on the left hand, or southerly track.

With C. N. R. at Port Colborne—One thousand (1,000) feet of Canada Cement Co's track, alongside Old Canal, is used for interchange purposes. Cars are delivered by both C. N. R. and N. St. C. & T. Ry. on same track. Care must be taken that operations of Canada Cement Co. are not interfered with.

PORT DALHOUSIE DIVISION

Time Table No. 52 — **NORTHBOUND** — Effective April 3rd, 1938, at 4 a.m.

Mls	STATIONS	Daily ex Sun	Daily ex Sun	Daily ex Sun and Holidays	Daily ex Sun and Holidays	Daily	Daily	Daily	Daily	Daily	Daily	Daily		Daily	Daily	Sat Only	Daily	Sat Only	Daily	Daily
		am	*am	am	am	am	am	am	am	am	pm	pm		pm	pm	pm	pm	pm	pm	pm
0.00	St. Catharines Terminal....Tel.Sid	5 45	6 35	6 56	7 26	7 56	8 51	9 56	10 56	11 56	12 26	12 56	And Every Thirty Minutes To	8 26	8 56	9 26	9 56	10 26	10 56	11 56
0.28	Geneva and St. Paul...Sid { Double	5 47	6 37	6 58	7 28	7 58	8 53	9 58	10 58	11 58	12 28	12 58		8 28	8 58	9 28	9 58	10 28	10 58	11 58
0.62	St. Paul and James....Tel.Sid { Track	5 50	6 40	7 01	7 31	8 01	8 56	10 01	11 01	12 01	12 31	1 01		8 31	9 01	9 31	10 01	10 31	11 01	12 01
0.71	James and King....Sid	5 51	6 41	7 02	7 32	8 02	8 57	10 02	11 02	12 02	12 32	1 02		8 32	9 02	9 32	10 02	10 32	11 02	12 02
0.91	James and Raymond....Sid	5 53	6 42	7 04	7 34	8 04	8 59	10 04	11 04	12 04	12 34	1 04		8 34	9 04	9 34	10 04	10 34	11 04	12 04
1.22	Lake and Louisa....Tel..Sid	5 55	6 44	7 06	7 36	8 06	9 01	10 06	11 06	12 06	12 36	1 06		8 36	9 06	9 36	10 06	10 36	11 06	12 06
1.61	Woodruff's Siding....Tel..Sid	5 58	6 45	7 09	7 39	8 09	9 04	10 09	11 09	12 09	12 39	1 09		8 39	9 09	9 39	10 09	10 39	11 09	12 09
2.33	Houtby's Siding....Tel..Sid	6 01	6 47	7 12	7 42	8 12	9 07	10 12	11 12	12 12	12 42	1 12		8 42	9 12	9 42	10 12	10 42	11 12	12 12
3.15	Barnsdale Siding....Tel..Sid	6 04	6 49	7 15	7 45	8 15	9 10	10 15	11 15	12 15	12 45	1 15		8 45	9 15	9 45	10 15	10 45	11 15	12 15
4.14	Lake Shore Road Siding....Sid	6 06	6 51	7 17	7 47	8 17	9 12	10 17	11 17	12 17	12 47	1 17		8 47	9 17	9 47	10 17	10 47	11 17	12 17
4.56	Canning Co. Siding....Tel..Sid	6 09	6 52	7 20	7 50	8 20	9 15	10 20	11 20	12 20	12 50	1 20		8 50	9 20	9 50	10 20	10 50	11 20	12 20
5.55	Port Dalhousie....Tel..Sid	6 14	6 56	7 27	7 57	8 27	9 22	10 27	11 27	12 27	12 57	1 27		8 57	9 27	9 57	10 27	10 57	11 27	12 27

PASSENGER TRANSFER POINTS

Northbound—Main Line at St. Catharines Terminal.
Thorold Coach Eastbound, at Geneva and St. Paul Streets.
Victoria Lawn Eastbound, at Geneva and St. Paul Streets.
Thorold Coach Westbound, at St. Paul and James Streets.
Victoria Lawn Westbound, at James and King Streets, except on 8.51 a.m. trip at Ontario Street Diamond.
Facer Street westbound, at Terminal Station.
Geneva-York Coach, at York and Louisa Streets.

SOUTHBOUND

Mls	STATIONS	Daily ex Sun	Daily ex Sun and Holidays	Daily ex Sun	Daily ex Sun and Holidays	Daily	Daily	Daily	Daily	Daily	Daily		Daily	Daily	Sat Only	Daily	Sat Only	Daily	Daily
		*am	am	am	am	am	am	am	am	pm	pm		pm	pm	pm	pm	pm	pm	am
0.00	Port Dalhousie....Tel.Sid	6 15	7 05	7 35	8 05	8 30	9 35	10 35	11 35	12 35	1 05	And Every Thirty Minutes To	9 05	9 35	10 05	10 35	11 05	11 35	12 35
0.99	Canning Co. Siding....Tel.Sid	6 20	7 10	7 40	8 10	8 35	9 40	10 40	11 40	12 40	1 10		9 10	9 40	10 10	10 40	11 10	11 40	12 40
1.41	Lake Shore Road Siding....Sid	6 22	7 12	7 42	8 12	8 37	9 42	10 42	11 42	12 42	1 12		9 12	9 42	10 12	10 42	11 12	11 42	12 42
2.40	Barnesdale Siding....Tel.Sid	6 25	7 15	7 45	8 15	8 40	9 45	10 45	11 45	12 45	1 15		9 15	9 45	10 15	10 45	11 15	11 45	12 45
3.22	Houtby's Siding....Tel.Sid	6 27	7 17	7 47	8 17	8 42	9 47	10 47	11 47	12 47	1 17		9 17	9 47	10 17	10 47	11 17	11 47	12 47
3.94	Woodruff's Siding....Tel.Sid	6 30	7 20	7 50	8 20	8 45	9 50	10 50	11 50	12 50	1 20		9 20	9 50	10 20	10 50	11 20	11 50	12 50
4.33	Lake and Louisa....Tel.Sid	6 32	7 22	7 52	8 22	8 47	9 52	10 52	11 52	12 52	1 22		9 22	9 52	10 22	10 52	11 22	11 52	12 52
4.89	St. Catharines Terminal....Tel.Sid	6 36	7 26	7 56	8 26	8 51	9 56	10 56	11 56	12 56	1 26		9 26	9 56	10 26	10 56	11 26	11 56	12 56
				Barn									Barn			Barn		Barn	Barn

NOTE—Operator on car leaving St. Catharines 6.56 a.m. will change cars at Barnesdale Siding with car leaving Port Dalhousie at 7.05 a.m.

*Call Dispatcher at Lake and Louisa and Register.

PASSENGER TRANSFER POINTS

Southbound—Victoria Lawn Eastbound, at Diamond.
Main Line, at St. Catharines Terminal.

SPEED RESTRICTIONS

Southbound Cars or Engines STOP before crossing street line at Welland Avenue.

SPRING SWITCHES

Barnesdale Siding—Both Ends.
Woodruff's Siding—Both Ends. } When 20 minute
Canning Co. Siding—Both Ends. } service is operated.

See Special Instructions on Page 16

FACER STREET DIVISION

Time Table No. 52 — **EASTBOUND** — Effective April 3rd, 1938, at 4 a.m.

Mls	STATIONS	Daily ex Sun	Daily ex Sun	Daily ex Sun	Daily ex Sun	Daily ex Sun	Daily ex Sun	Daily ex Sun	Daily ex Sun	Daily ex Sun	Daily ex Sun	Daily ex Sun	Daily ex Sun	Sun Only	Daily		Daily	Daily
		am	am	am	am	am	am	am	am	am	am	am	am	am	am		pm	pm
0.00	C.N.R. Station	6 09	6 29	6 49	7 09	7 29	7 49	8 09	8 29	8 49	9 09	9 29	9 49	.....	10 09	And Every Twenty Minutes To	11 09	11 29
0.85	William and St. Paul	6 14	6 34	6 54	7 14	7 34	7 54	8 14	8 34	8 54	9 14	9 34	9 54	.....	10 14		11 14	11 34
1.01	St. Paul and James....Tel	6 16	6 36	6 56	7 16	7 36	7 56	8 16	8 36	8 56	9 16	9 36	9 56	.....	10 16		11 16	11 36
1.32	James and Raymond	6 18	6 38	6 58	7 18	7 38	7 58	8 18	8 38	8 58	9 18	9 38	9 58	.....	10 18		11 18	11 38
1.92	St. Catharines Terminal....Tel	6 01	6 21	6 41	7 01	7 21	7 41	8 01	8 21	8 41	9 01	9 21	9 41	10 01	10 21		11 21	11 41
2.73	Niagara Street and Facer	6 05	6 25	6 45	7 05	7 25	7 45	8 05	8 25	8 45	9 05	9 25	9 45	10 05	10 05		11 25	11 45
3.26	Grantham Avenue	6 07	6 27	6 47	7 07	7 27	7 47	8 07	8 27	8 47	9 07	9 27	9 47	10 07	10 07		11 27	11 47

PASSENGER TRANSFER POINTS

Eastbound—Victoria Lawn Eastbound, Thorold Coach Eastbound and Geneva-York Coach, at William and St. Paul
Geneva-York Coach at Terminal Station.

WESTBOUND

Mls	STATIONS	Daily ex Sun	Daily ex Sun	Daily ex Sun	Daily ex Sun	Daily ex Sun	Daily ex Sun	Daily ex Sun	Daily ex Sun	Daily ex Sun	Daily ex Sun	Daily ex Sun	Daily ex Sun	Sun Only	Daily		Daily	Daily	Daily
		am	am	am	am	am	am	am	am	am	am	am	am	am	am		pm	pm	pm
0.00	Grantham Avenue		6 09	6 29	6 49	7 09	7 29	7 49	8 09	8 29	8 49	9 09	9 29	9 49	10 09	And Every Twenty Minutes To	11 09	11 29	11 49
0.53	Niagara Street and Facer		6 11	6 31	6 51	7 11	7 31	7 51	8 11	8 31	8 51	9 11	9 31	9 51	10 11		11 11	11 31	11 51
1.34	St. Catharines Terminal....Tel	5 55	6 15	6 35	6 55	7 15	7 35	7 55	8 15	8 35	8 55	9 15	9 35	9 55	10 15		11 15	11 35	11 55
1.65	Geneva and St. Paul	5 57	6 17	6 37	6 57	7 17	7 37	7 57	8 17	8 37	8 57	9 17	9 37	9 57	10 17		11 17	11 37	11 57
1.99	James and St. Paul....Tel	6 00	6 20	6 40	7 00	7 20	7 40	8 00	8 20	8 40	9 00	9 20	9 40	10 00	10 20		11 20	11 40	12 00
2.31	Ontario and King	6 03	6 23	6 43	7 03	7 23	7 43	8 03	8 23	8 43	9 03	9 23	9 43	10 03	10 23		11 23	Barn	Barn
2.45	Ontario and St. Paul	6 04	6 24	6 44	7 04	7 24	7 44	8 04	8 24	8 44	9 04	9 24	9 44	10 04	10 24		11 24		
3.26	C.N.R. Station	6 08	6 28	6 48	7 08	7 28	7 48	8 08	8 28	8 48	9 08	9 28	9 48	10 08	10 28		11 28		

NOTE—Double Track on Welland Avenue from Clark Street to Geneva Street.

PASSENGER TRANSFER POINTS

Westbound—Port Dalhousie Division Northbound, at St. Catharines Terminal.
Victoria Lawn and Thorold Coach Eastbound, at Geneva and St. Paul.
Victoria Lawn Westbound, at Ontario and King.
Thorold Coach Westbound, at Ontario and St. Paul.

SPEED RESTRICTIONS

On Raymond Street before crossing Clark Street STOP.

Page 15

Page 17

Page 16

PORT DALHOUSIE DIVISION — Special Instructions

All operators on Port Dalhousie Division are required to carry Train Order Book.

1. Port Dalhousie Division is in operation as a Local Line, and scheduled trains included in working time table do not require train orders. All train movements on this Division other than scheduled trains will be covered by train orders issued by the Dispatcher. Wherever possible, freight and work trains will be moved as sections of regular trains but must report to Dispatcher before moving as a section of a regular train. When movements are made in sections, flags will be displayed by day, and marker lights by night. Sections must not proceed until protecting signals are displayed by preceding section.

2. Within the limits of the City of St. Catharines, the sounding of whistles is prohibited except to give such signals as are necessary to train operation only, or except when necessary or advisable to prevent possible accident. (B.R.C. Order No. 46708).

3. Cars westbound on St. Paul Street, St. Catharines, may proceed from St. Paul Street to regular stop on James Street, with or against the traffic signal, if other traffic is clear.

4. The instructions in Time Table General Instructions, 13(b), will apply to all crossing sidings, and in addition, to avoid the possibility of a northbound first section leaving Lake and Louisa Streets before last section of a southbound movement on the same run has cleared Lake and Louisa Streets, the procedure to be followed is strict observance of the rule requiring sections displaying signals for a following section to protect such following section until into clear. Therefore, on Lake and Louisa Streets, it is necessary when southbound movements are operating in sections, that each section protect its following section until into clear at Lake and Louisa Streets, thereby avoiding the possibility of a northbound movement getting in between sections southbound.

5. Only last section of southbound trains will stop at Lock Street to take on or let off passengers, unless preceding sections have been instructed to stop by Inspector on duty in yards at Port Dalhousie.

6. When making stop at Lock Street, Port Dalhousie, street crossing must not be blocked. Cars carrying mail will be stopped at the near side of street or with front end at chalet platform.

7. When movements are in sections, southbound sections will not pass south switch at end of yards, until preceding section has passed Lock Street, unless instructed by inspector on duty.

8. West leg of "Y" at Welland Avenue and Geneva Street must NOT be used for freight movements.

9. Ontario Street Diamond—Stop before crossing. "Proceed" signal to be given by conductor of train from diamond. Operators of one-man cars will stop and proceed cautiously after making sure that crossing is clear. Port Dalhousie Division cars have right of way.

10. When cars are approaching, in either direction, the road at rear of Lakeside Park in Port Dalhousie, about 100 feet north of Lock Street, whistle or gong must be sounded.

11. Welland Vale Siding—Semaphore signal located 600 feet north of switch is for protection of trains on main track and trains entering or leaving Welland Vale Siding. Conductor of a train entering or leaving Welland Vale Siding must protect trains by this semaphore signal against all southbound trains. All southbound trains approaching Welland Vale Siding must approach semaphore signal prepared to stop regardless of indication.

YARD LIMITS

St. Catharines—St. Catharines Terminal via Welland Avenue to 150 feet west of Lake and Louisa Streets.
Port Dalhousie—Lock Street to end of Track.

RAILWAY CROSSINGS AT GRADE
(From Port Dalhousie)

Local Line, Ontario Street, St. Catharines—
Not Interlocked....................Mileage   3.88

TROLLEY BREAKERS—Shut Off Controllers

On James Street—150 feet north of Raymond Street.
On Geneva Street—100 feet south of Church Street.

TROLLEY CUT-OUT SWITCHES

On McKinnon's Siding.
On Welland Vale Siding, near McIntee Siding.
On Corbett's Siding.

SIDINGS AND TURN-OUTS
(From Port Dalhousie)

Connection to Port Dalhousie Freight Shed	Mileage
Tracks	0.05
Lead to Dock and Freight Shed Tracks	0.07
Canadian Canners Siding	0 86
Canning Factory Passing Siding—715 feet long...	0 92
Switches	1.06
Lake Shore Fruit Loading Spur	1.41
Barnesdale Passing Siding—912 feet long—Switches	2.32
	2.49
Barnesdale Loading Siding	2.82
Houtby's Passing Siding—374 feet long—Switches..	3.19
	3.26
Welland Vale and McIntee Coal Company Siding..	3.31
Ballast Pit Siding	3.49
McKinnon Industries Siding	3.80
W. S. Tyler Siding	3.84
McKinnon Columbus Chain Siding	3.85
Connection to Ontario Street Line	3.85
Woodruff's Passing Siding—608 feet long—Switches	3.89
(R. M. Stokes Coal Co.)	4.00
Parnell & Garland Siding	4.04
Connection to Lake Street Line	4.33
Material Yard, St. Catharines	4.69
Connection to Welland Avenue Double Track	4.71
Crossover—Welland Avenue Switches—	4.72
	4.74
End of Double Track—Welland Ave. and Geneva St.	4.87

LAKE SHORE DIVISION

Time Table No. 52

Effective April 3rd, 1938, at 4 a.m

Mls	STATIONS
0.00	St. Catharines Terminal...Tel..Sid
0.12	Lake Shore Junction.......Tel..Sid
1.33	Grantham Avenue................
1.45	Facer Street Siding............Sid
1.89	Carleton Street..................
2.48	Scott Street Siding............Sid
4.28	Welland Ship Canal..............
4.68	Lake Shore Siding.............Sid
4.82	End of Track....................

Regular Service to Grantham Avenue Only.—

(See Facer Street Division.)

No Regular Service Beyond Grantham Avenue.

See Page 18 for Special Instructions

Page 18

LAKE SHORE DIVISION and FACER STREET DIVISION
Special Instructions

BLOCK SIGNALS

1. **On St. Paul Street West**—West of Ontario Street—Red light indicates a car on St. Paul Street between Ontario Street and C. N. R. Station. Green Light indicates no car between Ontario Street and C. N. R. Station. Absence of light indicates signal out of order. This signal has no counting device and therefore does not provide for movements of more than one section under protection of signals.

2. **On Welland Avenue**—South side—Opposite Laughlin Spur. Trolley contactor located near Niagara Street Tower. Red Light indicates a car movement on Niagara Street. Green Light indicates car movement has cleared Niagara Street. Absence of light indicates signal out of order.

   Signals are for protection of all movements on Niagara Street, and freight trains will operate as sections of Facer Street cars.

   Motormen on eastbound freight trains, except when west of Geneva Street, cannot see signal. They must ascertain from Tower Operator the position of Facer Street cars before proceeding.

   When signals are out of order, eastbound cars will stop alongside of Niagara Street Tower and proceed only on instructions from Tower Operator.

3. Within the limits of the City of St. Catharines, the sounding of whistles is prohibited except to give such signals as are necessary to train operation only, or except when necessary or advisable to prevent possible accident (B. R. C. Order No. 46708). The boundary line between St. Catharines and the Township is Grantham Avenue.

4. Automatic Traffic Control Signals, St. Paul and James Streets—Westbound cars may proceed from St. Paul Street to stop on James Street with or against signal when other traffic is clear. Eastbound cars are governed entirely by automatic signals.

5. St. Catharines Terminal—All tracks are controlled by Operator in Tower at Niagara Street. Lake Shore or Facer Street signal to Operator is FOUR short whistles.

   Dwarf signals controlling switches on tracks in St. Catharines Terminal Yards are operated from Signal Tower situated at Niagara Street, and Motormen and Operators entering this area must make sure before passing these signals that they are set for "Proceed." Colour signal indications at night are: Red—STOP; Yellow—PROCEED.

6. All trains entering or leaving St. Catharines Terminal Yards must stop before crossing street line at Niagara Street.

7. Clark Street, St. Catharines, at west entrance to Car Shop Yard must not be blocked by cars left standing across it. When necessary to throw switches close to street, cars or locomotives must not block Clark Street.

8. Crossing of Welland Ship Canal Railway, Port Weller—Movements governed by distant and home semaphores and derails, controlled from tower at diamond crossing.

9. Welland Ship Canal Bridge, Port Weller—All trains will stop at "Stop" Board before crossing bridge. Westbound trains will approach "Stop" sign at lift bridge with extreme caution.

TROLLEY BREAKERS—Shut Off Controllers

On Geneva Street—100 feet south of Church Street.
On Raymond Street—100 feet west of Clark Street.
On Welland Avenue—At Head of Catherine Street—(Two)
On Welland Avenue—155 feet east of Geneva Street.
30 feet west of intersection of Welland Avenue and Niagara Street.
West of Welland Ship Canal Bridge, Port Weller.

TROLLEY CUT-OUT SWITCHES

On Port Weller Spur, Port Weller.

RAILWAY CROSSING AT GRADE

Welland Ship Canal Railway, Port Weller—
Interlocked . . . . .Mileage   4.20

SWING AND LIFT BRIDGES

Welland Ship Canal, Port Weller . . . . .Mileage   4.28

YARD LIMITS

St. Catharines—From St. Catharines Terminal to Carleton Street.
Port Weller—Carleton Street to End of Track.

SIDINGS AND TURN-OUTS

Car Shop Yards	Mileage
Facer Street Siding—812 feet long—Switches	{1.38
	{1.53
Scott Street Siding—776 feet long—Switches	{2.41
	{2.55
Port Weller Spur	3.98
Lake Shore Siding—1,260 feet long—Switches	{4.56
	{4.80

NIAGARA FALLS LOCAL DIVISION
SOUTHBOUND

Time Table No. 52   See Separate Time Table for Sunday.   Effective, April 3rd, 1938, at 4.00 A.M.

Mls.	STATIONS	am	am	am	am	am	am	am	am	am	am	am	am	pm	pm	pm	pm	L.L. pm	pm	L.L. pm	am	L.L. am	Sat. Only am
0.00	Bridge Street...........Sid						6 12	6 24	6 36	6 48	7 00	7 12	7 24	10 48	11 00		11 12	11 24	11 36	11 48	12 00	12 12	1 12
0.42	Queen St. Siding.........Sid			L.L.			6 15	6 27	6 39	6 51	7 03	7 15	7 27	10 51	11 03		11 15	11 27	11 39	11 51	12 03	12 15	1 15
0.81	Queen & Victoria Jct. Tel..Sid	5 32	5 41	5 47	5 53	6 05	6 17	6 29	6 41	6 53	7 05	7 17	7 29	10 53	11 05		11 17	11 29	11 41	11 53	12 05	12 17	1 17 Barn
1.47	Victoria Ave. Jct.........Sid	5 35	5 44	5 50	5 56	6 08	6 20	6 32	6 44	6 56	7 08	7 20	7 32	10 56	11 08		11 20	11 32	11 44	11 56	12 08	12 20	
2.08	Centre Siding...........Sid	5 38	5 47	5 53	5 59	6 11	6 23	6 35	6 47	6 59	7 11	7 23	7 35	10 59	11 11		11 23	11 35	11 47	11 59	12 11	12 23	
2.77	Main & Ferry Jct........Sid	5 41	5 50	5 56	6 02	6 14	6 26	6 38	6 50	7 02	7 14	7 26	7 38	11 02	11 14		11 26	11 38	11 50	12 02	12 14	12 26	
0.00	Main & Ferry Jct........Sid	5 41		5 56	6 08	6 20	6 32	6 44	6 56	7 08	7 20	7 32	7 44	11 02	11 14	11 26		11 38		12 02		12 26	
0.91	Winery Road	5 48		6 02	6 14	6 26	6 38	6 50	7 02	7 16	7 26	7 38	7 50	11 08	11 20	11 32		11 46		12 10		12 34	
3.24	Murray St. Siding........Sid		5 54		6 06	6 18	6 30	6 42	6 54	7 06	7 18	7 30	7 42	11 06	11 18		11 30		11 54		12 18		
4.48	Montrose................		6 00		6 12	6 24	6 36	6 48	7 00	7 12	7 26	7 36	7 48	11 12	11 24		11 36		12 00		12 24		

(column note: "And Every Twelve Minutes Until")

PASSENGER TRANSFER POINTS
Southbound—Main Line Eastbound, at Queen and Victoria Junction.
Bridge Coach, at Victoria Avenue Junction.
Lundy's Lane, at Main and Ferry Junction.

NORTHBOUND

Mls.	STATIONS	am	am	am	am	am	am	am	am	am	am	am	pm	pm	pm	pm	am	am	am	am	am
0.00	Montrose................		6 00		6 12	6 24	6 36	6 48	7 00	7 12	7 24	7 36	7 48	11 12	11 24		11 36		12 00		12 24	
1.24	Murray St. Siding.......Sid		6 06		6 18	6 30	6 42	6 54	7 06	7 18	7 30	7 42	7 54	11 18	11 30		11 42		12 06		12 30	
0.00	Winery Road	5 50		6 02	6 14	6 26	6 38	6 50	7 02	7 14	7 26	7 38	7 50	11 08	11 20	11 32		11 48		12 12		12 36
0.91	Main & Ferry Jct........Sid	5 56		6 08	6 20	6 32	6 44	6 56	7 08	7 20	7 32	7 44	7 56	11 14	11 26	11 38		11 56		12 20		12 44
1.71	Main & Ferry Jct........Sid	5 56	6 08		6 20	6 32	6 44	6 56	7 08	7 20	7 32	7 44	7 56	11 20	11 32	11 38	11 44	11 56	12 08	12 20	12 32	12 44
2.40	Centre Siding..........Sid	5 59	6 11		6 23	6 35	6 47	6 59	7 11	7 23	7 35	7 47	7 59	11 23	11 35	11 41	11 47	11 59	12 11	12 23	12 35	12 47
3.01	Victoria Ave. Jct........Sid	6 02	6 14		6 26	6 38	6 50	7 02	7 14	7 26	7 38	7 50	8 02	11 26	11 38	11 44	11 50	12 02	12 14	12 26	12 38	12 50 (Sat. Only)
3.67	Queen & Victoria Jct. Tel..Sid	6 05	6 17		6 29	6 41	6 53	7 05	7 17	7 29	7 41	7 53	8 05	11 29	11 41	11 47	11 53	12 05	12 17	12 29	12 41	12 53
4.06	Queen Street...........Sid	6 08	6 20		6 32	6 44	6 56	7 08	7 20	7 32	7 44	7 56	8 08	11 32	11 44		11 56	12 08	Barn	Barn	Barn	Barn	12 56
4.48	Bridge Street...........Sid	6 11	6 23		6 35	6 47	6 59	7 11	7 23	7 35	7 47	7 59	8 11	11 35	11 47		11 59	12 11					12 59

(column note: "And Every Twelve Minutes Until")

PASSENGER TRANSFER POINTS
Northbound—Lundy's Lane, at Main and Ferry Junction.
Bridge Coach, at Victoria Avenue Junction.
Main Line, at Queen and Victoria Junction.

See Special Instructions on Page 21

NIAGARA FALLS LOCAL DIVISION

Time Table No. 52 — SUNDAY SERVICE ONLY   Effective April 3rd, 1938, at 4 a.m.

SOUTHBOUND

Mls.	STATIONS	am	am	am	am	am	am	am	am	am	am	am	am	am	am	pm	pm	pm	pm	pm	pm	am
0.00	Bridge Street...........Sid	6 12	6 42	7 12	7 42	8 12	8 42	9 12	9 42	9 57		10 12	10 27	10 42	10 57	10 42	10 57	11 12	11 27	11 42	11 57	12 12
0.42	Queen Street Siding.....Sid	6 16	6 46	7 16	7 46	8 16	8 46	9 16	9 45	10 00	L.L.	10 15	10 30	10 45	11 00	10 45	11 00	11 15	11 30	11 45	12 00	12 15
0.81	Queen & Victoria Jct. Tel..Sid	6 19	6 49	7 19	7 49	8 19	8 49	9 19	9 47	10 02	10 02	10 17	10 32	10 47	11 02	10 47	11 02	11 17	11 32	11 47	12 02	12 17
1.47	Victoria Jct.............Sid	6 22	6 52	7 22	7 52	8 22	8 52	9 23	9 50	10 05	10 05	10 20	10 35	10 50	11 05	10 50	11 05	11 20	11 35	11 50	Barn	12 20
2.08	Centre Siding...........Sid	6 27	6 57	7 27	7 57	8 27	8 57	9 27	9 53	10 08	10 08	10 23	10 38	10 53	11 08	10 53	11 08	11 23	11 38	11 53		12 23
2.77	Main & Ferry Jct........Sid	6 32	7 02	7 32	8 02	8 32	9 02	9 32	9 56	10 11	10 11	10 26	10 41	10 56	11 11	10 56	11 11	11 26	11 41	11 56		12 26
0.00	Main & Ferry Jct........Sid		7 02		8 02		9 02		9 56		10 11	10 26	10 41	10 56	11 11	10 56	11 11	11 26	11 41			12 26
0.91	Winery Road		7 09		8 09		9 09		10 03		10 18	10 33	10 48	11 03	11 18	11 03	11 18	11 33	11 48			12 33
3.24	Murray Street Siding....Sid	6 35		7 35		8 35		9 35		10 13		10 28	10 43	10 58	11 13	10 58	11 13	11 28		11 58		
4.48	Montrose...............	6 41		7 41		8 41		9 41		10 19		10 34	10 49	11 04	11 19	11 04	11 19	11 34		12 04		

(column note: "And Every Fifteen Minutes Until")

PASSENGER TRANSFER POINTS
Southbound—Main Line Eastbound, at Queen and Victoria Junction.
Bridge Coach, at Victoria Avenue Junction.
Lundy's Lane, at Main and Ferry Junction.

NORTHBOUND

Mls.	STATIONS	am	am	am	am	am	am	am	am	am	am	am	am	am	pm	pm	pm	pm	pm	am	am
0.00	Montrose...............		6 41		7 41		8 41		9 49		10 19		10 34	10 49	11 04	11 19	11 04	11 19	11 34		12 04	
1.24	Murray Street Siding....Sid		6 49		7 49		8 49		9 54		10 24		10 39	10 54	11 09	11 24	11 09	11 24	11 39		12 09	
0.00	Winery Road		7 15		8 15		9 15		10 04		10 19	10 34	10 49	11 04	11 19	11 04	11 19	11 34		11 49	12 34
0.91	Main & Ferry Jct........Sid		7 22		8 22		9 22		10 11		10 26	10 41	10 56	11 11	11 26	11 11	11 26	11 41		11 56	12 41
1.71	Main & Ferry Jct........Sid	6 52	7 22	7 52	8 22	8 52	9 22	9 56	10 11	10 26		10 41	10 56	11 11	11 26	11 11	11 26	11 41 (L.L.)	11 41	11 56	12 11	12 41
2.40	Centre Siding..........Sid	6 57	7 27	7 57	8 27	8 57	9 27	10 00	10 15	10 30		10 45	11 00	11 15	11 30	11 15	11 30	11 45	11 45	12 00	12 15	12 45
3.01	Victoria Junction........Sid	7 02	7 32	8 02	8 32	9 02	9 32	10 03	10 18	10 33		10 48	11 03	11 18	11 33	11 18	11 33	11 48	11 48	12 03	12 18	12 48
3.67	Queen & Victoria Jct. Tel..Sid	6 06	6 36	7 06	7 36	8 06	8 36	9 06	9 51	10 06	10 21	10 36	10 51	11 06	11 21	11 36	11 51	11 51	12 06	12 21	12 51
4.06	Queen Street Siding.....Sid	6 08	6 38	7 08	7 38	8 08	8 38	9 08	9 53	10 08	10 23	10 38	10 53	11 08	11 23	11 38	11 53	Barn	12 08	Barn
4.48	Bridge Street...........Sid	6 11	6 41	7 11	7 41	8 11	8 41	9 11	9 56	10 11	10 26	10 41	10 56	11 11	11 26	11 41	11 56	12 11

(column note: "And Every Fifteen Minutes Until")

PASSENGER TRANSFER POINTS
Northbound—Lundy's Lane, at Main and Ferry Junction.
Bridge Coach, at Victoria Avenue Junction.
Main Line, at Queen and Victoria Junction.

See Special Instructions on Page 21

NIAGARA FALLS LOCAL DIVISION
Special Instructions

1. Switches and Sidings, other than those mentioned in "Special Instructions," are shown in column headed "Stations."

2. Cars or trains at all crossing points will wait on main line until opposing car or train is in sight, when both will enter opposite ends of siding at the same time and pass cautiously without stopping.

3. Double Track on Victoria Avenue, between Bridge Street and McDougall Avenue, will be used for right-hand operation and Spring Switches located at either end of Double Track will be set for right-hand operation. (See Section 13 (c) of General Instructions for precaution to be observed when cars are passing on Double Track).

4. Cars northbound on Stanley Street will come to a full stop before crossing Stanley Street to Livingstone Street. Southbound cars will come to a full stop on Livingstone Street before crossing Stanley Street. (B.R.C. Order No. 49417).

5. Bridge Street Grade—When Passenger cars are standing on Bridge Street, Operator must remain on car unless absolutely necessary to leave. Extra precautions must be observed to prevent car rolling down grade.

6. M.C.R. Crossing, Erie Avenue and Queen Street—Protected by electric signals of the "Color Light" type to govern movements over the crossing. Location and indications of signals, as follows:

On M. C. R. Tracks—"Color Light" Dwarf Signals located between tracks; southbound, 25 feet north of crossing, and northbound 275 feet south of crossing. Signals govern movements on both tracks.

On N. St. C. & T. Ry. Tracks—"Color Light" Type Signals located above the street curb. Northbound is suspended 16 feet above curb at southwest angle of Erie Avenue and Queen Street; southbound on mast in curb on west side of Erie Avenue, 150 feet north of crossing.

Light indications are as follows:
Red Light . . . . Stop.
Yellow Light . . . . Proceed with Caution.
Absence of Light . . . . . Signal out of Order.

Signals are controlled manually by M. C. R. trainmen from control box located in southwest angle of Erie Avenue and Queen Street. The normal indication is Yellow Light—"Proceed with caution" for the N. St. C. & T. Ry., and Red Light—"Stop" for the M. C. R.

When signals are out of order, movement over crossing must be made with extreme caution, cars first being brought to a stop and proceeding over crossing only when M. C. R. track is known to be clear.

7. M. C. R. Industrial Spur Crossing at Centre—Movements protected by conductors of M. C. R. trains.

8. All northbound cars operating on Lundy's Lane Division will come to a stop at the Presbyterian Church.

TROLLEY BREAKERS—Shut Off Controllers

At Niagara Falls Yards—Main Line, near Bridge Street—(Two Breakers).

RAILWAY CROSSINGS AT GRADE

	Mileage
M. C. R. Double Diamond Crossing, Erie Avenue and Queen Street—Not Interlocked	0.30
M.C.R. Industrial Spur at Centre—Not Interlocked	1.92

SIDINGS AND TURN-OUTS

	Mileage
Bridge Street Passing Siding	0.06
Queen Street Passing Siding	0.44
Double Track on Victoria Avenue—4,336 ft. long—	0.81 / 1.47
Victoria Avenue Wye Switch	1.53
Centre Siding	2.08
Ferry Street Siding	2.73
Lundy's Lane	2.77
Murray Street Siding	3.24
Falls View Siding	3.88

NIAGARA FALLS LOCAL DIVISION—(Motor Coach Route)
LOWER ARCH BRIDGE, QUEEN STREET, 4TH AVENUE

Time Table No 52   Effective April 3rd, 1938, at 4.00 a.m.

SOUTHBOUND

Miles	STATIONS	am	am	am	am	am	am	pm		pm	pm	am
0.00	International Rly. Terminal, Niagara Falls, N.Y.	6 58	7 58	8 58	9 58	10 58	11 58	12 58		10 58	11 58	12 58
2.20	North End Lower Arch Bridge, Niagara Falls, Ont...	7 10	8 10	9 10	10 10	11 10	12 10	1 10	And	11 10	12 10	1 10
3.10	Queen and Victoria Junction...Tel	7 15	8 15	9 15	10 15	11 15	12 15	1 15	Every	11 15	12 15	1 15
3.60	Bridge Street and Sixth Avenue	7 19	8 19	9 19	10 19	11 19	12 19	1 19	Hour	11 19	12 19	1 19
3.90	Huron Street and Fourth Avenue	7 21	8 21	9 21	10 21	11 21	12 21	1 21	Until	11 21	12 21	1 21
5.05	Victoria Avenue Junction	7 25	8 25	9 25	10 25	11 25	12 25	1 25		11 25	12 25	1 25
5.50	Tower Inn Terminal, Niagara Falls, Ontario...Tel	7 27	8 27	9 27	10 27	11 27	12 27	1 27		11 27	12 27	1 27 Gar

PASSENGER TRANSFER POINTS

Southbound—Main Line, at Queen & Victoria Jct.
Northbound and Southbound Cars, at Victoria Avenue Junction.

NORTHBOUND

Miles	STATIONS	Dly. Ex. Sun. am	am	am	am	am	am	pm	pm		pm	am
0.00	Tower Inn Terminal, Niagara Falls, Ontario...Tel	6 28	7 28	8 28	9 28	10 28	11 28	12 28	1 28		11 28	12 28
0.45	Victoria Avenue Junction	6 31	7 31	8 31	9 31	10 31	11 31	12 31	1 31	And	11 31	12 31
1.60	Huron Street and Fourth Avenue	6 35	7 35	8 35	9 35	10 35	11 35	12 35	1 35	Every	11 35	12 35
1.90	Bridge Street and Sixth Avenue	6 37	7 37	8 37	9 37	10 37	11 37	12 37	1 37	Hour	11 37	12 37
2.40	Queen and Victoria Junction...Tel	6 41	7 41	8 41	9 41	10 41	11 41	12 41	1 41	Until	11 41	12 41
3.30	North End Lower Arch Bridge, Niagara Falls, Ont.	6 46	7 46	8 46	9 46	10 46	11 46	12 46	1 46		11 46	12 46
5.30	International Rly. Terminal, Niagara Falls, N.Y.	6 57	7 57	8 57	9 57	10 57	11 57	12 57	1 57		11 57	12 57

PASSENGER TRANSFER POINTS

Northbound—Northbound and Southbound Cars, at Victoria Avenue Junction.
Main Line at Queen & Victoria Jct.

See Special Instructions for Motor Coaches on Page 23

ST. CATHARINES-THOROLD (Motor Coach Route)

Time Table No. 52   **EASTBOUND**   Effective April 3rd, 1938, at 4.00 a.m.

Mls	STATIONS	Daily ex Sun	Daily ex Sun	Daily ex Sun	Daily ex Sun	Daily ex Sun	Daily ex Sun	Daily ex Sun	Daily ex Sun	Daily ex Sun	Daily ex Sun	Daily ex Sun	Daily ex Sun	Daily	Daily	Daily	Daily		Daily	Daily	Daily
		am	am	am	am	am	am	am	am	am	am	am	am	am	am	am	am		pm	pm	pm
0.00	Ontario Street South and Rockcliffe........								8 10	8 30	8 50	9 10	9 30	9 50	10 10	10 30	10 50	And	10 50	11 10	11 30
0.71	William and St. Paul........................	5 54	6 14	6 34	6 54	7 14	7 34	7 54	8 14	8 34	8 54	9 14	9 34	9 54	10 14	10 34	10 54	Every	10 54	11 14	11 34
0.87	St. Paul and James................Tel	5 56	6 16	6 36	6 56	7 16	7 36	7 56	8 16	8 36	8 56	9 16	9 36	9 56	10 16	10 36	10 56	Twenty	10 56	11 16	11 36
1.21	St. Paul and Geneva......................	5 59	6 19	6 39	6 59	7 19	7 39	7 59	8 19	8 39	8 59	9 19	9 39	9 59	10 19	10 39	10 59	Minutes	10 59	11 19	11 39
1.62	Queenston and Thorold Road...........Tel	6 01	6 21	6 41	7 01	7 21	7 41	8 01	8 21	8 41	9 01	9 21	9 41	10 01	10 21	10 41	11 01	To	11 01	11 21	11 41
2.56	Lincoln Avenue..........................	6 04	6 24	6 44	7 04	7 24	7 44	8 04	8 24	8 44	9 04	9 24	9 44	10 04	10 24	10 44	11 04		11 04	11 24	11 44
3.46	Oak and Merritt.........................	6 08	6 28	6 48	7 08	7 28	7 48	8 08	8 28	8 48	9 08	9 28	9 48	10 08	10 28	10 48	11 08		11 08	11 28	11 48
3.91	Lybster Mill...........................	6 10	6 30	6 50	7 10	7 30	7 50	8 10	8 30	8 50	9 10	9 30	9 50	10 10	10 30	10 50	11 10		11 10	11 30	11 50
4.76	Town Line..............................	6 13	6 33	6 53	7 13	7 33	7 53	8 13	8 33	8 53	9 13	9 33	9 53	10 13	10 33	10 53	11 13		11 13	11 33	11 53
5.51	Thorold Station........................	6 16	6 36	6 56	7 16	7 36	7 56	8 16	8 36	8 56	9 16	9 36	9 56	10 16	10 36	10 56	11 16		11 16	11 36	11 56

PASSENGER TRANSFER POINTS

Eastbound—Facer Street, Victoria Lawn and Geneva-York Coach Eastbound, at William and St. Paul.
    Facer Street Westbound, at Geneva and St. Paul.
    Port Dalhousie Division Northbound, at Geneva and St. Paul.
    Main Line, at Geneva and St. Paul.

WESTBOUND

Mls	STATIONS	Daily ex Sun	Daily ex Sun	Daily ex Sun	Daily ex Sun	Daily ex Sun	Daily ex Sun	Daily ex Sun	Daily ex Sun	Daily ex Sun	Daily ex Sun	Daily ex Sun	Daily ex Sun	Daily ex Sun	Daily ex Sun	Daily	Daily	Daily		Daily	Daily	Daily	Daily
		am	am	am	am	am	am	am	am	am	am	am	am	am	am	am	am	am		pm	pm	pm	am
0.00	Thorold Station.......................	6 20	6 40	7 00	7 20	7 40	8 00	8 20	8 40	9 00	9 20	9 40	10 00	10 20	10 40	11 00	11 20		And	11 00	11 20	11 40	12 00
0.75	Town Line............................	6 23	6 43	7 03	7 23	7 43	8 03	8 23	8 43	9 03	9 23	9 43	10 03	10 23	10 43	11 03	11 23		Every	11 03	11 23	11 43	12 03
1.60	Lybster Mill.........................	6 26	6 46	7 06	7 26	7 46	8 06	8 26	8 46	9 06	9 26	9 46	10 06	10 26	10 46	11 06	11 26		Twenty	11 06	11 26	11 46	12 06
2.05	Oak and Merritt.....................	6 29	6 49	7 09	7 29	7 49	8 09	8 29	8 49	9 09	9 29	9 49	10 09	10 29	10 49	11 09	11 29		Minutes	11 09	11 29	11 49	12 09
2.95	Lincoln Avenue......................	6 32	6 52	7 12	7 32	7 52	8 12	8 32	8 52	9 12	9 32	9 52	10 12	10 32	10 52	11 12	11 32		To	11 12	11 32	11 52	12 12
3.89	Queenston and Thorold Road....Tel	6 35	6 55	7 15	7 35	7 55	8 15	8 35	8 55	9 15	9 35	9 55	10 15	10 35	10 55	11 15	11 35			11 15	11 35	11 55	12 15
4.30	St. Paul and Geneva.................	6 37	6 57	7 17	7 37	7 57	8 17	8 37	8 57	9 17	9 37	9 57	10 17	10 37	10 57	11 17	11 37			11 17	11 37	11 57	12 17
4.64	St. Paul and James................Tel	6 40	7 00	7 20	7 40	8 00	8 20	8 40	9 00	9 20	9 40	10 00	10 20	10 40	11 00	11 20	11 40			11 20	11 40	12 00	12 20
4.86	Ontario and St. Paul................	6 43	7 03	7 23	7 43	8 03	8 23	8 43	9 03	9 23	9 43	10 03	10 23	10 43	11 03	11 23	11 43			11 23	11 43	12 03	12 23
5.51	Ontario Street South and Rockcliffe....						8 07	8 27	8 47	9 07	9 27	9 47	10 07	10 27	10 47	11 07	11 27	11 47		11 27	Gar.	Gar.	Gar.

PASSENGER TRANSFER POINTS

Geneva-York Bus at Geneva and St. Paul.
Westbound—Victoria Lawn Westbound, at St. Paul and James.
    Facer Street Westbound, at Ontario and St. Paul.
    Port Dalhousie Division Westbound, at St. Paul and James.
    Main Line, at Geneva and St. Paul.
    NOTE—On Sundays, 10.20 a.m. and 6.20 p.m. trips ex Thorold operate down Academy Street and along Church to Ontario, thence to Glen Ridge.

See Special Instructions for Motor Coaches on Page 🖝 24

Page 23
Page 24

GENEVA-YORK MOTOR COACH

Time Table No. 52   Effective April 3rd, 1938, at 4.00 a.m.

Mls	STATIONS	Daily ex Sun	Daily ex Sun	Daily ex Sun	Daily ex Sun	Daily ex Sun	Daily ex Sun		Daily ex Sun	Daily	Daily		Daily
		am	am	am	am	am	am		am	am	am		pm
0.00	St. Paul and William	....	6 34	6 54	7 14	7 34	7 54	And	Sunday	10 34	10 54	And	11 34
0.16	St. Paul and James.....Tel	....	6 37	6 57	7 17	7 37	7 57	Every	Service	10 37	10 57	Every	11 37
0.50	St. Paul and Geneva........	....	6 40	7 00	7 20	7 40	8 00	Twenty	Starts	10 40	11 00	Twenty	11 40
0.80	Terminal Station.......Tel	6 22	6 42	7 02	7 22	7 42	8 02	Minutes	10 22	10 42	11 02	Minutes	11 42
2.00	Russell and York..........	6 28	6 48	7 08	7 28	7 48	8 08	To	10 28	10 48	11 08	To	11 48
3.30	St. Paul and William......	6 34	6 54	7 14	7 34	7 50	8 14		10 34	10 54	11 14		Garage

Leave Garage via Welland Avenue to Terminal—Return via York and Welland Avenue.

Church Trips on Sundays—Leaving Terminal Station 10.42 a.m. and 6.42 p.m. on Sundays, will proceed from Ontario to Church Street, to Academy, to St. Paul, thence regular route. Passengers for destinations on regular route between Church Street and Academy Street should be transferred to Victoria Lawn car at Ontario and Church. Passengers for Geneva-York Coach will be picked up by Victoria Lawn Car and transferred at Geneva and St. Paul.

An extra Church coach is operated, Sundays only, leaving Terminal Station at 10.32 a.m. and running 10 minutes ahead of regular coach.

PASSENGER TRANSFER POINTS

Facer Street, Victoria Lawn and Thorold Coach.
Eastbound, at William and St. Paul.
Main Line Eastbound, at Terminal Station.
Facer Street Eastbound, at Terminal Station.
Port Dalhousie Northbound, at York and Louisa.

NIAGARA-YORK MOTOR COACH

Mls	STATIONS	Daily ex Sun	Daily ex Sun	Daily ex Sun		Daily ex Sun
		am	am	am	And	pm
0.00	St. Paul and William........	7 04	7 24	7 44	Every	10 44
0.16	St. Paul and James.......Tel	7 07	7 27	7 47	Twenty	10 47
0.50	St. Paul and Geneva........	7 10	7 30	7 50	Minutes	10 50
0.90	Welland and Niagara........	7 12	7 32	7 52	To	10 52
1.20	Russell and Wiley..........	7 14	7 34	7 54		10 54
2.00	Russell and York..........	7 18	7 38	7 58		10 58
3.30	St. Paul and William.......	7 24	7 44	8 04		Garage

Leave Garage via Welland Avenue, Queen and regular route.

Return via York and Welland Avenue.

ROUTE—From William and St. Paul, via St. Paul to Niagara, to Maple, to Wiley, to Russell, to York, to Welland, to Queen, to Lake, to Ontario, to St. Paul.

COACH ROUTES—Special Instructions

1. Operators should frequently consult the latest copies of the "Highway Traffic Act," the "Public Vehicle Act," and "St. Catharines Traffic By-Law," in order to keep familiar with all regulations.
2. Operators must be prompt and endeavour to be on time. They must not, however, take chances. Proceed Safely—to be on time is never so important as to arrive safely.
3. Operators are required to bring their vehicle to a dead stop before crossing any railroad track. Gears shall not be shifted on railroad tracks.
4. Door must be kept closed when bus is in motion and Operators shall make sure that bus is at a dead stop before door is opened. Door must be closed before vehicle is started.
5. Operators must never leave bus unattended with motor running, and not on street with motor stopped unless absolutely necessary.
6. Operators wishing to pass a bus going in opposite direction shall signal by flashing lights twice. Never signal driver of approaching vehicle by waving the hand.
7. Do not Coast—Always use engine as a brake on hills.
8. All street signals and highway signs governing the operation of traffic shall be carefully observed.
9. Operators shall make such tests and inspections, before leaving garage, as are necessary to satisfy themselves that bus is in proper condition. See that tires are properly inflated, horn is working, and that fire extinguishers and necessary road tools are in place, including jack, jack handle, tire wrench, etc.
10. Make frequent inspection of bus for external defects. Make sure that license plates are in place; that all lights are burning; that tires are properly inflated; that horn is operating and that proper destination sign is displayed.
11. Operators are expected to keep the inside of bus in a reasonably clean and respectable condition.
12. Busses must always be started in low gear. This is essential to properly protect clutch and drive mechanism.
13. On busses equipped with air brakes, air gauge should be checked frequently to see that there is sufficient air pressure to efficiently operate brakes. If on account of frequent stops, air pressure should drop to a point where efficient brake application cannot be made, bus should be stopped at curb until air gauge indicates sufficient pressure for safe operation.

GENERAL INSTRUCTIONS

1. Employees will be governed by the General Instructions and Special Instructions applying to the Division on which they are operating, and must rigidly adhere thereto.

2. All trains will stop at the near side of Streets which are regular stops, unless otherwise ordered or indicated by stop signs.

3. All cars and trains will stop at the near side of such streets, in various municipalities, as are declared by municipal by-law to be "Through" streets, and are indicated by "Stop" signs.

4. All trains will stop in towns and cities when changing direction from one street to another.

5. Operators must not open doors of one-man, or safety type cars when car is in motion, and doors must be closed before car is started. Interurban cars with door control must have doors closed before car is started, and doors kept closed until car is stopped.

6. Only qualified trainmen and signalmen in the employ of this Company are permitted to operate a hand-operated interlocking plant; other persons who tamper with mechanism provided to protect a railway crossing commit a breach of the criminal code and will be rigorously prosecuted.

7. Passenger trainmen will be required, while on duty, to wear the standard uniform, including cap, designated by the Company.

8. Motormen or operators are forbidden to relinquish control of their cars to conductors, or others, except with the knowledge and approval of the Dispatcher or in cases of extreme emergency.

9. Smoking is not permitted in Local Line cars and buses. Passengers who persist in smoking after being asked to refrain should be courteously requested to leave the car or bus at next stop. Smoking is permitted in smoking compartments of interurban cars.

10. **Standard Time and Inspection of Watches**—All passenger and freight trainmen must, while on duty, be provided with an approved watch. The minimum grade of watch acceptable and approved for use on this railway must be of reputable manufacture and have 17 or more jewels. It must be fitted with a plain Arabic standard dial and be lever set, and if in open case, must wind at the figure "12." It must be of size 16 or larger.

Watches must be examined and approved by the Company's designated Watch Inspector every January and July, and watch-rating card (Form 777) must be secured and carried in all instances by employees.

When watches are cleaned, receipts or certificates showing the date must be secured and presented to the Watch Inspector at the next semi-annual inspection.

All passenger and freight trainmen must report to Dispatcher and receive standard time before going on duty.

All other employees whose duties require them to operate a car or train over any Division must carry a watch and report to Dispatcher, and receive standard time before proceeding over any Division.

11. **Bulletins—Train Registers—Train Orders—**

(a) Passenger and freight trainmen and others concerned with train operation will be advised by circular of the issuance of Bulletins affecting train movements, and will promptly thereafter read the same carefully and sign as having done so. Bulletins will be displayed at the following points: St. Catharines Terminal; Office of Supervisor of Freight Train Service, St. Catharines; Thorold Station; Niagara Falls Terminal; Electrical Department Headquarters and Car Shops Office, St. Catharines.

(b) Train Registers—A book or form which may be used at designated stations for registering signals displayed, the time of arrival and departure of trains and such other information as may be prescribed. Train Registers will be kept at the following points: St. Catharines Terminal; Thorold Station; Niagara Falls Terminal and Port Colborne. **It shall be the duty of the Conductor or Operator to register and to note carefully whether all trains and their sections due have arrived or left.**

(SPECIAL NOTE)—A register is also kept at Lincoln Junction for the registration of extra trains between Lincoln Junction and C. N. R. Merritton Station, only.

(c) A train must not leave its initial station on any Division, or a junction, or pass from one of two or more tracks to a single track, without train order, and until it has been ascertained whether all trains due have arrived or left.

12. **Reporting Delays—**

(a) Conductors will note the duration of delays to service at various diamond crossings, and at signal crossings, including swing bridges, and will report by telephone to Dispatcher the cause and duration of each delay.

13. **Special Precautions—**

(a) Protection of Trains on Sidings—When trains operate on spurs or sidings, off of main track, at such distances as will prevent observation of signals carried by trains on main track, conductor of train must leave a trainman stationed at junction of spur or siding and main track, for the purpose of observing signals displayed by trains on main track and protecting his train.

(b) At sidings used for meeting purposes, it is the duty of a conductor or operator whose train or section is in clear, but carrying signals protecting following section to protect such following section until in clear, by holding opposing train with danger signals, or until Dispatcher may modify the order.

When trains are operating in sections at sidings, named in train order for meeting or passing a train, or at meeting points shown in Time-Table in underscored bold face type, it is the duty of the conductor or operator on the last section to give hand proceed **signal** (using white hand lantern at night on interurban divisions) to the motorman or operator in charge of the first section of the opposing train; and the motorman or operator of the first section of the opposing train before entering main track at sidings used for meeting purposes, must receive hand proceed signal from conductor or operator in charge of last section of train operating in sections.

(c) When passing trains or cars on double track, sound gong and reduce speed, prepared to stop, keeping sharp lookout for persons suddenly appearing from behind the rear end of train or car on opposite track.

14. **Torpedo and Fusee Signals**—The explosion of two torpedoes is a signal to proceed at restricted speed. The explosion of one torpedo will indicate the same as two, but the use of two is required.

One case containing torpedoes and fusees is allotted to each freight motorman and one case to each freight conductor; also one case to the conductor or operator of the first and last section of each passenger train. They will be held responsible for the use of fusees and torpedoes and must report to Supervisor of Freight Train Service or Inspector when the same are used.

15. **Special Movements**—When movements of passenger cars are being made from terminus of run to car barns, or as special cars, roller signs must read "Car Barns" or "Special."

16. **Telephones and Signals**—Telephone and Signal Boxes must be kept locked, and passenger and freight trainmen must see that boxes are locked upon leaving same.

17. **Portable Telephones**—Portable Telephones are stored in Trainmen's Room, St. Catharines Terminal. Operators of interurban trains departing from St. Catharines Terminal will secure a portable telephone from Trainmen's Room and report number to Dispatcher. Operators in charge of interurban trains concluding their runs at St. Catharines will return portable telephone to Trainmen's Room and report number to Dispatcher.

18. **Trolley Breakers**—These are located on the various Divisions at the points listed in Special Instructions, and motormen and operators must shut off power when passing under them.

(Continued on Page 26)

Page 26

General Instructions

(Continued from Page 25)

Trolley Pans at swing bridges are the equivalent of breakers, and must be treated accordingly.

Trolley cross-overs at diamonds are the equivalent of breakers, and must be treated accordingly.

19. **Restricted Speed at Switches, Etc.**—Proceed at greatly reduced speed, prepared to stop immediately when passing over facing tongue switch points, spring controlled switches, and under trolley pan switches.

20. **Bad Weather Conditions**—Proceed at greatly reduced speed, prepared to stop immediately over special work that may be interferred with by snow, ice, sleet, etc. Proceed at reduced speed over flooded tracks. Do not attempt to pass over track flooded, should water be up to bottom of motor cases.

21. **Switching at Stations and Yards**—When switching under conditions which make it necessary to disturb cars being loaded or unloaded, great care must be taken to warn all persons in the vicinity of same, and to give them opportunity to get out of danger before cars are moved. When cars are so moved, they must be returned to the original position, or placed in an equally convenient place for loading or unloading.

22. **Backing Cars**—When necessary to back cars, conductor or operator must change controls and operate car from rear end.

23. **Clearance—St. Catharines Terminal**—Under the provisions of Board of Railway Commissioners Order No. 35139, dated 19th May, 1924, trainmen are prohibited from riding the tops or sides of cars whilst operating through or past St. Catharines Terminal.

24. **Brake and Sander Equipment**—(a) See Rule 2, "Special Rules governing the handling of air brakes." Always try air brake before starting, after changing ends of car or locomotive.

(b) Report to Dispatcher, sander not properly working, or insufficient supply of sand, and make note in Defect Book.

25. **Accidents**—In case of accident, passenger and freight trainmen will immediately make a report thereof on Form SC 695, for the information of the Company's Solicitor and his advice thereon, handing same to the Officer in charge of train service on the Division concerned who will forward it to the Solicitor. Bus accidents should be reported on Form 6023 and should also be handed to the Officer in charge of the bus on the Division concerned in order that he may forward the report to the Solicitor. Where completion of the forms would delay the Company's Officers being advised of the accident, employees should report by telephone or otherwise and complete the Form as promptly as possible.

26. **Witnesses**—In case of accident employees should obtain the names of any witnesses, including passengers, and give the names and addresses on either Form SC 695 or Form 6023 for the information of the Solicitor.

27. **Lost Articles** — Conductors or Operators should go through their cars or coaches at Terminals and pick up any articles left by passengers. Any such articles picked up or handed to Operators by other persons should be turned in at first opportunity either to Baggageman, Dispatcher or Car Shop. Along with article should be given the number of car or coach on which found, the Division, time and name of person finding it. Great care is to be taken in answering enquiries concerning articles supposed to have been left on cars or coaches. If enquiries are made directly to crews in regard to any specific article lost, person so enquiring should be politely referred either to Superintendent's Office, St. Catharines, or if at Niagara Falls, to Inspector there.

28. **Operation of Passenger Cars Coupled**—When cars are operated coupled in multiple unit trains, proceed signal is given by air communicating signal whistles. Each conductor is required to first make certain that all steps are clear and no passengers boarding or alighting, then the proceed signal will be given. The cock that controls each whistle at each end of each car must be left open so that all whistles sound in all cars when a whistle is given; thereby permitting conductors in cars other than the first car to hear signals as given. Proceed signals will, therefore, be given from each car and the conductor on the first car will give his signal last.

Motorman is required to receive a proceed signal from each car before starting. If necessary, he will use his car whistle or horn, giving four short whistle blasts for "call for signals" should it be necessary to repeat communicating cord signals to start the train.

Conductors in each car are required to see that their front doors and step plates are closed to prevent passengers from alighting on the left hand side.

Conductors on cars, other than the first car, will pay close attention for electric buzzer signals given by passengers on push buttons, indicating that they wish train to stop at next station or flag stop, and will relay passenger's buzzer signal by giving stop signal to motorman by means of air communicating signal whistles.

Conductor of first car is in charge of the train.

29. **Fires—Damage to Company's Property**—Damage by fire or other cause to Company's property must be promptly reported on Accident Form SC 695, giving full details as to date, division, car number, place, etc.

30. **Head and Signal Lamps**—It shall be the duty of conductors, operators and motormen to see that their trains or locomotives are equipped with proper headlamps and marker lamps, and kept lit between sunset and sunrise. Each freight trainman while on duty between these hours must carry a white hand-lantern, and motormen and conductors of freight trains must each have a red hand-lantern lit and available for use between sunset and sunrise.

Headlamps for cars and locomotives, and white and red hand-lanterns for use on passenger trains, are numbered and will be used only on correspondingly numbered cars and locomotives. Motormen and operators of passenger and freight trains will make sure upon taking out cars or locomotives that they are equipped with properly numbered headlamps and white and red hand-lanterns, and upon returning to car barns they will remove these lamps and place them in the proper receptacle provided.

Conductors and operators on local and interurban divisions will see that their cars are equipped with a red and a white hand-lantern. On interurban divisions and Port Dalhousie Division, the red hand-lantern will be kept lit between sunset and sunrise and displayed on the bracket provided for that purpose in the rear vestibule of the car. The same will apply on local line divisions operating in sections. The white hand-lantern will be lighted only when emergency requires and will remain in the custody of motorman or operator.

In the event of a headlamp becoming out of order, if another headlamp cannot be procured, a while light must be displayed in its place.

31. **Lights in Cars**—When changing poles at night, cars must not be left in darkness.

Lights must be extinguished during daylight hours.

32. **Issuance of Train Orders**—To obtain train orders at telephone stations, conductors will call the Dispatcher who will give such orders as are necessary. The conductor when taking the order will write same plainly in his train order book, and when he has finished writing the order he will repeat it to the Dispatcher who will complete the order, if correct, by giving the initials of the Superintendent and the time of completion, which initials and time shall be promptly written on the order. When the order has been properly completed, the conductor taking the train order shall then sign his name to the order, after which it is in full force and effect. The motorman will then read the order to the conductor who has taken the order, sign his name to the order, and take one copy for his use, before train starts, or is moved.

(Continued on Page 27)

General Instructions

(Continued from Page 26)

THE FOLLOWING RULES TAKE EFFECT JULY 5th, 1931, AND SUPERSEDE PREVIOUS RULES AND INSTRUCTIONS INCONSISTENT THEREWITH:

Approved by Order No. 46785, Dated June 11th, 1931, by The Board of Railway Commissioners for Canada.

33. **Train Orders**—One-man car operators will sign train orders in the space marked "conductor." The original copy of train order will be torn out at the end of each trip for deposit in box provided. Train orders once in effect, continue so until fulfilled, superseded or annulled. Any part of an order specifying a particular movement may be either superseded or annulled. Time of train's arrival fulfilling a train order or schedule, will be reported at once by telephone to Dispatcher by conductor or operator.

Stations at which a schedule is first timed on any division is an initial station for that schedule, and for any extra train whose movement on that division commences at that station. A train must not leave its initial station on any division, or a junction, or pass from one of two or more tracks to a single track, without a train order, and until it has been ascertained whether all trains due have arrived or left.

34. **Train Registers**—One-man car operator must enter information on train register, giving train number, car number, section, and signals carried, and time, and sign his name in the space headed "conductor." See General Instruction 11 (b), page 24, Employees' Time-Table.

Except by train order authority, no train can depart from a register station and enter upon single track until the conductor or operator has signed his name on the train register in the column headed "Remarks," opposite the registration of the train to be met or due prior to departure.

35. **Signals**—(a) Employees whose duties may require them to give signals, must have the proper appliances, keep them in good order and ready for immediate use.

(b) Flags of the prescribed color must be used by day, and lights of the prescribed color by night.

(c) Day signals must be displayed from sunrise to sunset, but when day signals cannot be plainly seen, night signals must be used in addition. Night signals must be displayed from sunset to sunrise.

36. **Flagman's Equipment**—(a) Flagmen must be equipped, for daytime, with a red flag on a staff, at least six torpedoes and five red fusees; and for night time, or when weather or other conditions obscure day signals, with a red light, a white light, a supply of matches, at least six torpedoes and five red fusees.

(b) Fusees and torpedoes are to be carried on all cars and trains, except City Lines, St. Catharines, including Port Dalhousie Division and Niagara Falls Local Lines.

37. **Fusee and Torpedo Signals**—A train finding a fusee burning red at or near its track must stop and then proceed at restricted speed. (Restricted Speed—Proceed prepared to stop short of train, obstruction, or anything that may require the speed of a train to be reduced.)

The explosion of two torpedoes is a signal to proceed at restricted speed. The explosion of one torpedo will indicate the same as two, but the use of two is required.

Torpedoes must not be placed at stations or on public crossings.

38. **Distance Required Between Following Trains**—Trains running in the same direction must keep not less than 1,200 feet apart except in closing up at stations or meeting points. When the view is obscured by curves, fog, storms or other causes, train must be kept under such control that it can be stopped within the range of vision. Motormen of sections following must have their trains under full control, prepared to stop at flag stations, crossings and passing sidings, expecting to find the preceding train stopped, or running at reduced speed.

39. **Protection of Standing Cars**—A train should not be stopped on a curve and permitted to stand on a curve, if practicable to avoid it. Cars must not be left standing on a grade without brakes being fully applied, including hand brake, and, if necessary, wheels blocked, when motorman and conductor, or one-man car operator, has to be absent from car. Controller reverse key must be removed and retained in possession of motorman or one-man car operator.

40. **Rear End Protection**—(a) When a train is moving under circumstances in which it may be overtaken by another train, the flagman (conductor, rear end brakeman or one-man car operator) must take such action as may be necessary to insure full protection by day or by night. When the view is obstructed, lighted fusees must be thrown off at intervals. When day signals cannot be plainly seen owing to weather or other conditions, night signals must be used. One-man car operators are responsible for the protection of their trains.

(b) When a train stops on the main track under circumstances in which it may be overtaken by another train, the flagman (conductor, rear end brakeman or one-man car operator) must go back immediately with flagman's signals, a sufficient distance from the train to insure full protection, at least:

In daytime, if there is no down grade toward train within one mile of its rear, and there is sufficiently clear view of rear from an approaching train...1,000 feet
At other times and places, including curves and other obstructions of vision, if there is no down grade toward train within one mile of its rear......1,500 feet
If there is a down grade towards the train within one mile of its rear, or weather conditions are stormy and vision obscured..2,000 feet

Controller reverse key must be removed and retained in possession of one-man car operator.

The flagman (conductor, rear end brakeman or one-man car operator) must, after going back a sufficient distance from the train to insure full protection, take up a position where there will be an unobstructed view of him from an approaching train of, if possible, 1,000 feet. Then, place two torpedoes not more than 200 or less than 100 feet apart on the rail on the same side as the motorman of an approaching train, and when necessary in addition displaying a lighted fusee. If recalled before another train arrives he must in addition to the two torpedoes, **leave a fusee burning red at the point he returns from,** and while returning to his train (when snow plows or sweepers may be running, curvature, weather, or other conditions governing) a fusee burning red must be placed at such points or times as the flagman may find necessary to insure full protection. One-man car operators are responsible for protection of their trains.

The flagman must always on the approach of a train display stop signals and, if not already done, place two torpedoes on the rail as before described, and then return 300 feet nearer the protected train.

One-man cars on Divisions, except City Lines, St. Catharines, Port Dalhousie Division and Niagara Falls Local Lines, are equipped with portable telephone. When the one-man car operator has complied with the duty of flagman, he may return to his car to use portable telephone, when safety will permit, **leaving a fusee burning red half-way in distance between torpedoes and rear of train.**

The front of a train must be protected in the same way when necessary by the front brakeman or, if there is no front brakeman, by the motorman.

41. **One-Man Car Front End Protection**—The front of a one-man car stopped on main track must be first protected when it is known by train order or by time-table schedule, that the direction of the movement of next train approaching will be towards the front of standing one-man car. After protection of front end has been completed, rear end must be protected as prescribed.

42. **Use of Portable Telephones**—Operators of first and last sections on Divisions except Local Lines, St. Catharines, Port Dalhousie Division and Niagara Falls Local Lines, will see that their car, when taking charge of same, is equipped with portable telephone and phone connection rods, and test by making call to Dispatcher.

43. **One-Man Car Operator Responsible For Switches**—Operators will be held strictly responsible for handling of switches. See Rule 105, Revised General Rules and Instructions, and Bulletin.

Page 28

(44)

WHISTLE SIGNALS

SOUND	INDICATION
(a) One Short	Stop. Apply Brakes.
(b) Two Long	Release Brakes. Proceed.
(c) One Long—Three Short	Flagman protect rear of Train.
(d) Four Long	Flagman return from west or south.
(e) Five Long	Flagman return from east or north.
(f) Three Long	When running, train parted; to be repeated until answered by hand flag or lamp signal for "train has parted". Answer to hand flag or lamp signal for "train has parted".
(g) Two Short	Answer to any signal not otherwise provided for.
(h) Three Short	When train is standing, "back". Answer to hand or lamp signal "back", and communicating signal when train is standing "back".
(j) Four Short	Call for signals.
(k) One Long—Two Short	To call attention of all trains met or passed, sectionmen, bridgemen, and others interested, to signals displayed for following Section. If not answered by a train, the train displaying signals must stop and ascertain the cause.
(l) Two Long—Two Short	"Two Long—Two Short must be sounded at least 80 rods (one-quarter mile) from every public road crossing at grade, and the car or engine bell kept ringing until the crossing is passed". In addition, the following will apply in connection with the use of bell: The car or engine bell must be rung when a car or engine is about to move, and while moving about stations.
(m) One Short—One Long	When double heading air brakes have failed on leading engine, and second engine is to take control. Answer, One Short—One Long to be given by second engine as soon as it has control of air brakes.
(n) Two Short—One Long	Answer to whistle signal calling attention to signals displayed for following section.
(o) One Long Whistle	Approaching stations, junctions, draw bridges, railway crossings at grade, and meeting points. (Extracts from Order No. 44,195 Board of Railway Commissioners: "Motorman approaching any siding used for meeting purposes will blow one long blast of the whistle in all respects as required when approaching a regular station. This signal is to be given at whistle boards located in advance of each siding. Should the motorman fail to give one long blast of whistle, the conductor must take immediate action to stop the train. The conductor on passenger trains shall answer such blast with one communicating signal, if there is a "hold order", or if a train is to be met or passed, or if an order is to be received, and with two short blasts if the train is to proceed. Should the conductor fail to answer, motorman must stop train before reaching siding").
(p) Succession of Short Sounds	Alarm for persons or live stock on track.

(45) Maintenance of Way Flagging Rules for Impassable Track

(Extract from Order No. 40391 Board of Railway Commissioners, dated February 23rd, 1928)

1. A yellow flag by day, or a yellow light by night, on the right-hand side of the track, indicates track or trolley wire is in bad order, or men at work 800 feet in advance, and train must operate at six miles an hour until it passes the same kind of signal on the left-hand side of the track; and when men are at work during stormy, foggy, or smoky weather conditions, flagmen must be placed in addition to the signals referred to.

2. Before undertaking any work which will render the main track impassable, or if rendered impassable from any cause or defect, trackmen, bridgemen, or other employees of the company shall protect the same as follows:

   (a) Send out a flagman in each direction with stop signals at least—

   1000 feet in daytime, if there is no down grade towards the obstruction within one mile, and there is a clear view of 1000 feet from an approaching train;

   1500 feet at other times and places, if there is no down grade towards the obstruction within one mile;

   2000 feet if there is a down grade towards the obstruction within one mile.

   (b) The flagman must, after going the required distance, from the obstruction, to ensure full protection, take up a position where there will be an unobstructed view of him from an approaching train, if possible, of 1000 feet. The flagman must display a red flag by day and a red light by night, and remain in such position until recalled or relieved.

3. Trains stopped by flagman, as per Rule 2, shall be governed by his instructions and proceed to the working point, or working point signal, as the case may be, and there be governed by signal or instructions of the foreman in charge.

4. When train order or bulletin protection is to be provided, a flagman must be sent out as per instructions in Rule 2; flagman protection to remain until confirmation is received of protection being provided by train order or bulletin. The defective or working point must then be marked by signals placed in both directions as follows:

   (a) Yellow flags by day and in addition yellow lights by night, 800 feet from the defective or working point; red flags by day and in addition red lights by night, 400 feet from the defective or working point, on the same side of the track as the motorman of an approaching train, and there is a clear view of at least 1000 feet.

5. When weather or other conditions obscure day signals, night signals must be used in addition.

6. Flagmen must each be equipped for day time with a red flag, and for night time and when weather or other conditions obscure day signals, with a red light and a white light and a supply of matches.

(46) Special Rules Governing the Handling of Air Brakes

1. *To All Employees*—Employees must be thoroughly conversant with the Brake and Signal Equipment, and report promptly any trouble or defects.

2. *Terminal Test*—The motorman and conductor are responsible for knowing that a proper Terminal Test of train brakes has been made before starting from terminal stations. Motormen must personally handle brake valve, when making all tests.

3. *Running Test*—Motormen on passenger trains must make a Running Test when leaving a terminal or any point where consist of train has been changed (at a speed not less than 15 m.p.h. when practicable) by making a brake application sufficient to insure the proper control and safety of train.

4. *Road Test*—When the brake pipe on any train has been uncoupled, brakes must be applied and released from motorman's brake valve after re-coupling and before starting out. Trainmen must see that brakes behind point of separation operate properly.

5. *Double Heading, Assisting and Pusher Service*—When two or more motor cars or engines are coupled in any train, all hose must be coupled and brakes tested, and operated from the leading motor car or engine. Maximum air pressure must be maintained on all motor cars or engines, and brake valve cut-out cocks closed on all motor cars except the leading motor car or engine. In the case of the leading motor car giving up the train short of the destination of the train, a test of the brakes must be made to see that the same are operative from the motorman's valve of the motor car remaining with train.

6. *Emergency Application*—Brakes must be applied in emergency only when necessary to avoid accident.

7. *Observing Air Gauges*—Air Gauges must be observed frequently to insure the maximum pressure be maintained at all times.

8. *Cutting Out Brakes*—Brakes must not be cut out unnecessarily. The car immediately behind leading motor car or engine must always have its brakes cut in and operative, and brakes must not be cut out on more than two consecutive cars on any train.

9. *Setting Out Cars*—When cars are set off at any point, auxiliary reservoirs must be bled and hand brakes applied.

10. *Standing on Grades*—When necessary for a train to stand on a grade for over five (5) minutes, air brakes must be released and train held by hand brakes.

11. *Calling for Brakes*—A call for brakes from a motorman when running must be promptly responded to by each trainman opening a conductor's valve, and then applying hand brakes. Conductor's valves must not be closed until train stops.

   The Audible Signal (calling for brakes) is one short blast of whistle.

12. *Percentage of Operative Brakes*—Passenger trains must have 100 % of brakes operative when leaving terminals, and must not be run with less than 85% at any time.

   Mixed and freight trains must have at least 90% of brakes operative when leaving terminals, and must not be run with less than 85% at any time.

Page 30

Niagara, St. Catharines & Toronto Railway

MILEAGE CHART, 1938

Main Line Division— Mileage
  Car Barn to St. Catharines Terminal (Opposite Bumping Posts)... 0.42
  Car Barn to C.N.R. Station—Via Raymond, James, King, Ontario and St. Paul Streets 1.53
  St. Catharines Terminal to Niagara Falls—Bumper at New Terminal to Bumper at New Terminal, Niagara Falls................13.05
  St. Catharines Terminal to St. Catharines Terminal (Uptown Loop)—Via Geneva, St. Paul, James, Raymond and Welland Avenue.. 1.54

Grantham Division—
  Terminal to Port Dalhousie East—Point Opposite Main Line Bumper, St. Catharines Terminal, to Bumper at Port Dalhousie.... 2.93

Welland Division—
  Car Barn to St. Catharines Terminal (Opposite Bumping Posts):... 0.42
  St. Catharines Terminal to Centre of Station, Thorold... 4.84
  Thorold to Port Colborne—C/L Station, Thorold, to C/L Platform, Port Colborne...........................18.59

Lake Shore Division—
  Car Barn to St. Catharines Terminal (Opposite Bumping Posts)... 0.42
  St. Catharines Terminal to Stop 50—Bumper on Lake Shore Division, St. Catharines, to West Side Public Road............... 4.82

Victoria Lawn Division—
  Car Barn to King and Ontario—Yard Switch at Raymond (West of Clark) Via Raymond, James and King, to South (North) Switch
    King and Ontario... 0.60
  King and Ontario Streets to McKinnon's—North Switch at King and Ontario to Bumper Near Carleton Street................. 1.02
  King and Ontario to Victoria Lawn—South Switch at King and Ontario to End of Track (Victoria Lawn)..................... 2.48
  McKinnon's to St. Paul and James—Bumper at McKinnon's to West Switch at St. Paul and James................. 1.36
  St. Paul and James to Car Barn—West Switch at St. Paul and James to Yard Switch on Raymond, West of Clark.............. 0.48
  Victoria Lawn to St. Paul and James—End of Track (Victoria Lawn) to East Switch at St. Paul and James................. 2.12
  McKinnon's to Victoria Lawn—Bumper on Ontario at Carleton to End of Track (Victoria Lawn) 3.51

St. Catharines and District—Facer Street Division—
  Car Barn to Ontario and St. Paul... 0.74
  Ontario and St. Paul to C.N.R. Station—Bumper at C.N.R. Station... 0.79
  King and James to Car Barn—South Switch on James at King to Yard Switch on Raymond........................ 0.37
  C.N.R. Station to Car Barn—Bumper at C.N.R. Station to Yard Switch on Raynond........................ 1.49
  Car Barn to Terminal—(Entrance to Yards From Welland Avenue)... 0.45
  Terminal to Grantham Avenue—Terminal Yard Cross-Over East of Geneva on Welland Avenue to C/L Grantham Avenue........ 1.33
  Grantham Avenue to Carleton Street—C/L Grantham Avenue to C/L Shelter on Carleton Street................. 0.56
  Grantham Avenue to St. Paul and James—C/L Grantham Avenue to West Switch on St. Paul at James (Via Geneva and St. Paul) 2.00
  St. Paul and James to Grantham Avenue—West Switch at St. Paul and James to C/L Grantham Avenue (Via James and Raymond) 2.26
  St. Paul and James to Car Barn—West Switch at St. Paul and James to Yard Switch on Raymond Street...................... 0.48
  Car Barn Yard, St. Catharines—East Switch to West Switch... 0.11
  Ontario and St. Paul to James and St. Paul—West Switch at Ontario and St. Paul to West Switch at James and St. Paul.......... 0.22
  C.N.R. Station to Ontario and St. Paul—Bumper C.N.R. Station to West Switch at Ontario and St. Paul..................... 0.79

Port Dalhousie Division—
  Car Barn to Terminal—Yard Switch on Raymond (West of Clark to West Switch on Welland Avenue)........................ 0.38
  Terminal to Car Barn (Via Geneva, St.Paul, James and Raymond) West Switch on Welland Ave. at Geneva to Yard Switch on Raymond 1.08
  Port Dalhousie to Terminal—C/L Platform, Port Dalhousie, to West Switch on Welland Avenue at Geneva................ 4.89
  Louisa Street Cut-Off—Street Line Welland Avenue to Street Line Catherine Street................................. 0.06

Niagara Falls Local Line—
  Car Barn to Queen and Victoria—Switch on Main Line at Car Barn to Switch on Queen at Victoria........................... 0.43
  Queen and Victoria to Bridge Street—C/L Platform at Bridge Street to Switch on Queen at Victoria........................... 0.79
  Bridge Street to Montrose—C/L Platform Bridge Street to C/L Shelter, Montrose................................. 4.47
  Bridge Street to Main and Ferry—C/L Platform Bridge Street to Switch at Main and Ferry......................... 2.78
  Bridge Street to Winery Road—C/L Platform Bridge Street to Winery Road, Lundy's Lane............................ 3.69
  Queen and Victoria to Main and Ferry—Switch on Queen at Victoria to Switch at Main and Ferry........................ 1.99
  Victoria Junction to Montrose—Victoria Avenue Junction Switch to C/L Shelter, Montrose 2.99
  Victoria Junction to Winery Road—Victoria Avenue Junction Switch to Winery Road 2.21
  Montrose to Queen and Victoria Avenue Junction—C/L Shelter to Switch on Queen at Victoria......................... 3.68
  Winery Road to Queen and Victoria Avenue Junction—Winery Road to Switch on Queen at Victoria..................... 2.90
  Main and Ferry to Montrose C/L Shelter... 1.69
  Main and Ferry to Winery Road... 0.91
  Victoria Junction to Terminal—Victoria Avenue Junction Switch to Terminal 0.44
  Queen and Victoria to Victoria Avenue Junction—Switch on Queen at Victoria to Victoria Avenue Junction..................... 0.69

NOTE:—The Above Mileage Covers Only Train Operation—Bus Mileage Recorded From Speedometer.

Top: Steamer *Garden City* at Port Dalhousie, c1905.
(J.J. WIGT COLLECTION)

Bottom: NS&T car 61 being used as a one-man car on the Welland line, where left-side boarding and alighting were then the norm. Substation Junction, Thorold, September 27th 1941.
(J.D. KNOWLES)

Opposite Top: Car 51 at an unknown location (probably Port Dalhousie–Lakeside Park), c1902.
(J.J. WIGT COLLECTION)

Opposite Middle: NS&T car 130 on Grantham Sub at Port Dalhousie East, Saturday, July 4th 1953.
(JOHN F. HUMISTON T2685)

Opposite Bottom: Cars 65, 67 and 60 in mu train and 82 following. Niagara Falls (southbound on Victoria at Queen), summer 1943.
(DICK VINCENT)

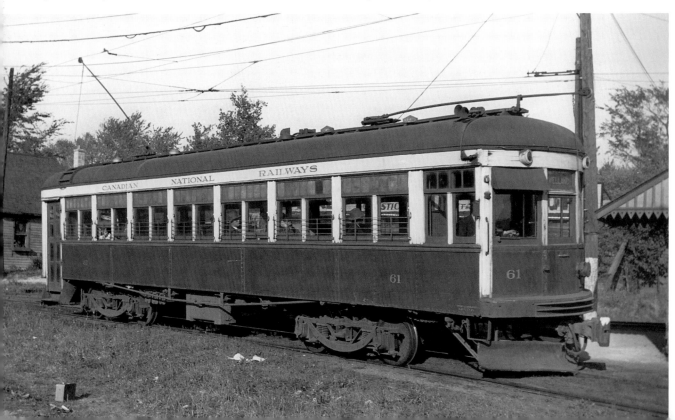

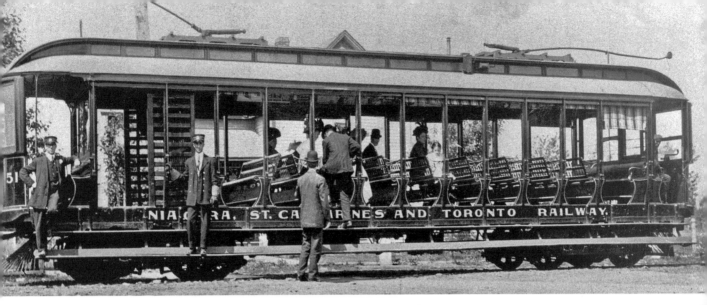

Top: Car 131 on tail track at Port Dalhousie (Lakeside Park at right), on a 1940 fantrip.
(FRED ANGUS COLLECTION)

Bottom: NS&T train 197, cars 132-135 on Victoria Avenue south of Stamford Street, Niagara Falls, Ontario, 3:00 PM, Saturday, July 20th 1946.
(JOHN F. HUMISTON S7221)

Top: Car 83 on Louisa Street, St. Catharines on an excursion, July 29th 1956.
(R.J. SANDUSKY)

Bottom: NS&T train 197, cars 132-135, to St. Catharines at Stop 70, Bridge Street, Falls Subdivision, Niagara Falls, Ontario. Saturday, July 20th 1946.
(JOHN F. HUMISTON S7222)

Top: NS&T car 130 on Grantham Sub at Port Dalhousie East, Saturday, July 4th 1953.
(JOHN F. HUMISTON T2686)

Bottom: Line car 31, Elm Street, Humberstone, c1955.
(JOHN F. BROMLEY COLLECTION)

INDEX

Photo references are set in *semibold italic* type. *IBC*=Inside Back Cover, *IFC*=Inside Front Cover, *OFC*=Outside Front Cover and *OBC*=Outside Back Cover.

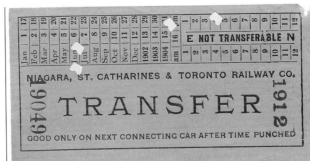

Top: NS&T car 325.
(ANTHONY J. KRISAK, COLLECTION OF RICHARD A. KRISAK)

Bottom: 300-series car on Facer Street, c1945.
(BRO. BERNARD POLINAK, S.J., COLLECTION OF RICHARD A. KRISAK)

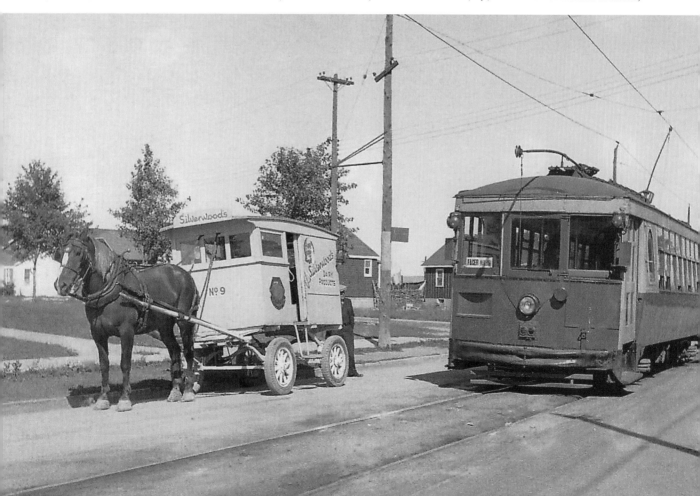